Ethics and Health Care

Who should have access to assisted reproductive technologies? Which one of many seriously ill patients should be offered the next available transplant organ? When may a surrogate decision-maker decide to withdraw life-prolonging measures from an unconscious patient? Questions like these feature prominently in the field of health care ethics and in the education of health care professionals. This book provides a concise introduction to the major concepts, principles, and issues in health care ethics, using case studies throughout to illustrate and analyze challenging ethical issues in contemporary health care. Topics range widely, from confidentiality and truthfulness to end-of-life care and research on human subjects. *Ethics and Health Care* will be a vital resource for students of applied ethics, bioethics, professional ethics, health law, and medical sociology, as well as students of medicine, nursing, and other health care professions.

JOHN C. MOSKOP is Professor of Internal Medicine and Wallace and Mona Wu Chair in Biomedical Ethics at the Wake Forest School of Medicine in Winston-Salem, North Carolina. He chairs the Clinical Ethics Committee at Wake Forest Baptist Medical Center and serves on the Ethics Committee of the American College of Emergency Physicians. He is the author of more than 100 articles and book chapters on a broad range of topics in bioethics.

Cambridge Applied Ethics

Titles published in this series

Ethics and Health Care

An Introduction

JOHN C. MOSKOP
Wake Forest School of Medicine

CAMBRIDGE
UNIVERSITY PRESS

CAMBRIDGE
UNIVERSITY PRESS

University Printing House, Cambridge CB2 8BS, United Kingdom

One Liberty Plaza, 20th Floor, New York, NY 10006, USA

477 Williamstown Road, Port Melbourne, VIC 3207, Australia

4843/24, 2nd Floor, Ansari Road, Daryaganj, Delhi - 110002, India

79 Anson Road, #06-04/06, Singapore 079906

Cambridge University Press is part of the University of Cambridge.

It furthers the University's mission by disseminating knowledge in the pursuit of education, learning and research at the highest international levels of excellence.

www.cambridge.org
Information on this title: www.cambridge.org/9781107601758

First published 2016

A catalogue record for this publication is available from the British Library

Library of Congress Cataloging in Publication data
Moskop, John C., 1951– , author.
Ethics and health care : an introduction / John C. Moskop.
   p.   ;   cm. – (Cambridge applied ethics)
Includes bibliographical references and index.
ISBN 978-1-107-01547-0 (hardback) – ISBN 978-1-107-60175-8 (paperback)
I. Title. II. Series: Cambridge applied ethics.
[DNLM: 1. Bioethical Issues – United States.   2. Delivery of Health Care – ethics – United States.   3. Ethics, Clinical – United States.
4. Organizational Case Studies – United States.   WB 60]
RA427.25
174.2–dc23

2015033131

ISBN 978-1-107-01547-0 Hardback
ISBN 978-1-107-60175-8 Paperback

For Ruth, with love and thanks

Contents

Preface

My goal for this book is to provide an engaging and concise introduction to the expanding field of health care ethics. The volume is designed to be accessible to university undergraduates, but detailed enough for graduate and professional school students and health care professionals in practice. Because it is an introduction to health care ethics, I have avoided stating and defending my own position on controversial moral issues and complex case examples. Rather, I have attempted to provide essential conceptual and factual information about the issues discussed, a fair statement of commonly held positions, and a review of central moral arguments. This approach, I hope, will enable readers to understand why the issues and cases are challenging, to engage in careful moral reasoning and deliberation about them, and to formulate and defend their own conclusions.

The book is divided into four parts. The five chapters of Part I offer basic information about health care ethics. These chapters provide an account of the role of ethics in health care, a brief history of health care ethics and clinical ethics consultation in the United States, a review of leading methods of moral reasoning in health care, and an examination of the relationships between law and ethics and between culture and ethics in health care. Part II examines the moral foundations of the therapeutic relationship between patients and health care professionals. Each of the six chapters in this part focuses on a central moral feature of that relationship, including privacy and confidentiality, truthfulness, informed consent to treatment, surrogate decision-making for patients who lack decision-making capacity, respect for professional boundaries, and responsible stewardship of health care resources. Part III is devoted to ethical issues in health care at the beginning and at the end of life. The seven chapters in this part explore the topics of assisted reproductive technologies, abortion, maternal-fetal conflict, advance care planning and advance directives, moral conflicts in end-of-life care, medical futility, and aid in dying. The three chapters of Part IV examine three additional areas of major interest and attention in health care ethics: biomedical research on human subjects, human genetics, and organ transplantation. Each of the four parts of the book begins with a brief introduction that includes a summary of the content of its individual chapters.

The twenty-one chapters of the book share a common format. Each chapter begins with a case example that poses a moral question or problem for the stakeholders in that situation. Many of these cases are drawn from the literature of medicine and bioethics; others are adapted from my experiences as a clinical ethics consultant and from experiences shared with me by clinical colleagues. The chapter then addresses its topic in various ways, including examination of key concepts and facts, description of major positions or approaches, and review of relevant moral considerations. Each chapter concludes with a case analysis that brings the content of the chapter to bear on the case example and invites readers to use that content to choose and defend a course of action for that case.

My primary focus in the book is on ethical issues in the provision of health care for individual patients, not on issues in public and population health. I do, however, address legal and health policy issues that guide personal health care throughout the volume, and I examine moral issues in biomedical research on human subjects in Chapters 19 and 20.

In addition to the references contained within each chapter, the Further Reading section at the end of the book offers suggestions for readers seeking additional information about the topics discussed in each chapter. This list includes both classic sources and notable recent publications on these topics.

Finally, just a few words about the grammatical and linguistic conventions I have adopted for this volume. I use single quotation marks to indicate that I am referring to a term, not using the concept signified by that term, and to indicate a quotation within another quotation. I use double quotation marks for direct quotations, for short titles, and as "scare quotes" to indicate the use of a term in a special or questionable way. I use italics for the case examples that begin each chapter, for book titles, for foreign words, and for special emphasis on a term. Some authors stipulate a distinction between the terms 'ethical' and 'moral', but I view those terms as roughly synonymous and use them interchangeably.

Acknowledgments

This volume is a product of many years devoted to teaching, scholarship, and professional service in the field of health care ethics. I am most grateful to the institutions that have given me the opportunity to serve on their faculties, the Brody School of Medicine at East Carolina University and the Wake Forest School of Medicine. My faculty colleagues in bioethics and medicine at those institutions have been invaluable mentors, instructors, and collaborators throughout my career. I could not have written this book without them, and I owe them a great debt of gratitude. My students over the past thirty-five years have been a continuing source of encouragement and inspiration; their interest and their commitment to learning and practicing the ethics of health care give meaning and worth to my endeavors. I am also grateful for financial support at different stages of my research from the Kulynych Family Foundation and from the Wake Forest University Center for Bioethics, Health, and Society.

I owe heartfelt thanks to Hilary Gaskin and Rosemary Crawley, my editors at Cambridge University Press, for their expert guidance, and especially for their patience with this overcommitted professor! My colleague Gerardo Maradiaga and my wife Ruth Moskop have read the entire book in manuscript. I am deeply grateful for their many valuable suggestions and for their steadfast support and encouragement throughout this project. Many thanks, Ruth, for graciously tolerating my spending so many weekends at the office writing – I hope that you will be happy to see me more often on Saturday and Sunday!

Part I

Ethics in health care
Role, history, and methods

The five chapters in Part I of this volume provide a general introduction to the field of health care ethics, including its purpose, history, methods, and relation to the domains of law and culture. The account of the nature, scope, and limits of health care ethics provided in these chapters is designed to set the stage for examination of the multiple specific topics in ethics and health care in the subsequent chapters of the book.

Chapter 1, "The role of ethics in health care," begins with a description of several concepts of ethics, common sources of moral guidance, and methods for resolving moral disagreements. It then considers the relation of ethics and health care, arguing that ethical issues are especially prominent in health care. This prominence is a result both of the importance of the human interests at stake and of the complexity of many treatment decisions. Ethics can guide difficult choices in health care, but decisions also depend on factual information, and even the most careful moral reasoning may not produce a unique and definitive "correct" solution.

Chapter 2, "A brief history of health care ethics and clinical ethics consultation in the United States," describes the emergence of health care ethics as a new field of inquiry and practice in the latter half of the twentieth century. This review highlights major changes in the US health care system during this period. It also identifies three high-profile events that called public attention to moral issues in medical research and practice: investigative reports condemning the decades-long Tuskegee Study of Untreated Syphilis in poor black men, the US Supreme Court abortion decision in *Roe* v. *Wade*, and the New Jersey Supreme Court *Quinlan* decision on rights to refuse life-sustaining medical treatment. Chapter 2 also outlines the development of the practice of clinical ethics consultation in US health care facilities. From its origins in the 1970s, clinical ethics consultation has become a widely available service designed to help health care professionals, patients, and families make difficult moral choices about medical treatment.

Chapter 3, "Methods of health care ethics," summarizes a variety of different approaches that scholars have proposed for moral reasoning in health care settings. These approaches recommend different theoretical tools and strategies to guide moral deliberation, including basic principles, paradigmatic cases, moral rules, and moral virtues. This chapter also describes a simple, step-by-step procedure for analyzing health care ethics cases.

Chapter 4, "Law and ethics in health care," is devoted to the relationship between law and ethics as guides to choice and action in health care. Recognizing that some health care professionals are inclined to look first to the law for direction, this chapter begins by considering the option of sole reliance on the law as a strategy for decision-making. It also examines a very different option, namely, sole reliance on ethics as one's guide to action. The chapter offers reasons why both of these options are unsatisfactory, and it proposes an alternative strategy, that of recognizing legal rules and standards as one among multiple morally significant but fallible action guides.

Part I concludes with Chapter 5, "Culture and ethics in health care." This chapter examines the role of cultural beliefs and values in health care. It points out the increasingly multicultural composition of contemporary societies and the growing frequency of culture-based disagreements about what health care to provide and accept. Chapter 5 describes three different responses to cultural disagreements, namely, moral imperialism, moral relativism, and moral negotiation. It considers strengths and weaknesses of each of these responses and argues for the overall superiority of moral negotiation. In order to negotiate cultural disagreements productively, Chapter 5 recommends that health care professionals adopt a "culturally humble" approach, including a respectful attitude toward patients and colleagues, attention to the cultural beliefs and values of others, and a commitment to communication in order to understand others' concerns and to seek agreement on a plan of care.

1   The role of ethics in health care

Case example

Metropolitan Medical Center (MMC) is a private, not-for-profit 500-bed acute care hospital. MMC clinicians and administrators are wrestling with a serious problem. Over the past year, MMC has admitted eight different patients who presented to the MMC Emergency Department with severely damaged heart valves that have required valve replacement surgery. In each of these patients, the damaged valve was the result of endocarditis, a bacterial infection of the inner surface of the heart, including the heart valves. All of the patients report intravenous (IV) injection of a homemade liquid preparation of Opana® (oxymorphone hydrochloride), a potent narcotic pain medication designed for oral ingestion. All of the patients are from the same nearby town, all are indigent, and none have health insurance. Despite strong warnings from their physicians that continued IV drug use would likely cause reinfection of the implanted heart valves, four of the patients have returned to MMC with recurrence of endocarditis requiring repeat valve replacement.

MMC medical staff members have sharply divided opinions about how to respond to these patients. Several cardiovascular surgeons have argued that these patients should be warned that they will not be offered repeat surgery if they continue IV drug use and present to the hospital a second or third time with damaged heart valves due to endocarditis. Several infectious disease specialists have argued that these patients are suffering from an addictive disease and that they are therefore not responsible for their condition and should receive life-prolonging surgery. A psychiatric consultant reports that these patients meet statutory criteria for involuntary commitment and treatment for their substance abuse, but that no substance abuse treatment facilities are currently willing to accept them for the extended treatment they require.

The president of MMC has charged the chief medical officer (CMO) to develop and implement a consistent approach to caring for these patients. What approach should MMC adopt?

As mentioned in the Preface, the aim of this book is to provide a concise introduction to fundamental concepts, methods, topics, and arguments in health care ethics. Each chapter begins with a case example in which health care professionals, patients, or others confront a specific moral problem or question in a health care setting, and each chapter ends with an analysis of that case. This first chapter will examine basic concepts of ethics and health care and will consider the role and significance of ethics in health care relationships and practices.

What is ethics?

One might claim that the answer to this simple question is so obvious that it needs no discussion. We frequently encounter the terms 'ethics,' 'morality,' 'ethical,' and 'moral' in our daily lives; popular media outlets regularly feature stories about moral conflict, moral failure, and, occasionally, moral heroism in health care, business, politics, and other areas of public and private life. Many times each day, we make decisions and take actions that have moral significance, although we usually do not consciously consider the moral dimension of our decisions and actions.

Despite the ubiquity of ethics in our lives, when I ask students, in the first meeting of an ethics course, to give me a concise definition of ethics, I am virtually always met with silence and puzzled looks. The students appear to share the view expressed by US Supreme Court justice Potter Stewart in a pornography case – Justice Stewart wrote that he would not attempt to define pornography, but claimed "I know it when I see it."[1]

Although they may not realize it, my students' initial reluctance to propose a definition of ethics may reflect the fact that 'ethics,' 'morality,' and related terms are commonly used in several different ways. 'Ethics' can refer to various members of a family of related concepts. Among the various concepts of ethics are (at least) the following:

1. A set of rules or principles for human behavior, as, for example, the Ten Commandments, or the American Medical Association's Principles of Medical Ethics.

---

[1] *Jacobellis v. Ohio* 1964.

2. A field of scholarly inquiry within philosophy, theology, and other disciplines, including various methods and theories (for example, Aristotelian ethics and Islamic ethics).
3. The state of a person's character, as, for example, "Mother Teresa is a paragon of ethics."
4. A feature of human choice and action, as, for example, "Abusing that disabled person was unethical."

Each of these different but related concepts of ethics will figure in this book. Although they are different, all of them address questions of what kind of people we should be, what actions we may or should undertake, and how we should relate to one another and to the world around us. Some scholars maintain that there is a significant difference in meaning between the terms 'ethics' and 'ethical' on the one hand, and 'morality' and 'moral' on the other. These terms may have slightly different shades of meaning, but I believe that they are very commonly used as synonyms, and therefore I will use them interchangeably throughout the volume.

Sources of moral guidance

If we recognize that ethics offers guidance about what kind of person we should be and how we should act, an obvious follow-up question is "Where does this moral guidance come from?" Unlike the first question mentioned above, students have a number of ready answers to this second question. Many credit their parents or teachers for providing this guidance, some cite the role of their religion and its doctrines, others recognize the influence of their peers and their cultural communities, still others appeal to social norms, especially norms embodied in the law, and a few mention the inner voice of conscience. Students with particular backgrounds may add that moral philosophy, or the moral standards and principles of their profession, offer further guidance.

In today's diverse and multicultural societies, all of these sources, and many others, offer valuable moral advice. This multiplicity of guides can encourage us to lead thoughtful and committed moral lives, but it also poses an obvious problem. In a variety of situations in which we confront a difficult moral choice, different sources of guidance on which we rely may disagree about what we should do, and none of these sources is likely to have a convincing claim to priority or infallibility. How, then, should we determine what to do when our trusted sources of moral guidance disagree? This problem can arise for individuals seeking to make a responsible decision and carry it out, and it can obviously also arise when two or more people disagree about what joint action they should take, as, for example, a physician and patient considering what treatment plan they should adopt for that patient's illness. Because contemporary societies are culturally, religiously, and morally pluralistic, we frequently confront uncertainty and disagreement about what course of action to pursue. What can we do in such situations?

Resolving moral disagreements

Recognizing the fact of moral disagreement need not result in moral stalemate or paralysis; when we confront a difficult situation, we may recognize that doing nothing as well as taking some action is a conscious choice with significant consequences. We may, therefore, attempt to resolve the disagreement. Methods for resolving moral conflicts include rational argument, what I will call "moral persuasion," and negotiation and compromise. When these methods are unsuccessful, it may sometimes be appropriate to resort to a kind of coercion. In other situations, the parties may conclude that they cannot reach an agreement and therefore cannot engage in a joint endeavor. Let's consider each of these options in turn.

Rational argument. The most powerful method for resolving moral disagreement is appeal to a compelling rational argument. The proponent of one conclusion about how to resolve a disagreement may be able to present an argument showing that that conclusion follows, according to established rules of formal logic, from premises that both parties accept as true. Refusal to accept the conclusion of such a compelling moral argument would be an irrational decision. In many, if not most situations of moral disagreement, however, it may not be possible for either party in the dispute to construct a logically valid argument from shared premises. So, this method of resolution of disagreement will not be available in those situations.

"Moral persuasion." The proponent of one position in a situation of moral disagreement might appeal, not to a compelling rational argument, but rather to characteristics of his or her position that she believes will be attractive or persuasive to other parties, and invite them to embrace that position because of those attractive characteristics. One might, for example, claim that a particular course of action will likely have certain beneficial consequences, or that it is the kind of action a virtuous person would choose. Even if such invitations to view the action in a positive way do not constitute a logically sound argument, they may persuade others to endorse that course of action.

Negotiation and compromise. Despite the fact of moral pluralism and the frequent occurrence of moral uncertainty and disagreement, we obviously also have strong interests in making and acting on moral choices, both individually and jointly. If health care professionals and their patients, for example, cannot agree on a treatment plan for the patient's illness, central interests and goals of both parties will likely be frustrated. When we encounter differences in moral beliefs and preferences, therefore, we often choose to examine the situation more thoroughly, in an effort to find a course of action that both parties can accept and undertake together. Such an examination may uncover shared values and goals that can form the basis for agreement, or it may motivate the parties to accept limitation of some individual preferences in order to achieve common goals. A process of moral negotiation and compromise may achieve agreement on a joint course of action that is not optimal for either party, but that does enable the parties to work together to achieve shared goals.

Coercion. If a moral disagreement cannot be resolved, one party may attempt to force the other to act in a particular way. Though such a coerced action obviously does not resolve the moral disagreement, it may be morally justifiable in certain contexts, especially contexts in which one party has legitimate authority over another. Consider, for example, the relationship of parents and their minor children. Parents and children sometimes disagree about whether the children should be permitted to act in certain ways. When these disagreements cannot be resolved, it may be permissible for parents to constrain the behavior of their children, based on the parents' considered judgment. Such authority relationships also commonly exist in employment settings. In entering military service, for example, a person may agree to be bound by the orders of a superior officer.

Agreeing to disagree. Even the best efforts of the parties to resolve moral disagreements by means of rational argument, moral persuasion, and negotiation and compromise have no guarantee of success. The moral beliefs and values of the parties may be so deep-seated and divergent that there is little or no basis for agreement on a common course of action. Unless one party has legitimate authority over the other, therefore, the parties may decide that they can only agree to disagree. As a consequence of this decision, the parties will not be able to cooperate on a course of action in the situation about which they disagree. Patients, for example, may refuse treatments recommended by their physicians, and physicians may refuse to provide services requested by their patients.

This book will identify and examine central ethical issues and problems in health care. It will review and evaluate a variety of reasons, arguments, and procedures offered to address those issues and problems. The book is designed to give readers an understanding of the issues and arguments, and to enable them to engage in moral deliberation and to develop and defend a considered position on those ethical issues.

What is health care?

Like ethics, the concept of health care may seem so obvious and well understood that it requires little further discussion. In developed nations, virtually every resident receives health care services periodically throughout his or her life, usually beginning on or before the day of one's birth and ending on the day of one's death. Health care serves a variety of widely recognized and related purposes, including the prevention and treatment of illness and injury, the relief of pain and suffering, the preservation and restoration of physical and mental function, and the preservation and restoration of physical form. We also recognize that health care includes a variety of services in multiple settings, from physician office visits for preventive care and health maintenance, to emergency department treatment for acute illnesses and injuries, to ongoing care for chronic or progressive illnesses such as diabetes or heart disease, to major surgery and intensive care for catastrophic conditions such as multiple trauma or organ failure.

The broad scope and national prominence of the health care systems of the United States and other developed nations deserve brief mention here. Health care provides employment to millions of people in a variety of health care professions and related occupations. It is a major sector of the US economy, with projected national health expenditures of 2.9 *trillion* dollars in 2013, or 17.2 percent of the entire US gross domestic product (GDP).[2] More than 90 percent of these expenditures are for health care services provided to individual patients, including hospital and nursing home care, the services of physicians, nurses, dentists, and other professionals, and prescription drugs and other medical products. The primary focus of this book, therefore, will be on ethical issues in personal health care. In addition to personal health care services, the US health care system also includes public health activities and biomedical research, and Chapter 19 of this volume is devoted to ethical issues in biomedical research on human subjects.

How is ethics related to health care?

Health care is clearly a major focus of human effort and resource investment in the United States and around the world, on a par with education, national security, manufacturing, agriculture, transportation, and government. Ethical issues arise in all of these areas, but judging from the number and intensity of public debates, nowhere else is attention to ethical issues more prominent than in health care. Why does ethics play such a conspicuous role in the health care arena? How can attention to ethical issues inform and guide the choices and actions of health care professionals and patients?

One probable reason for the sustained attention to ethics in health care is the significance of the values and interests health care serves. We rely on health care to protect us, if possible, from untimely death, disability, suffering, and disfigurement. These are clearly not trivial matters, but rather some of the most basic interests of every human being. Because these interests are so important, both individuals and groups are willing to devote considerable time, energy, and resources to health care decisions and practices.

Despite the importance of the human values at stake in health care, we would not need to pay much attention to ethical issues if most or all of our health care choices and their likely consequences were clear, and the best choices were obvious. More often than not, however, when basic values are at stake in health care, the opposite is true. Serious health conditions are

---

[2] Sisko et al. (2014).

often complex and difficult to understand. Alternative treatment plans may also be complicated, with multiple interventions and a variety of different possible consequences, both beneficial and harmful. The actual outcome of a proposed treatment for an individual patient may be very uncertain.

Consider, for example, the situation of Mr. Johnson, a 50-year-old man who seeks treatment for new symptoms of dizziness and vivid visual hallucinations. Diagnostic imaging studies reveal a brain tumor, and a biopsy confirms the diagnosis of a virulent form of brain cancer. An oncologist breaks this bad news to Mr. Johnson, explains what is known about this form of cancer, and describes several alternative treatment options, including whole brain radiation treatments, intrathecal chemotherapy (a series of injections of chemotherapy drugs directly into the cerebrospinal fluid), and provision of palliative medications designed to ameliorate the symptoms of the disease. The first two treatment plans offer a small chance of remission of the cancer and of extended survival, but they also have side effects of different kinds and significant risks of severe complications. Whole brain radiation may cause cognitive disability, and intrathecal chemotherapy may cause severe headache, nausea, and vomiting. Palliative treatments may relieve symptoms and enhance Mr. Johnson's quality of life, but only temporarily, if the cancerous tumor grows as expected. Mr. Johnson finds the prospects for success of the more aggressive, possibly life-prolonging treatment options unimpressive, in relation to their recognized complications and side effects, but his wife and two children urge him to choose the treatment that maximizes his chances of survival.

Mr. Johnson has had little experience with serious illness, and he initially feels overwhelmed by the complexity and gravity of his situation and his treatment choices. He may struggle to make treatment choices that require trade-offs between conflicting prudential and moral values. He wants to avoid a premature death, but is also reluctant to accept the pain and suffering of a long and rigorous course of treatment that offers only a limited chance of prolonging his life. His own individual preference may be to focus on palliative care to improve his quality of life, but he may not want to hurt his family members by refusing their request that he accept aggressive anticancer therapy. He may wonder how expensive the proposed treatments are, how much of those expenses his health insurance will cover, and whether he should commit his family's life savings to paying for his treatment.

This case illustrates the centrality of the values at stake in health care, the complexity of health care choices, and the unavoidable uncertainty of health care outcomes. Recognizing that he faces choices that are difficult and will change his life significantly, Mr. Johnson will very likely seek and be guided by the advice of his physicians, and perhaps also of other professionals who are caring for him. These professionals, in turn, have embraced a responsibility to serve the health care needs of their patients. In Mr. Johnson's case, that responsibility includes advice and assistance in coming to terms with his condition and making treatment decisions with important medical and moral consequences. That assistance should include a clear explanation of his illness and of the available treatment options, and the best available information about the likely outcomes of the different options for prolongation of life, preservation of function, and quality of life. The information that Mr. Johnson's physicians should provide to him includes both important factual information about his condition and identification and estimation of the value of different anticipated treatment outcomes. If Mr. Johnson's physicians conclude that one treatment option is superior to the others, they should also recommend that option and explain the reasons for their recommendation. This guidance will be of great importance to Mr. Johnson in making his decision, whether or not he chooses to accept a recommendation that his physicians have offered.

Public officials and health care facility executives frequently confront moral and policy decisions that are as complex, difficult, and serious as the treatment decisions facing Mr. Johnson and his caregivers. Consider, for example, the response of hospitals worldwide to the 2014 epidemic of Ebola virus disease (EVD) in West Africa. Faced with the real prospect that a patient with EVD may seek care for this virulent and often lethal illness at their facility, hospital officials around the world confronted decisions about how they would respond. Despite initially limited information about effective prevention and treatment for EVD, failure to prepare might have fatal consequences for both patients and staff. Difficult decisions included:

1. Which staff members should assume the considerable risk of caring for EVD patients?
2. How much, and what kind of, personal protective equipment (PPE) should hospitals procure?

3. What training in PPE use and EVD treatment should hospitals provide, and for whom?

4. Should restrictions be imposed on the freedom of movement of hospital staff who care for an EVD patient, in order to prevent disease transmission to third parties?

5. May hospitals deny specific treatments to EVD patients on the grounds that the expected benefit of those treatments for the patients is disproportionate to the expected risk to the clinicians providing the treatments?

6. May hospitals refuse to admit EVD patients because their care is too expensive, or, in the event of a local EVD epidemic, because hospital resources are inadequate to care for new patients?

It is important to recognize that defensible answers to these questions will depend on several different kinds of information, including information about the natural history, transmission, and treatment of EVD, hospital resources, and the moral interests of EVD patients, other hospital patients, and health care professionals. Public officials confront comparable problems in deciding about isolation of EVD patients, quarantine of others who may have been exposed to the Ebola virus, and restrictions on travel from the epidemic region.

This book is designed to enable readers to identify central moral issues in health care, understand essential concepts in bioethics, recognize the role of factual information in moral deliberation, and engage in effective moral reasoning. I believe that this knowledge and these skills will help readers to develop and defend reasonable solutions to difficult and significant moral problems frequently encountered in health care.

I hasten to add, however, that I do not view ethics as a panacea or "magic bullet" able to achieve a unique and definitive solution to all of the thorny moral problems in contemporary health care. That would be a highly desirable outcome, but, like most scholars in this field, I believe that it is not within the power of the discipline of ethics to achieve. Instead, I acknowledge that ethics has clear limits. For example, ethics is clearly interdependent with other disciplines and bodies of knowledge. Defensible solutions to significant problems in health care rely on moral considerations, to be sure, but they also rely on various other kinds of information. In the case described above, for example, Mr. Johnson and his physicians need empirical information about the likely consequences of different treatment plans in order to evaluate those plans. Even the best scientific information and the most thorough evaluation of the relevant moral considerations may not demonstrate that one treatment plan is clearly superior to all others. A careful reasoning process, however, may enable Mr. Johnson to eliminate at least some options as worse than others.

Case analysis

In the case described at the beginning of this chapter, MMC confronts a difficult decision about whether to provide repeat heart valve replacement surgery for patients whose valve damage is the result of IV drug use. The MMC president has delegated the task of developing and implementing a consistent institutional procedure for the treatment of future patients with this condition to the CMO.

Let's suppose that the CMO begins this task by convening a meeting of interested medical staff members who hold different views. At the meeting, she asks her colleagues to state their reasons for the views they hold.[3] Each group offers multiple reasons for its conclusion. The cardiovascular surgeons who oppose repeat valve replacement argue that these patients have been clearly informed about the grave risks of continuing IV drug use, and so they should assume responsibility for their own life and health by refraining from this dangerous practice. They point out that there are clearly diminishing returns from repeat surgeries – second and subsequent cardiac surgeries are riskier and significantly less likely to be successful. If these patients continue their drug use, the likelihood of repeat infection and severe heart damage is very high. The surgeons appeal to an analogous situation, noting that patients with liver failure who continue to use alcohol or drugs are routinely not accepted as candidates for liver transplantation, because this behavior will result in failure of a transplant organ. They point out that surgeons' decisions not to offer surgery are routinely honored at MMC, and they contend that this deference to surgical judgment should also apply to the decision not to operate on these patients.[4] Finally, they argue that, in addition to their reduced prospects for success, repeat surgeries on these patients impose significant burdens and costs on MMC staff, other

[3] For more detailed statements of these arguments, see DiMaio et al. (2009) and Hull and Jadbabaie (2014).
[4] For a discussion of this prerogative of surgeons, see Wicclair and White (2014).

patients, and the institution as a whole. These surgeries may limit or delay surgical procedures for other patients, they pose a risk of intraoperative transmission of HIV, hepatitis, and other infections to surgeons and surgical staff, and, because these patients are indigent, the costs of their treatment will be borne by MMC and will adversely affect the financial health of the institution at a time of increased competition and reduced reimbursement.

The infectious disease (ID) physicians who support repeat valve replacement surgery also offer multiple reasons for their position. They argue that IV drug use should not be understood as a moral failing, but rather as an addictive disease. Because patients with this disease lack the capacity to control their behavior, denying life-sustaining treatment to them is an unjustified form of blaming the victim for his or her predicament. At the very least, they maintain, these patients should be offered drug rehabilitation treatment that includes detoxification and relapse prevention strategies. These physicians challenge claims that repeat surgery has little or no value, asserting that surgery can prolong life and that rehabilitation therapy offers hope for overcoming addictive disease. Finally, they point out that many, if not most, of the patients treated at MMC suffer from conditions that are largely the result of unhealthy behaviors, including smoking, overeating, and failure to adhere to treatment recommendations. Because we do not deny treatment to these other patients, they argue, it would be arbitrary and unfair to single out IV drug users and deny beneficial treatment to them alone.

At the meeting, advocates of both positions acknowledge some significance in the arguments offered by their opponents, but neither group is convinced by those arguments and willing to change its view. The CMO informs them that she has accepted a responsibility, on behalf of the institution, to formulate and implement a consistent approach to the care of these patients, and that she will enforce adherence to this policy by MMC medical and clinical staff. She then requests suggestions for elements of the policy on which both sides can agree. The ID physicians propose that all patients who present with this condition be offered comprehensive drug rehabilitation services, and that MMC fund the development of these services in the community it serves. Some surgeons and hospital administrators express concern about the cost of these services, but most are in favor of this requirement. The surgeons, in turn, propose that their decisions to deny valve replacement surgery to these patients be honored, especially in situations when the patient's overall medical condition is grave and the risk of major surgery is therefore very high. Several ID physicians acknowledge that this major surgery should not be offered in some cases; they propose, in response, that the decision to forgo this surgery not be made by individual surgeons, but rather by a small group of physicians that includes a cardiovascular surgeon, an ID specialist, a psychiatrist, the chair of the institutional ethics committee, and the CMO herself. Several surgeons object to this proposal as an undue limitation of their professional prerogatives, but several others express willingness to share responsibility for these difficult decisions. The CMO expresses interest in these suggestions, and she appoints a small working group to draft a description of this procedure and to develop medical criteria to guide decisions about these surgeries. She approves the resulting policy draft and informs all MMC staff that they will be expected to adhere to the new policy.

In this situation, the CMO addresses a difficult problem for her institution by examining moral arguments for different positions, engaging in a process of negotiation and compromise, and then implementing a policy mandating a standard approach to making treatment decisions for these patients. How would you evaluate her approach to resolving a moral dispute? Can you suggest a better way to address this problem?

2   A brief history of health care ethics and clinical ethics consultation in the United States

Case example

On April 15, 1975, 21-year-old Karen Ann Quinlan attended a friend's birthday party at a bar near her home in New Jersey. Karen was on a strict diet at the time, and she was also taking the anti-anxiety drug diazepam (Valium®). After several drinks at the party, Karen felt faint, and friends took her home and put her to bed. When they checked on her fifteen minutes later, she had stopped breathing. They attempted to revive her and called for assistance. Emergency medical technicians arrived, continued cardio-pulmonary resuscitation efforts, and transported Karen to a nearby hospital, where she was placed on a mechanical ventilator.

Karen remained hospitalized, on ventilator support, for the next several months, but she did not regain consciousness. Neurologists diagnosed her condition as a "persistent vegetative state," a form of irreversible unconsciousness caused by lack of oxygen to her brain during the time when she was not breathing. Karen did, however, retain some brain activity. She did not meet established brain-oriented legal and medical criteria for death (sometimes called "brain death"), since those criteria require a finding of "irreversible cessation of total brain function." Her physicians were convinced that Karen could not survive without ongoing ventilator support.

Karen's parents, Joseph and Julia Quinlan, had consented to all recommended life-sustaining treatments for their daughter during the first three months of her hospitalization. By the end of July 1975, however, they reached the conclusion that Karen would not want continuing life-sustaining treatment in a state of permanent unconsciousness. The Quinlans were devout Roman Catholics; after consultation with their parish priest, they requested that Karen's ventilator support be discontinued and that she be allowed to die. Karen's physicians responded that they could not honor this request, on the grounds that removing Karen's ventilator support would be a form of euthanasia that would be immoral, illegal, and contrary to medical standards of care. Karen was a patient at St. Claire's Hospital, and the hospital supported the physicians' decision to continue ventilator support. What should have been done to resolve this disagreement?[1]

With the rapid expansion of health care services in the United States in the decades immediately following World War II, patients, health care professionals, and the American public at large confronted new and challenging moral questions about what treatments should be offered and provided, especially near the beginning and the end of human life. A new field of intellectual inquiry, variously called "medical ethics," "bioethics," "biomedical ethics," and "health care ethics," emerged to address these questions.[2] The growing field of health care ethics provided a body of knowledge and methods of practical reasoning that made possible a new practice, called "clinical ethics consultation," in US hospitals and other health care facilities. Clinical ethics consultation is now a very widely available service to assist professionals and patients when they confront ethics questions in health care. This chapter will provide a brief review of the history of health care ethics and of clinical ethics consultation in the United States.

The new field of health care ethics

Attention to the moral responsibilities of physicians dates back to the establishment of medicine as a profession in classical antiquity, as demonstrated in the Oath of Hippocrates and other Hippocratic writings.[3] Through the intervening ages, a few physicians wrote treatises on their professional duties, and the American Medical Association (AMA) adopted a "Code of Medical Ethics" at its inaugural convention in 1847.[4] Theologians in several faith traditions, including Roman Catholicism and Judaism, offered analyses of the duties of physicians and patients in specific situations.[5] Ethics in medicine and health care was not, however, viewed as a distinct field of

---

[1] For a more detailed account of Karen's story, see Pence (2004) or Quinlan and Quinlan (1977).

[2] Representative titles of early books include *Ethics in Medicine* (Reiser et al. 1977), *Contemporary Issues in Bioethics* (Beauchamp and Walters 1978), *Health Care Ethics: A Theological Analysis* (Ashley and O'Rourke 1978), and *Principles of Biomedical Ethics* (Beauchamp and Childress 1979).

[3] See Hippocrates (1923).   [4] American Medical Association (1847).

[5] See, for example, Kelly (1958) and Jacobovitz (1975).

inquiry, with its own specific problems, resources, and methods, until well into the second half of the twentieth century.

Several scholars, most notably David Rothman and Albert Jonsen, have offered book-length accounts of the origins of the new field of bioethics.[6] They argue that bioethics emerged in response to a convergence of events and trends in American society and health care. Health care in the United States experienced explosive growth in the years following World War II.[7] Greatly increased public spending for biomedical research fueled the development and dissemination of a wide variety of new and powerful medical treatments. For the first time in history, medical treatments and technologies, including mechanical ventilation, artificial nutrition and hydration, and organ replacement therapies, could exert significant control over the time and manner of death for patients with a variety of catastrophic illnesses.

Post-World War II public financing programs also subsidized community hospital construction and the rapid expansion of medical education. Employer-provided private health insurance programs increased access to health care for American workers and their families, and establishment of the public Medicare and Medicaid health insurance programs in 1965 did the same for elderly and many indigent Americans. All of these developments made a growing array of new medical technologies accessible to an increasing number of American patients. These technologies offered substantial benefits for many patients, but they also caused serious complications and side effects, imposing severe burdens of suffering and disability on other patients. Treatment innovations prompted physicians to pose a new question: "Now that we can, with increasing hope of success, use new technologies to prolong the lives of catastrophically ill patients, *must* we always attempt to do so?" Nothing in their training equipped physicians to answer this question confidently, and so they sought assistance with new and difficult ethical problems.[8]

American society at large was also undergoing major changes during this period. The civil rights movement, the anti-Vietnam War movement, and the feminist movement of the 1960s and 1970s urged Americans to question authority, to embrace political activism, and to recognize individual rights. Social critics began to question the paternalistic tradition in American

---

[6] Rothman (1992) and Jonsen (1998).   [7] Starr (1982).
[8] See Veatch (1976) for an early analysis of these problems.

health care, in which physicians made treatment decisions and patients played a mostly passive role. The 1960s witnessed the emergence of a new legal responsibility of physicians to obtain their patients' informed consent to treatment.[9] Following its recognition in US law, proponents of the emerging field of health care ethics emphasized informed consent as a paradigm of patients' moral rights to active participation in decisions about their health care.

Finally, three high-profile events in the early and mid-1970s focused substantial public attention on moral problems in health care. The first of these was a 1972 Associated Press exposé of the Tuskegee Study of Untreated Syphilis, a 40-year-long series of clinical trials in rural Alabama on African-American men with syphilis.[10] The Tuskegee Study was roundly condemned, both for failing to obtain the informed consent of the subjects to participation in this research and for withholding effective antibiotic treatment from the subjects when that treatment became available in the late 1940s. Tuskegee became an enduring symbol for African-American distrust of the US health care system, and it evoked a formal apology to the research subjects from President Bill Clinton in 1997. In a more immediate response to the disturbing revelations of the Tuskegee Study, the US Congress in 1974 established a National Commission for the Protection of Human Subjects of Biomedical and Behavioral Research.[11] Congress charged the Commission to propose regulations for the protection of human research subjects and to develop guidelines for research ethics. Several years later, the National Commission published *The Belmont Report: Ethical Principles and Guidelines for the Protection of Human Subjects of Research*.[12] This report contains the first published statement of what has become widely known as the principle-based approach to moral reasoning in health care.[13]

The second high-profile event was the announcement, on January 22, 1973, of the US Supreme Court decision on abortion in *Roe* v. *Wade*.[14] The Court's decision, giving Constitutional protection to a woman's right to abortion, evoked a heated moral and political debate over abortion policy

---

[9] See Faden et al. (1986) for an account of this history.   [10] See Jones (1981).

[11] National Research Act (1974).

[12] National Commission for the Protection of Human Subjects of Biomedical and Behavioral Research (1978).

[13] For more on the principle-based approach, see Chapter 3, "Methods of health care ethics." For more on research ethics, see Chapter 19, "Research on human subjects."

[14] *Roe* v. *Wade* (1973).

that continues to the present day. Many prominent philosophers and theologians have contributed to this debate, offering analyses of the rights and duties of women, the moral status of the fetus, and the proper role of law in regulating reproductive decisions.[15] Subsequent years brought the introduction of assisted reproductive technologies, including *in vitro* fertilization, gestational surrogacy, and prenatal genetic diagnosis. Each of these options had its proponents and opponents, and the control of human reproduction became a major topic area for the new field of health care ethics.[16]

The third high-profile event of the 1970s was the widely publicized case of Karen Ann Quinlan described at the beginning of this chapter.[17] The Quinlan case is generally acknowledged to have brought end-of-life treatment decisions "out of the closet" and into the consciousness of the American public.[18] In response to Karen's predicament, state legislatures, beginning with California in 1976, enacted statutes recognizing a new mechanism for refusing unwanted life-sustaining treatment, the "living will."[19] The Quinlan case was followed by a series of legal cases defining the scope and limits of "the right to die," culminating in 1990 with the first US Supreme Court decision on end-of-life care in the case of Nancy Cruzan.[20] From their beginnings in *Quinlan*, end-of-life treatment decisions have been a major focus of bioethical attention.[21]

The above-described events focused American public attention on a variety of moral issues in health care. Confronted with these novel issues, legislators enacted new statutes, and courts established new precedents. Scholars in theology, philosophy, medicine, law, and other disciplines proposed methods for addressing bioethical issues, offered analyses of specific problems, and defended solutions to those problems. To support these activities, a variety of professional institutions and scholarly resources began to appear. In 1969, a group of physicians and ministers founded the Society for Health and Human Values (SHHV), the first

---

[15] For an account of the early history of debates over reproductive decision-making, see Jonsen (1998): 282–321.

[16] For more on ethical issues in reproduction, see Chapter 12, "Assisted reproductive technologies," Chapter 13, "Abortion," and Chapter 14, "Maternal-fetal conflict."

[17] *In re Quinlan* (1976).   [18] See Fried (1976).   [19] Natural Death Act (1976).

[20] *Cruzan v. Director, Missouri Department of Health* (1990).

[21] For more on ethical issues in treatment near the end of life, see Chapters 15–18 of this volume.

professional association devoted to moral issues in health care. Research institutes in bioethics were established, including the Hastings Center in 1969 and the Kennedy Institute of Ethics at Georgetown University in 1971. Scholarly journals were founded, beginning with the *Hastings Center Report* in 1971 and the *Journal of Medicine and Philosophy* in 1976. Also beginning in the 1970s, US medical schools hired faculty to develop and teach courses in bioethics.[22] By the latter half of the 1970s, several anthology textbooks of bioethics were in print.[23] A four-volume *Encyclopedia of Bioethics* was published in 1978,[24] and a book-length approach to bioethical reasoning, *Principles of Biomedical Ethics*, by Tom Beauchamp and James Childress, appeared in 1979.[25] By the end of the 1970s, then, health care ethics was well on its way to recognition as a significant and independent field of scholarly inquiry.

In the subsequent decades, health care ethics has continued its steady expansion and has become a standard part of health care professional education in the United States. The Liaison Committee on Medical Education, the accreditation agency for US and Canadian schools of medicine, has, for example, required ethics instruction in medical education for many years. The literature of health care ethics continues to grow, with dozens of scholarly journals now in publication, and the *Encyclopedia of Bioethics* now in its fourth edition.[26] In 1998, the SHVV joined with two other professional associations, the Society for Bioethics Consultation (SBC) and the American Association of Bioethics (AAB), to form the American Society for Bioethics and Humanities (ASBH), whose annual meetings attract hundreds of bioethics scholars, teachers, and students. The chapters of this book describe significant developments and multiple ongoing debates on a wide variety of health care ethics topics.

Precursors to clinical ethics consultation

As the number and complexity of ethical questions in health care increased, early commentators offered tentative ideas about potential sources of advice and guidance in addressing those questions. In 1975, pediatrician

---

[22] Veatch and Sollitto (1976).

[23] See, for example, Gorovitz et al. (1976), Reiser et al. (1977), and Beauchamp and Walters (1978).

[24] Reich (1978).   [25] Beauchamp and Childress (1979).   [26] Jennings (2014).

Karen Teel suggested that hospital "ethics committees" could be established for this purpose; her suggestion received widespread attention when it was cited by the New Jersey Supreme Court in its 1976 *Quinlan* decision.[27] Ethics committees have in fact become a standard feature in US hospitals and the primary provider of ethics consultation today, but in 1975 they were virtually unknown. No guidelines existed regarding the structure or function of ethics committees, and a 1983 report of a national survey of 602 hospitals estimated that only 1 percent of US hospitals had ethics committees.[28]

Before the advent of hospital ethics committees, however, at least three other types of committees with ethics-related functions were operating in specific health care settings in the United States. In 1962, an institutional committee became the subject of a lengthy article in *LIFE* magazine entitled "They Decide Who Lives, Who Dies."[29] In that article, journalist Shana Alexander reported on the Admissions and Policy Committee of the Seattle Artificial Kidney Center. Several years earlier, Dr. Belding Scribner's invention of an implantable device enabling regular access to a patient's circulatory system allowed him to provide long-term hemodialysis to patients with end stage renal disease (ESRD). Scribner secured funding for a nine-bed dialysis center, but treatment candidates quickly exceeded the center's capacity, and so an Admissions and Policy Committee of anonymous community members was created to decide which medically suitable candidates would be offered dialysis. The Committee used a variety of informal criteria, including age, gender, marital status, number of dependents, income, educational background, occupation, past accomplishments, and future potential, to make their selections.[30] Alexander's article called public and scholarly attention to the Committee's methods. Critics objected to its use of "social worth" criteria to make these life-and-death treatment decisions, with one commentary asserting that "the Pacific Northwest is no place for a Henry David Thoreau with bad kidneys."[31] In 1972, Congress was persuaded to respond to this dramatic example of scarcity of a life-prolonging medical treatment by adding funding for treatment of virtually all patients with ESRD to the Medicare health insurance program.

[27] Teel (1975).   [28] Youngner et al. (1983).   [29] Alexander (1962).
[30] For another account of this issue, see Jonsen (1998): 211–217.
[31] Sanders and Dukeminier (1968).

A very different type of committee, called an institutional review board (IRB), was mandated by the National Institutes of Health (NIH) in 1966 for all institutions conducting federally funded research on human subjects.[32] IRBs were given a specific charge, namely, to review protocols for proposed research on human subjects within their institution and to determine whether that research satisfies federal regulations for the protection of the research subjects. Because IRBs were in operation in medical schools and research hospitals in the 1970s, this committee-based mechanism may have suggested itself as a model for review of clinical ethics problems. Although IRBs and hospital ethics committees both address ethical issues, their functions are otherwise quite different. IRBs perform a required prospective review of all federally funded human subjects research and are governed by specific federal regulations; ethics committees provide ethics consultation upon request in individual clinical cases as a voluntary service and are free to develop their own procedures and guidelines for this practice.

Several commentators describe yet another kind of ethics committee operating in some Catholic hospitals by the early 1970s. Establishment of these committees, called "medico-moral" or "medical-moral" committees, was recommended by both the US and Canadian Catholic bishops in 1971.[33] These committees were initially created to ensure that Catholic hospitals observed Church doctrine on such matters as contraception, abortion, sterilization, and euthanasia. In 1974, A. R. Kosnik proposed a more expansive charge for these committees, including staff education and inter-professional communication, in addition to interpretation and enforcement of Catholic religious directives.[34] Lappetito and Thompson report that many of these committees expanded their mission in the 1980s and evolved into institutional ethics committees with the three standard functions of ethics education, ethics-related policy development, and clinical ethics consultation.[35]

The initial impetus for ethics consultation

As noted above, the idea of a hospital ethics committee first received widespread attention when the New Jersey Supreme Court, in its highly publicized 1976 *Quinlan* decision, endorsed a suggestion by Teel that such a

---

[32] For more on the history of protection of human research subjects, see Rothman (1992): 85–100.

[33] Anonymous (1983).   [34] Kosnik (1974).   [35] Lappetito and Thompson (1993).

committee could assist physicians in making difficult ethical decisions.[36] Both Teel and the Court proposed a consultative role for ethics committees in individual clinical cases, but the nature of the role each envisioned for these committees was significantly different. Teel opined that ethics committees could help physicians by "exploring all of the options for a particular patient" and by "diffus[ing] responsibility for making these judgments." The Court, in contrast, assigned to the committee the task of confirming the patient's prognosis, in these words: "If that consultative body agrees that there is no reasonable possibility of Karen's ever emerging from her present comatose condition to a cognitive, sapient state, the present life-support system may be withdrawn." Early commentaries noted this confusion about the proper role of ethics committees and proposed "Prognosis Committee" as a more appropriate title for the task assigned to such committees by the New Jersey Supreme Court.[37] Despite this confusion about roles, the *Quinlan* Court's endorsement of "ethics committees" likely encouraged their establishment in some US hospitals. Reflecting on the Quinlan case and on several early reports describing ethics committee activities, the President's Commission for the Study of Ethical Problems in Medicine, in its landmark 1983 report *Deciding to Forego Life-Sustaining Treatment*, suggested that institutions give "serious consideration" to establishing ethics committees to review treatment decisions made on behalf of patients who lack decision-making capacity.[38]

A second major impetus for the creation of institutional ethics committees emerged out of the hotly debated issue in the 1980s of life-sustaining treatment for severely ill newborns. Similar to the debate over life-sustaining treatment for adults, a highly publicized case triggered both public awareness and policy responses to this issue. In 1982, an infant known only as "Baby Doe" was born in Bloomington, Indiana, with Down syndrome. Baby Doe also had esophageal atresia, a surgically correctable condition in which food is prevented from entering the stomach. His parents refused permission for the surgery, a circuit court judge upheld their refusal, the Indiana Supreme Court decided not to review that decision, and Baby Doe died six

---

[36] See Teel (1975) and *In re Quinlan* (1976).

[37] Medical Society of New Jersey, Association of Osteopathic Physicians and Surgeons, New Jersey Hospital Association (1977).

[38] President's Commission for the Study of Ethical Problems in Medicine and Biomedical and Behavioral Research (1983b): 164.

days after birth.[39] Outraged by this case, President Ronald Reagan directed the Department of Health and Human Services to notify health care providers that failure to provide life-sustaining treatment to handicapped infants was a violation of federal anti-discrimination law. Subsequent regulations required posting of public notices in hospitals, established a hotline to report violations of the law, and granted federal investigators access to hospital records to investigate potential violations. This federal action evoked strong objections from medical and hospital professional associations, multiple legal challenges, new federal legislation, and a series of revisions to the "Baby Doe regulations."[40]

The mechanism of case review by hospital committees assumed a central role in the evolution of the Baby Doe controversy. Medical and hospital professional associations proposed that, instead of direct federal intervention, hospitals create "infant bioethical review committees" to examine all decisions to forgo life-sustaining treatment of handicapped neonates.[41] After earlier versions of the Baby Doe regulations were overturned by the courts, revised federal regulations endorsed the use of hospital committees, then called "infant care review committees," as a first forum for review of non-treatment decisions, and recognition of those committees remained in the final Baby Doe rules issued on April 15, 1985, and still in effect.[42] These regulations provided a strong incentive for hospitals with neonatal intensive care units to establish infant care review committees. Although establishment of such committees was never mandatory, it offered a clear way for hospitals to demonstrate their intention to comply with federal and state regulations regarding treatment for severely ill newborns. In mail surveys conducted by the American Hospital Association's Society for Patient Representatives, responding hospitals reported a doubling (to 60 percent) of hospital ethics committees between 1983 and 1985; the survey authors attribute this increase to hospital efforts to respond to the Baby Doe regulations.[43]

Early obstacles and strategies

By the mid-1980s, hospital ethics committees and the practice of clinical ethics consultation were gaining a clear foothold in US hospitals. Because they were still novel concepts, however, the purpose and role of ethics

[39] Weir (1983).   [40] Moskop and Saldanha (1986).   [41] Wallis (1983).
[42] Department of Health and Human Services (1985).   [43] Anonymous (1985).

committees and ethics consultation were not yet well defined or understood. A 1986 *Handbook for Hospital Ethics Committees*, published by the American Hospital Association, identified case consultation, policy development, and education as the three core functions of ethics committees and offered practical guidance for establishing and sustaining ethics committees.[44]

Despite their growing numbers during this period, several obstacles stood in the way of establishing ethics committees and developing clinical ethics consultation services. Ethics consultation was designed as a way to bring moral advice to bear on difficult questions in the clinical setting, but this practice required a new kind of interaction between ethics and medicine, and early attempts to facilitate that interaction revealed a gap between the cultures of the two disciplines. On the one hand, physicians expressed concern that ethics consultants would intrude into their private relationships with patients, would usurp their authority, and would inappropriately scrutinize and criticize their actions. Some physicians argued that ethics consultation could be a valuable service, but that it should be provided by fellow health care professionals.[45] On the other hand, professional ethicists confessed unfamiliarity and discomfort with the role of clinical consultant and questioned whether the existing model of medical consultation by specialist physicians was the best model for their role as ethics advisors.[46]

Over time, clinical ethics consultation services developed various strategies to overcome these obstacles. To reassure reluctant physicians, consultants emphasized that their services were purely voluntary and provided only in response to a request for assistance from a health care professional, patient, or family member. The stated goal of ethics consultation was to provide useful advice and to assist in reaching agreement on a morally justifiable course of action, not to criticize or sanction health care professionals for unethical behavior. Ethics consultants also emphasized that they did not assume decision-making authority and that such authority remained in the hands of the primary stakeholders. Thus, ethics consultation services sought to provide timely, knowledgeable, and user-friendly assistance in addressing difficult ethics questions. Insofar as they were successful in this endeavor, clinicians came to recognize their value and request their assistance.

Consultation services also sought to overcome the initial reluctance of ethics scholars and teachers to participate in this activity. Health care

---

[44] Ross et al. (1986).   [45] See Siegler (1979) and La Puma and Schiedermayer (1991).
[46] See Fleetwood et al. (1989) and Barnard (1992).

professionals invited ethicists into various clinical settings, helping them to become familiar with medical terminology and clinical routines. Many ethics committees used small groups or teams to provide ethics consultation, thereby allowing ethicists to observe the consultation process and to develop skills for interacting with health care professionals, patients, and families and for communicating consultation suggestions or recommendations by means of the patient's medical record. The small group model remains the most popular way to provide ethics consultation, with two-thirds of consultation services reporting use of this model in the most recent national survey.[47]

As they labored to establish the practice of ethics consultation in the 1980s, early proponents also undertook professional activities to inform and support their efforts. A Society for Bioethics Consultation (SBC) was founded in 1986, and the SBC sponsored annual conferences on ethics consultation issues until it merged in 1998 with the SHHV and the AAB to form the American Society for Bioethics and Humanities (ASBH). Three new journals also emerged in quick succession. The first, the *HealthCare Ethics Committee Forum* (*HEC Forum*), appeared in 1989, with a mission to address ethical issues of interest to institutional ethics committee members. The second and third, the *Journal of Clinical Ethics* (1990) and the *Cambridge Quarterly of Healthcare Ethics* (1992), both focus on clinical ethical issues confronted by health care professionals. Clinical ethics consultants thus came to enjoy an increasing number of professional and scholarly resources in organizing and providing consultation services.

Growing recognition and core competencies

The year 1991 marked a turning point in the evolution of clinical ethics consultation. In that year, the Joint Commission on Accreditation of Healthcare Organizations (JCAHO), the accreditation agency for US and Canadian acute care hospitals, adopted a new patient rights standard that required hospitals seeking accreditation to provide institutional mechanisms to address ethical issues in patient care.[48] Although the new JCAHO standard did not specify a particular type of mechanism, most US hospitals have relied on institutional ethics committees to fulfill this function. This

[47] Fox et al. (2007).   [48] Heitman and Bulger (1998).

action by JCAHO made ethics consultation a virtual requirement in all but the smallest US hospitals.

Another turning point for ethics consultation came in 1998 with the publication of *Core Competencies for Health Care Ethics Consultation*, a consensus report of a twenty-one-member joint task force of the SBC and the SHHV.[49] This widely discussed report offered a definition of ethics consultation, recommendations about the consultation process and the proper roles of ethics consultants, and a descriptive catalog of the knowledge and skills necessary for effective ethics consultation. The *Core Competencies* report provided an initial set of benchmarks for ethics consultation and was a point of departure for much of the subsequent scholarly activity on this topic.[50] Building on the *Core Competencies* report, a Clinical Ethics Task Force of the ASBH authored *Improving Competencies in Clinical Ethics Consultation: An Education Guide* (2009).[51] This guide is designed to give novice ethics consultants a comprehensive introduction to the subject matter of clinical ethics.

A national survey conducted in 1999–2000 and published in 2007 confirmed the wide availability of clinical ethics consultation in US hospitals.[52] In that survey, 81 percent of responding hospitals reported that they had an ethics consultation service, and another 14 percent reported that they were in the process of developing one. Clinical ethics consultation has thus evolved, over a forty-year period, from a bare idea into a standard practice in US hospitals. Standards and models for ethics consultation continue to evolve; for example, the ASBH published a revised second edition of the *Core Competencies for Healthcare Ethics Consultation* report in 2011 and approved a *Code of Ethics and Professional Responsibilities for Healthcare Ethics Consultants* in 2014.[53] Ongoing debate centers around whether and how to establish standards and processes for the credentialing of individual clinical ethics consultants and for the accreditation of ethics consultation training programs.[54]

---

[49] Society for Health and Human Values – Society for Bioethics Consultation Task Force on Standards for Bioethics Consultation (1998).

[50] See, for example, Aulisio et al. (2003).

[51] American Society for Bioethics and Humanities Clinical Ethics Task Force (2009).

[52] Fox et al. (2007).

[53] American Society for Bioethics and Humanities (2011) and American Society for Bioethics and Humanities (2014).

[54] See, for example, Dubler et al. (2009) and Engelhardt (2009).

Case analysis

When Karen Ann Quinlan's physicians refused her parents' request to discontinue mechanical ventilation and allow Karen to die, Joseph and Julia Quinlan obtained legal counsel and took their request to a New Jersey trial court, where it was opposed by her physicians and by a guardian *ad litem* appointed to represent Karen's interests. National news outlets highlighted the case, and it captured wide public attention. In November 1975, the trial court judge ruled that Karen's ventilator support should be continued, arguing that her own wishes were unknown, that there was no established constitutional right to die, and that this was a medical decision that should be made by Karen's physicians.

Joseph and Julia Quinlan appealed this decision, and the New Jersey Supreme Court agreed to hear the case on an expedited basis, without intervening appeals court review. In January 1976, that court overturned the trial court decision. The New Jersey Supreme Court ruled that Karen had a right to refuse life-prolonging treatment in her debilitated condition, and that her father should be authorized to make that decision on her behalf, since she lacked the ability to make the decision herself.

Still reluctant to carry out this decision, Karen's physicians did not immediately discontinue ventilator support, but rather attempted to wean her gradually off the ventilator. Contrary to their testimony at trial that she could not survive without the ventilator, Karen did regain the ability to breathe on her own and was transferred to a nursing home. She survived for more than ten years in the nursing home, but never regained consciousness. Karen died on June 13, 1986, with her mother Julia at her side.

Some forty years later, the New Jersey Supreme Court decision in the Quinlan case may seem self-evident to readers today, given the long-established consensus view that patients have a fundamental right to refuse unwanted medical treatment, including life-prolonging measures. What features of that historical context motivated Karen's physicians, hospital representatives, and New Jersey public officials to oppose her parents' wishes so strongly?

3   Methods of health care ethics

Case example

Ms. Carlson is a 45-year-old woman who was recently diagnosed with amyotrophic lateral sclerosis (ALS), also known as Lou Gehrig's disease, a severe and eventually fatal neuromuscular disorder that causes progressive weakness and loss of control of one's muscles. Ms. Carlson was admitted to University Hospital three days ago for treatment of persistent and painful leg cramps, a common symptom of ALS. Two days of drug treatment and physical therapy have eased her muscle cramps and restored Ms. Carlson to her level of health and function before this hospitalization. Dr. Yates, her attending neurologist, informs her that she is now ready for discharge from the hospital. Ms. Carlson responds that she is deeply grateful for the excellent medical and nursing care that she has received in the hospital and that she believes that she can benefit further from several additional days in the hospital. Dr. Yates replies that the urgent medical reason for her admission to the hospital, her severe leg cramps, is under control, and so there is no further need for inpatient treatment. Ms. Carlson agrees that the leg cramps are much better, but she adds that she feels weak and is not confident that she can safely care for herself in her apartment, where she lives by herself. Therefore, she says, she will not agree to leave the hospital. Should Ms. Carlson remain in the hospital?

The previous chapter described the emergence of health care ethics in the United States as a new field of inquiry prompted in part by several high-profile events in the 1970s. Scholars responded to the growing public and professional interest in ethical questions about medical treatment by developing and recommending a number of different approaches to moral reasoning in health care contexts. This chapter will describe the first and most widely discussed approach to moral reasoning in health care, the principle-based approach of Tom Beauchamp and James Childress. It will then offer briefer descriptions of several alternative approaches, including the case-based approach of Albert Jonsen and Stephen Toulmin, the systematic, rule-based approach of Bernard Gert, Charles Culver, and Dan Clouser, the virtue-based approach of Edmund Pellegrino and David Thomasma, and the "postmodern" approach of H. Tristram Engelhardt, Jr. Finally, it will suggest a simple practical method for analyzing moral questions in health care that can draw on the resources of all of these approaches.

A principle-based approach

As mentioned in the previous chapter, the first detailed theoretical approach to moral reasoning in health care appeared in the United States in the late 1970s. In 1979, philosopher Tom Beauchamp and theologian James Childress, faculty colleagues at Georgetown University's Kennedy Institute of Ethics, published the first edition of *Principles of Biomedical Ethics,* their book-length account of what has come to be known as the principle-based approach to health care ethics, or "principlism."[1] For a decade or more, Beauchamp and Childress's approach was the only well-developed, generally available method for analysis of moral issues in health care, and so it was widely studied and applied by both scholars and health care professionals. As we shall see, a variety of competing approaches have been proposed over the years, but the principle-based approach is likely still the most commonly cited and used method for analyzing moral issues and cases in health care.

The central thesis of the principle-based approach is that four general principles – respect for autonomy, nonmaleficence, beneficence, and justice – provide an analytic framework for addressing moral problems in health care. Beauchamp and Childress assert that these principles are both basic and universal, claiming that they are part of "the common morality," that is, "the set of universal norms shared by all persons committed to morality."[2] They claim further that "observation [of these principles] is essential to realize the objectives of morality."[3] The remainder of this section will describe these four principles and their role in guiding moral reasoning in health care.

[1] Beauchamp and Childress (1979). *Principles of Biomedical Ethics* is now in its seventh edition, published in 2013.
[2] Beauchamp and Childress (2013): 3.   [3] Beauchamp (2007).

Respect for autonomy

The first of the four principles, respect for autonomy, can be expressed in several different ways. Here are two formulations:

1. "Honor the choices and actions of autonomous persons."
2. "Assist persons in making and carrying out autonomous choices."

The first of these formulations asserts what is sometimes called a "negative duty," or a "duty of forbearance." This statement, in other words, instructs us to refrain from interfering with autonomous choices and actions, and so we can fulfill this duty simply by leaving other people alone. In contrast, the second formulation of the principle asserts a "positive duty." To fulfill that duty, one must do more than refrain from interfering with another's choices and actions. Rather, one must take positive action to promote autonomous choice and action. Beauchamp and Childress endorse both of these formulations of the principle of respect for autonomy.[4]

Several prominent sources provide support for this principle. The eminent German moral philosopher Immanuel Kant, for example, argued for the unique moral status of persons as rational agents who can make moral choices. Kant concluded that we must respect the moral agency of persons by treating them as ends in themselves, not as mere means to the ends of others.[5] Respect for individual freedom of thought, association, and movement are also basic tenets of the liberal Western political tradition that were incorporated by the founding fathers into the US system of law and government. One cannot, however, trace the origins of the principle of respect for autonomy back to antiquity; this principle does not appear in the Hippocratic Oath or in other pre-modern writings on medical ethics.

Despite their assertion that respect for autonomy is a basic ethical principle, proponents also recognize that it is clearly limited in several ways. As expressed above, the principle applies only to "autonomous persons." This limitation indicates an obvious need to determine whether a person is autonomous, that is, able to make and act on his or her choices. That determination is discussed under the heading "decision-making capacity" in Chapter 8, "Informed consent." Even if a person does clearly have the capacity to make and act on his or her own choices, proponents of this principle generally recognize several justified reasons for constraining that

---

[4] Beauchamp and Childress (2013): 107.   [5] Kant (1959).

person's actions. Health care professionals may, for example, act to prevent a person from inflicting harm on a third party, and they are not required to honor a person's request to use resources to which that person is not entitled.

Nonmaleficence

In its simplest form, the second of the four principles, nonmaleficence, asserts the following: "Do not inflict harm." At first impression, this principle may seem so obvious that it could go without formal expression. In fact, however, it is virtually impossible for contemporary health care professionals to abide by this simplest formulation of the principle of nonmaleficence. The powerful and invasive therapies routinely provided in contemporary health care offer significant benefits of cure and relief of symptoms, but they also frequently cause harmful complications and side effects. A 2009 commentary in the *Journal of the American Medical Association* (*JAMA*), for example, suggested that the overall *benefits* of the US health care system might not outweigh the aggregate health *harm* it imparts.[6] Because advanced technological health care has significant potential for harm as well as benefit, a more defensible contemporary formulation of the principle of nonmaleficence is: "Do not provide treatments likely to cause more harm than benefit."

Unlike respect for autonomy, the principle of nonmaleficence does have clear origins in antiquity; early statements can be found in the Greek writings on medicine attributed to Hippocrates.[7] A later Latin formulation of the principle, "*Primum non nocere*," usually translated as "Above all [or 'First of all'], do no harm," was often cited as a fundamental moral principle of medicine.[8] The principle of nonmaleficence is affirmed in one form or another by a wide variety of philosophical and religious systems of ethics. For example, Gert's philosophical moral theory discussed below asserts that the fundamental purpose of morality is to minimize evil or harm. No fewer than four of the Ten Commandments of Judaism and Christianity prohibit specific harms to others (murder, adultery, theft, and deception).

Though the moral duty to avoid causing harm is very widely recognized, the meaning and scope of the concept of harm is much more controversial.

---

[6] Kilo and Larsen (2009).   [7] Hippocrates (1923).   [8] Jonsen (1977).

Consider just one prominent example: The practices of euthanasia and assisted suicide are condemned by many medical professional associations and individual practitioners, presumably because killing is viewed as a type of harm.[9] Patients who request euthanasia or assistance in dying, however, presumably do so because they view these practices not as harmful, but rather as clearly beneficial in their particular circumstances. Disagreements like this one raise obvious questions about whose judgments about harm should be honored and how the principle of nonmaleficence should be applied in these situations.

We have noted that infliction of harm, as, for example, the side effects of cancer chemotherapies, may be justified by expected benefits like remission of the cancer or prolongation of the patient's life. There may also be instances in which infliction of harm is justified without any expected benefit to the person who is harmed. Perhaps the most obvious example of this is the practice of nontherapeutic research on human subjects. In this type of research, consenting subjects agree to accept a risk of harm caused by experimental treatments, without any expectation of benefit to themselves. The justification for these nontherapeutic studies appeals to potential benefits to future patients from the knowledge gained by the studies.[10]

Beneficence

The principle of nonmaleficence, as described above, creates a negative duty. That is, this principle directs us to refrain from actions likely to cause more harm than benefit. The principle of beneficence articulates a corresponding positive duty, namely, "Act for the benefit of others." To fulfill the principle of beneficence, therefore, one must take action to promote the interests of another person.

Like nonmaleficence, the principle of beneficence has ancient roots; the Hippocratic Oath, for example, includes the following pledge: "I will apply dietetic measures for the benefit of the sick according to my ability and judgment . . ."[11] Also similar to nonmaleficence, many philosophical

---

[9] See Chapter 18, "Aid in dying," for further discussion of this issue.

[10] See Chapter 19, "Research on human subjects," for further discussion of the ethics of clinical research.

[11] Oath of Hippocrates (1995).

and religious theories of ethics endorse specific duties of beneficence. Utilitarian theories of ethics, for example, assert that the single overarching principle of ethics is to maximize the overall beneficial consequences of one's actions. The second of Jesus's two "Great Commandments," "You must love your neighbor as yourself," grounds multiple duties to care for others in Christian theology.[12]

As is the case with the other principles, multiple questions can be raised about the meaning and scope of the principle of beneficence. Opportunities to act for the benefit of others are unlimited and so could consume literally all of anyone's time, energy, and material resources. Assuming that the total devotion of one's life to helping others is not morally required, there must be clear limits to the obligations of beneficence. Beauchamp and Childress appeal to the concept of social reciprocity to justify limited duties of beneficence, arguing that benefits we have received from others establish obligations to benefit those others in return.[13] They also argue that health care professionals incur specific duties of beneficence that are not shared by all, based on their professional roles and relationships and on particular benefits bestowed on them by society.

Just as individual beliefs about what constitutes a harm can and do vary, so also do beliefs about what constitutes a benefit. When health care professionals and patients disagree about what treatment is beneficial, whose opinion should prevail? US health policy addresses this question in several different ways. On the one hand, professionals must respect the informed refusal of treatment by patients who have decision-making capacity, no matter how beneficial a professional believes the recommended treatment would be.[14] This obligation gives respect for patient autonomy priority over efforts to secure patient benefits. On the other hand, health care professionals may refuse to provide certain treatments they judge to be ineffective, harmful, or morally unjustified, despite patient requests for those treatments.[15] These and other policies articulate social decisions about the scope and limits of professional duties of beneficence.

---

[12] Mark 12:31; Matthew 22:39.   [13] Beauchamp and Childress (2013): 213.

[14] See Chapter 8, "Informed consent," for detailed discussion of patient rights to informed consent and refusal of treatment.

[15] See Chapter 10, "Professionalism," and Chapter 17, "Medical futility," for further discussion of these professional prerogatives.

Justice

The fourth and final basic principle of biomedical ethics recognized by Beauchamp and Childress is justice, but these authors are quick to acknowledge that "no single moral principle is capable of addressing all problems of justice."[16] Rather, Beauchamp and Childress offer a pluralistic account of justice that affirms a single "formal" principle of justice and then makes use of six different "material" principles of justice as "resources" for decisions about the distribution of the benefits and costs of health care among the members of a particular population.[17]

The formal principle of justice, generally attributed to Aristotle, can be expressed as follows: "Treat equals equally, and unequals unequally."[18] Stated in this brief way, the principle seems enigmatic, but the underlying idea is quite simple. This formal principle of justice directs us to be *consistent* in our decisions and actions, in the following way: If people are equal in all morally relevant respects, we should treat them in the same way, or equally, and if people are unequal in those respects, we should treat them in different ways, or unequally. This general instruction seems both obvious and uncontroversial.

The principle is purely formal, however, and not substantive. It does not generate substantive conclusions about what course of action is just because it says nothing about what information or attributes are morally relevant in comparing people for the purpose of deciding how to treat them. In deciding how to allocate a scarce health care resource among a group of patients, for example, any or all of the following patient characteristics, among others, might be viewed as relevant: urgency of need for the resource, likelihood and magnitude of expected benefit from the resource, personal responsibility for one's medical condition, ability to adhere to a treatment regimen, and ability to pay for the resource. To make a decision about fair allocation of this resource, we need additional guidance about which of these characteristics are in fact morally relevant, and about their significance relative to one another. Material principles of distributive justice, and the theories that explain, defend, and apply those principles, offer

[16] Beauchamp and Childress (2013): 250.

[17] 'Distributive justice' is the term used to refer to moral decisions about the allocation of specific benefits and burdens among the members of a group or population.

[18] Aristotle (1999).

guidance about what characteristics are relevant and how they are relevant. Beauchamp and Childress acknowledge the following six material principles of justice and appeal to them in examining specific questions about the allocation of health care benefits and costs:

1. A utilitarian principle: "To each person according to rules and actions that maximize social utility."
2. A libertarian principle: "To each person a maximum of liberty and property resulting from the exercise of liberty rights and participation in fair free-market exchanges."
3. A communitarian principle: "To each person according to principles of fair distribution derived from conceptions of the good developed in moral communities."
4. An egalitarian principle: "To each person an equal measure of liberty and equal access to the goods in life that every rational person values."
5. A "capabilities" principle: "To each person the means necessary for the exercise of capabilities essential for a flourishing life."
6. A "well-being" principle: "To each person the means necessary for the realization of core dimensions of well-being."[19]

Inclusion of justice among the basic principles of health care ethics highlights the fact that contemporary professionals, patients, institutions, health care systems, and societies confront pressing and complex problems of distributive justice. To address these problems, Beauchamp and Childress appeal to not one, but multiple material principles of distributive justice, and they assert that no one of these principles is sufficient. Because these principles emphasize different and sometimes conflicting values and claims, however, their conclusions about specific allocation problems will also often be different and in conflict with one another. This consequence raises the obvious problem of how to choose among them when material principles of justice and their conclusions diverge.

Using the principles

Identifying and describing the four basic principles is an essential step, but only the first step in the principle-based approach to health care ethics. As the above summary account of the principles makes clear, each of the

[19] Beauchamp and Childress (2013): 253.

principles is morally significant, but none is absolutely binding. In other words, each principle can be overridden by still more compelling moral considerations in particular circumstances. Beauchamp and Childress describe this feature of the principles by claiming that they generate *prima facie* obligations, that is, obligations that must be fulfilled unless they conflict with an obligation of equal or greater moral force.

How, then, can health care professionals, patients, and other stakeholders determine which course of action is morally superior, when principles or obligations appear to be in conflict? Beauchamp and Childress acknowledge that the four principles are very general and so cannot by themselves provide clear answers to particular moral questions. To provide more concrete guidance, they argue, the principles must be *specified*. Specification of the principles is the development of more concrete rules to direct moral choice and action. The principle of respect for autonomy, for example, is specified by the moral rule "Honor the informed refusal of treatment by patients who have decision-making capacity." That rule can be further specified as follows: "Honor the informed refusal of treatment by patients who have decision-making capacity, unless treatment of a patient's condition is necessary to prevent a serious threat to the public health." Much if not most of the work of health care ethics, for this approach, is the formulation and justification of moral rules that give specific content to the general principles.

Even specific moral rules may give conflicting advice, however, and difficult moral problems may not have established rules that provide specific direction about how to resolve them. In those difficult choice situations, Beauchamp and Childress appeal to a process of "weighing and balancing" competing moral considerations.[20] This process involves reflection on the reasons for competing courses of action, but also on more intuitive qualities like compassion and moral discernment. Beauchamp and Childress argue that moral agents should seek maximal agreement or coherence among the overarching moral theories, general principles, specific moral rules, and particular judgments they affirm, a state of internal moral harmony philosopher John Rawls called "reflective equilibrium." They recognize, however, that conscientious and reasonable agents may still disagree about how to resolve complex and controversial moral problems.[21]

---

[20] Beauchamp and Childress (2013): 19–24.   [21] Beauchamp and Childress (2013): 24–25.

Alternatives to principles

Since the appearance of the principle-based approach to health care ethics in the late 1970s, scholars have developed and recommended a variety of other approaches to addressing and resolving moral questions in health care, often in direct response to "principlism." This section will provide summary descriptions of four widely discussed alternative approaches to health care ethics: a case-based approach, a systematic, rule-based approach, a virtue-based approach, and a "postmodern" approach.

A case-based approach

In contrast to the "top-down" approach that moves from very general principles to the examination of moral problems in specific health care situations, theologian Albert Jonsen and philosopher Stephen Toulmin have articulated and defended a "bottom-up" approach that begins with moral judgments about specific cases.[22] Jonsen observes that the case is "the unit of health care and the unwaning center of attention of its providers."[23] The case-based, or "casuistic," approach to moral reasoning asserts that our most confident and most widely shared moral judgments are about the right or best course of action in specific cases, not about general principles. Moral deliberation in health care, therefore, should begin with these paradigm cases as examples and should reason by analogy from these cases in order to resolve questions posed by novel cases. This "analogical" method requires careful description of the case at issue, identification of similarities of that case to paradigm cases, and use of those paradigm cases as moral precedents for the resolution of the current case. Proponents of the case-based approach point out that it has roots in the casuistic tradition of analysis in sixteenth- and seventeenth-century Roman Catholic moral theology.[24] It is also the foundation of the common law tradition in British and American jurisprudence, in which judges use past cases as precedents in making decisions about subsequent cases.

Attention to cases is indeed a central feature of health care, since a fundamental goal is attending to the health needs of individual patients. Recognizing that central feature, the next section of this chapter will describe

---

[22] Toulmin (1981), Jonsen (1986), Jonsen and Toulmin (1988).   [23] Jonsen (1986).
[24] Jonsen and Toulmin (1988).

a simple method for ethics case analysis. We do, moreover, sometimes have strong and widely shared moral intuitions about how to resolve moral questions in particular cases. Proponents of the case-based approach argue that the moral reasoning process should rely solely, or at least primarily, on those settled judgments about paradigm cases. Critics raise several kinds of questions about this approach, however. John Arras, for example, asks who identifies and interprets the moral problems to be addressed and the paradigm cases used to resolve them.[25] If health care professionals dominate these tasks, they may neglect the views of health system "outsiders" and thereby perpetuate ingrained prejudices. Critics also question whether case-based reasoning by analogy can completely exclude the use of principles. They point out that judgments about similarities between cases depend on the identification and evaluation of morally significant features the cases have in common, as, for example, access to a scarce medical resource. These common features, critics argue, amount to implicit principles of moral relevance and direction; they might, for example, identify and endorse criteria for allocating that scarce resource. Case-based and principle- or rule-based approaches may, therefore, be best understood as complementary and not mutually exclusive.

A systematic, rule-based approach

The case-based approach described above argues for the primacy of moral judgments about particular cases, not general principles. A systematic, rule-based approach to moral reasoning in health care developed by philosopher Bernard Gert, in collaboration with physician Charles Culver and philosopher Dan Clouser, is also sharply critical of principlism.[26] Gert argues that the principles proposed by Beauchamp and Childress do little more than identify general topics in health care ethics and do not provide usable guides to moral choice and action. Gert offers an alternative approach based on the general theory of ethics he developed and refined over more than four decades.[27] From its beginnings, Gert based his theory on an account of the common morality; Beauchamp and Childress followed his lead in appealing to the common morality as the source of the principles they endorse. Both approaches assert that the common

---

[25] Arras (1991).   [26] Gert et al. (2006).   [27] Gert (1970).

morality is universally binding and is accepted by all rational persons, but they offer very different accounts of its content. Gert argues that "the hard-core foundation of morality" is the avoidance or lessening of the evils or harms of death, pain, disability, loss of freedom, and loss of pleasure.[28] Based on this foundation, Gert maintains that the common morality consists of: (1) rules prohibiting actions that cause harm, (2) ideals encouraging the prevention or relief of harm, and (3) a procedure for determining when it is justifiable to violate a moral rule.[29] Gert recognizes the following ten basic moral rules:

1. Do not kill.
2. Do not cause pain.
3. Do not disable.
4. Do not deprive of freedom.
5. Do not deprive of pleasure.
6. Do not deceive.
7. Keep your promise. (Do not break your promise.)
8. Do not cheat.
9. Obey the law. (Do not break the law.)
10. Do your duty. (Do not neglect your duty.)[30]

To decide whether an action is morally permissible or morally required based on this approach, one must first describe the morally relevant features of the situation to determine whether that action would violate one of these moral rules. Gert provides an additional set of ten questions designed to identify the morally relevant features of the situation.[31] If the action would violate a rule, one must also determine whether the violation is justifiable in that situation. Gert proposes a procedure for determining whether a rule violation is justified. Violation of a rule is justified, he argues, only if an impartial rational person would agree that anyone in the same situation would be justified in breaking that rule, and if there is public knowledge that this kind of violation of the rule is allowed. In

---

[28] Gert rejects the view that promoting good is the goal of morality; he claims that gaining goods is far less important than avoiding evils. See Gert et al. (2006): 13.

[29] Gert objects to the description of his approach as "rule-based," pointing out that it recognizes moral ideals as well as rules. In fact, however, rules play a dominant role in his approach to moral reasoning. For example, only rules, and not ideals, generate moral duties and justify punishment for failure to obey them. See Gert et al. (2006): 12.

[30] Gert et al. (2006): 36.   [31] Gert et al. (2006): 39–40.

other words, exceptions to obeying the moral rules in specific circumstances must be publicly recognized and permitted for anyone in those circumstances.

Gert argues that his approach provides a procedure for making moral choices in difficult cases that is more systematic and less dependent on unsupported appeals to moral intuition than either the principle-based or the case-based approach. He acknowledges that his procedure cannot provide a single correct resolution to every moral conflict, but he does claim that it can explain why a conflict is unresolvable. Critics question whether the moral system Gert describes is an accurate and complete account of a universally accepted common morality, or rather a debatable theory about what should be our most fundamental moral rules and procedures.[32]

A virtue-based approach

All of the approaches to moral reasoning described thus far in this chapter focus on the use of particular theoretical tools – principles, paradigm cases, or rules – to guide moral choice and action in specific situations. In contrast, the virtue-based approach to health care ethics asserts that the most important moral task is becoming a particular type of person, namely, a person of good moral character, or a person of virtue. Proponents of this approach argue that instilling moral virtues in both professionals and patients will enhance their relationships and will prevent moral transgressions. Moral philosophers and theologians have proposed multiple different virtue-based theories over the centuries, and so it is no surprise that contemporary scholars offer different accounts of the essential health care virtues. Based on their account of the nature and ends of medicine, for example, Edmund Pellegrino and David Thomasma identify eight central virtues of physicians: fidelity to trust, compassion, *phronesis* (practical wisdom), justice, fortitude, temperance, integrity, and self-effacement.[33] Drawing on Carol Gilligan's account of women's distinctive perspectives on the moral life, nurse scholars have proposed approaches to nursing ethics based on the feminist virtue of caring.[34]

If moral character is understood as a person's disposition or commitment to choose and to act for the right reasons, then the development of

[32] See, for example, Arras (2009).   [33] Pellegrino and Thomasma (1993).
[34] See Gilligan (1982), Stephany (2012).

character is indeed essential to the moral life of individuals and their communities. Having the disposition to act for the right reasons is not sufficient for moral action, however, because moral action also requires the ability to determine what the right reasons for action in particular situations are. Virtue-based theories may guide moral reasoning by inviting reflection on whether a just or a compassionate health care professional, for example, would act in a particular way. Just as principles may conflict in specific situations, so also may virtue-based inclinations. Emphasis on justice in access to care may, for example, suggest a different course of action than emphasis on compassion for a patient's suffering. Approaches that emphasize the development of virtue and those that focus on action-guiding moral tools may, therefore, be complementary and important elements of a comprehensive health care ethics.

A "postmodern" approach

The "postmodern" approach to health care ethics challenges a central claim of all of the above-described approaches, namely, the claim that there is universal acceptance of, or a compelling rational argument in support of, a set of basic principles, moral rules, case-based moral judgments, or virtues. Philosopher-physician H. Tristram Engelhardt, Jr, the primary proponent of this postmodern approach over the past three decades, argues that the modern philosophical project of creating a rational, objective, and universally binding foundation for any substantive moral theory has failed.[35] The postmodern situation, therefore, is one of moral pluralism, that is, great diversity in people's fundamental moral beliefs and values, without an objective method to determine which beliefs and values are correct and which are mistaken. Given the lack of compelling rational arguments for particular moral conclusions, Engelhardt argues that there is only one alternative to abandoning ethics entirely and relying instead on coercion to impose one's will on those who disagree. That alternative is to resolve moral disputes by peaceable negotiation, seeking agreement with others on solutions to moral disputes. Such agreement, when it is reached, does not amount to moral truth in any objective sense, but it does honor the claims of the moral agents involved to make and act on their own moral choices without coercion.

---

[35] Engelhardt (1996).

In view of the limits of moral argument in the postmodern world, Engelhardt proposes a major reinterpretation of Beauchamp and Childress's four basic principles of health care ethics. In place of the principle of respect for autonomy, Engelhardt offers what he calls "the principle of permission." This principle asserts that a necessary condition for moral authority in a pluralistic society is respect for the right of moral agents to give their permission, or agreement, to a joint course of action in a common endeavor.[36] Engelhardt acknowledges that the principles of nonmaleficence, beneficence, and justice all address central areas of moral concern in health care. Because there are fundamental disagreements about what constitutes harm, benefit, and justice, however, he argues that use of these principles as a guide to collective action will require that the actors have a shared understanding of the meaning and implications of these principles. Persons who hold very different moral beliefs and values (whom Engelhardt refers to as "moral strangers") will have few opportunities for mutually agreeable joint activity. In contrast, "moral friends," persons who have a large number of shared and substantive moral commitments, can cooperate on a wide variety of moral projects. Engelhardt himself has embraced one such community of shared moral belief and practice, the traditional Christianity of Orthodox Catholicism. In *The Foundations of Christian Bioethics*, Engelhardt examines the implications of Orthodox Catholic moral doctrine for choices in health care.[37]

Persistent disagreement and debate in the United States about controversial health policy issues lend credence to Engelhardt's claims about moral pluralism in contemporary secular societies. Another sign of this moral pluralism is the frequency of conflict about the right or best treatment plan in particular clinical situations. In these conflict situations, clinical ethics consultants may be able to facilitate enough shared understanding of the situation and identify enough shared moral commitments to help the primary stakeholders reach a mutually agreeable resolution of the conflict. Those shared moral commitments may include acceptance of the principles, moral rules, or ideals of virtuous behavior recommended by the approaches described in this chapter. If the moral views of the interested parties are too divergent, however, they may not be able to reach agreement

[36] Engelhardt (1996): 109.   [37] Engelhardt (2000).

on a common course of action. The postmodern approach emphasizes this limitation of moral reasoning, but the proponents of the other approaches discussed above also acknowledge that their approaches cannot resolve all disagreements between informed and conscientious moral agents.

A simple method for case analysis

The approaches described in this chapter offer multiple strategies for analyzing and resolving moral questions in health care. Many of these are complementary strategies, that is, they offer different but compatible ways to understand and evaluate problems. Other strategies endorse competing principles or values and may suggest incompatible conclusions. Each approach has its strong proponents and its critics. A thorough and comparative evaluation of each of these approaches would require a separate book of its own on the theoretical foundations of health care ethics. Because I believe that each approach has significant strengths and weaknesses, my own preference is to choose and use strategies that appear well suited to the moral problem at hand, rather than embrace and rely solely on just one of these approaches.[38]

In providing clinical ethics case consultations and in case-based ethics teaching, I use a simple, non-technical problem-solving method to identify relevant information and assess alternative courses of action.[39] Many of the case analyses presented in the chapters of this book are at least implicit illustrations of this method. The method includes the following six steps:

1. Identify the moral problem.
2. Gather relevant information.
3. Identify the available options and their likely consequences.

---

[38] The case analysis method described in this section thus assumes a pluralistic moral theory that recognizes moral appeals of several different kinds and relies on intuitive moral judgments about the relative significance of those appeals in specific cases. Philosopher Baruch Brody develops and defends a pluralistic moral theory of this kind in his book *Life and Death Decision Making* (Brody 1988).

[39] I believe that versions of this generic method are used in multiple settings. I was first introduced to it in a brief account provided by Andrew Jameton in his 1984 nursing ethics textbook (Jameton 1984: 66–68). Jonsen, Siegler, and Winslade describe and apply a different method for ethics case analysis (called "the four topics method") in their volume *Clinical Ethics* (Jonsen et al. 2006).

4. Identify and evaluate arguments for and against the available options.
5. Choose a course of action and defend it.
6. Carry out the chosen action and assess its consequences.

Let's consider each of these steps in more detail. Although the method is described as a sequential, step-by-step process, actual moral analysis and deliberation may often require moving back and forward among the steps, as new information, new options, or new moral arguments are identified. Each of the first four steps is open-ended, in the sense that it could be pursued and refined indefinitely. There are, of course, practical limits on the process of moral deliberation, but I believe that careful attention to each of the following steps can enhance that process and its conclusions.

Identify the moral problem

In order to analyze and resolve a moral problem, one must have at least a rough idea of what the problem is. In some situations, the problem may be obvious; for example, parents may not agree on what treatment their young child should receive for a serious illness, and so professionals may not know what treatment to provide. In other situations, the problem may be difficult to articulate; a member of a health care team may feel uneasy about a proposed treatment plan, but not be able to say exactly why. In still other situations, some of the stakeholders may view the problem in one way, and others may see it in a very different way. In the situation of the parents who disagree about treatment for their child, for example, some may state the key question as "Who has the final authority for making this decision?" and others as "Which treatment is in this child's best interests?" In most situations, there are at least several different ways to state the problem, and often there are several related but distinguishable problems at issue. Careful formulation of different ways to state the moral problem and recognition of different moral problems encountered in the situation are valuable first steps in the understanding and analysis of a difficult case.

Gather relevant information

Effective moral reasoning cannot occur in an informational vacuum. In other words, analysis of an ethics question requires attention not only to moral reasons, but also to important factual information about the situation. Interested parties must, therefore, identify and gather that factual information in order to gain an adequate understanding of the situation and the problem. Some of that information may already be in hand, other information may be readily available, and still other information may be difficult or impossible to obtain. Relevant information typically is of various kinds, including the following:

- the condition and prognosis of the patient
- the identity of the various stakeholders in the situation (e.g., the patient, members of the health care team, the patient's authorized surrogate decision-maker, the patient's family, the health care facility)
- beliefs, values, and desires of the stakeholders[40]
- the time frame (e.g., an emergency, an urgent situation, a long-standing problem)
- institutional policies
- professional standards of practice
- applicable regulations, statutes, or common law precedents

Factual information of these kinds is not only relevant, but often essential to an effective reasoning process. To take an obvious example, unless one knows that a patient has expressed a particular treatment choice, one cannot decide whether to honor that choice. Knowledge that honoring a patient's request for assistance in suicide is a felony under state law is clearly relevant to a physician's decision about how to respond to that request.

Identify the available options

Based on their understanding of the moral problem and the situation in which it has arisen, the interested parties can identify various courses of action that could be taken to address the problem. Some of these options may be obvious, and others may be imaginative, "out-of-the-box" ideas that had not been initially apparent to the stakeholders. Some may be interim steps

---

[40] Another approach to moral reasoning in health care, called narrative ethics, focuses on eliciting and interpreting the narratives, or stories, of both patients and health care professionals. This narrative ethics approach asserts that attention to personal stories about illness enables us to understand one another's beliefs, values, and desires more fully and thereby to care for one another more effectively. See, for example, Hunter (1991), Charon and Montello (2002), and Frank (2013).

designed to gather additional relevant information, as, for example, a meeting of family members and health care team members to provide new information and share ideas about treatment for an unconscious patient with a life-threatening illness. Others may be more conclusive or final responses to the moral problem; for example, a physician's decision to honor or to deny a young adult patient's request for surgical sterilization. As alternative courses of action are identified, it will also be useful to consider the expected consequences of each course of action, including both desired and undesired outcomes, and both short-term and long-term outcomes.

Identify and evaluate arguments

Informed by an understanding of the moral problem or question, the significant facts of the situation, and the available response options, the interested parties can undertake the central task of identifying and evaluating moral reasons for and against the several possible courses of action. The parties may identify a wide variety of moral considerations, and they may appeal to one or more of the approaches to moral reasoning described earlier in this chapter. The following questions can guide this task:

- What moral principles, rules, rights, duties, or values are relevant in this situation?
- Do other cases offer a precedent for action in this situation?
- Do any institutional policies or laws bear on the situation?
- What is the moral significance of the likely consequences of alternative courses of action?
- What is the moral significance of the moral beliefs and preferences of the various stakeholders in the situation?
- How do all of these moral considerations count for or against the alternative courses of action?
- If moral reasons for different courses of action are in conflict, which reasons are more persuasive, and why?

Choose a course of action and defend it

Scholarly and public debate about controversial ethical issues may persist for decades, but patients' health care needs typically require a prompt response, and so those who are responsible for a patient's care cannot deliberate indefinitely. Rather, based on their analysis of the situation and the available options, they must eventually choose the course of action that they believe is morally preferable. Out of respect for all of the stakeholders in the situation, the deciding parties should be prepared to defend the course of action that they have chosen. Because moral reasoning is fallible, I believe that they should also acknowledge moral considerations that may convince other reasonable and conscientious people to disagree with their conclusion.

Carry out the chosen action and assess its consequences

In most US hospitals, clinical ethics consultants are available to assist interested parties in addressing moral problems that arise in the care of patients, but ethics consultants do not have the authority to take action or to require others to take action. Instead, the primary stakeholders in the clinical situation retain the authority to make and carry out decisions about what treatments to provide and to accept. That authority is sometimes shared by two or more of the stakeholders, as, for example, the patient and the attending physician, and is sometimes held by one party. Once the authorized person or persons have reached a decision, they should carry out the chosen action. Because the expected consequences of the action will usually be an important consideration in making the decision, the stakeholders will want to know whether the actual outcome of the chosen action is in fact what was expected, or something different. They can then use the actual outcome to assess both their clinical and their moral reasoning, and that assessment can inform reasoning in subsequent situations.

Case analysis

Ms. Carlson and her attending physician Dr. Yates disagree about whether she should be discharged from the hospital after several days of inpatient treatment for severe and painful muscle cramps. Dr. Yates observes that the cramping problem for which she was admitted to the hospital has been treated successfully and concludes that she has no further need for the high level of care provided to hospital inpatients at the present time. Ms. Carlson agrees that the leg cramps are much better, but she adds that she still feels weak and knows that she will benefit from several more days of excellent inpatient care from her physicians and nurses. She is, therefore, unwilling to leave the hospital.

The case analysis method outlined in the previous section suggests a series of steps for examining this situation. The first step in the process is identification of the moral problem. Perhaps the most obvious way to state the problem in this case is: "Should Ms. Carlson be discharged from the hospital today, or should she remain an inpatient?" Not surprisingly, there are other obvious ways to state the problem, for example: "Who has the most compelling moral claim to access to the resource of an inpatient bed in this situation?" "How should decisions about allocation of this resource be reached?" "Who should have the final authority to allocate this resource?"

The second step in the process is gathering relevant information. Obviously relevant in this case is information about Ms. Carlson's diagnosis, her current medical condition and ability to care for herself, her need for continuing health care, her understanding of her situation, and her wishes about treatment. Also relevant is information about Dr. Yates's assessment of Ms. Carlson's need for additional hospital-based care and about alternatives to hospital care for her. Additional kinds of information that may be relevant are the hospital's policies on patient transfer and discharge, the medical needs of patients waiting in the hospital's emergency department for an inpatient bed to become available, the willingness of relatives or friends of Ms. Carlson to support and assist her at her apartment or in another setting, and the limitation of coverage in Ms. Carlson's health insurance policy to inpatient treatment that is medically necessary. Would you find the above kinds of information relevant in making a decision about what to do in this case? What other information would you want to obtain?

Identification of available options is the next step in this process. A variety of both interim and "final" options to resolve the problem are likely to be available. Interim options might be efforts to gather additional information about the situation, as, for example, obtaining a second medical opinion about Ms. Carlson's current condition or an ethics consultation to provide advice about the moral issues at stake. The final decision can be viewed as an "either–or" choice, that is, either honor Ms. Carlson's request to remain in the hospital, or require her to leave the hospital despite her unwillingness to do so. These two dichotomous options, however, can each be further described in at least several different ways. For example, a decision to honor Ms. Carlson's request might include specific conditions, for example, a limit of one or two more days in a convalescent care unit of the hospital to arrange transfer to an extended care facility or to arrange home health services for her. A decision to discharge or transfer Ms. Carlson could include offering her a choice among several options for continuing care that have been identified by her hospital-based case manager. The foreseeable consequences of each of the available options can also be described, including consequences for Ms. Carlson, other patients, Dr. Yates, hospital staff, and the hospital itself.

The next step in the process is identification of moral reasons for and against the available options. This step can make use of one or more of the different approaches to moral reasoning described in this chapter. Relying on the principle-based approach, for example, one might consider how the principle of respect for autonomy should be further specified to address the question of whether inpatients' refusals to leave the hospital should be honored, and if so, under what circumstances. One might also conceive the situation as requiring balancing of principles in conflict, as, for example, balancing Ms. Carlson's wishes and the benefits to her of additional inpatient care against the hospital's interest in control over the resources it owns and in just allocation of those resources to all of the patients it serves. A case-based approach might ask the stakeholders to consider how requests like that of Ms. Carlson have been addressed in the past. Under what circumstances have inpatient requests for extended stay in the hospital been granted, and when have those requests been denied? Comparison of those situations with that of Ms. Carlson might then guide the decision in her case. Gert's systematic rule-based approach would direct the interested parties to determine which of the ten moral rules applies in this situation and to consider whether there is sufficient justification for violation of the relevant rules. A virtue-based approach might ask the involved parties to consider what action in this situation a moral role model would choose, or what action would best exemplify the central values of this institution. Finally, Engelhardt's postmodern approach might focus on the question of "permission" in this case, asking, for example, "Must Ms. Carlson obtain the permission of hospital staff for the continued use of hospital resources?" and "May hospital staff forcibly remove Ms. Carlson from the hospital if she refuses to leave voluntarily?"

Based on the factual information gathered and the moral reasons assessed in the preceding steps, the interested parties must eventually take the next step of deciding about how to proceed. Notice that in this case, deferring a decision about discharge or transfer for Ms. Carlson is a *de facto* decision to honor her request to remain in the hospital. The decision might be based on a negotiated agreement among all of the stakeholders, as, for example, a joint decision to allow Ms. Carlson to remain in the hospital one more day while arrangements for home health services are completed, or perhaps a decision to transfer her to a short-stay rehabilitation facility for physical therapy to help her cope with the weakness associated with her condition. If, however, an agreement cannot be reached, the decision may ultimately turn on questions of legal authority, such as whether and under what circumstances the hospital may force a patient to accept discharge, and whether the hospital chooses to invoke that authority in this case. Whatever the resolution of the situation, it will likely be instructive to observe the outcome of the decision, to learn whether the expected consequences did occur, and to consider whether the actual consequences lend support to the decision that was made.

4 Law and ethics in health care

Case example

Dr. Ames, a psychiatrist in private practice in a medium-sized California city, is caring for Ms. Warren, a 25-year-old single woman who was diagnosed four years ago with bipolar disorder. Dr. Ames and Ms. Warren have had monthly outpatient appointments over the past six months. At her first visit, Dr. Ames prescribed one of the standard medications for this condition, and he has been monitoring his patient's progress since then. At today's visit, Ms. Warren reports that she has felt very sad for the past week and has started to think that her condition is hopeless and that her life may not be worth continuing. This is the first time that she has mentioned any thoughts of suicide in her sessions with Dr. Ames.

Dr. Ames knows that it is not unusual for a depressed patient to have suicidal thoughts and that it is very difficult to predict whether a patient who expresses such thoughts will actually commit suicide. He also knows that if Ms. Warren does commit suicide while under his care, he may be at significant risk of malpractice liability for failing to prevent her suicide. Dr. Ames could prevent her from committing suicide, at least in the short term, by involuntarily committing her to a psychiatric hospital, but commitment may not improve her longer-term prospects for survival and control of her illness. Involuntary commitment would be a major disruption of Ms. Warren's life, and she would likely view this action as a betrayal of her trust by Dr. Ames. Taking this action, therefore, would very likely undermine their therapeutic relationship. Should he nevertheless commit her, to reduce her risk of suicide and his risk of liability?

When confronted with difficult questions about what to do, health care professionals may look both to ethics and to the law for guidance. Professor Kenneth de Ville, in fact, reports that the most common and often the first question asked by physicians and medical students in ethics discussions is "What does the law say?"[1] Clinicians may inquire about their legal

---

[1] De Ville (1994).

responsibilities for many reasons. Like Dr. Ames in the case above, they presumably want to avoid malpractice liability, and so they may seek information about the law in order to protect themselves from an adverse judgment. They may also view the law as offering clear direction about how to resolve complex problems. Despite the inclination of health care professionals to inquire about their legal rights, duties, and risks, de Ville concludes that primary reliance on the law is not a reliable approach to addressing the moral issues that confront them.

What, then, is the optimal relationship between legal and ethical reasons as a guide to health care professional practice? This chapter will consider two simple, initially tempting, and very different ways to understand the roles of law and ethics in health care. I will argue that both of these options are ultimately misguided and then offer a more defensible alternative approach.

Option 1: sole reliance on the law

Physicians and medical students whose first question about a difficult situation is "What does the law say?" might describe their decision-making strategy as follows: "Just tell me what the law requires, or what the legally safest course of action is. That's what I will do, and that's all I need to know!" The fact that many health care professionals are quick to inquire about the legal implications of different courses of action suggests that sole or primary reliance on the law is a tempting guide to action. Why is this option initially tempting, and why is it ultimately unsatisfactory?

The option of sole reliance on the law is attractive to health care professionals for several reasons. When they confront an important and difficult decision, clinicians naturally seek to minimize uncertainty and cognitive dissonance about what to do. In such situations, however, there is often unavoidable uncertainty about the consequences of different possible courses of action, and there are often conflicting moral considerations, without any definitive way to resolve the conflicts among them. In contrast, clinicians may view legal rules as giving clear and unambiguous direction, for example, "You *must* obtain the patient's informed consent to treatment," or "You *may not* euthanize a patient." Moreover, professionals may see legal rules as an expression of the social will, at least in a state with a fundamentally just system of government. Finally, they may recognize that the law demands obedience and punishes those who disobey. Thus, understanding legal rules and carefully adhering to them gives clinicians maximal protection against criminal and civil liability.

Despite the above-described attractive features of exclusive reliance on the law as a guide to action for health care professionals, this option is ultimately unsatisfactory, for several other persuasive reasons. First, although the law provides clear direction in some circumstances, it does not offer any explicit guidance about how to address many other morally significant decisions in health care. Enacting a law typically requires strong social support for a particular course of action. When a moral issue is in dispute, as is often the case in health care, the law is typically silent, allowing individuals to choose and act in multiple different ways. In fact, some laws explicitly protect the rights of both patients and health care providers to make their own health care choices without legal infringement. To take just one notable example, both the common law and statutory law in the United States protect both a woman's right to choose abortion and a health care professional's right not to provide or participate in abortion procedures. When the law does not dictate a course of action, both patients and professionals must turn to other sources of guidance to decide what to do in specific circumstances.

Second, even if the law does provide specific direction, it is not always the best guide to action, in health care or in other contexts. History offers multiple examples of unjust laws, as, for example, laws permitting involuntary sterilization for eugenic purposes and laws denying voting rights to women. Laws whose purposes are beneficent may have unintended harmful consequences. For example, legal rules requiring life-sustaining treatment of newborns with critical illnesses were enacted in the United States in the 1980s to prevent medical neglect of some vulnerable patients, but had the unintended consequence of preventing professionals and parents from choosing to forgo harmful treatment for other infants.[2] When laws are flawed, so also is simple reliance on them as guides to action. Rather, conscientious health care professionals may have a moral responsibility to participate in efforts to revise or repeal such laws and may also have a responsibility to engage in civil disobedience in order to protect their patients from harm.

Finally, although health care professionals have a justifiable interest in protecting themselves from malpractice liability, self-protection is not

[2] See Moskop and Saldanha (1986) and Kopelman et al. (1988).

always an appropriate or overriding goal. In many situations, absolute self-protection from liability is impossible, because all of the reasonable treatment options pose some legal risk. If an orthopedic surgeon treating a patient with a severe fracture of the leg decides against an operation to repair the fracture, and the fracture does not heal properly, the patient may claim that her poor outcome is the result of the surgeon's mistaken decision not to operate. If the surgeon does decide to operate, and the patient suffers a significant complication from the surgery, the patient may claim that her injury was caused by the surgeon's failure to perform the procedure correctly. In this situation, then, the surgeon can choose the course of action that he or she believes will be less risky, but cannot choose a course of action that will eliminate all malpractice risk.

In a few situations, liability may not be an issue, because all of the reasonable choices have legal protection. Consider, for example, the situation in which a physician faces a decision whether she should report a patient who has a medical condition that might impair his ability to drive to the state Department of Motor Vehicles. In North Carolina, state law grants physicians immunity from liability if they decide to report these patients *and also* if they decide not to report.[3] Thus, the physician in this situation must base her decision on grounds other than minimization of liability risk.

In still other situations, it may be morally appropriate, or even morally required, that health care professionals accept some increased liability risk in order to prevent harms to or secure benefits for patients or others. A pulmonologist, for example, may choose to honor his patient's prior request not to receive long-term ventilator support near the end of life, despite the fact that the patient can no longer express this request and the patient's family insists that ventilator support be continued. The pulmonologist may believe that the family will seek damages for his failure to follow their directions, but nevertheless choose the course of action that honors the patient's wishes and promotes the patient's best interests.

Option 2: sole reliance on ethics

Morally responsible health care professionals who recognize that the law is not always a reliable guide to action may adopt a very different approach to

[3] North Carolina General Statutes § 20–9.1.

resolving moral questions in their practice. They may articulate this approach as follows: "My primary duty as a health care professional is to do the right thing for my patients. If I am making morally sound decisions, I don't need to worry about what the law says." Why is this a tempting option for some health care professionals, and why is it ultimately unsatisfactory?

Health care professionals may be attracted to the option of sole reliance on ethics for several reasons. They may view their moral responsibilities to patients as having priority over legal responsibilities. As noted in Chapter 10, "Professionalism," appeals to professionalism in health care emphasize a duty to place patient interests above self-interest; professionals who embrace this duty wholeheartedly may disregard their own liability risks in their efforts to serve the interests of their patients. Many health care professionals resent what they view as the intrusion of lawyers and the law into their practices; these strong negative attitudes may motivate professionals to minimize the influence of legal rules on their decisions. Finally, professionals may survey their moral and legal responsibilities and come to the conclusion that morally justified or required decisions are also generally legally permissible. If that is the case, these professionals may choose to use moral reasons to guide their actions with the expectation that this strategy will not run afoul of the law.

Each of the above reasons has some plausibility, but there are also very good reasons why health care professionals (and everyone else) should not simply ignore or disregard their legal responsibilities. First, health care professionals may share in a general, *prima facie* moral duty to obey the law. The American Medical Association's "Principles of Medical Ethics" recognize such a duty in the following words: "A physician shall respect the law and also recognize a responsibility to seek changes in those requirements which are contrary to the best interests of the patient."[4] Though it acknowledges that laws may sometimes not be in the best interests of patients, this statement nevertheless asserts a general duty to obey the law. That duty may be defended in several ways. It may, for example, be based on a broader duty of allegiance that all citizens owe to their state and its system of government and law, assuming that the government is legitimate and the legal system is a just one. The duty to obey the law may also be based on the benefits one enjoys as a resident of a state with an ordered

---

[4] American Medical Association (2001b).

system of laws and public services. Finally, a general duty to obey the law may be defended based on the unfairness of being a "free rider," that is, one who benefits from the lawful behavior of others but does not obey the law oneself.

As noted above, the fact that one's legal responsibilities overlap significantly with one's moral responsibilities may be a reason for paying primary attention to moral responsibilities. This overlap may also, however, be a good reason for paying attention to the law as a guide to one's moral responsibilities. The law may, in other words, serve as a reflection of a society's central moral convictions about what actions should be required and proscribed. Legal rules may thus help health care professionals identify and define the scope and limits of their moral as well as their legal duties. Examples of laws that also express moral convictions about health care include standards for informed consent to treatment, confidentiality regulations, protections and requirements for "Good Samaritan" interventions by health care professionals, and measures to protect the health of the public from dangerous illnesses.

Health care professionals also have an important prudential reason to attend to their legal as well as their moral responsibilities. Although morally sound practice is *generally* consistent with the law, moral and legal duties may *occasionally* conflict with one another. When this is the case, disregarding the law in order to pursue other goals may expose a health care professional to substantial personal risk. Consider, for example, E. A. Rybak's description of the situation US obstetricians confront when one of their patients requests a vaginal delivery after a previous Cesarean section delivery.[5] Although vaginal birth after Cesarean (VBAC) is an increasingly uncommon patient preference, Rybak acknowledges that it is a reasonable choice for a woman who wishes to avoid multiple Cesarean procedures. VBAC does, however, pose an increased risk, to one in 2000 cases, of a catastrophic injury to the infant during delivery, even if the physician's delivery technique is flawless. If the newborn does suffer such an injury, the parents are likely to bring suit on behalf of the injured patient and to receive a multi-million dollar jury award, even if the obstetrician did not violate the standard of care. Given the magnitude of this liability risk, Rybak concludes that obstetricians may refuse patient requests for VBAC in

[5] Rybak (2009).

order to protect themselves. Exposing oneself to this probability and magnitude of risk, he argues, goes beyond self-sacrifice to potential self-destruction of one's career, and it is not morally required. Rybak does not attempt to pinpoint the appropriate tipping point in these conflict situations between acting to benefit a patient and acting to protect oneself from liability risk, and others may well challenge his claims about the amount of liability risk obstetricians should assume in honoring their patients' requests. Nevertheless, unless one asserts that health care professionals must assume any amount of risk to themselves in order to provide a benefit to their patients, some magnitude of adverse consequences for the professional may provide sufficient justification for defensive practice, that is, actions taken to protect oneself from liability.

What's the alternative?

In this chapter, I have argued that health care professionals should not rely solely on the law to guide their practice, but neither should they disregard the law entirely and rely exclusively on moral considerations. What, then, is the appropriate relationship of law and ethics as guides to action? As discussed in Chapter 1, "The role of ethics in health care," health care professionals, and nearly everyone else in today's world, depend on multiple different sources for moral guidance, including family members, friends, mentors, religious doctrines, moral philosophy, cultural values, and professional principles, among others. Each of these sources can provide valuable counsel, but the content of their advice may differ, and none of these sources is infallible. Legal rules can also serve as important, but not infallible, guides to action.

This chapter has identified several persuasive reasons for the importance of attention to the law, including a general duty of citizens to respect the law, the significance of legal rules as an expression of basic moral convictions of a society, and the potentially serious adverse consequences for professionals of violating legal rules, including legal standards of care. Health care professionals should, therefore, inform themselves carefully about the legal rules that apply to their practice. Because legal rules are frequently a reflection of widely held moral beliefs in states with just systems of government, legal and other sources of guidance will often be in harmony. When these sources agree, professionals can follow their guidance with reasonable confidence that their action is justified, and the situation will not present a moral problem.

As we have seen, however, legal rules or liability risks occasionally suggest or dictate courses of action that may undermine moral goals, such as honoring patient choices or securing patient benefits. These situations pose significant moral conflicts for health care professionals. Should they follow the legally "safe" course of action, or should they assume some risk of civil or criminal liability in order to honor the wishes or promote the best interests of their patients? There are persuasive reasons for both of these alternatives. On the one hand, health care professionals affirm moral principles of respect for autonomy, nonmaleficence, and beneficence. As discussed in Chapter 10, "Professionalism," calls to professionalism in health care, like the Physician Charter, emphasize the "primacy of patient welfare," that is, a fundamental professional commitment to subordinate one's personal interests to the welfare of one's patients.[6] Reliance on these principles will incline professionals to resolve conflicts between personal interests, including avoiding legal risk, and patient interests in favor of the patient.

On the other hand, widely accepted principles also endorse health care professional rights and duties that may conflict with patient interests. As noted above, the AMA Principles of Medical Ethics assert a general physician duty to respect the law. In addition to the patient-centered duties ascribed to professionalism, there is also wide recognition, in statutes and professional association policies, that health care professionals have a right to conscientious refusal to provide some treatments or services that violate their personal moral convictions. As discussed above, physicians may also have a right to refuse to provide treatments that subject them to substantial risk of malpractice liability.

When professional and patient interests conflict, therefore, "Act to promote patient welfare" may be a valuable rule of thumb, but it does not appear to be an absolute duty. Guidelines exist for specific conflict situations; for example, scholars who defend health care professional rights to conscientious refusal of treatment have articulated specific conditions under which such refusals should and should not be permitted.[7] There is,

---

[6] ABIM Foundation, ACP–ASIM Foundation, and European Federation of Internal Medicine (2002).

[7] See Wicclair (2011).

however, no general formula for resolving these conflicts, and there is no single, widely accepted measure to compare the significance of the different interests at stake. Instead, individual health care professionals in these situations must evaluate the various values and interests in conflict and decide which claims should determine their course of action.

Studies suggest that some physicians are willing to assume a measure of liability risk in order to serve the interests of their patients, and others are much more risk averse.[8] Wherever professionals decide to strike the balance between patient benefit and self-protection, they should do so based on accurate information about their legal duties and realistic estimation of their liability risks. A decision not to provide a particular treatment in order to limit one's potential liability may be reasonable if the risk is genuine and significant, but not if the decision is based on inaccurate "horror stories" about catastrophic damages.

Case analysis

At their monthly therapy session, Ms. Warren expresses suicidal thoughts to her psychiatrist Dr. Ames for the first time. How should Dr. Ames respond to this disclosure by his patient? If he believed that Ms. Warren was in imminent danger of harming herself as a result of her mental illness, Dr. Ames would have good reason to admit her to a psychiatric hospital, with or without her consent, to protect her from harm and to provide continuing treatment for her condition. Although the lifetime suicide risk for persons with affective disorders is estimated at 6 percent,[9] Ms. Warren's initial mention of suicidal thoughts does not warrant the conclusion that she is in imminent danger. Involuntary hospitalization, with its increased observation of patients and restrictions on their behavior, would reduce her risk of suicide in the short term, but it would have several other harmful consequences for Ms. Warren, including loss of her liberty, probable loss of her trust in Dr. Ames, and increased reluctance to seek psychiatric care in the future.

Considering only Ms. Warren's interests, therefore, involuntary commitment to a psychiatric hospital does not appear to be the best plan for her continuing treatment. If Ms. Warren does commit suicide while under

---

[8] See, for example, McCrary et al. (1992) and Studdert et al. (2005).   [9] Inskip et al. (1998).

Dr. Ames's care, however, her relatives are quite likely to bring and win a suit against him for damages due to his failure to prevent her suicide, despite the fact that accurate prediction and effective prevention of suicide are both extremely difficult.[10] May Dr. Ames commit Ms. Warren in order to reduce the risk of this adverse consequence for himself?

Before taking this action, Dr. Ames should surely consider whether there are other, less restrictive ways to reduce her risk of suicide and his own liability risk. He might, for example, explain that he is concerned that she may harm herself and recommend that she accept voluntary hospitalization for intensive treatment of her depressed mood. Assuming that she retains decision-making capacity and accepts this recommendation, a voluntary hospitalization will presumably reduce her risk of suicide. It is, however, very likely that she will view this option as too great a disruption of her daily life and refuse hospitalization. Dr. Ames might also recommend more frequent outpatient therapy sessions in order to monitor Ms. Warren's condition more closely and intervene if her condition worsens. Assuming that Ms. Warren agrees with this plan, closer monitoring may also reduce her risk of suicide. Given the unpredictability of suicide, however, it may not offer a significant reduction of that risk. Finally, Dr. Ames might decide that the liability risk to himself of continuing to treat Ms. Warren has become too great and seek to transfer her care to another provider or to terminate their relationship in some other way. He may not, however, find another psychiatrist willing to accept a "high-risk" patient, and his decision to seek termination of their relationship may be viewed by Ms. Warren as a devastating rejection that reinforces her feelings of worthlessness.

Although Dr. Ames's concerns about his liability risk in making treatment decisions for Ms. Warren may seem crass and insensitive, Jacob Appel argues that psychiatrists caring for suicidal patients face a genuine moral dilemma in balancing self-protection and patient interests.[11] To resolve this dilemma, Appel proposes enactment of statutes that provide immunity from liability for psychiatrists whose patients commit suicide in outpatient settings. Such a statute would enable Dr. Ames to continue outpatient treatment for Ms. Warren without concern about liability risk to himself if she should commit suicide. Is Appel's proposal a morally justifiable policy solution to this clinical ethics problem?

---

[10] Appel (2012).   [11] Appel (2012).

5 Culture and ethics in health care

Case example

Dr. Jordan is a neonatologist providing intensive care for Baby Sanjay, a 2-week-old premature infant with a large unilateral cerebral hemorrhagic infarct (a blood clot in the brain causing bleeding and tissue damage). Because his lungs are not fully developed, Baby Sanjay is currently dependent on a mechanical ventilator to support his breathing. Dr. Jordan believes that Baby Sanjay has a fairly good chance of survival (60–70 percent) with continuing intensive care. It is very probable, however, that he will be both physically and mentally disabled. At this early stage of Baby Sanjay's development, the degree of his eventual disability is still highly uncertain. It could be mild to profound, and there is a small chance he would survive without disability. Dr. Jordan has provided intensive care for hundreds of infants with medical conditions like Baby Sanjay, and he is committed to preserving the lives and promoting the health and well-being of his patients.

Baby Sanjay's parents are citizens of India; his father is working temporarily in the USA, but they plan to return to India shortly. They visit their son frequently and are very concerned about his serious medical problems. After hearing that, if he survives, Baby Sanjay will probably be mentally and physically disabled, the parents have asked Dr. Jordan to discontinue ventilator support and allow the baby to die. They explain that in their home city in India, disabled people face severe discrimination; little education, rehabilitation, or health care is available to them. Therefore, they prefer to allow Baby Sanjay to die rather than to live what they believe will be a life of profound suffering and indignity.

To evaluate the parents' request, Dr. Jordan consults several of his colleagues who received their medical training in India. They corroborate the parents' claim that mentally disabled persons, and their families, suffer great discrimination and receive little support in India. How should Dr. Jordan respond to the parents' request?[1]

---

[1] Adapted from a case reported in Kopelman and Kopelman (2007).

The ubiquity of cultural diversity

Until the twentieth century, most of the world's people lived and died within their own community, region, or nation and had little contact with foreigners or "strangers." Developments in travel, technology, communication, politics, and economics since that time have transformed this situation in all but the world's poorest and remotest regions. Increasing global study and work opportunities, and responses to the plight of political and economic refugees, have made the United States, Canada, and western European nations distinctly multicultural societies. In addition to the many immigrants with multiple national, racial, and ethnic origins living in North America and Europe, "native" North Americans and Europeans commonly identify themselves as members of several subcultures, based on shared religious belief (e.g. orthodox Judaism), region (e.g. "Southern culture"), age (e.g. youth culture), gender (e.g. feminist culture), sexual orientation (e.g. gay culture), and even professional affiliation (e.g. biomedical culture). Identification with one or more cultural groups and participation in cultural practices are central to the personal identity and self-concept of most people. I will use the term 'culture' in this chapter in a broad sense to refer to the complex and changing set of relationships, practices, beliefs, and values generated and widely shared within a national, racial, religious, or other social group.[2]

When everyone in a homogeneous community has the same cultural beliefs, values, and practices, they are very likely to agree about how to work together to achieve their common goals. Because people of different cultures and subcultures often do not share important beliefs, values, and practices, they are likely to disagree about what goals to pursue or how to pursue them. And, because decisions about health care are among the most important choices most people confront, cultural disagreements about health care are common occurrences in contemporary multicultural societies. Some of these disagreements have persisted for decades. One prominent example of a longstanding disagreement is the reluctance of health care professionals to comply with the parental refusal of blood transfusions for their minor children by members of the Jehovah's Witness religious community.[3] Another widely discussed example involves a cultural practice

---

[2] This description of culture is adapted from Hunt (2001).

[3] See, for example, Dixon and Smalley (1981).

of modification of the female genitalia known as "female circumcision." In the 1990s, US physicians reported requests from recent African immigrants for this procedure. In response, the AMA and other health care organizations argued that the practice is more accurately described as "female genital mutilation" and that it should not be offered or condoned, but some have questioned this conclusion.[4] How, then, should health care professionals and patients address these culture-based disagreements? This chapter will examine several moral responses to cultural diversity in health care.

Moral responses to cultural diversity

When culture-based disagreements arise in health care, as in other settings, several different moral responses are possible. I proceed now to a description and evaluation of three common responses, which I will call "moral imperialism," "moral relativism," and "moral negotiation."

Moral imperialism

Proponents of the position I will call "moral imperialism" typically identify strongly with the moral convictions of their own cultural tradition. They may, for example, make the following assertion: "My culture's moral beliefs are true and must therefore be respected; other cultural beliefs (insofar as they disagree with mine) are false and may be disregarded."

An obvious advantage of this position is its ability to simplify moral decision-making for its adherents, since it enables them to rely entirely on their own beliefs and to discount the beliefs of those who have different views. If, moreover, one can provide *compelling reasons* for one's moral beliefs, then everyone *ought to* accept and respect them.

The challenge for moral imperialists, however, is to provide reasons or arguments powerful enough to compel the agreement of others. Mere assertion of the truth of one's beliefs is obviously not enough to convince others, nor is simple appeal to intuition or to one's own personal experience. The historical record certainly suggests that no one national culture has a monopoly on moral truth, but rather that all are susceptible to immoral practices, including slavery, persecution, genocide, and unjust aggression.

[4] See Council on Scientific Affairs, American Medical Association (1995).

Similar charges can be brought against racial, religious, and other cultural groups. Without compelling arguments for his or her own position, the moral imperialist's out-of-hand rejection of another culture's moral claims seems disrespectful, even dehumanizing to members of the "foreign" culture.

Moral relativism

The general response to cultural disagreements that I will call "moral relativism" stands in stark contrast to moral imperialism. Rather than asserting the truth of one set of cultural beliefs, the moral relativist questions the ability to make any cross-cultural moral claims. The moral relativist may thus state this position as follows: "There is no legitimate way to evaluate or criticize the moral beliefs of another culture. Each culture's moral beliefs are valid for that culture."

Moral relativists obviously show substantial respect for and deference toward the moral beliefs of persons of different cultures. Moral relativists may be inspired by recognition of the great diversity of beliefs and practices across different cultural groups, but it is important to note that this position goes beyond the empirical evidence for wide cultural diversity to make the claim that different cultural beliefs and practices cannot be evaluated outside of their own cultural context. It thus resists the imperialistic or ethnocentric tendency to assume that one's own beliefs are correct and to impose those beliefs on "primitive" or "inferior" cultures.

Acceptance of moral relativism rules out any criticism of the beliefs of another culture. At least some cross-cultural moral judgments, however, appear to be both meaningful and legitimate – there is, for example, strong consensus in support of judgments like "slavery is wrong" and "human sacrifice is wrong." Despite their differences, people of different cultures also have significant beliefs and values in common; they can appeal to these shared values and beliefs to reach agreement on moral questions and to cooperate on common projects. The relativistic position may thus underestimate our ability to make and defend cross-cultural moral judgments.

Moral negotiation

A third general response to culture-based moral disagreement I will call "moral negotiation." Proponents of moral negotiation make the following assertion: "People of different cultures can seek and often achieve moral agreement based on shared beliefs, values, and methods of reasoning." Rather than insistence on their own culture's beliefs or immediate deferral to the beliefs of a different culture, "moral negotiators" seek engagement with members of other cultural groups to find a mutually agreeable course of action.

The moral negotiation response has considerable strengths. It recognizes that people of all cultures have the ability to reason and to work together in mutually respectful ways. This approach encourages a process of dialogue and negotiation. It enables participants to come to a greater understanding of both another's and one's own guiding beliefs and values; that mutual understanding may reveal common ground and facilitate a solution to the disagreement that both parties can accept. For these reasons, I believe that it is clearly preferable as a general response to situations of cultural conflict to either moral imperialism or moral relativism.

Moral negotiation is not without its weaknesses, however. It offers the attractive prospect of resolving moral conflict by mutual agreement, but there is no guarantee that a negotiated solution can be found to every conflict. As Chapter 16 discusses in greater detail regarding moral conflicts over treatment near the end of life, there are multiple potential causes of conflict, and some of these causes are more amenable to resolution than others. If a disagreement is the result of lack of knowledge about the significance of a cultural practice, for example, simply sharing information about that practice may resolve the disagreement. If, however, the disagreement is the result of deep-seated and fundamental value commitments that are in opposition to one another, the prospects for agreement are much poorer. And, even if a process of moral negotiation is able to achieve agreement between the parties to a dispute, there is no guarantee that that agreement is the "right" or "best" solution in any final or absolute sense.

Recognizing that resolution of a moral conflict is not guaranteed, how should proponents of moral negotiation of culture-based disagreements proceed when a negotiated resolution to the disagreement eludes them? Available options may include the following:

1. Keep trying! With additional reflection and dialogue, a new course of action that all can accept might be identified. As a patient's medical condition evolves, for example, it may become easier to rule out some treatment alternatives and reach agreement on others.

2. Seek help! Knowledgeable advisors may be able to shed new light on a dispute. A minister or rabbi, for example, may help to interpret how religious doctrines should guide health care choices. Most US hospitals offer ethics consultation services to assist in resolution of moral issues that arise in patient care.

3. Agree to disagree! The parties may conclude that they will not reach agreement on a common course of action and decide to end their relationship.

4. Implement one's own decision! In many situations, one person has the authority to impose his or her own choice on others. A military officer, for example, may order soldiers under his command to undergo vaccination against a potential biological weapon, despite their stated wish to forgo that treatment.

5. Defer to the other's decision! This may be one's only option when one is in a subordinate position, as, for example, a minor child subject to the decisions of his or her parents.

6. Appeal to a higher authority! When conflict is intractable and neither party has clear authority over the other, one or the other may appeal to a higher level of authority. One party may, for example, petition a court to review the dispute and decide the issue.

None of the above options is foolproof from either a practical or a moral point of view, but any one of them might represent the best course of action in a given situation.

Responsibilities of "culturally humble" health care professionals

The increasing cultural diversity of patients in recent years has not been lost on medical educators. The US Accreditation Council for Graduate Medical Education (ACGME), for example, makes explicit reference to cultural diversity in its description of core competencies for residency education in internal medicine, in these words: "Residents are expected to demonstrate … sensitivity and responsiveness to a diverse patient population, including but not limited to diversity in gender, age, culture, race, religion, disabilities, and sexual orientation."[5] For a number of years, US medical

---

[5] Accreditation Council for Graduate Medical Education (2013).

schools addressed this subject matter under the rubric of "cultural competence," with classes describing the health-related beliefs and practices of cultural groups whose members were likely to be represented in the local patient population.[6] This factual information might help physicians and other health care professionals recognize and respond to the culture-specific preferences of their patients, but the "cultural competence" approach has also been criticized as inadequate and potentially misleading.[7] Limited general knowledge about cultural practices, it is argued, may encourage stereotyping and manipulation of patients, rather than sensitivity and responsiveness to the complex and changing cultural beliefs and practices of individual patients.

These critics propose "cultural humility" as a more appropriate goal for health care professional education. Culturally humble professionals are, first of all, aware of the content and limits of their own cultural orientation. Because they cannot aspire to mastery of the complex and evolving cultural practices of their patients, they seek to engage patients in dialogue, in order to understand and respond to each individual patient's goals and preferences. The concept of cultural humility provides a strong foundation for the moral negotiation approach to resolving culture-based conflicts. In this section, therefore, I will propose three basic responsibilities of culturally humble health care professionals: respect, cultural awareness, and communication.

Respect

Respect for other persons is certainly not limited to health care settings, but it is essential for effective therapeutic relationships. Health care professionals demonstrate basic respect by recognizing that people of all cultures are moral agents whose interests and preferences should be sought and cannot simply be disregarded, although they may not always be honored. Professionals should also show basic respect for the people with whom they work, recognizing that they are also moral agents and acknowledging their interests and responsibilities.

---

[6] See, for example, Crandall et al. (2003).
[7] See, for example, Tervalon and Murray-Garcia (1998) and Hunt (2001).

Cultural awareness

Health care professionals may be inclined to disregard or ignore the cultural commitments of their patients; they may view culture as unimportant to treatment of patients' medical conditions and rely exclusively on the "hard data" of physical findings and diagnostic test results. This approach reflects a commonly held assumption of the medical culture, namely, that empirical data transcends culture and should be the sole basis for treatment decisions, rendering cultural and social information irrelevant and distracting.[8]

The culturally humble professional, in contrast, recognizes the significance of cultural values for medical treatment decisions and thus seeks out information about the patient's cultural orientation. The ability to recognize that a patient has specific cultural beliefs and to identify the content of those beliefs may depend, at least in part, on a basic familiarity with different cultures. A culturally humble clinician, however, will not assume that a particular patient subscribes to all of the commonly held beliefs of a racial or ethnic group or religious community, but will elicit the individual patient's beliefs through appropriate questions.

Communication

Demonstrating respect for patients as moral agents, achieving an understanding of patients' cultural beliefs and values and of how those beliefs and values bear on medical treatment decisions, and negotiating resolution of disagreements all depend heavily on successful communication. Professionals must be able to both give and receive information in effective and culturally sensitive ways, including information about patients' medical conditions and treatment options and information about patients' values, goals, hopes, fears, and desires. Shared understanding of all this relevant information provides the basis for continuing discussion in an effort to find a mutually agreeable treatment plan.

Like cultural sensitivity, the ACGME has identified communication skills as a core competency that must be taught and evaluated in medical resident training. The relevant standard reads as follows: "Residents are expected to: communicate effectively with patients, families, and the

---

[8] See Taylor (2003).

public, as appropriate, across a broad range of socioeconomic and cultural backgrounds ..."[9]

I have, in summary, proposed that health care professionals respond to the cultural diversity of their patients by embracing responsibilities to demonstrate basic respect for patients as moral agents, to identify the significant cultural beliefs and values of patients, and to communicate effectively with patients in order to achieve a shared understanding of the patient's situation and to reach agreement on a treatment plan.

Case analysis

Dr. Jordan and Baby Sanjay's parents disagree about what treatment plan to pursue for this gravely ill premature infant. Dr. Jordan projects that his patient has a good chance for long-term survival, and he therefore recommends continuing intensive care. Baby Sanjay's parents are deeply concerned about the probable mental and physical disability of their son and the poor quality of life he is likely to have in their home city in India. They request discontinuation of life-sustaining treatment to allow Baby Sanjay to die.

Both Dr. Jordan and the parents appear to have the infant's best interests at heart, but they have very different views about what those best interests are and how to achieve them. They may also have other considerations in mind. Dr. Jordan, for example, may be concerned that his failure to provide continuing intensive care could be professionally and even legally risky, since it could be viewed as a kind of medical neglect of his patient. Baby Sanjay's parents may be concerned not only for Sanjay, but also for themselves and their other children, since the whole family may suffer from hostile attitudes toward a disabled member and from the significant costs of providing ongoing medical care for Sanjay.

This situation highlights substantial cultural and social differences between the United States and India. The material resources and average standard of living of the two societies are very different, and those resource differences are reflected in their health care systems. In the United States, for example, neonatal intensive care is routinely provided for infants like Baby Sanjay. In India, neonatal intensive care is a much scarcer resource,

---

[9] Accreditation Council for Graduate Medical Education (2013).

and most infants with conditions like Baby Sanjay do not have access to intensive care and so die very soon after birth. As the parents report, cultural beliefs and attitudes toward people with disabilities are also very different in the two countries. US law prohibits discrimination on the basis of disability and requires public and private entities to provide accommodation of various kinds for people with disabilities. In contrast, some traditions in India view disabilities as punishment for past transgressions, and so may view persons with disabilities and their families as morally suspect.

How, then, should Dr. Jordan respond to this situation? Let's assume that, over the two weeks since Baby Sanjay's birth, he has met with the parents on multiple occasions and has kept them informed about the baby's condition. He has explained the anticipated benefits and risks of harm of the treatments he has provided and has asked the parents about their hopes, fears, and preferences regarding Baby Sanjay's condition and its treatment. He has listened carefully to their concerns and their request that life-sustaining measures be withdrawn, and he has asked the parents to share their reasons for this request. He has also sought advice from his colleagues regarding the accuracy of the parents' statements about the treatment of disabled people in India, and he has learned that their account is accurate.

Dr. Jordan might explore with Baby Sanjay's parents whether there are ways to avoid the negative long-term consequences of continuing intensive treatment that they envision. He might, for example, propose to the parents that they consider remaining in the United States to enable Baby Sanjay to take advantage of the medical and educational resources available to him in the US. Or, he might suggest that the parents relinquish custody of Baby Sanjay, allowing him to remain in the US when they return to India. The parents may not, however, be able or willing to emigrate to the United States, and they may not agree to relinquish custody of their son. If he and the parents cannot resolve their disagreement, Dr. Jordan might seek direction from a court regarding whether he should continue to provide life-sustaining treatment for Baby Sanjay or should honor the parents' refusal of treatment for their child.

In the case on which this description is based, a dramatic change in the medical condition of the patient resulted in agreement on how to proceed.[10]

---

[10] Kopelman and Kopelman (2007).

The infant suffered additional severe brain injury, making his chance for survival much lower and the probability of severe disability much greater. In light of this new development, the medical team agreed to honor the parents' request for discontinuation of life-sustaining treatment, and the infant died shortly thereafter.

If Baby Sanjay's condition had remained stable, however, whose preference about how to proceed should have been followed? Chapter 9, "Surrogate decision-making," and Chapter 16, "Moral conflicts in end-of-life care," provide additional information that may help to answer this question.

Part II

Moral foundations of the therapeutic relationship

Therapeutic relationships between patients and professionals are at the center of health care; they are the primary mechanism for realizing its cherished goals of health, healing, and comfort. Part II of this volume examines six moral foundations of these therapeutic relationships:

- respect for patient privacy and confidentiality
- truthful communication
- informed consent to treatment
- surrogate decision-making for patients who lack decision-making capacity
- respect for professional boundaries
- responsible stewardship of health care resources

These six foundations are widely recognized as essential for the provision of effective, equitable, and respectful health care.

Chapter 6, "Privacy and confidentiality," first examines the meaning of these concepts and their application in health care settings. Then it argues that respect for privacy and confidentiality preserves patient autonomy, promotes beneficial treatment outcomes, and protects patients from harm. The chapter acknowledges that respect for privacy and confidentiality may be limited by other duties, including duties to obey the law and to protect both patients and third parties from harm.

Chapter 7, "Truthfulness," explores professional duties to communicate truthfully with patients. It bases these duties on respect for patients' rights to know about their condition and its treatment, the ability of patients to accept even bad news, and the benefits to patients of making decisions based on a clear understanding of their condition, prognosis, and treatment alternatives.

Chapter 7 describes and endorses an account of what it means to be truthful that was proposed by physician Richard Cabot. It distinguishes duties to provide truthful information from duties to protect the confidentiality of that information, and it recognizes that patients may choose to waive their right to receive personal health information.

Chapter 8 is devoted to examination of patient rights to give or withhold, and professional duties to obtain, informed consent to medical treatment. After a brief summary of the legal origins and moral foundations of informed consent, the chapter describes the three essential elements of informed consent, namely, the patient must have the capacity to consent, the health care professional must provide relevant information about the treatment decision, and the patient must be free to choose. The chapter concludes with a review of recognized exceptions to the duty to obtain the patient's informed consent to treatment, including emergency situations, treatment of patients who lack decision-making capacity, patient waiver of consent, and treatment that is required in order to protect the health of the public.

Chapter 9 explores the role of surrogate decision-makers in choosing treatment for patients who lack decision-making capacity. It begins with an argument that knowledgeable and willing surrogates are the most appropriate decision-makers for these patients and then considers who should be authorized to serve in this capacity. The chapter reviews three standards that are widely recommended to guide surrogates' choices, the expressed preferences standard, the substituted judgment standard, and the best interests standard. Finally, it argues that surrogate decision-makers should have broad but not absolute authority, and that health care professionals should intervene to protect their patients from surrogate decisions that are clearly harmful or unreasonable.

Chapter 10 considers the concept of professionalism and its application to health care. After brief review of different senses of the term 'profession', this chapter presents Edmund Pellegrino's argument that therapeutic relationships in health care are morally distinctive in five different ways. The moral demands of these relationships impose significant responsibilities on health care professionals, and the general term 'professionalism' is often used to refer to that set of moral responsibilities. The chapter then examines a specific topic within the broad domain of professionalism, the recognition and enforcement of professional boundaries. It offers a description and rationale for four categories of professional boundaries: personal boundaries, commercial boundaries, inter-professional boundaries, and integrity boundaries.

Chapter 11 is devoted to resource stewardship, a responsibility of health care professionals that has received increasing recognition over the past two decades. This chapter reviews professional association statements affirming a duty of stewardship and offers a brief history of the recent rapid growth of resource-intensive care in the US health care system. It then proposes a general description of health care resource stewardship based on the stewardship parables of the New Testament. The chapter then examines the following five criteria for responsible stewardship of health care resources:

1. Do not use resources fraudulently.
2. Do not use resources wastefully.
3. Choose the most cost-effective treatment.
4. Do not provide "low-value" treatment, that is, treatment whose expected benefit is less than its expected cost.
5. Develop and use fair procedures to allocate unavoidably scarce resources.

Chapter 11 concludes with a review of four types of resource allocation: rationing, triage, gatekeeping, and "gaming the system."

6   Privacy and confidentiality

Case example

Dr. Adams is an emergency physician on duty during the early morning hours this Sunday in the Emergency Department (ED) of a community hospital in a small Midwestern city. The ED receptionist informs Dr. Adams that a woman is on the telephone anxiously inquiring whether her 20-year-old daughter Alice, an undergraduate student at the local university, is a patient in the ED. The woman reports that her daughter's roommate has informed her that Alice has not returned to her room as expected; the roommate does not know where Alice is or what has happened to her. The caller adds that she has attempted to contact Alice by cell phone, but her calls have not been answered.

Alice was, in fact, transported to the ED several hours earlier by friends after she fell at a party and could not get up. When Dr. Adams first saw her, she was tearful and unsteady. When he asked what happened, she said, "I drank way too much and took some pills. I am so ashamed; please don't tell anyone about this, especially my mom!" Shortly thereafter she lost consciousness, and she is now receiving initial evaluation and treatment for acute alcohol poisoning or a drug overdose. The receptionist asks Dr. Adams to speak with the caller. Should he do so? If he does speak with her, what, if anything, should he tell her about Alice?

Ancient origins, contemporary significance

Protection of patient confidentiality is among the most ancient of the moral responsibilities embraced by health care professionals. The famous medical oath attributed to Hippocrates, for example, includes this pledge: "What I may see or hear in the course of treatment or even outside of treatment in regard to the life of men, which on no account one must spread abroad, I will keep to myself, holding such things shameful to be spoken about."[1] Unlike several of the other injunctions contained in the Hippocratic Oath, however, this commitment to protect patient confidentiality is not just a matter of historical interest. Rather, it remains a staple of contemporary medical oaths and codes of ethics of health care professional associations world wide. To cite just two examples, the *ICN Code of Ethics for Nurses*, most recently revised by the International Council of Nurses in 2012, includes this statement: "The nurse holds in confidence personal information and uses judgment in sharing this information."[2] The current version of the AMA's "Principles of Medical Ethics," a document described as "the essentials of honorable behavior for the physician," contains the following principle: "A physician shall respect the rights of patients, colleagues, and other health care professionals, and shall safeguard patient confidences and privacy within the constraints of the law."[3]

These statements are representative examples of the consensus view that respect for patient confidentiality is a fundamental professional responsibility in health care. They also raise important conceptual and moral questions. For example, the AMA "Principles of Medical Ethics" statement makes reference to both "confidences" and "privacy," prompting the question whether these terms are synonymous or refer to different concepts. Both of the above confidentiality statements indicate that personal health information can sometimes be disclosed, prompting questions about the proper scope and limits of respect for patient confidentiality. This chapter will examine the concepts, moral foundations, and limits of respect for patient privacy and confidentiality.

Key concepts

To show proper respect for patient privacy and confidentiality, health care professionals must have a clear understanding of the meanings of these concepts. Although privacy and confidentiality have overlapping meanings, there are also important differences between them. Both terms can be used to describe matters of fact (e.g., "a private room," "a confidential report"), but our interest in this context is in their normative uses in the assertion of values, rights, and obligations.

---

[1] Oath of Hippocrates (1995).   [2] International Council of Nurses (2012): 2.
[3] American Medical Association (2001b).

Privacy

The term 'privacy' has three important, and different, uses in health care contexts, sometimes called physical privacy, informational privacy, and decisional privacy.[4] Physical privacy refers to important personal interests in freedom from unwanted contact with others or exposure of one's body to others. Privacy in this sense is unavoidably limited in health care, since accurate diagnosis and effective treatment of medical conditions often require physical examination and physical contact with or manipulation of the body of the patient. Patients accept this loss of physical privacy in order to obtain the benefits of health care, but they expect health care professionals to limit physical contact and exposure to what is necessary for effective diagnosis and treatment.

Informational privacy refers to important personal interests in preventing disclosure to others of information about oneself, especially sensitive or embarrassing personal information. Informational privacy is also unavoidably limited in health care, since health care professionals must obtain multiple kinds of health-related information from their patients in order to understand their health conditions and provide effective treatment. Once again, patients are generally willing to disclose personal health information in order to receive appropriate treatment, but they expect health care professionals to protect this information from any unnecessary further disclosure.

Decisional privacy refers to important personal interests in making and carrying out decisions about one's own life without interference from others. US courts have appealed to a right to privacy in this sense to protect patient access to contraception[5] and abortion,[6] and to uphold patient refusal of life-sustaining treatment.[7] Because rights to decisional privacy protect patient control over health care choices, they are closely linked to rights to informed consent to treatment and to participation in biomedical research. Informed consent is examined in Chapters 8 and 19; the remainder of this chapter will focus on issues of physical and informational privacy.

---

[4] Allen (1995).   [5] *Griswold* v. *Connecticut* (1965).   [6] *Roe* v. *Wade* (1973).
[7] *Bouvia* v. *Superior Court* (1986).

Confidentiality

Like informational privacy, the term 'confidentiality' refers to the protection of sensitive information. In health care settings, professionals accept a duty of confidentiality when they pledge to protect the personal health information of their patients. Health care providers respect confidentiality by refraining from disclosing personal health information to others who have no right to the information and by refraining from accessing patient information without authorization. Providers can violate this duty both intentionally and inadvertently. An unscrupulous physician might, for example, intentionally violate confidentiality by selling information about a celebrity patient to a journalist. A nurse might inadvertently violate confidentiality by discussing a patient's condition with a co-worker in a public area of a hospital, where it is overheard by visitors and other patients.[8]

Moral foundations

Moral grounds for affirming a professional duty to respect patient privacy and confidentiality can be found in several of the foundational principles of bioethics articulated by Beauchamp and Childress, including respect for autonomy, beneficence, and nonmaleficence.[9] The principle of respect for autonomy affirms the special status of persons as moral agents able to make morally significant choices and carry them out. Consider, for a moment, how a person's freedom of choice and action would be compromised if one had little or no control over others' access to one's person or access to sensitive information about oneself. Without at least some degree of privacy and confidentiality, one would be constantly subject to the intrusions of others, and one's freedom of choice and action would be severely constrained. Thus, a reasonable degree of physical and informational privacy is a necessary condition for effective personal autonomy.

The principle of beneficence expresses a central professional commitment to act for the benefit of one's patients. Health care's ability to benefit patients relies heavily on an effective therapeutic relationship between

[8] See Ubel et al. (1995).
[9] Beauchamp and Childress (2013). For a description of these principles, see Chapter 3, "Methods of health care ethics."

patients and professionals, and the effectiveness of that relationship relies in turn on mutual trust. If patients are confident that their health care providers will protect their physical privacy and their personal information, they will be more likely to seek care and to communicate health-related information openly and accurately. Communication of this information is often essential to making a correct diagnosis of the patient's illness and to providing effective treatment. Patients who trust their health care providers are also more likely to accept and adhere to the treatment plan those providers recommend. In all of these ways, respect for privacy and confidentiality contributes to the goal of benefiting patients.

Closely related to the affirmative professional duty to act for the benefit of patients is a negative duty, to refrain from actions that harm patients, or at least to refrain from actions whose potential harms exceed their potential benefits. This duty is expressed by the principle of nonmaleficence. Professional respect for patient privacy and confidentiality plays a significant role in preventing potential harms. Failure to protect physical privacy violates patients' interests in modesty and subjects patients to unwelcome invasion of their personal space. Failure to protect personal health information may result in a variety of harms. Public disclosure that a patient is a victim of a sexual assault, for example, may subject that person to acute embarrassment or shame. Disclosure that a person has AIDS may result in ostracism, stigmatization, and discrimination. The principle of nonmaleficence thus provides an important additional reason for protecting patient privacy and confidentiality.

Evidence for the significance of patient privacy and confidentiality may also be found in a variety of federal and state laws and regulations enacted to protect these values. Most prominent among these in the United States is a set of federal regulations implemented under the Health Insurance Portability and Accountability Act of 1996 (HIPAA).[10] Though the impetus for these regulations was a perceived threat to patient confidentiality posed by electronic transmission of medical records, the HIPAA privacy regulations require health care providers to protect the confidentiality of personal health information (PHI) recorded or transmitted in any form, including electronic, written, and oral communication. Under these regulations, providers must obtain the patient's written authorization to use or disclose

---

[10] US Department of Health and Human Services, Office for Civil Rights, no date.

PHI. There are, however, notable exceptions to this requirement; providers may use and disclose PHI without patient authorization for "treatment, payment, and health care operations" activities, and for twelve "national priority purposes," including public health and abuse and neglect reporting requirements, law enforcement purposes, and organ, eye, and tissue donation activities. Depending on their severity, violations of HIPAA privacy regulations may subject health care providers to civil and criminal penalties.

Moral limits

The previous section offered several reasons for the moral significance of patient privacy and confidentiality. Those reasons provide strong grounds for recognizing professional duties to protect privacy and confidentiality. These duties are best understood, however, as *prima facie*, not *absolute*, duties. In other words, health care professionals must fulfill these duties *unless* there are stronger moral duties that require professionals to override them. What, then, are the stronger moral duties that can override patient privacy and confidentiality?

The AMA principle of medical ethics cited above suggests one such duty when it asserts that "a physician . . . shall safeguard patient confidences and privacy *within the constraints of the law*" (emphasis added). By qualifying its principle in this way, the AMA appeals to an implied professional duty to obey the law that may override the duty to protect patient confidentiality.[11] There are, in fact, laws in most jurisdictions that require health care professionals to report various kinds of personal health information, including diagnoses of serious communicable diseases and cancers, medical findings that suggest abuse or neglect of children or dependent adults, gunshot and knife wounds, and poisonings, among others. These laws typically require reporting to government officials, often public health, social services, or law enforcement officers. Enactment of these reporting requirements presumably reflects a social choice that important public purposes like protection of the public's health and prosecution of serious crimes should override protection of patient confidentiality.

---

[11] For further discussion of the duty to obey the law, see Chapter 4, "Law and ethics in health care."

Another professional duty often cited to justify overriding patient privacy and confidentiality in particular circumstances is the duty to protect third parties from harm. Health care professionals sometimes acquire information about a patient indicating that that patient poses a significant risk of harm to others. This information may take various forms. For example, a neurologist providing medical care for a patient with a newly diagnosed seizure disorder may recognize that there is a high risk that this patient will have a seizure while driving, lose control of his vehicle, and cause a serious accident. The neurologist may conclude that she should inform the appropriate authorities of the risk posed by this patient, and statutes in most US states either permit or require physicians to report such information to the state agency that issues driver's licenses, enabling those agencies to suspend the patient's driver's license until he or she no longer poses a significant risk as a driver. Other examples of this duty to protect third parties may include informing others of risks to them from the behavior of a person with severe psychiatric illness, and informing a wife of a patient with a recently acquired HIV infection of the risk of infection posed by sexual relations with her husband. It should be noted that this duty to protect third parties from harm depends on a judgment by a health care professional that a patient's condition or behavior does in fact pose a significant risk to others.

A third duty that may be invoked to override patient privacy and confidentiality is the duty to protect patients themselves from harm. A psychiatrist may, for example, decide to alert the family members of a patient with severe depression that the patient is seriously contemplating suicide. In such a situation, the psychiatrist may conclude that the patient has lost decision-making capacity and needs the help of family members to prevent self-infliction of grave harm. Disclosure of personal health information to surrogate decision-makers is, in fact, generally required for children and other patients who lack decision-making capacity, so that surrogates can make informed treatment choices on behalf of these patients. Moral issues in surrogate decision-making are discussed in greater detail in Chapter 9.

Like the professional duty to protect patient privacy and confidentiality, the three general duties to disclose patient information described above are best understood as *prima facie* duties; that is, all of them have moral weight, but none is absolutely binding. This poses an obvious question for health care professionals. "When these *prima facie* duties conflict in a particular situation," a professional may ask, "how do I decide which one takes precedence? In other words, how do I determine which one is my *actual* duty in that situation?" The person posing this question may hope for a simple rule or algorithm for determining which *prima facie* duty should take precedence in this, or any, situation requiring a moral choice. If such a rule or algorithm were discovered or invented, moral judgment would become a matter of applying it to reach a conclusion. Given the complexity of these questions and the limits of ethical theory, however, no such algorithm has emerged, nor is one likely to do so. Instead, professionals must rely on careful assessment of a variety of factors, including relevant concepts, factual information, and moral considerations, in deciding which of two or more conflicting duties has the most compelling reasons in its favor.

In complex moral choice situations, it may be impossible to conclude that one alternative is demonstrably morally superior to all others. Certain choices may be clearly preferable to others, however, and guidelines may assist in the evaluation of the available alternatives. Several such guidelines can help professionals reach decisions about whether to protect or override patient confidentiality. First, clinicians should consider both the *magnitude* and the *probability* of the consequences of different alternatives. If, for example, the harm to persons exposed to a patient with an infectious disease is both very severe and very probable, the case for disclosing this condition may be morally compelling. Second, when *prima facie* duties are in apparent conflict, clinicians should seek strategies that allow them to satisfy all of the conflicting duties before choosing to fulfill one by overriding others. Should a physician be able to convince a reluctant patient to consent to the disclosure of personal information for an important reason, for example, the physician will not have violated the patient's confidentiality. Finally, when considering whether to disclose confidential information for a patient's own benefit, professionals should pay close attention to whether the patient has decision-making capacity. Overriding the confidentiality of a patient who retains decision-making capacity for that patient's own good is a kind of "hard paternalism" that is difficult to justify.[12]

---

[12] An action is paternalistic when it interferes with a person's presumed rights, freedoms, or interests for that person's own good (Dworkin 2014). Most commentators view "soft paternalism," that is, actions taken to protect a person from harm when that person is unable to make an informed or voluntary choice, as justified. A "hard paternalistic"

Case analysis

The situation described at the beginning of this chapter poses obvious questions about confidentiality for Dr. Adams. May (or should) he inform the caller that Alice is a patient in the ED? Or, must he protect the confidentiality of Alice's health information?[13]

Several kinds of information are likely to be important to Dr. Adams in deciding how to proceed in this situation. He recognizes that information about Alice's condition is highly sensitive; she does not want others, and especially her mother, to know that she has gone on a drinking binge and may have taken a drug overdose. If Alice were still conscious and able to understand and respond to his questions, he could inform her that her mother is inquiring about her and ask for permission to tell her mother where she is, but he cannot do that now. Dr. Adams may appreciate a mother's natural and deep concern for her daughter's safety, but he may also want to confirm the identity of the caller and her relationship to his patient, perhaps by asking for specific information that the mother should know. The caller may very well be Alice's mother, but might also be someone else impersonating the mother in order to obtain information about Alice's condition. Dr. Adams may also want to assess the urgency and gravity of Alice's medical condition – for example, is she unstable and at serious risk of death from acute alcohol or drug toxicity? He may also want to know whether the hospital's confidentiality policy addresses the subject of telephone inquiries about hospital patients, and, if it does, what responses to such requests are permitted or recommended. Finally, he may want to consider whether disclosure of Alice's health information may be required in order to obtain informed consent for her treatment from a surrogate decision-maker.

At least the following three options are available to Dr. Adams:

1. He may decline the receptionist's request that he speak with the caller, perhaps advising the receptionist to inform the caller that the hospital does not respond to telephone requests for information about ED patients.

---

action, in contrast, overrides the wishes of a person who retains the ability to make informed and voluntary choices for him or herself, and so is considerably more difficult to justify.

[13] For a discussion of multiple privacy and confidential issues encountered in the emergency department, see Moskop et al. (2005).

2. He may agree to speak with the caller and inform her that Alice is a patient in the ED, but that he cannot disclose any medical information about her over the telephone.

3. He may agree to speak with the caller, inform her that Alice is a patient in the ED, describe her condition, request additional information about Alice's health, and seek the caller's participation in making decisions about her treatment.

How should Dr. Adams evaluate each of these options?

The first option has the advantage of protecting the confidentiality of Alice's health information, and it also respects her apparently sincere and fervent request to him not to disclose this embarrassing information. Failure to disclose Alice's whereabouts, however, will subject her mother to continuing anxiety about her daughter's safety. Perhaps more importantly, unless the emergency exception to informed consent applies in this situation, Dr. Adams may have a responsibility to obtain consent for Alice's treatment from a surrogate decision-maker, and, as her nearest relative, her mother may be her legally authorized surrogate. If Alice's condition is critical, it may be cruel not to inform her mother and give her a chance to be near her daughter.

The second option provides a truthful answer to the mother's urgent question, and so presumably relieves her anxiety about her daughter's whereabouts. It may also protect the confidentiality of the specific information about Alice's condition. Informing the mother that Alice is a patient in the ED, however, will give her a serious new cause for concern about her daughter's health. In addition, if Dr. Adams does not give Alice's mother any information about her daughter's condition, he cannot secure her surrogate consent for treatment.

Carrying out the third option would enable Dr. Adams to respond fully to the obvious concern expressed by Alice's mother for her daughter's safety and health. It would also enable him to obtain the mother's surrogate consent to her daughter's treatment. It does not, however, honor Alice's explicit request for protection of the confidentiality of her health information. Moreover, if Alice's condition is not serious, she may not need immediate treatment, but only a period of observation.

Each of these courses of action has its advantages and disadvantages – which one should Dr. Adams choose? I believe that careful attention to the facts of the situation should strongly influence Dr. Adams's choice. For example, if he judges that Alice's medical condition is critical and that she may well not survive, he will have several powerful reasons for disclosing the situation to her mother. First of all, Dr. Adams may conclude that, when Alice requested that he keep her condition confidential, she did not understand the gravity of the situation. Second, he may believe that it will be highly important, to both Alice and her mother, that her mother be with her in this critical situation, especially if she does not survive. Finally, Dr. Adams may recognize the value of including Alice's mother, as her closest family member, in major decisions about her treatment.

In contrast, if Dr. Adams judges that Alice's condition is improving with treatment that has already begun and that she is therefore not in danger of death or serious disability, he may conclude that there is not a compelling reason to provide information about Alice's condition to her mother and that he should therefore honor Alice's request that he keep her condition confidential. It may, however, be difficult for Dr. Adams to form a clear or confident opinion about the seriousness of Alice's condition; how, in your judgment, should that uncertainty affect his decision?

7   Truthfulness

Case example

Twenty-two-year-old Annie was brought by friends to the ED of a small Virginia hospital. She fell while horseback riding, was kicked by her horse, and lay in a field for several hours. Despite initial IV therapy, her blood pressure remains very low, and an abdominal tap reveals that she is bleeding very rapidly into her abdomen.

Though she is in shock, Annie remains awake and alert. She asks Dr. Smith, the emergency physician caring for her, "Is it a serious injury? Will I live?"

Dr. Smith responds, "Everything will work out, Annie. It may be a little rough for a bit, but it will work out."

"Are you sure?" she asks. "Please, tell me honestly."

Dr. Smith is very concerned about Annie's unstable condition, and he is unsure how she will do. What should he say to her?[1]

Past and present

In twenty-first-century Anglo-American societies, truthfulness is widely acknowledged as a central professional responsibility of physicians. Professional standards regarding truthfulness have, however, undergone significant change over the past century, and what constitutes truthful communication is still a matter of some controversy. Other cultures, moreover, endorse somewhat different approaches to communication between physicians and patients. This chapter will examine the meaning and justification of truthfulness in the therapeutic relationship.

In an article published in 1903, physician Richard Cabot states the "rule for truth-speaking" he was taught as a Harvard medical student: "When you are thinking of telling a lie, ask yourself whether it is simply and solely

[1] Anonymous (1981).

90

for the patient's benefit that you are going to tell it. If you are sure that you are acting for his good and not for your own profit, you can go ahead with a clear conscience."[2] As this rule illustrates, the medical profession of that era condemned self-serving lies, but approved lies told for the benefit of patients. Notice that the rule authorizes the physician to judge whether truthful or deceptive information will do more good for the patient, and to base his or her disclosure on that judgment.

This rule Cabot cites appears to have persisted well into the twentieth century. In a survey of 200 Chicago physicians published by Oken in 1961, almost 90 percent of the respondents reported that they generally withheld information about a cancer diagnosis from their patients.[3] These physicians cited various reasons for withholding this information, including a belief that the patients would not want to know and a desire to maintain the patients' hope for recovery and their cooperation with treatment.

Professional standards and practices regarding information disclosure changed rapidly during the last third of the twentieth century. This period witnessed growing acceptance of a duty to obtain informed consent to treatment that was first articulated in American case law in 1957 (see Chapter 8, "Informed consent"). This duty required physicians to inform the patient about his or her condition and its recognized treatment options as a necessary condition of obtaining a valid informed consent. Informed consent was one cornerstone of a patient rights movement that rejected traditional attitudes of deference to physician "orders" and demanded a more active role for patients.[4]

Revisions made by the AMA to its "Principles of Medical Ethics" during this period reflect growing recognition of a professional duty of truthfulness. The version of this document adopted in 1957 makes no mention of honesty or truthfulness.[5] A revision of the document adopted in 1980 includes, as its second principle, "A physician *shall deal honestly with patients and colleagues*, and strive to expose those physicians deficient in character or competence, or who engage in *fraud or deception*" (emphasis added).[6] The wording of this principle is strengthened in the current version of the "Principles," adopted in 2001: "A physician shall uphold the standards of professionalism, *be honest in all professional interactions,* and strive to report physicians deficient in character or competence, or engaging in *fraud or*

---

[2] Cabot (1903).   [3] Oken (1961).   [4] See, for example, Veatch (1972).
[5] American Medical Association (1957).   [6] American Medical Association (1980).

deception, to appropriate entities" (emphasis added).[7] The American College of Physicians (the US medical professional association of specialists in internal medicine) devotes an entire section to the topic of "Disclosure" in the 2005 fifth edition of its "Ethics Manual." That section includes an assertion that "Information should be disclosed whenever it is considered material to the patient's understanding of his or her situation, possible treatments, and probable outcomes. This information often includes the costs and burdens of treatment, the experience of the proposed clinician, the nature of the illness, and potential treatments."[8]

Do these changes in official statements of professional ethics regarding disclosure reflect a corresponding change in physician practice? One study offers impressive evidence that such a change in practice did occur. In 1977, Novack and colleagues administered a questionnaire to physicians in Rochester, New York, about their practice regarding disclosure of a cancer diagnosis; the questionnaire was almost identical to the one used by Oken in the 1961 study described above.[9] Ninety-eight percent of the 278 respondents in this latter study reported that their general policy is to disclose a cancer diagnosis to the patient, an almost complete reversal of the predominant practice reported sixteen years earlier.

The case for truthfulness

Are there compelling moral reasons for the shift in professional standards and practice regarding truthfulness described in the preceding section? If so, what are those reasons? I will argue that a persuasive moral case for truthfulness can be made by appealing to bioethical principles of respect for autonomy, nonmaleficence, and beneficence.

Respect for autonomy

Patients seek health care for many reasons, including, to be sure, treatment and prevention of illness and relief of pain and suffering. Another important reason for seeking care, for most patients, is a desire to understand their health condition. To achieve that understanding, patients typically

---

[7] American Medical Association (2001b).   [8] Snyder and Leffler (2005).
[9] Novack et al. (1979).

want to know whether they have a particular disease, what are their treatment options, and what is the likely outcome of the disease, both with and without treatment. To fulfill patients' desires to understand their health condition, physicians must provide truthful and relevant information about diagnosis, treatment, and prognosis. Without such information, patients cannot make meaningful choices about what treatment to accept. Thus, truthful communication respects patients' basic rights to know about their health condition and to make treatment choices based on that knowledge.[10] In contrast, a physician's decision to withhold significant medical information or to deceive a patient about his or her health condition is likely to be viewed as a sign of disrespect, a judgment that the patient lacks moral worth and therefore has no claim on important information about him or herself and no right to make important health choices based on that information.

Nonmaleficence

As described in Chapter 3, the principle of nonmaleficence has its origins in the ancient medical pledge to "do no harm," and is best understood today as a commitment to refrain from actions that are likely to cause more harm than benefit. To apply this principle to the topic of truthfulness, therefore, we must address the question whether a practice of truthfulness is likely to cause more harm than benefit, or vice-versa. The prevailing early twentieth-century view described by Richard Cabot emphasized the harmful effects of truthful disclosure, especially of bad news, in provoking anxiety and depression, and so recommended against disclosure. To test this view, Cabot undertook an "experimental" practice of truthful disclosure, and he reports his conclusion in dramatic fashion: "It has been, on the whole, the most interesting and surprising experiment that I have ever tried. The astounding *innocuousness of the truth* when all reason and all experience would lead one to believe that it must do harm, has surprised me even more than the remarkable tolerance of febrile patients for alcohol" (italics in original).[11] If Cabot's experience is representative of the consequences of truthful communication in other health care

---

[10] For further discussion of disclosure requirements for informed consent, see Chapter 8.
[11] Cabot (1903).

contexts, most patients and their loved ones are resilient enough to accept and deal with the truth about their health, even when the news is bad.

Truthful disclosure may sometimes cause harm, but so, obviously, may a practice of deception. As Cabot also points out, if a patient discovers a physician's attempt to deceive him or her, that patient is likely to mistrust everything the physician says, causing irreparable damage to their therapeutic relationship. Failure to disclose important health information may also cause harm. If, for example, a patient is not informed that his or her illness is terminal, the patient may not attend to important business or relationship matters before death, and those lost opportunities may result in major financial or emotional harm.

Beneficence

A finding that truthful communication is benign or innocuous supports the conclusion that this practice is morally permissible. A finding that truthfulness has significant benefits for patients supports the stronger conclusion that this practice should be morally recommended or required. The practice of truthfulness can, in fact, contribute to good outcomes for patients in several different ways. Patients' confidence that health care professionals are being open and honest with them is essential to building strong and trusting therapeutic relationships, to convincing patients to accept and adhere to recommended treatments, and thus to realizing the benefits those treatments can provide. Truthful communication about the patient's condition and the likely outcomes of treatment alternatives also enables patients to choose and achieve realistic health and life goals. For example, truthful and sensitive communication about expected treatment outcomes for a patient with advanced cancer may enable the patient to choose palliative treatments that enhance quality of life and avoid treatments whose likely harms clearly outweigh potential benefits. In these situations, truthful disclosure helps patients to understand the limits of health care, discourages unrealistic expectations, and so avoids the potential disappointment and frustration of medicine's failure to realize those expectations.

Taken together, I believe that these arguments make a strong case for recognizing truthfulness as a basic responsibility of health care professionals. Many other questions remain to be answered, however, including: What exactly does it mean to be truthful, or to practice truthfulness? What are the scope and limits of the duty of truthfulness in health care communication? How does truthfulness relate to the professional responsibility to keep personal health information confidential? How should different cultural values and practices affect the duty of truthfulness? The remainder of this chapter will be devoted to addressing these important conceptual and moral questions.

The concept, scope, and limits of truthfulness in health care

Consider the following situation: Mr. Hudson, a 60-year-old farm worker, visits a family physician in his small town with symptoms of persistent abdominal pain, nausea, fatigue, and dark urine. The family physician suspects a malignancy and refers Mr. Hudson to an oncologist in a neighboring city. The oncologist examines him and performs several diagnostic tests, including an abdominal magnetic resonance imaging (MRI). At a follow-up visit four days later, the oncologist makes the following statement: "Mr. Hudson, I am sorry to tell you that you have advanced cancer of the pancreas, and it has metastasized to your liver and lymph nodes. None of our standard cancer treatments, including chemotherapy, radiation therapy, and surgery, is effective for your condition. Most patients with your condition are dead within three months. I will send this information to your family doctor." Then he leaves the room.

   Did this oncologist fulfill his professional responsibility to communicate truthfully with Mr. Hudson? I believe that many people would insist that he did not. If confronted with this judgment, however, the oncologist might respond that he did provide Mr. Hudson with the essential information about his condition, the lack of effective treatment alternatives, and the prognosis, and that everything he told Mr. Hudson was absolutely true. Assuming that the oncologist is correct about the truth of his statements, how can we conclude that his communication was not a truthful one?

   To answer this question, we must first recognize the significant difference between truthful communication and a true statement or series of true statements. Even if each of the oncologist's statements is literally true, they may not give Mr. Hudson a clear or adequate understanding of his medical condition and its consequences. The oncologist's intention may be to "state the facts" as he sees them, or, if he is a malicious person, to cause

Mr. Hudson pain, but in either case, the most likely outcome is that Mr. Hudson will leave the doctor's office both confused and frightened.

If truthfulness is more than simply uttering true statements, what more is required? In his "experimental study" of truth-telling in medicine, Richard Cabot offers the following perceptive answer to this question: "By telling the truth I mean doing one's best to convey to another person the impression that one has about the matter in hand ... *A true impression,* not certain words literally true, is what we must try to convey ... What is often called the simple truth, the 'bald truth' or the 'naked truth' is often practically false – as unrecognizable as Lear naked upon the moor. It needs to be explained, supplemented, modified" (emphasis in original).[12]

Cabot's account clearly suggests much of what is wrong with the oncologist's disclosure. Though literally true, it is drastically incomplete. The oncologist offers no explanation of pancreatic cancer, or of what is meant by 'metastasis to other organs', even though Mr. Hudson is unlikely to understand this medical term. He mentions several treatments that are not effective for Mr. Hudson's condition, but appears to assume that cure or remission of the cancer is the only appropriate goal of treatment, and so does not discuss other goals of care and treatments that can achieve those goals. He bluntly states a very poor prognosis for survival, but does not elaborate further on survival probabilities, and does not address other issues likely to be of great interest to Mr. Hudson, including prospects for relieving his pain and other symptoms, how the disease is likely to progress, and the potential benefits of palliative and hospice care. Finally, his brief disclosure and abrupt departure may convey to Mr. Hudson that his own feelings and concerns are unworthy of the physician's attention and that he is being abandoned to his fate.

If, as Cabot proposes, truthfulness is conveying one's own impression or understanding of a situation, one can fail to be truthful by offering an incomplete or misleading explanation. One can also fail to convey one's own impression of a situation by offering *too much* information, and so Cabot's account also suggests appropriate *limits* on the kind and amount of information professionals should disclose. Cabot offers a colorful description of these limits: "I am not recommending that we should explain to every mother in full detail the etiology, pathology, course, and prognosis of her baby's illness. I have never tried that experiment, and I should suppose

---

[12] Cabot (1903).

it would be a very stupid, useless, and probably harmful thing to do. I do not believe in cramming information down people's throats or trying to tell them what they cannot understand properly, any more than I believe in button-holing every acquaintance in the street, and giving him a detailed account of what I consider his faults and failings."[13] Just as rough half-truths can mislead a patient, so also can "snowing" the patient with large amounts of technical or insignificant information, so that the patient cannot appreciate what information is most relevant and important. "Full disclosure" of all medical information is thus neither a practical nor a desirable goal.[14]

In his thoughtful analysis of duties of truthfulness, theologian Dietrich Bonhoeffer argues that these duties depend on the nature of the relationship between two persons, and so "telling the truth" requires a correct appreciation of one's relationship with another.[15] Though he does not apply it to health care, Bonhoeffer's observation is clearly relevant in the health care domain. Professional duties of confidentiality obviously impose limits on information disclosure. As described in Chapter 6, confidentiality is the duty *not* to provide a patient's personal information to persons who have *no* right to that information, such as curious strangers or identity thieves. Truthfulness, in contrast, is the duty *to* provide accurate medical information to persons who *do* have a right to that information, such as the patient, the surrogate decision-maker for a patient who lacks decision-making capacity, other professionals caring for the patient, and the patient's health insurance provider.

Another important limit of the professional duty of truthfulness is derived from the purpose of the therapeutic relationship. Health care professionals and patients form relationships to accomplish specific goals, most notably to understand and respond to the health needs of the patient. Professional duties of disclosure are thus appropriately limited to information that serves those specific goals, that is, information about the patient's health condition and treatment. Health care professionals have no duty, for example, to disclose information about their own personal lives, even if patients request such information, and professional boundaries restricting self-disclosure are designed to keep personal and professional relationships separate and distinct.[16]

---

[13] Cabot (1903).   [14] Epstein et al. (2010).   [15] Bonhoeffer (1965).

[16] See Chapter 10, "Professionalism," for additional discussion of professional boundaries.

Appeal to respect for patient autonomy is a major argument for the professional duty of truthfulness, but patient autonomy also imposes a significant additional limitation on that duty. When patients prefer not to receive information, professionals are not required to provide that information to them. Patients have a right to their own health-related information, but they may waive that right, and if they do so, professionals may, and indeed should, respect their decision not to be informed. There is, in other words, no general duty to receive health information, although there may be specific duties in some circumstances, as, for example, when a person's health condition poses a significant risk to another person.

This limitation on duties to disclose health information provides a strategy for dealing with different cultural beliefs and practices regarding disclosure of certain kinds of information. There is significant evidence that a number of national and ethnic cultures have beliefs and desires regarding information disclosure that are markedly different from the predominant views in North America and western Europe. In Japan, China, and other Asian nations, for example, elderly patients may routinely rely on family members to receive information about serious illness and make treatment decisions on their behalf.[17] Carrese and Rhodes report that Navajo Indians strenuously avoid discussion of "negative information," including serious illness and death.[18] When patients from these cultures prefer not to receive information about their health condition and its treatment, professionals have no duty to disclose that information to them. As Freedman points out, however, one cannot assume from the bare fact that a patient is a member of a particular cultural group that that patient would in fact choose to follow that group's cultural norms about information disclosure.[19] Freedman proposes that professionals adopt a strategy of "offering truth" in these circumstances, asking patients how much information they wish to receive about their condition and treatment, and respecting their decision about how much they want to know.

Case analysis

In this case, Annie asks Dr. Smith two direct and straightforward questions about her injury, namely, "Is it a serious injury? Will I live?" Not entirely

---

[17] See Ruhnke et al. (2000), Cong (2004), and Fan and Li (2004).
[18] Carrese and Rhodes (1995).   [19] Freedman (1993).

satisfied with his initial, somewhat vague response that "everything will work out," Annie asks Dr. Smith again, "Are you sure? Please, tell me honestly." Annie's questions put Dr. Smith in a difficult situation. The seriousness and persistence of her questions clearly suggest that Dr. Smith's opinion is important to her, and the urgency of the situation seems to require a prompt response.

What are Dr. Smith's options? If he decides to give a direct answer to her question, "Are you sure (that I will live)?" he has only two choices: "Yes, I am sure," or "No, I am not sure." Each answer has strengths and weaknesses. On the one hand, the positive answer would reinforce Dr. Smith's strong desire that Annie will survive and so presumably is an answer that he would very much like to give her. He may also interpret her questions as a request for reassurance, and he may believe that a reassuring positive response will calm and comfort her, and perhaps even increase her chances of survival. On the other hand, Dr. Smith recognizes that he is in fact not sure that she will survive. Thus, a negative response would most accurately reflect his impression of the current situation, and so it would satisfy his felt desire and obligation to be truthful. There are several good reasons for Dr. Smith's uncertainty about the outcome. Annie's injuries are clearly serious, but their exact nature and extent are still unknown. Initial efforts to stabilize her blood pressure have not been successful, and she is still in shock. Emergency surgery will be required for definitive diagnosis and treatment of her injuries, but the surgical team has not yet arrived in the ED. Given her circulatory instability, Annie could suffer a cardiac arrest at any moment, and, if the source of her internal bleeding has not been repaired, cardiopulmonary resuscitation efforts may not be successful.

Another option for Dr. Smith would be to refrain from answering Annie's question. Dr. Smith might believe that is inappropriate for Annie to put him "on the spot" in this way, and so might conclude that he has no duty to answer her question. He might simply remain silent. He might respond with his own question, perhaps "Why do you ask?" Or, he might offer a different observation, perhaps "We are doing everything we can to treat your injury." Remaining silent would avoid a deceptive response, but it would still deny Annie the information she is requesting. Silence would offer no reassurance to Annie of Dr. Smith's concern, and Annie would likely feel his silence as a withdrawal or distancing from her at this vulnerable time. Annie's response to the question "Why do you ask?" may help Dr. Smith understand the reason for her question, but it may also suggest that Annie is not entitled to Dr. Smith's opinion unless she has a very good reason for requesting it. A statement that the team is doing its best may provide some reassurance, but it does not answer Annie's repeated questions about her prognosis.

Dr. Smith has only a few moments to decide what to do. How would you advise him?

Annie's story appeared in 1981 as an anonymous first-person narrative contribution to "A Piece of My Mind," a regular feature of short narrative articles about the practice of medicine in *JAMA*.[20] The narrator recounts that, after some anxious moments, Annie does go to surgery. The surgeons repair a severely lacerated liver and remove a ruptured kidney. Post-surgical complications require numerous blood transfusions, but two weeks later, Annie is recovering nicely. In conversation with Annie and her parents, Dr. Smith (my pseudonym) recalls his ED conversation with Annie, and is amazed that she remembers every word he said. Then he adds with a flourish, "When I found that you had abdominal bleeding and I still couldn't bring up your blood pressure with two IVs, I have to admit that I thought you were a goner."

Annie seems shocked to hear this and says, "Don't you remember? You said that you were sure I would live. I remembered that promise all the time! I put a great deal of weight on what you said, and you ..." The article concludes with this sentence: "Suddenly, for the first time since the accident, and to everyone's surprise, tears are in her eyes and she is weeping; she is inconsolable because I lied to her."

Would your advice to Dr. Smith change, in light of this reported outcome?

[20] Anonymous (1981).

8 Informed consent to treatment

Case example

Fifty-seven-year-old Mr. Evans arrives at the Emergency Department of a large teaching hospital complaining of chest pain, cough, and shortness of breath. Chest x-rays are obtained, and they reveal a large pleural effusion (a buildup of fluid between the layers of tissue that line the lungs and the chest cavity). Mr. Evans is admitted to the hospital and is assigned to a general internal medicine inpatient team. The team concludes that a thoracentesis (removal of accumulated pleural fluid with a needle inserted between the ribs) should be done to allow Mr. Evans's lungs to expand more freely, making breathing easier, and to obtain a fluid sample for testing. The senior resident asks Dr. Collins, the first year resident on the team, to perform the thoracentesis, and she agrees. Dr. Collins has observed this procedure on multiple occasions, but she has never performed a thoracentesis before. In obtaining Mr. Evans's consent, must she inform him that this will be the first time she has performed this procedure?

Origins and moral grounds

First introduced in the United States more than half a century ago, informed consent to medical treatment is now generally recognized as a fundamental moral and legal right of patients. This chapter will examine the origins, moral grounds, and essential elements of informed consent. It will also describe recognized exceptions to the professional duty to obtain the patient's informed consent.

The concept of informed consent has its origins in medical law. Early twentieth-century cases in the United States recognized a right to consent to proposed treatment, articulated in a classic statement by Justice Benjamin Cardozo in 1914: "Every human being of adult years and sound mind has a right to determine what shall be done with his own body; and a surgeon who performs an operation without his patient's consent commits an assault, for which he is liable in damages."[1] Cardozo refers to assault, and early consent cases relied on legal concepts of assault and battery, understood in this context as the intentional, nonconsensual, and offensive touching of a patient by a physician.

In a series of cases beginning in 1957, US courts expanded the established duty to obtain a patient's consent into a duty to obtain an *informed* consent, that is, to obtain consent *after* providing specific information about the proposed treatment to the patient.[2] Most of these more recent informed consent cases rely on the legal concept of negligence, or failure to satisfy a professional standard of care, rather than assault and battery. The professional standard in these cases is a standard regarding what information should be given to patients about the proposed treatment and its expected benefits, risks, and alternatives.

Although its origins are in the law, leading scholars in the emerging field of medical ethics in the 1970s embraced the doctrine of informed consent and emphasized its importance as a remedy for paternalistic attitudes and practices then common among physicians.[3] These scholars viewed informed consent as a valuable mechanism for encouraging a more equal relationship between patients and physicians and a more active role for patients in making treatment decisions.

What, then, are the moral grounds for recognizing a patient right to informed consent to medical treatment, and a provider duty to obtain that consent? Commentators acknowledge two primary moral grounds, namely, respecting patient autonomy and promoting patient well-being.[4]

The role and value of informed consent in respecting patient autonomy is readily apparent and thus needs little explanation. A right to informed consent (and its corollary, informed refusal of treatment) gives patients the final say regarding what treatment they will receive, recognizing that they are moral agents entitled to make important choices about their own lives. Informed consent thus expresses basic convictions about the distinctive moral status of human persons, as well as the fundamental value ascribed to individual freedom in democratic societies.

---

[1] *Schloendorff* v. *Society of New York Hospital* (1914). For more information about early twentieth-century consent decisions, see Faden et al. (1986): 119–125.

[2] See Faden et al. (1986): 125–140.   [3] See Ramsey (1970) and Veatch (1972).

[4] See Brock (1987) and Beauchamp and Childress (2013).

Informed consent also plays an important role in promoting patient well-being, or, in principle-based language, in fulfilling the principle of beneficence. Medical treatment decisions can have multiple and profound positive or negative consequences for patients, including life or death, mental and physical function or disability, beauty or disfigurement, and comfort or suffering. Patients clearly have a strong interest in these outcomes of treatment, but their treatment preferences can differ because they have different personal beliefs, values, and goals. Whether chemotherapy or amputation will be a better treatment option for a patient with sarcoma (a malignant tumor of the leg), for example, will likely depend on that patient's beliefs and attitudes about physical function, longevity, disfigurement, pain, and risk-taking. Physicians have expert knowledge about the probable benefits and risks of different treatments, but patients are most knowledgeable about their own values, preferences, and goals. Because both of these kinds of knowledge are essential for making good medical treatment choices, a shared decision-making process will be most effective. Requiring informed consent enables the patient to make choices in light of his or her own values and interests, and treatments chosen based on those values and interests are most likely to achieve the best outcome for that patient.

Essential elements

In order for a patient to provide an informed consent to medical treatment, three essential elements must be present. First, the patient must have the *capacity* to make a treatment decision. Second, the patient must have the *information* he or she needs to make an informed choice. Third, the patient must make the treatment decision *voluntarily*. Let's examine each of these three essential elements of informed consent in turn.

Decision-making capacity

The first essential element of an informed consent is patient decision-making capacity. In seeking a patient's informed consent to a particular treatment, health care professionals must assess whether the patient has the ability to make that decision. The terms 'competence' and 'incompetence' are also frequently used in the medical literature and in practice settings to refer to patients' abilities to make treatment decisions. It is important to recognize that the term 'incompetence' is also used to refer to a court's determination that a person lacks the ability to make legally effective decisions, resulting in the appointment of a legal guardian with authority to act on behalf of the incompetent person. These clinical and judicial decisions have obvious similarities, but they are also significantly different. To avoid confusion, in this chapter I will use the term 'decision-making capacity' to refer to patients' abilities to make medical treatment decisions.

How do health care professionals determine whether a patient has the capacity to make a treatment decision? In most situations, the answer is obvious – either the patient is clearly able to understand the choice at hand and to engage fully in the decision-making process, or the patient is clearly unable to participate in decision-making, due to unconsciousness, advanced dementia, delirium, or some other incapacitating condition. In still other situations, however, when patients are conscious but have compromised mental status, clinical judgments about capacity are more difficult. To guide capacity evaluation in these latter situations, scholars have identified the following four more specific abilities that are necessary for decision-making capacity:[5]

1. *The ability to understand information relevant to the treatment decision at hand.* Patients must have at least a basic grasp of their medical condition, treatment alternatives, and the expected benefits and risks of those alternatives, to make a treatment decision.

2. *The ability to appreciate the significance of that information for one's own situation.* In addition to a theoretical understanding of treatment-related information, patients must recognize that this information applies to their own situation. A patient with severe anorexia nervosa, for example, may affirm the importance of nutrition for a starving person, but fail to recognize that this description applies to her own current condition.

3. *The ability to reason, evaluating information about treatment options in a logical way to reach a decision based on one's own preferences and values.* Patients must be able to engage in a process of considering treatment options and choosing a treatment option based on its consistency with their beliefs and values and its ability to achieve their goals.

[5] See Grisso and Appelbaum (1998) and Appelbaum (2007).

4. *The ability to express a choice.* Patients must be able to communicate their treatment choice, so that professionals can act on it. A few medical conditions, such as global paralysis or profound depression, may render patients unable to express a treatment choice.

A variety of different capacity evaluation tools have been developed to assist clinicians in assessing a patient's decision-making capacity.[6] Questions in these evaluation tools enable a more systematic and structured assessment of the specific abilities listed above.

Several other features of decision-making capacity judgments are important to recognize. First, decision-making capacity is a *threshold* judgment – that is, a patient either has or does not have sufficient capacity to consent to a particular treatment. In this respect, decision-making capacity is like pregnancy; a patient cannot be "partially pregnant" or be "partially capable." Second, decision-making capacity is a *task-* or *context-specific* judgment – that is, it is a determination that a patient can consent to *this particular* treatment in *this particular* context. Thus, a patient may have capacity to make a simple treatment decision, but lack the capacity to make a more complex decision. Because capacity judgments are context-specific, they are also *time-specific* – that is, a patient may lack capacity to make a treatment decision at one time, perhaps because he is acutely psychotic, and regain that capacity at a later time, after the psychotic episode has passed.

Finally, most (but not all) commentators maintain that capacity judgments should be *consequence-* or *risk-specific* – that is, the appropriate threshold for capacity to make a treatment choice should vary with the likely consequences of that choice.[7] In other words, a higher threshold for capacity should be required when a patient makes a choice that poses a higher risk of harm. This "sliding scale" approach to capacity judgments has a result that some find paradoxical, namely, a patient may have sufficient capacity to consent to a highly beneficial treatment for a life-threatening medical condition, but lack the capacity to refuse the very same treatment. Thus, a patient with acute appendicitis may have sufficient capacity to consent to an appendectomy, but not to refuse that same procedure. The justification for this approach appeals to a tension between patient

---

[6] Sessums et al. (2011).

[7] For different conclusions on this issue, see Buchanan and Brock (1989) and Wicclair (1991).

autonomy and patient well-being, the two major values underlying the determination of decision-making capacity and informed consent generally. On the one hand, we want to respect the autonomy of patients who *have* decision-making capacity by recognizing that capacity and obtaining their informed consent to treatment. On the other hand, we want to promote the well-being of patients who *lack* decision-making capacity by *not* honoring "incompetent" choices that will have predictably harmful consequences. A risk-specific, sliding-scale approach to capacity evaluation is intended to enable clinicians to strike an appropriate balance between those two moral goals.

Information disclosure

The second essential element of an informed consent is communication to the patient of appropriate information about the treatment decision at hand. Unless patients have at least some knowledge about treatment alternatives and their expected consequences, any choice among them will be blind and therefore virtually meaningless. Important questions include what kinds of information, and how much information, must be communicated to patients in order to satisfy this informational requirement.

Among the *kinds* of information generally required for an informed consent are the following:

1. the patient's medical condition, and the expected consequences of that condition without treatment;
2. the reasonable or standard treatment alternatives for that condition;
3. the significant expected benefits and harms of the treatment alternatives, and their probabilities; and
4. in most cases, a treatment recommendation.[8]

Other kinds of information sometimes included in this list of required disclosures are the financial cost of the treatment alternatives and the experience of the treating physician with particular procedures. Kinds of information that need *not* be communicated include harms that are very minor or are very unlikely, or that are so widely known that the patient would already be aware of them.

[8] Brock (1987).

How much information of the kinds listed above must be communicated to the patient? Most US states recognize one or the other of two different legal standards of information disclosure.[9] The older standard, called the *professional standard*, requires health care professionals to communicate that amount of information that other professionals with similar training and experience would communicate in similar situations. This standard relies on customary professional practice, but it may give inadequate attention to *patients'* views about what information they should receive. The newer standard, called the *reasonable person standard*, directs professionals to provide the amount of information that a reasonable person would want to have in order to make a treatment decision in the given situation. Although this standard does adopt a patient-oriented approach, it does not require professionals to tailor their communication to what each particular patient would want to know, but rather to the desires of a hypothetical reasonable person. Satisfying the informational desires of each individual patient would serve the moral ideal of giving each patient the most fully informed choice, but it would likely impose a substantial burden on health care professionals to identify all of the possibly idiosyncratic informational preferences of each of their patients. Providers should, however, encourage patients to ask questions if they want additional information.

Voluntary choice

The third essential element of an informed consent is that the patient's treatment choice be voluntary, that is, under the patient's own control. A "coerced consent" is obviously a consent in name only, not a morally or legally effective agreement to treatment. A voluntary choice does not, however, mean a choice free from any influences whatsoever; such a choice would presumably be totally random. Rather, there are multiple possible influences on patients' treatment choices, many of them morally innocuous and others morally dubious. Health care professionals must, therefore, recognize which influences on patient choice are permissible and which are impermissible.

As noted above, a recommendation regarding which treatment to accept is, in most cases, one of the kinds of information that patients

---

[9] Faden et al. (1986).

expect and that physicians and other health care professionals should provide. That recommendation typically has a strong influence on patient choice, but not an impermissible influence. Rather, patients desire professional guidance of this kind in making treatment decisions, and they retain the ability to accept or reject these treatment recommendations. If a patient decides to reject a physician's recommendation to pursue a particular course of treatment, may the physician attempt to influence the patient's decision in any other way? Assuming that the physician had good reasons for making that treatment recommendation, I suggest that he or she may, and indeed should, discuss the situation further in order to confirm that the patient has an adequate understanding of his options and of the reasons why the physician believes that the recommended treatment is superior to the alternatives. In other words, physicians, as well as family members and others, may seek to persuade the patient to accept a particular treatment. Such efforts at rational persuasion are permissible, provided that they are not so prolonged, insistent, or unwelcome that the patient feels unable to resist.

The antithesis of respecting patients' voluntary choice of treatment is, of course, imposing treatment on an unwilling patient by overt *physical force*. Such coerced treatments clearly lack informed consent. There are other less blatant, but also impermissible violations of this essential element of informed consent. Short of physical force, one might compel a patient's acceptance of treatment by threatening the patient with unacceptable consequences. For example, a physician may obtain consent under *duress* by telling an anxious patient that he will discharge the patient from the hospital without any treatment unless the patient accepts the physician's treatment recommendation. A more subtle, but still morally problematic influence on patient choice is *manipulation*.[10] A health care provider may seek to manipulate the consent situation to elicit a desired decision from the patient. Such manipulation may take a variety of forms, including limiting the information shared with the patient, slanting or "framing" the information in favor of one option, or taking advantage of a particular fear of the patient. Though the patient may not be aware that he or she has been manipulated, successful manipulation nevertheless robs that patient of a genuine choice among treatment alternatives.

[10] Rudinow (1978).

Exceptions

Patient rights to informed consent to treatment are arguably among the most important expressions of bioethical principles of respect for autonomy and of beneficence. Despite their moral significance, however, these rights are not absolute. Rather, several exceptions to the duty to obtain a patient's consent to treatment are morally defensible, including exceptions for emergency treatment, for patients who lack decision-making capacity, for patient waiver of consent, and for public health requirements. Some commentators also endorse a so-called "therapeutic privilege" exception to informed consent. This section will describe each of these exceptions to informed consent and consider reasons for permitting them.

Emergency treatment

Probably the most well-known exception to informed consent, the emergency exception applies when immediate treatment is necessary to prevent death or serious harm to a patient.[11] It should be recognized that this description applies only to those few situations in which initiation of treatment cannot be delayed without grave risk of harm. When this is the case, taking the time to inform the patient about his or her condition, treatment options, and their expected consequences will delay the needed treatment and thus likely defeat its purpose. In such circumstances, therefore, providers may initiate treatment immediately, based on the *presumption* that the patient would, if time allowed, consent to treatment to preserve life or to prevent serious harm. Even in such an emergency situation, however, this presumption of consent can be defeated by the patient's explicit refusal of a particular treatment. To honor treatment refusals in such circumstances, however, providers may need at least a short period of time to assess whether the patient has sufficient decision-making capacity to refuse a potentially highly beneficial treatment.

Patients who lack decision-making capacity

If a patient lacks the capacity to make a treatment decision, obviously there can be no moral or legal duty to obtain that patient's consent to

[11] Moskop (1999).

treatment. Recognizing this exception does not, however, permit a provider to treat such a patient at his or her own sole discretion. Rather, if the patient's lack of decision-making capacity is temporary, and treatment can be safely delayed, the provider should seek to restore the patient's capacity and then obtain his or her consent to treatment. If the patient cannot be restored to capacity, the provider must ordinarily obtain consent to treatment from a surrogate decision-maker authorized to act on behalf of the patient. The scope and limits of surrogate decision-making will be examined in Chapter 9.

Patient waiver of consent

Recognizing that patients have a *right* to informed consent to treatment does not imply that patients also have or should accept a *duty* to give informed consent. Rather, patients may choose to *waive* their right to informed consent.[12] That is, they may ask *not* to receive certain kinds of information about their treatment options, preferring either to make a decision without that information or to rely on someone else, perhaps a close relative or the treating physician, to make the decision on their behalf. Health care professionals may honor these waivers of the right to consent, provided that they have determined that the patient has decision-making capacity and is aware that he or she has the right to be informed and to make a treatment decision. Professionals may, of course, choose not to accept a patient's request to make a treatment decision on the patient's behalf, if they are unwilling to assume that responsibility.

Public health requirements

Medical treatment is sometimes beneficial not only, or even primarily, for the patient receiving the treatment. This is the case when a patient's medical condition poses a serious threat to the health of others. Public health law in most jurisdictions recognizes two major types of such threats, serious communicable disease and severe mental illness. These laws permit isolation and compulsory treatment of patients with serious communicable diseases like Ebola virus disease, multi-drug-resistant tuberculosis, and

---

[12] King (1993).

severe acute respiratory syndrome (SARS), to prevent transmission of those serious diseases to others. Patients with severe mental illness who are judged to be dangerous to themselves or to others are subject to involuntary commitment to an institution and involuntary treatment of their illness. When compulsory treatment is administered for public health purposes, health care professionals should still inform patients about the nature of the treatment provided and the reason why it is required.

"Therapeutic privilege"

Some commentators recognize another exception to informed consent with the enigmatic title "therapeutic privilege."[13] According to this exception, health care providers may withhold otherwise essential information about a proposed treatment if they judge that disclosure of that information would in itself cause serious harm to the patient. The anticipated harm must be a result of the disclosure itself, not from the potential that the disclosure may cause the patient to refuse a beneficial treatment. Although therapeutic privilege is often included in lists of recognized exceptions to the duty to obtain informed consent, it has also been sharply criticized. Critics argue that it is extremely difficult to predict accurately that the act of giving a patient information about his or her condition and treatment will cause significant harm, or be more harmful than withholding that information from the patient. If a patient is so fragile or unstable that he or she cannot cope with material information about his or her condition and treatment, that patient is very likely to lack decision-making capacity. Thus, the justifiability of therapeutic privilege as an independent exception to informed consent remains in doubt.

Case analysis

This case poses an obvious question about what information Dr. Collins should communicate to Mr. Evans in order to obtain his informed consent to thoracentesis. Presumably Dr. Collins should tell Mr. Evans about his pleural effusion, describe the proposed thoracentesis, explain the expected benefits of this procedure (namely, easier breathing and obtaining a sample

---

[13] Berger (2005).

of pleural fluid for testing, to determine the cause of this condition), and review significant potential complications or side effects of the procedure (for example, pain and a punctured lung). Should she also inform him that this will be the first time she has performed this procedure?

It appears that the two primary legal standards for information disclosure described above offer different answers to this question. Judging from an admittedly small sample, that is, internal medicine residents with whom I have discussed this issue, my impression is that most residents do not disclose to patients that they are performing a procedure like thoracentesis for the first time. If, therefore, the appropriate standard is the customary practice of professionals with similar training and experience in similar circumstances, the professional standard may not require this disclosure. When asked to defend their decision not to disclose their lack of experience performing a new procedure, these resident physicians have offered a variety of reasons, including (1) this information will cause the patient (and the resident?) unnecessary anxiety; (2) this information will cause patients to request that residents not perform the procedure and thus deprive them of this valuable learning opportunity; (3) the number of times the resident has performed the procedure is not significant information, since thoracentesis is in any case a low-risk procedure; and (4) the patient should already know that this is a teaching hospital where residents gain experience performing procedures. At least some of these reasons seem morally relevant and significant; we do want to avoid causing patients unnecessary anxiety, and we do want resident physicians to gain experience in performing important medical procedures. Are they sufficient to justify nondisclosure?

A persuasive case can be made that use of the reasonable person standard of information disclosure would generate a different answer to the question of what should be disclosed in this situation. That is, the hypothetical reasonable person may well want to know that a resident will be performing a thoracentesis on him or her for the first time, for at least the following two reasons: (1) The patient may conclude that a resident with no experience is more likely to perform the procedure incorrectly or more clumsily, thus causing more pain and a greater chance of a serious complication like a punctured lung. (2) The patient may want the opportunity to decide whether to allow the resident to gain this experience or to request a more experienced provider. If, for either of these reasons, a reasonable person would want to know that a resident would be performing a procedure on him or her for the first time, this standard would require disclosure of that information.

As this case illustrates, providers and patients can have different interests in consent situations, and the two different disclosure standards may reflect those different interests. There are, however, other ways to address at least some of those interests. For example, the content and style of communication in this situation might allay rather than evoke anxiety in patients. Suppose the senior resident explains to Mr. Evans that Dr. Collins will perform the thoracentesis under her close supervision and with her careful instruction, and that the supervisor will take over the procedure at the first sign of any problem. That approach is likely to allay Mr. Evans's anxiety about a failed procedure, and so make it more likely that he will agree to this plan. If patients are more likely to agree to allow residents to gain needed experience under these conditions, then residents need not fear that disclosure will prevent them from learning the procedural skills that they, and their patients, need. Thus, a thoughtful disclosure in this setting may satisfy both the patient's right to receive relevant information and the resident's interest in gaining essential experience.

Finally, residents who choose not to disclose their lack of experience with a procedure report that patients sometimes ask them how often they have performed a proposed procedure, and add that, when patients ask this specific question, they have a responsibility to respond truthfully. The fact that some patients ask this question indicates that those patients believe this information to be significant for their treatment decision. If patients who are insightful and bold enough to ask deserve a truthful response, should this information also be provided to patients who are less knowledgeable or more timid?

9   Surrogate decision-making

Case example

Ms. Tina Cartrette is a 28-year-old woman with severe intellectual disability (also known as cognitive disability or mental retardation). Ms. Cartrette also has cerebral palsy and a seizure disorder. She has been a resident of a long-term care facility since she was 5 years old, and has never been able to sit up, walk, talk, dress, or bathe herself. Ms. Cartrette is fed through a tube inserted directly into her stomach. She has been hospitalized five times in the past year for urinary tract infections, which, in her case, cause high fever and seizures.

When Ms. Cartrette reached the age of 18, she was declared legally incompetent, and her mother, Ms. Diane Arnder, was appointed to serve as her legal guardian. Ms. Arnder lives in a distant city; she calls the residential care facility regularly to check on Ms. Cartrette and visits her daughter about twice a year.

Twelve days ago, Ms. Cartrette was hospitalized once again with a high fever and uncontrolled seizures. She received IV antibiotics and medications to control her seizures, but the medications led to respiratory depression, and, with Ms. Arnder's consent, Ms. Cartrette was intubated, placed on a mechanical ventilator, and transferred to the Medical Intensive Care Unit (MICU). She remains in the MICU on ventilator support. Dr. Friedland, Ms. Cartrette's attending physician, has discussed her treatment options with Ms. Arnder. Dr. Friedland told Ms. Arnder that continuing ventilator support could make Ms. Cartrette permanently ventilator-dependent, but removal of the ventilator would probably result in her death. After discussions with her husband and her pastor, Ms. Arnder has requested that the ventilator be withdrawn, explaining that she does not want to see her daughter suffer any longer. Most of the members of Ms. Cartrette's treatment team (including Dr. Friedland, several nurses, and a social worker) are willing to honor this request, but one of the residents disagrees. He points out that Ms. Cartrette is neither *terminally ill nor unconscious, and he asserts that she should not simply be allowed to die. How should the team proceed?*[1]

The moral issue, and the available options

As noted in Chapter 8, a patient's lack of decision-making capacity is a generally recognized exception to the legal and moral duty to obtain the patient's informed consent to medical treatment. If a patient is unable to make a treatment decision, health care professionals obviously cannot rely on such a decision to guide their actions. How, then, should professionals determine what care to provide for these patients? Even though patients who lack decision-making capacity cannot make choices at a particular time, they may have expressed preferences about medical treatment in the past, and they may regain the ability to make treatment choices in the future. How, if at all, should a person's past preferences and the prospect of future choices guide his or her treatment in the present? Patients without decision-making capacity cannot express or actively pursue their interests, but they still have important interests. How, and to what extent, should health care professionals identify and promote those interests? These questions highlight the moral significance of making treatment decisions for incapacitated patients. Several potential options for addressing these situations can be identified and evaluated, as follows:

Option 1: no consent, no treatment!

A simple, but generally unsatisfactory option would be to conclude that, because no informed consent can be obtained from the patient, no treatment can be provided. This option would provide maximal respect for the patient's physical privacy, understood as freedom from invasion of a person's body or personal space without that person's permission, but such respect for privacy would come at a very high price. The price, failure to provide medical treatments that can prevent grave harm to the person and can greatly enhance the person's welfare, seems disproportionately high in comparison to the value of protecting personal privacy, whenever the need for treatment is unambiguous.

[1] Sabo (2001).

Option 2: wait for the patient to regain decision-making capacity!

Many different conditions (e.g., delirium, intoxication, and depression) can interfere with a person's ability to make decisions, and the loss of decision-making capacity may be temporary. When this is the case, and when medical treatment can be delayed without causing significant harm, waiting until the patient regains capacity and then securing the patient's informed consent to a proposed treatment is a morally attractive solution. This option enables the health care provider to honor the patient's autonomous choice and provide beneficial treatment. This option is available, however, only when loss of decision-making capacity is temporary. If loss of capacity is permanent, waiting for a patient to regain capacity will be endless, and this option will be identical to option 1 above. If the loss of capacity is not permanent but of long duration, and treatment is urgently needed, delay will result in serious harm to the patient.

Option 3: let the physician decide!

A third option would be to allow physicians to make treatment decisions on behalf of their patients who lack decision-making capacity. Several good reasons can be offered in support of this option. Their training and experience enables physicians to identify and evaluate the likely outcomes of treatment alternatives, and physicians pledge to act for the benefit of their patients. Still other reasons, however, count against giving this authority to physicians. Very often, the physician caring for a patient with a serious injury or illness that has rendered the patient incapable of making treatment choices is a hospitalist or other specialist who has never met the patient before. In these circumstances, the physician will have no prior knowledge of the patient's values, preferences, or goals, and so will not be able to base treatment decisions on that information. Even if the physician did know the patient before he or she lost decision-making capacity, the physician's values and interests may be significantly different from those of the patient. The physician, for example, may place a high priority on life prolongation, but the patient may prefer to forgo life-prolonging treatment in order to ease the burden of caregiving on her family. These reasons suggest that reliance on physicians may not be the best option for making treatment decisions when patients lack decision-making capacity.

Option 4: identify a surrogate decision-maker!

This option proposes that we identify and authorize a third party, called a surrogate decision-maker, to make treatment decisions on behalf of incapacitated patients. Like patients who retain decision-making capacity, this surrogate decision-maker can confer with the patient's physician or other health care professionals about the patient's condition and treatment alternatives, and can use that essential information to guide his or her treatment decision. Unlike most physicians, who do not have detailed knowledge of their patients' wishes, goals, and values, the surrogate decision-maker can, at least ideally, be someone who knows the patient very well and who is willing and able to make treatment decisions based on that knowledge of the patient. This fourth option appears to be most likely both to honor the patient's own preferences and to achieve the best treatment outcome. Choice of this option raises an important further question: Who should serve as surrogate decision-makers?

Who should serve as surrogate decision-makers?

I suggested above that an optimal surrogate decision-maker for an incapacitated patient is someone who knows the patient well, who is willing to take on this responsibility, and who will make decisions based on knowledge about the patient's present situation and about the patient's values and preferences. Who is, in fact, most likely to have all of these characteristics? Early commentators concluded that the patient's next of kin, or another close family member, is generally the most appropriate surrogate decision-maker.[2] This conclusion was based on the belief that a close family member is best situated to know the patient well and is most likely to care for and about the patient. Choosing a family member as the patient's surrogate also respects family privacy and shared responsibility within the family unit. Not all patients have close family members, however, and the law has long provided mechanisms for appointment of legal guardians to make decisions on behalf of patients judged incompetent in a court proceeding. Over the past two decades, many jurisdictions have also enacted laws enabling persons to designate a person of their own

---

[2] See President's Commission for the Study of Ethical Problems in Medicine and Biomedical and Behavioral Research (1983a) and Hafemeister and Hannaford (1996b).

choice to serve as their surrogate decision-maker, or "health care agent," should they lose decision-making capacity. Patients can make this designation by means of a document called a "health care power of attorney." This document is discussed in more detail in Chapter 15, "Advance care planning and advance directives."

For many years, physicians in the United States had some discretion in choosing which family member to recognize as surrogate decision-maker. In recent years, however, most US states have enacted statutes that create a hierarchical list of persons authorized to serve as surrogate decision-makers for patients who lack decision-making capacity.[3] In 2007, for example, the state of North Carolina revised its informed consent statute by adding the following hierarchy of surrogates:

1. a health care agent appointed by the patient via a health care power of attorney
2. a legal guardian appointed by a court of competent jurisdiction
3. an "attorney-in-fact" appointed by the patient via a general power of attorney that includes authority to make health care decisions
4. the patient's spouse
5. a majority of the patient's reasonably available parents and adult children
6. a majority of the patient's reasonably available adult siblings
7. a person who has an established relationship with the patient, who is acting in good faith on behalf of the patient, and who can reliably convey the patient's wishes[4]

The North Carolina statute goes on to state that, if none of the above persons is reasonably available, the patient's attending physician may treat the patient without consent, provided that a second physician confirms the need for treatment.[5] In other words, this statute defaults to option 3 above, reliance on the physician's treatment decision, when no suitable third party surrogate is available. Statutes in most jurisdictions also explicitly recognize parents as the "natural guardians" of their minor children and authorize parents to make treatment decisions for those children.

---

[3] American Bar Association (2014).   [4] North Carolina General Statutes § 90–21.13.

[5] This statute appeals to physician discretion in determining the necessity for treatment, and so its language appears to be broad enough to authorize physicians caring for patients who lack an authorized surrogate also to forgo treatments they do not deem necessary or appropriate.

The above list is hierarchical in the sense that a person becomes an authorized surrogate only if no one higher on the list is available. The list is notable for several reasons. It gives highest priority to persons who have been expressly chosen to serve as surrogates, either by the patient him or herself or by court action to protect the interests of an incompetent person. It then recognizes family members, in order of the closeness of their relationship to the patient. If no one in the above categories is available, the statute explicitly authorizes surrogate decision-making by a person who fits a more general description, which could include a more distant relative, a friend, or a personal caregiver. As life expectancy increases, more very elderly patients outlive all of their close relatives, and this last category becomes increasingly important.

How should surrogates make decisions?

Let's assume that a reasonable procedure is in place to identify a surrogate decision-maker for an incapacitated patient, that this procedure has been followed, and that the designated surrogate is available and willing to make treatment decisions for the patient. Should the surrogate be free to make any treatment decision he or she prefers, for any reason he or she may have? Must the physician and other health care professionals respect any treatment decision the surrogate makes? In other words, should the surrogate's authority to choose be absolute?

I have argued that reliance on a surrogate is generally the best option for making treatment decisions for patients who lack decision-making capacity, because a good surrogate is most likely to know what treatment the patient would prefer and to make treatment decisions based on that knowledge. This is not always the case, however; an adult child, for example, may be a patient's closest relative, but that child may have had no contact with her parent for many years and may have very powerful ill feelings toward that parent. As this example illustrates, the legally authorized surrogate may not, in fact, know the patient well, and may not have the patient's wishes or best interests at heart. For this reason, the authority of surrogates should not be absolute. Rather, health care professionals should be able to challenge surrogate decisions in at least some circumstances. If that is the case, how can professionals determine when they should honor, and when they should challenge, a surrogate's choice?

Are standards available to guide surrogate choices, and also to assess whether those choices are appropriate?

There are, in fact, three standards for surrogate decision-making that are widely recognized in the legal, medical, and bioethics literature: the expressed preferences (or advance directives) standard, the substituted judgment standard, and the best interests standard.[6] Commentators generally describe these standards as an ordered set. In other words, a surrogate should apply the first standard, if possible; if not, then the second standard; and if neither the first nor the second can be applied, then the third. What specific guidance does each of these three standards offer?

The expressed preferences (advance directives) standard

According to this standard, surrogates should make treatment decisions that are in accordance with any specific preferences previously expressed by the patient, when he or she had decision-making capacity. The rationale for this standard is obvious: if a person has clearly stated his or her treatment wishes in advance, we should respect that person's autonomous choices. People can express their treatment preferences in a variety of ways, including, among others, informal conversations with their chosen health care agent, and formal, written living wills.[7] Many people do not express treatment preferences in advance, however, making this standard inapplicable for those people. And, some treatment preferences expressed by a person may be difficult to interpret or to apply to a given medical condition, prompting surrogates to seek additional sources of guidance.

The substituted judgment standard

If a patient has not expressed specific treatment preferences in advance, this standard instructs the surrogate to base treatment decisions on a judgment about what the patient would choose, if he or she had decision-making capacity. To make this judgment, the surrogate should apply his or her knowledge of the patient's goals, values, and beliefs to the patient's current situation. The obvious intent of this standard, like the expressed

---

[6] See Hafemeister and Hannaford (1996a), American Medical Association (2001a), and Brock (1991).

[7] For further discussion of living wills, see Chapter 15, "Advance care planning and advance directives."

preferences standard, is to direct surrogates to make the treatment decision that the patient would most likely make if he or she could do so. Notice that this standard can be applied only if the person had previously formulated and held goals, values, and beliefs, and if the surrogate is informed about these features of the person's life.

The best interests standard

Some human beings, as, for example, infants and profoundly cognitively disabled people, have not formulated or expressed goals, values, or beliefs. Some surrogate decision-makers, as, for example, a social worker who has been appointed legal guardian for an incapacitated homeless person without known relatives, may have no knowledge of the goals, values, or beliefs of the now-incapacitated person. In these situations, the expressed preferences and substituted judgment standards cannot be applied, and surrogates are instructed to apply the best interests standard. According to this standard, the surrogate should choose treatments that will promote the patient's overall well-being. Because well-being is a broad and somewhat vague concept, however, this standard provides, at best, very general guidance. Well-being can include prolongation of life, preservation, restoration, or enhancement of mental and physical function, physical appearance, and quality of life, and relief of pain and suffering. When treatment alternatives offer different combinations of expected benefits and harms, it may be difficult to determine which alternative is most beneficial on the whole, and thus the best interests standard may not offer clear guidance about what treatment decision to make.

Applying the standards

The three standards described above have been widely endorsed and adopted as guides to surrogate decision-making. They can also serve as criteria for assessing the adequacy of the treatment decisions surrogates actually make for incapacitated patients, but there are clear limits to their usefulness for this latter purpose.

The expressed preferences standard directs surrogates to honor a person's stated wishes regarding future treatment, but assessing whether surrogates do in fact honor those wishes will depend largely on how they were expressed. If the wishes were communicated verbally to the person's appointed health care agent, for example, health care professionals will depend on the agent to report those wishes accurately in order to determine whether they are being carried out. If the wishes were expressed in a written advance directive, that document will serve as an independent statement of the patient's wishes and a check on the surrogate's decisions, but it may be difficult to apply a general statement of treatment preferences in a living will to a specific medical situation. If a living will does express a clear preference for a particular treatment plan in a particular situation, many advance directive statutes allow physicians to act on the preferences expressed in the living will without seeking or obtaining surrogate consent for that action.

The substituted judgment standard directs surrogates to base treatment decisions on knowledge of the patient's goals, values, and beliefs. Because the surrogate is presumed to have a better understanding of those goals, values, and beliefs than the health professionals caring for the patient, once again the professionals will largely depend on the surrogate to apply that knowledge in good faith to the treatment decisions at hand. To challenge decisions under this standard, professionals would presumably have to conclude that the surrogate's decisions were contrary to known or probable goals, values, or beliefs of the patient.

The best interests standard directs surrogates to make treatment choices that promote the overall well-being of the patient. This standard does not depend on specific knowledge about the patient, but rather on general measures of well-being. Because those measures are broad, vague, and not clearly commensurable with one another, however, they can be used to defend a wide variety of treatment decisions.

What conclusions can be drawn about the role of these surrogate decision-making standards? I believe that the standards offer useful guidance to surrogates making treatment decisions, instructing them to focus on the expressed or presumed preferences of the incapacitated patient, or, if preferences cannot be determined, on the patient's well-being. The role of these standards as grounds for assessing or challenging surrogate decisions is more limited. The standards rely heavily on surrogates' presumed superior knowledge of the patients they represent and on their evaluation of treatment alternatives. Because people have a wide variety of different treatment preferences, goals of care, values, and beliefs, surrogate decisions based on these characteristics can fall within a broad range of reasonable alternatives.

That range is not unlimited, however, and so the authority of surrogates is not absolute. In their thoughtful analysis of surrogate decision-making standards, Rhodes and Holzman argue that health care professionals should respect a surrogate's treatment decision unless they conclude that the decision is *unreasonable*.[8] Consider, for example, the case of parents who refuse life-saving surgery on their 10-year-old child for acute appendicitis, claiming that this illness is a punishment inflicted by God. Such a decision is so clearly and seriously detrimental to the child's welfare that it constitutes an instance of medical neglect. In situations like this one, health care professionals may and indeed should intervene to protect their patients from harm.

When health care professionals conclude that a surrogate's decision is neglectful or otherwise unreasonable, how should they proceed? Several different courses of action may be worth pursuing. A natural first response would be to review the relevant information with the surrogate, check the surrogate's understanding of the situation, address any misunderstandings, and seek agreement on a treatment alternative acceptable to both the treating professionals and the surrogate. If an ethics consultation service is available, any of the interested parties may request a consultation. Ethics consultants can provide an independent evaluation of the surrogate's decision and offer reasons why it is either justifiable or unreasonable. Ethics consultants may also identify additional treatment alternatives and help the interested parties find a mutually acceptable treatment plan. In some situations, especially when a physician recognizes that expert or public opinion about a particular treatment is divided, the physician may inform the surrogate that he or she is unwilling to carry out the surrogate's treatment choice and suggest that the surrogate seek to transfer the patient to a physician who will honor that choice. If the physician or other professional is convinced that the surrogate's choice is clearly unreasonable, he or she may petition a court to override the surrogate's choice, to appoint a legal guardian for the patient, or, if the surrogate is the patient's legal guardian, to remove the existing guardian and appoint a successor

---

[8] Rhodes and Holzman (2004).

guardian. Finally, if the need for treatment is urgent (as, for example, if there is evidence that the child's appendix has ruptured and emergency surgery is required), a physician may choose to override the surrogate's decision on his or her own authority. The appropriateness of each of these approaches will depend largely on the particular circumstances.

Case analysis

In this case, Ms. Cartrette's severe intellectual disability prevents her from understanding her health condition or making treatment decisions. Ms. Arnder, her mother and legal guardian, has decided that ventilator support should be withdrawn, with Ms. Cartrette's death as the expected outcome. The members of Ms. Cartrette's health care team are not in agreement about honoring Ms. Arnder's decision; most, including Dr. Friedland, Ms. Cartrette's attending physician, are willing to do so, but one resident asserts that Ms. Cartrette should not be allowed to die. Is Ms. Arnder's decision a proper exercise of her authority as Ms. Cartrette's surrogate decision-maker, or is it an unreasonable and neglectful decision that Ms. Cartrette's caregivers should challenge?

Because Ms. Cartrette has never been able to express any preferences, goals, values, or beliefs, the expressed preferences and substituted judgment standards cannot be applied in this situation. The best interests standard directs Ms. Arnder to choose the treatment plan that will promote Ms. Cartrette's well-being, but we have noted that well-being is a broad concept that includes many kinds of consequences, including survival, mental and physical function, and pain and suffering. Because there is no uniform method to measure and compare these different kinds of consequences, there is room for significant difference of opinion about what treatment, and what likely outcome, is in a patient's best interests. Ms. Arnder would likely defend her choice on the grounds that the pain, suffering, and limited quality of life associated with permanent ventilator dependence and recurrent infections and seizures outweighs the benefits to Ms. Cartrette of prolongation of life. Is this a reasonable choice? The resident would likely respond that Ms. Cartrette's acute condition can be treated, that she can be restored to her prior condition, and that her life, although limited, has value and should be protected. Are these sufficient grounds for challenging Ms. Arnder's decision?

Because this case eventually entered the legal system, its facts and outcome are matters of public record. According to news reports and court rulings, the treatment team in this situation did seek an ethics consultation, and Dr. Stell, the ethics consultant at Carolinas Medical Center in Charlotte, North Carolina, discussed the situation with members of the team and concluded that honoring Ms. Arnder's decision was in Ms. Cartrette's best interests.[9] At Ms. Arnder's request, the team did withdraw ventilator support, and also discontinued tube feeding and antibiotics. Contrary to their expectations, Ms. Cartrette resumed breathing on her own when the ventilator was removed. Shortly thereafter, someone notified the North Carolina Governor's Advocacy Council for Persons with Disabilities about Ms. Cartrette's situation, and that organization filed a petition seeking emergency reinstatement of life-prolonging medical treatments. A court order to restore these treatments was issued. At a hearing two weeks later, a clerk of court concluded that Ms. Arnder's decisions were neglectful and potentially harmful, removed Ms. Arnder as Ms. Cartrette's guardian, and appointed a successor guardian.

With the support of the hospital, Ms. Arnder appealed this decision, and an appeals hearing took place three months later. The presiding judge concluded that the clerk of court in the initial hearing had misinterpreted the North Carolina natural death statute, and that Ms. Arnder's actions did not constitute neglect. He therefore reinstated Ms. Arnder as Ms. Cartrette's guardian. Ms. Arnder decided once again to forgo life-prolonging treatment for Ms. Cartrette, and she died some days later.

In this case, two court officials reached different conclusions about the appropriateness of a surrogate's decision. Which conclusion do you find more persuasive?

---

[9] Stell (2001).

10 Professionalism: responsibilities and privileges

Case example

Dr. George Gayle has just completed the final stage in his formal medical training, a fellowship in medical oncology, and has joined a local multispecialty medical practice. He is a devoutly religious man and is a leading member of a large Christian congregation. Because his religious faith is such a central part of his life, Dr. Gayle would like to incorporate his spiritual beliefs into his professional practice.

Dr. Gayle informs his physician colleagues that he intends to address spiritual issues with his patients in several ways, including asking all of his patients about their own spiritual beliefs and practices, inviting patients to pray for healing with him, encouraging patients to take advantage of the health benefits of prayer and of other religious practices, inviting patients to visit the Sunday school course he teaches, and helping patients with serious illness understand that there is meaning in life and hope for the future. May he engage in these activities with his patients?

Over the past two decades, professionalism has become a major topic of discussion in medicine and health care. Commentators warn that the increasing commercialization and bureaucratization of health care is undermining the professionalism of physicians and other health care professionals.[1] In response, professional associations have adopted formal statements pledging support for principles of professionalism, and professional schools have expanded professionalism instruction for their students.[2] This chapter will examine the concept of professionalism and consider its moral significance in health care. It will then focus on one specific application of the concept of professionalism, namely, the identification and enforcement of professional boundaries.

---

[1] See, for example, Ludmerer (1999) and ABIM Foundation et al. (2002).

[2] See ABIM Foundation et al. (2002) and Swick et al. (1999).

Conceptual issues

Despite general agreement about the importance of professionalism in health care, there is considerably less consensus on the meaning of this term. In its most general sense, 'professionalism' is defined as "the conduct, aims, or qualities that characterize or mark a profession or a professional person."[3] As this definition indicates, understanding what is meant by professionalism requires a prior understanding of the concepts of a profession and a professional. But these latter concepts have many meanings, and they are associated with many kinds of "conduct, aims, and qualities." Consider, for example, the following ways in which a person may be considered a professional:

1. The person receives payment for his work, e.g., a professional painter, a professional basketball player.
2. The person is licensed or certified to perform his work, e.g., a licensed electrician.
3. The person has had an advanced education, in a "professional school," e.g., an architect.
4. The person engages in intellectual rather than manual labor, e.g., a university professor, a research scientist.
5. The person belongs to a group that creates and enforces its own standards of competence, e.g., an attorney.
6. The person belongs to a group that has sole control over a socially valuable activity (a "professional monopoly"), e.g., a certified public accountant.
7. The person "professes" (that is, publicly affirms) special duties and high moral standards, e.g., a priest or minister.

All of the above "professional criteria" apply to physicians, and most of them apply to other health care professionals, such as nurses, pharmacists, and physical therapists. Though all these criteria reflect common uses of the terms 'profession' and 'professional,' they differ markedly in their moral significance. Some criteria, like embracing high moral standards, are morally praiseworthy; others, like advanced education and intellectual labor, are morally neutral; and still others, like self-regulation and a

---

[3] Professionalism (1969).

professional monopoly, may be morally questionable if they promote the interests of professional groups at the expense of others.

To make substantive claims about the moral importance of professionalism, therefore, one must consider not only the specific profession in question, but also identify the morally significant features of that profession. Let's turn, therefore, to consideration of the distinctive moral features of professionalism in medicine and health care.

The moral significance of professionalism in health care

Is there something morally distinctive about medicine and health care that confers special urgency or importance on professionalism in those areas of human activity? Edmund Pellegrino, a leading physician, scholar, and educator in the field of bioethics over the past half-century, has made a persuasive case for the moral significance of professionalism in health care.[4] Pellegrino identifies five characteristics of the relationships between health care professionals and patients that give those relationships special moral import:

1. Health care professionals care for people who are vulnerable; patients are usually sick, injured, or suffering, and so are dependent on the knowledge and skill of their professional caregivers.
2. Health care professionals protect and promote fundamental human values of life, health, physical and mental functioning, and relief of pain and suffering.
3. The professional–patient relationship requires a distinctive kind of intimacy in which patients disclose confidential personal information and give health care professionals access to private parts of their bodies for examination and treatment.
4. Due to their vulnerability, patients must trust in the knowledge, skill, and good intentions of professionals, and professionals must rely on the trust of their patients in order to care for them effectively.
5. Health care professionals "profess," or promise, to act for the benefit of their patients and to place patient interests before self-interest.

These five characteristics, Pellegrino argues, make health care a morally distinctive enterprise. Recognizing them can help us to understand appeals

[4] Pellegrino (1983).

to professionalism in health care as efforts to keep professionals true to their commitments to act for the good of their patients and to refrain from exploiting patient vulnerability. These professional commitments impose limits, or boundaries, on appropriate professional behavior.

Pellegrino emphasizes the moral obligations of health care professionals, but he also recognizes the moral agency of both patients and professionals.[5] Just as respect for patients imposes obligations on professionals, so also can respect for the moral agency and integrity of professionals impose limits on the demands that patients may make on their services. The remainder of this chapter will focus on one application of professionalism in health care, that is, the recognition and enforcement of professional boundaries. We will consider how these boundaries create both obligations and privileges for health care professionals.

Professional boundaries in health care

Laws, regulations, professional guidelines, and institutional policies have established a variety of professional boundaries in health care to define and encourage appropriate behavior, and to discourage or prohibit inappropriate behavior, in therapeutic relationships. Some boundaries are designed to protect patients from harm, such as exploitation or substandard care. Other boundaries are designed to protect the health care professions and individual professionals from harm, such as loss of a profession's identity, or violation of an individual professional's moral integrity. Because professional boundaries impose limits on the behavior of both clinicians and patients, however, they are also subject to criticism and challenge. Some recommended boundaries may, for example, unduly interfere with personal freedom of action and association. Other boundaries may limit patient access to needed services.

Boundary rules have been proposed and adopted to guide a wide variety of professional activities. General boundary rules, moreover, may apply in different ways in specific contexts. To account for these different applications, we can make use of a distinction between boundary *crossings* and boundary *violations* proposed by Nadelson and Notman.[6] A boundary crossing is a morally permissible action that does not comply with a general

---

[5] Pellegrino (2006).   [6] Nadelson and Notman (2002).

boundary rule. A boundary violation is a morally objectionable failure to observe a professional boundary. Consider, for example, the general boundary rule against physical contact between physicians and patients except as needed during physical examination and treatment. Holding a fearful patient's hand while disclosing a diagnosis of a serious illness may be considered a morally benign boundary crossing, while sexual touching of an anesthetized patient would be a morally objectionable boundary violation.

In the remainder of this chapter, I will examine four major categories of professional boundaries in health care: "Personal Boundaries," "Commercial Boundaries," "Inter-professional Boundaries," and "Integrity Boundaries."

Personal boundaries

Professional boundaries in this category are the most widely recognized and addressed in public policy and in the medical literature. The rationale for these boundaries is to establish a clear distinction and separation between the professional relationships clinicians have with their patients and the personal relationships they have with family and friends. This separation is viewed as essential for several reasons. It calls attention to the very different purposes and goals of these two kinds of relationships, and to significant risks of harm if the two kinds of relationship are combined. Vulnerable patients who are dependent on a professional's care may, for example, be subjected to sexual exploitation by an unscrupulous professional, without clear rules prohibiting sexual contact between patients and professionals. Even if there is no intention to exploit a patient, combining professional and personal relationships may adversely affect the quality of care. For example, the emotional bond between a professional and a close family member may hamper the professional's ability to assess the family member's health condition objectively and treat it appropriately. Personal boundaries also protect professionals from patient efforts to pry into a professional's personal life or to enter into a personal relationship with the professional.

Examples of personal boundaries, in addition to the prohibition of sexual relations between patients and professionals and treatment of immediate family members, are rules against entering into business agreements or partnerships with patients, rules against disclosing personal problems to patients, and rules limiting acceptance of expensive gifts from patients.[7] While small gifts from patients may be a morally benign expression of a patient's gratitude for a professional's good care, expensive gifts are more likely to be a kind of bribe or "quid pro quo," with the expectation of special favors from the professional. Commentators also warn about the potential for personal social networking sites like Facebook to blur the boundary between personal and professional relationships, and they advise against professionals entering into online "friend" relationships with their patients.[8]

Although the above-mentioned personal boundaries are well established in health care, there are also controversial questions about their limits. Consider the following example. Laws and professional standards in most jurisdictions prohibit sexual contact between professionals and their patients. Should that prohibition extend to sexual contact between professionals and *former* patients? Potential for exploitation, though diminished, may still exist, but the parties may feel great affection for one another and claim that they should have the freedom to enter into an intimate personal relationship. The *AMA Code of Medical Ethics* addresses this question by asserting that physicians must, at a minimum, terminate the physician–patient relationship before initiating a dating, romantic, or sexual relationship with a patient and adding that "sexual or romantic relationships with former patients are unethical if the physician uses or exploits trust, knowledge, emotions, or influence derived from the previous professional relationship."[9]

Another complex question for this category of professional boundaries is the role of spiritual and religious issues in the professional–patient relationship.[10] On the one hand, religion and spirituality are deeply personal domains, and so one might argue that they should not enter into professional relationships in health care. On the other hand, spiritual and religious beliefs and practices may contribute to health and well-being, and so one might argue that a holistic approach to health care should include its spiritual dimension. Analysis of the case described at the beginning of this chapter will examine this question in greater detail.

---

[7] Nadelson and Notman (2002).   [8] See, for example, Guseh et al. (2009).
[9] American Medical Association (1990).   [10] Post et al. (2000).

Commercial boundaries

Commentators frequently cite the pervasive influence of large health care corporations as a serious threat to professionalism in medicine.[11] To achieve their corporate goals of increasing sales and profits, these commercial interests may offer strong financial inducements to professionals or may impose strict limitations on the services they provide. These inducements and limitations may in turn create major conflicts of interest for professionals, requiring them to choose between self-interest and the best interests of their patients. The rationale for this category of professional boundaries, therefore, is to limit and manage these conflicts of interest by distinguishing morally acceptable from unacceptable business practices in health care.

Some commercial boundaries in health care have been recognized for many years. Examples of these longstanding boundaries are the prohibition of fee-splitting (that is, payment of a "kick-back" fee to a physician who refers a patient to another physician), limits on physician ownership of ancillary services to which they refer patients, and the prohibition of unionization of physicians to secure increased benefits for themselves through collective bargaining. More recent commercial boundaries include the prohibition of managed care contracts in which physician compensation is directly linked to individual decisions to limit procedures or referral to specialists, and restrictions on the giving and accepting of gifts to professionals from pharmaceutical and medical device and supply companies.

Financial inducements, gifts, and practice restrictions may all modify professional practice to the detriment of patients, and so may undermine the basic professional commitment to act for the benefit of patients. Commercial boundaries are designed to protect that professional commitment. As long as professionals are compensated for their services, and health care resources are limited, however, there will be inevitable conflicts and tradeoffs in determining who should receive what benefits, and who should pay what costs, in the provision of health care. Commercial boundaries must, therefore, strike a balance between regulation of commercial practices that undermine basic values of health care and acceptance of legitimate market mechanisms within virtually all of today's health care

---

[11] See, for example, Kassirer (2000), Lundberg (1990), Rothman (2000), and Sullivan (1999).

systems. Chapter 11, "Resource stewardship," will address these issues of resource allocation in more detail.

Inter-professional boundaries

Contemporary health care in the developed world is a highly complex practice that involves multiple different professionals, including physicians, nurses, clinical psychologists, allied health professionals, pharmacists, and many others. In order to achieve the goals of the system, it is essential that these professional groups each accept responsibility for their respective practice domains and also understand and cooperate with one another to provide the full range of health care for patients. Inter-professional boundaries serve the purpose of defining the scope of practice of the various health care professions and of regulating interaction among those professions. Inter-professional boundaries thus protect the identity of the different health care professions and enable them to work together effectively to promote the interests of the patients they serve.

Examples of inter-professional boundaries include statutes and institutional credentialing policies that specify the scope of practice of different health care professionals and of different medical specialists, and guidelines that describe appropriate and inappropriate referral from one professional to another. Inter-professional boundaries also address other kinds of interaction between different professionals; in response to past abuses, for example, many health care facilities and professional associations have adopted policies designed to identify and prevent disruptive or abusive behavior by physicians toward nurses or other professionals.[12]

Inter-professional boundary rules can also be highly controversial. A notable historical example is the relationship between physicians and chiropractors. The "Principles of Medical Ethics" adopted in 1957 by the AMA includes the following statement: "A physician should practice a method of healing founded on a scientific basis; and he should not voluntarily associate professionally with anyone who violates this principle."[13] Based on this principle, the AMA asserted that any professional association of physicians with chiropractors, including making and accepting referrals and engaging in joint research, was a violation of medical ethics. The AMA

[12] American Medical Association (2000).   [13] American Medical Association (1957).

defended this principle as a measure that protects patients from ineffective or harmful treatment, but chiropractors argued that it was a self-interested attempt to protect medicine's professional monopoly. Several groups of chiropractors sued the AMA, and in 1987 a federal court ruled that the AMA's policy directing physicians not to work with or refer patients to chiropractors was an illegal business practice, and required the AMA to publish a statement that its members were free to associate professionally with chiropractors.[14]

Integrity boundaries

Boundaries in this category serve two primary purposes. Some of these boundaries are efforts to protect the moral integrity of an entire professional group, usually by proscribing actions that would violate central values of that profession. Examples of this type of integrity boundary are professional policy statements and practice standards prohibiting physician participation in capital punishment, euthanasia, and assisted suicide, on the grounds that these practices are incompatible with the physician's role as healer. These "profession-wide" integrity boundaries are similar to the inter-professional boundaries described above, but their focus is on preserving a profession's basic values, rather than regulating its relation to other professional groups.

Other integrity boundaries are designed to protect the moral integrity of individual professionals, usually by permitting professionals to refuse to provide specific health care services that violate their personal moral convictions. Examples of this second type of integrity boundary are statutes and institutional policies that give health care professionals a right of "conscientious objection," that is, refusal to provide or participate in certain types of care, such as abortion or sterilization.

Several of the integrity boundaries mentioned above are subjects of intense moral debate. Chapter 13 examines the perennial issue of abortion, and Chapter 18 addresses the ongoing debate over the practices of physician-administered euthanasia and physician-assisted suicide. These debates turn, in large measure, on disagreements about whether these practices are more likely to provide significant benefit to patients or subject them to serious harm.

[14] Getzendanner (1988).

Professional rights to conscientious objection are also hotly debated. This issue pits the interests of patients in accessing health care services against the interests of professionals in abiding by their own moral convictions. Opponents of conscientious objection argue that honoring these claims restricts patients' freedom to choose their medical treatment and denies them the benefits of that treatment.[15] Proponents argue that health care professionals should not be forced to violate their conscientiously held beliefs and that medical treatment requires the consent of both the professionals who provide it and the patients who receive it.[16] If one accepts Pellegrino's assertion that health care professionals promise to act for the benefit of patients and to place patient interests before self-interest, one might conclude that health professionals must honor patient requests for treatment and must therefore sacrifice their own moral integrity to serving their patients' expressed interests. That is not Pellegrino's own conclusion, however; rather, he argues that professionals and patients must communicate their values and beliefs to one another and seek relationships that preserve the moral integrity of each.[17]

If we acknowledge that both professionals and patients have a strong interest in preserving their own personal moral integrity, and neither has an absolute right to impose his or her will on the other, how can these conflicts be resolved? One approach would be to formulate general guidelines and apply them to specific situations to determine whose interests ought to take precedence in those situations. Several commentators and professional association committees have attempted this task and have reached a similar conclusion, which Dan Brock calls the "conventional compromise" position on conscientious objection.[18] This position accepts a professional right to conscientious objection, but imposes specific limits on that right. It asserts that professionals may refuse to provide a range of health services. The range of services that professionals may refuse to provide is not fully specified, but it typically includes morally controversial services like abortion, and it excludes refusals based on prejudice, refusal to provide core services within a particular specialty, and refusal of emergency

---

[15] See, for example, Charo (2005) and Savulescu (2006).

[16] See, for example, Sulmasy (2008) and Cherry (2012).   [17] Pellegrino (2006).

[18] See Brock (2008), Wicclair (2011), Committee on Ethics, American College of Obstetricians and Gynecologists (2007), and Committee on Bioethics, American Academy of Pediatrics (2009).

care. According to the conventional compromise position, when professionals do refuse to provide a health care service, they must nevertheless provide information to the patient about all standard services for the patient's condition, including the service to which they object, and they must refer the patient to another qualified professional who does not object to the requested service.

Case analysis

As a devoutly religious man, oncologist Dr. George Gayle expresses an intention to address spiritual issues with his patients in several different ways. Are the practices he contemplates justifiable actions within the therapeutic relationship, or are they unjustifiable violations of a professional boundary separating professional and personal spheres of life?

Based on the importance of religious faith in his own life, Dr. Gayle undoubtedly believes that addressing spiritual and religious issues with his patients can provide significant benefits to many or perhaps most of them, and he looks forward to securing those benefits for his patients. If asked about these benefits by his physician colleagues, he might describe very positive experiences with patients during his residency and fellowship training in which responding to the spiritual needs of patients provided real comfort to them and greatly strengthened his relationship with them. He might also point out that patients with cancer and other life-threatening diseases frequently raise questions about spiritual issues, asking why this hardship has occurred to them and how their illness should affect their understanding of the value and meaning of their life. These are natural and important concerns, he believes, and physicians should not avoid or neglect them.

Dr. Gayle is likely correct in his belief that patients commonly have spiritual concerns and that addressing those concerns can enhance patient well-being. Nevertheless, there are also significant reasons for questioning whether the various actions he proposes are appropriate. Though some patients may welcome discussion of spiritual issues or shared prayers with their caregivers, others will likely view this as an unwelcome intrusion into a personal and private domain. They may find these actions uncomfortable, but be reluctant to express their discomfort for fear of offending or alienating the physician on whom they feel dependent. They may also find Dr. Gayle's assertions about the truth of religious beliefs or the value of religious or spiritual practices presumptuous, since his training and expertise is in medicine, not theology, and, for most patients, not in their own religious or spiritual beliefs. Some patients will find Dr. Gayle's actions offensive, arguing that the physician from whom they seek health care violates an important professional boundary when he subjects them to proselytizing for his own religious faith.

Dr. Gayle proposes several different practices, and these practices may have significantly different goals and significance. Asking patients about their spiritual beliefs and practices, sometimes called "taking a spiritual history," may help physicians determine whether the patient has an important social support network, for example, and may identify particular treatment preferences that are based on religious beliefs, such as the refusal of blood products by Jehovah's Witness patients. General discussions about expectations and hope will be important for many patients with grave illnesses, but invitations by one's physician to prayer and to Sunday school are much more likely to be viewed by patients as unwelcome proselytizing.

Which practices, then, should Dr. Gayle pursue? Physician-bioethicist Daniel Sulmasy offers the following advice on addressing spiritual issues within the therapeutic relationship: "Physicians should not ignore the spiritual needs of their dying patients, but neither should they overestimate their skills in addressing these needs. What physicians should be able to do is to take a spiritual history, elicit a patient's spiritual and religious beliefs and concerns, try to understand them, relate the patient's beliefs to decisions that need to be made regarding care, try to reach some preliminary conclusions about whether the patient's religious coping is positive or negative, and refer to pastoral care or the patient's own clergy as seems appropriate."[19]

---

[19] Sulmasy (2006).

11   Resource stewardship

Case example

Dr. Moore is a gastroenterologist working in a large multi-specialty private medical practice. One of his long-term patients is Father Nolan, a 54-year-old Episcopal priest with chronic hepatitis C virus (HCV) infection. Father Nolan contracted this infection more than twenty-five years ago, probably through a blood transfusion, and he has had slowly progressive liver injury over the past two decades. Until very recently, the only available drug treatment regimen for HCV infection was lengthy, arduous, and only partially effective. Father Nolan began this treatment regimen five years ago, but suffered severe complications and had to discontinue the treatment.

A new drug, sofosbuvir, has just been approved for the treatment of HCV infection. The early evidence suggests that this new drug is a genuine medical breakthrough. Treatment with a combination of sofosbuvir and other medications is short in duration, is well tolerated, and has a more than 95 percent cure rate. Dr. Moore would prescribe the new drug for Father Nolan right away, but for one stumbling block – the cost of the treatment regimen is about $140,000. Father Nolan has private health insurance; his parish provides this insurance to its staff through a non-profit insurer that specializes in health insurance plans for small religious institutions. In an attempt to control its costs, the insurance company has placed strict limits on who can be reimbursed for this drug, reserving it for only those patients with severe liver disease who need immediate treatment. The company has decided that its many other chronic HCV patients can wait until competing drugs now being developed by other manufacturers enter the market over the next few years, and the subsequent competition drives down drug prices.

Father Nolan does not meet his insurer's strict conditions for receiving the new HCV treatment. He is not acutely ill, but he does have continuing symptoms caused by liver damage, including fatigue, loss of appetite, and swelling in his lower body. Dr. Moore believes that his patient would clearly benefit from receiving the new treatment as soon as he can. He is considering several options. He could report exaggerated symptoms to the insurance company in order to make Father Nolan eligible to receive the new treatment. He could inform Father Nolan about the new treatment and about the insurance company's decision not to cover it in his case. Or, he could decide not to mention the new drug treatment, continue to provide symptomatic treatment, and wait for the expected release of new HCV drugs and for a change in the insurance company's treatment eligibility rules. How should he proceed?[1]

Resource stewardship is the most recently recognized, and therefore probably the least well understood, of the moral foundations of the therapeutic relationship examined in Part II of this volume. In 1997, the Board of Directors of the American College of Emergency Physicians (ACEP) approved a new document developed by its Ethics Committee, entitled "Code of Ethics for Emergency Physicians."[2] Previously, ACEP had endorsed the American Medical Association's "Principles of Medical Ethics,"[3] but the "Code of Ethics for Emergency Physicians" includes a new and distinct set of ten "Principles of Ethics for Emergency Physicians," which it describes as "fundamental moral responsibilities of emergency physicians." Several of the new ACEP principles of ethics are similar to principles in the AMA list, but others are entirely different. Among the novel principles in ACEP's list is the following: "Emergency physicians shall serve as responsible stewards of the health care resources entrusted to them." This is, to my knowledge, the first formal statement of a duty of resource stewardship in the ethics code of a professional society of physicians or other health care professionals. In its description of this duty, the ACEP Code observes that "the emergency physician has dual obligations to steward resources prudently while honoring the primacy of the patient's best medical interests."

One year later, in the 1998 fourth edition of its "Ethics Manual," the American College of Physicians also recognized a duty of resource stewardship, in the following passage:

> Physicians must promote their patients' welfare in an increasingly complex health care system. This ... includes stewardship of health care resources so that finite resources can meet as many health care needs as possible, whether in the physician's office, the hospital, the nursing home, or home care.[4]

---

[1] For further information about this treatment for HCV, see Brennan and Shrank (2014).
[2] American College of Emergency Physicians (1997).
[3] American Medical Association (1980).   [4] American College of Physicians (1998).

The AMA has also recognized a duty of resource stewardship, but its recognition came much later. In 2012, it issued "Opinion 9.0652 – Physician Stewardship of Health Care Resources."[5] That opinion includes the following description:

> Physicians' primary ethical obligation is to promote the well-being of individual patients. Physicians also have a long-recognized obligation to patients in general to promote public health and access to care. This obligation requires physicians to be prudent stewards of the shared social resources with which they are entrusted. Managing health care resources responsibly is compatible with physicians' primary obligation to serve the interests of individual patients.

These representative professional association statements indicate growing acceptance of a duty of resource stewardship, but they also suggest several important questions. Why did appeals to this duty emerge in the late 1990s? What exactly is meant by a duty of stewardship? Why is stewardship a duty of health care professionals? Each of the above statements links stewardship with the duty to promote the best interests of individual patients – how do these two duties relate to one another? This chapter will explore the origins, meaning, proposed criteria, and scope of the duty of resource stewardship.

Origins of the duty

A brief look back at the recent history of health care can shed light on the emergence of a professional duty of resource stewardship. Over the past century, health care in the United States and the rest of the developed world has undergone a remarkable transformation.[6] In the first half of the twentieth century, health care was largely a cottage industry, with care provided by individual practitioners in patients' homes or in small physician offices. Available treatments were limited, inexpensive, and "low-tech," and patients usually paid for their care in cash out of pocket.

Following World War II, however, health care entered an era of major innovation and expansion, with rapidly increasing public and private spending on biomedical research and easier access to care via personal

---

[5] American Medical Association (2012).

[6] For a detailed account of this transformation, see Starr (1982).

health insurance. The investment in research produced multiple new and effective treatments in every medical specialty, and the growth of health insurance made those new treatments available to larger numbers of patients. By 1980, *New England Journal of Medicine* editor Arnold Relman proclaimed the emergence of "the new medical-industrial complex" – US health care had become a highly complex, multi-billion dollar industry.[7]

The US health care system enjoyed extraordinary success and prosperity during this period, but it also confronted two persistent problems. First, despite the growth of private and public systems of health insurance, forty to fifty million US residents still lacked insurance and easy access to health care, and this contributed to significant health disparities.[8] Second, spending on health care increased relentlessly, consuming an ever-larger share of the entire US economy, and straining the budgets of both public and private payers.[9] By 1992, presidential candidate Bill Clinton asserted that the United States faced a "crisis" in health care and pledged to reform the US health care system.[10] Despite Clinton's election victory, his complicated plan for national health care reform never gained much support in a divided US Congress. Instead, employers and government turned to market-based managed care organizations to control their health care costs. These organizations employed various mechanisms to "manage," and usually to restrict, the choices of both patients and health care providers. Managed care plans grew rapidly in the 1990s, but the restrictions they imposed were highly unpopular.[11] Strong public and professional backlash against managed care resulted in multiple legislative restrictions and widespread rejection of managed care health insurance options.

Prior to this time, the prevailing opinion was that health care professionals should make treatment decisions based only on the best interests of their individual patients, and should leave decisions about the allocation of health care resources to health system officials and to legislators.[12] It was in this late-1990s period, however, that appeals to a professional duty of resource stewardship began to appear. By then, there was growing consensus that the long and steady growth in US health care spending was unsustainable, and so cost containment was essential. A major government initiative to control costs, the Clinton health care plan, had failed, and

---

[7] Relman (1980).   [8] Schroeder (2001).   [9] Altman and Levitt (2002).
[10] Clinton (1992).   [11] See Block et al. (1996), Church (1997), and Greene (2003).
[12] See, for example, Levinsky (1984), Abrams (1986), and Sulmasy (1992).

market-based managed care initiatives were under sustained attack. If neither government nor the market could (or should?) control the costs of health care, commentators and professional societies proposed that health care professionals, and especially physicians, should assume this responsibility.[13] Although payments to physicians are a relatively small proportion of total personal health care expenditures, physicians' *decisions*, about diagnostic testing, treatment, referral to other providers, and hospitalization, among others, are major determinants of the use and the cost of care.

In one obvious sense, physicians are in the best position to determine whether a test or a treatment that they are considering for a patient would be a good use of resources, including the necessary personnel, medical supplies, medical equipment, and the money to pay for those personnel, supplies, and equipment. Physicians can make these decisions based on their first-hand knowledge of the patient, his or her medical condition, the different treatment options, and the likely consequences of those options. Recall that, except for their own time and effort, the resources in question in these treatment decisions almost always do not belong to the physicians who prescribe their use, but rather to whoever will pay for them, usually a government- or employer-funded insurance program, and often the patients themselves. These payers make multiple decisions about the resources they control, as, for example, what treatments are covered under Medicare or under a private health insurance plan, and what treatment an individual patient is willing to pay for. They may also, however, call on health care professionals to make wise use of their resources as a condition of authorizing those professionals to allocate those resources for the care of their patients.

Concepts and criteria

The term 'steward' is used in a variety of different ways – think, for example, of wine stewards in restaurants, cabin stewards on cruise ships, and shop stewards in unionized factories. More similar to the contemporary use of stewardship language in health care, however, are prominent appeals in Christian theology. The New Testament records several parables about

---

[13] See American College of Emergency Physicians (1997), American College of Physicians (1998), and Larkin et al. (1998).

stewardship told by Jesus to his disciples.[14] In these parables, a wealthy man entrusts resources to servants and later demands an accounting from each servant of the resources entrusted to him, praising those who used the resources to increase the master's possessions and condemning those who failed to do so. Christians interpret these parables as exhortations to make wise use of God's creation, including both individual and shared resources. In similar fashion, calls to resource stewardship in health care direct professionals to make wise, or prudent, or responsible use of the health care resources entrusted to them. This claim seems obvious – of course we want health care professionals to be responsible and to practice the virtues of wisdom and prudence. The claim is also quite vacuous, however, because it does not specify what constitutes responsible, wise, or prudent use of health care resources. To make resource stewardship a useful guide to action, more substantive principles or criteria are needed. Choosing more specific criteria for resource use, and defending those criteria, are much more difficult and controversial tasks, however.

There are surely multiple ways to approach the task of giving content to a duty of health care resource stewardship; here is one such approach: In the Biblical parables cited above, stewards are praised and rewarded for using resources to further the interests of their masters, who are the owners of the resources. The lesson of these parables seems clear – Christians should recognize that they are not owners but stewards of God's creation and should use the resources available to them in accordance with the divine will. If we apply this general understanding of stewardship (namely, attending to the interests or wishes of the resource owner) to health care, we can conclude that health care professionals should use the resources entrusted to them to promote the interests or carry out the wishes of the resource owners.

Who, then, are the owners of the resources devoted to health care, and what are their interests and wishes? There are, of course, multiple owners of these resources, both public and private, and both corporate and individual. And, these owners have multiple interests and wishes, sometimes shared and sometimes unique or distinctive. If the interests and wishes of these resource owners were highly diverse, it would presumably be impossible to formulate criteria that are both substantive and broadly

---

[14] See, for example, Luke 19:11–27 and Matthew 25:14–30.

applicable, and professionals would instead have to examine each situation individually. If, however, the various owners of health care resources have many substantive *shared* interests and wishes, it may be possible to identify at least some general criteria of stewardship based on those shared interests.

There are, in fact, a number of important interests and goals that are shared by virtually all the major owners of resources devoted to health care, including public health insurance programs like Medicare and Medicaid, private-industry-funded health plans, public and private health care facilities, manufacturers of pharmaceuticals, medical devices, and medical equipment, and individuals who purchase health care for themselves and their families. Perhaps most prominent among these shared interests is the provision of safe and effective health care services for the individual patients who need and can benefit from them. Also very prominent for corporate public and private payers is promotion of the overall health of a group of people, as, for example, all of the members of a health maintenance organization, or all of the employees and their dependents covered under an employer-provided health insurance plan. All of these resource owners also share an obvious interest in achieving their goals of promoting individual and population health in the least costly way, in order to conserve their limited resources and to insure their solvency and their continued existence. (For-profit health care corporations have an additional, distinctive goal for controlling spending, namely providing a return on investment to their private owners or their shareholders.) Finally, the major owners of health care resources appear to be willing to honor at least some choices of both patients and health care professionals, even if those choices do not optimize health outcomes, conserve resources, or maximize profits.[15]

Even though the interests described above are widely shared, an obvious problem with using them to identify specific criteria for making steward-ship decisions is the fact that the different interests can and often do conflict with one another. Because that is the case, a decision that promotes one interest (for example, providing a very expensive new chemotherapy treatment that benefits an individual patient) may interfere with achieving

---

[15] For example, hospital Do Not Resuscitate orders policies very often require that patients or their representatives agree to Do Not Resuscitate orders, even when physicians believe that a resuscitation attempt would be futile.

another interest (for example, initiating a local smoking cessation program to improve the health of a specific population). Nevertheless, scholars have proposed a number of candidate criteria to guide resource use, including refraining from fraud and from wasteful services, choosing the most cost-effective treatment option, avoiding the use of marginally effective or "low-value" treatments, and rationing unavoidably scarce resources fairly. Let us consider each of these criteria in turn.

Fraud

The most obvious and least controversial criterion for health care resource stewardship is the prohibition of fraud. Professionals commit fraud when they collect fees for services never provided, or when they provide services under false pretenses – an egregious example of the latter would be pre-scribing narcotic drugs, without a medical indication, to drug dealers, in return for an under-the-table payment. These actions are a kind of theft of health care resources; they are widely condemned and are recognized as criminal offenses. Despite this condemnation, however, fraud remains a major problem for health care systems around the world. In the United States, for example, the Department of Health and Human Services fraud investigation programs recovered $19.2 billion in fraudulent public health insurance payments over the five-year period ending in 2013. The US Department of Justice opened criminal or civil health care fraud investigations of almost 3000 health care providers in fiscal year 2013.[16]

Medical waste

If health care professionals may not commandeer health care resources by fraud, it seems equally clear that they should not use resources in a wasteful manner. In fact, one of the major reasons for the conclusion that physicians should have unilateral authority to deny medically futile treatment is the assertion that providing futile treatment wastes whatever resources are required for that treatment (see Chapter 17, "Medical futility"). The challenge for applying the concepts of waste and futility, however, is articulating material criteria to determine when an

---

[16] US Department of Health and Human Services and US Department of Justice (2014).

intervention is wasteful or futile. Consider the following definition of 'medical waste' offered by economist Victor Fuchs: "any intervention that has no possible benefit for the patient or in which the potential risk to the patient is greater than potential benefit."[17] There are many examples of medical treatments that research has shown to be either worthless or positively harmful; physicians no longer offer those treatments and routinely refuse patient requests for them.[18] Moreover, in some health care contexts, such as surgery, physicians have considerable discretion to refuse a requested surgical intervention on the grounds that surgery is more likely to harm than to benefit the patient.[19]

Nevertheless, Berwick and Hackbarth estimate that non-beneficial treatment is a major contributor to waste in the US health care system, along with fraud, administrative complexity, and failures of care delivery, care coordination, and pricing.[20] Medically wasteful treatment is clearly a significant problem, but most health care services do offer at least some prospective benefit. And, it is easier to recognize in retrospect that a treatment *did not* produce a benefit than to identify prospectively that a treatment *will not* produce a benefit. Fuchs offers the following example: A patient has been experiencing frequent headaches over the past month. One possible cause of these headaches is a brain tumor or lesion, but the physician believes this cause is unlikely (less than a 10 percent chance). A magnetic resonance imaging (MRI) scan would likely identify a brain tumor or lesion, if one is present, but at an approximate cost of $5000.[21] The patient is very anxious about her headaches and reports that she is having trouble accomplishing daily tasks.

In this case, the MRI scan does not appear to be a "necessary" or "essential" treatment for the patient's headaches. Nevertheless, it does appear to offer some benefit – it provides evidence for or against one possible cause of the patient's headaches. If a tumor or lesion is discovered, specific treatment can be offered, and if no tumor or lesion is identified, that result may help to relieve the patient's anxiety. Because it has some

---

[17] Fuchs (2009).

[18] One notable example is the drug laetrile, once called "the perfect chemotherapeutic agent." Multiple studies in animal and human subjects over several decades failed to show that laetrile has any benefit as an anti-cancer treatment. See American Cancer Society (2014).

[19] Wicclair and White (2014).   [20] Berwick and Hackbarth (2012).   [21] Bebinger (2012).

benefit, the procedure is not "medically wasteful." If waste is understood in the strict sense of treatment that has no expected benefit at all, the injunction to refrain from wasteful treatment has very strong support, but may also have only limited application.

Cost-effective treatment

Another proposed criterion for responsible stewardship of health care resources appeals to the concept of cost-effective treatment. To illustrate this concept, bioethicist Lynn Jansen offers the following example: "Two treatments ... exist for a given medical condition. Both treatments are effective and neither has been shown to be superior to the other, but one treatment is considerably more expensive."[22] In this example, both treatments are effective, and so neither one is medically wasteful. The less expensive treatment (a generic rather than a brand-name prescription medication, for example) is more cost-effective, however, because it accomplishes the desired result at a lower cost. Because the outcome of the two treatments is similar, the "extra" resources used to provide the more expensive treatment do not produce any additional benefit, and so those extra resources are used wastefully. Jansen concludes that "the duty of stewardship ... is a duty that applies primarily to this domain. Considerations of good stewardship direct health care providers to select the most cost-effective response among the eligible options ..."[23]

As is the case with medically wasteful treatment, judgments about cost-effectiveness are heavily dependent on the availability of information comparing the effectiveness of different treatment options. Commentators, therefore, call for increased funding for comparative effectiveness research.[24] Because the various outcomes of different treatments for the same condition are often similar but not identical, and because outcomes may vary for different sub-categories of patients, cost-effectiveness criteria will also require some mechanism for dealing with these differences. Consider, for example, two treatments for end-stage renal disease (ESRD), in-center hemodialysis and home peritoneal dialysis.[25] Both are effective

---

[22] Jansen (2013).   [23] Jansen (2013).

[24] See, for example, Aaron (2008) and Fuchs (2009).

[25] In hemodialysis, the patient's blood is filtered through a medical device called a dialyzer to remove wastes and excess fluid, usually during a three-to-five hour dialysis

treatments, that is, both replace the essential functions of the kidneys and preserve the lives of ESRD patients, and both are currently in wide use. Studies report that the cost of hemodialysis in the United States is 30–50 percent higher than the cost of peritoneal dialysis, and so the latter clearly appears to be the more cost–effective of these two treatments.[26] The large majority of dialysis patients in the US receive hemodialysis, however, probably because it requires significantly less self-administered care than peritoneal dialysis.[27] How should professionals apply a cost-effectiveness criterion of stewardship in this instance? Should they offer only peritoneal dialysis? Should they offer both options but strongly encourage patients to choose peritoneal dialysis? Because treatment for most US patients with ESRD is covered under the public Medicare program, the patients them-selves will not pay more for hemodialysis than peritoneal dialysis. Should physicians explain the cost consequences to the Medicare program of their treatment choice and urge them to choose the treatment that will conserve resources for the program?

Economically wasteful/marginally beneficial/low-value treatment

Recall Fuchs's definition of 'medical waste' as services that confer no benefit at all or are positively harmful to patients. Fuchs also offers a second definition of waste in health care, which he calls "economic waste." He defines 'economic waste' as "any intervention for which the value of the expected benefit is less than expected costs."[28] Notice that interventions of this kind do provide benefits, and so they require a determination that these benefits are less valuable than, or are not worth, the resources used to produce them. Other commentators describe these "economically wasteful" treatments as "marginally beneficial" or "low-value" treatments.[29] Another proposed criterion for responsible stewardship of resources directs professionals to determine when a treat-ment's expected benefits are not worth its costs, and to refrain from providing these marginally beneficial or low-value treatments.

session three times a week. In peritoneal dialysis, patients use a catheter to introduce a solution called dialysate into their peritoneal (abdominal) cavity several times per day. Dialysate draws blood-borne wastes and excess fluid out of the blood vessels that line the peritoneal cavity, and then it is removed from the body.

[26] Karopadi et al. (2013).   [27] Collins et al. (2013).   [28] Fuchs (2009).
[29] See, for example, Ubel and Arnold (1995) and Jansen (2013).

This criterion is likely more difficult to apply, and more controversial, than those described above. To use it, a professional must assign values, or acceptable prices, to expected benefits. Suppose, for example, that the expected benefit of a newly approved chemotherapy regimen for patients with advanced pancreatic cancer is three months additional survival. At what price point should an oncologist conclude that this benefit is not worth the cost? For many years, cost-benefit analyses of new medical treatments have employed a threshold of $50,000 per quality-adjusted life-year gained, but recent authors claim that that threshold is too low in the US context.[30] Moreover, neither professionals, nor policymakers, nor patients are comfortable "putting a price on life" in making treatment decisions.

In fact, both health care professionals and patients in the United States have multiple incentives to provide and receive more rather than fewer treatments.[31] US medical training has, at least until very recently, emphasized meticulousness, thoroughness, and zeal in keeping patients from harm and securing benefits for them, rather than parsimony in the use of resources. Fee-for-service payment, aggressive marketing of new drugs and medical devices to professionals, and a desire to minimize liability risk all encourage professionals to provide more rather than fewer treatments. Because their out-of-pocket payments are limited, US patients with health insurance want all treatment that offers some benefit, no matter how costly. Patients want and expect high-technology treatments, and direct-to-consumer marketing prompts them to request "new and improved" drug treatments.

To counteract these strong incentives for more treatment and more spending, physician-bioethicist Howard Brody proposed in 2010 that the professional associations of the various medical specialties develop a new kind of practice guideline designed to discourage overtreatment.[32] Brody challenged each medical specialty society to develop a "top five list" of diagnostic tests or treatments that are very commonly ordered, are expensive, and do not "provide any meaningful benefit to at least some major categories of patients for whom they are commonly prescribed." Brody's term 'no meaningful benefit' is clearly meant to include medical waste ("no benefit"), and perhaps also economic waste ("benefit not worth the cost"). Organized medicine accepted Brody's challenge – by mid 2014, more

---

[30] Neumann et al. (2014).   [31] Emanuel and Fuchs (2008).   [32] Brody (2010).

than sixty US medical specialty societies had developed and published "top five lists" of tests and procedures to avoid, as part of the "Choosing Wisely" campaign organized by the American Board of Internal Medicine (ABIM) Foundation.[33]

The top five lists of the Choosing Wisely campaign give professionals valuable information about overused and wasteful or low-value services, but use of this information to avoid these services is voluntary. Is this information sufficient to counteract the multiple incentives to provide more rather than fewer services? If it is not, more powerful incentives for changes in practice will be necessary. Additional options may include insurance plan rules that limit or deny coverage for questionable treatments, and financial incentives that reward physicians for making decisions to forgo those treatments.[34]

If health care professionals accept as a criterion of resource stewardship that they should refrain from or avoid economically wasteful or low-value services, how should they apply this criterion? Recall the example described above of the patient with frequent headaches. Suppose the physician seeing this patient considers an MRI scan, but judges that this is a low-value diagnostic test that she should not order. How should she proceed? Should she simply not mention the MRI scan and offer other options for treatment of the patient's headaches? Should she mention that an MRI scan could be done, but explain that it is unlikely to provide valuable information and that she will not refer the patient for this test? Should she mention the MRI scan and discourage its use, but agree to refer the patient if she strongly desires it? The first of these options is likely the simplest, unless the patient asks for an MRI, but it is also the least transparent. Honoring the patient's informed request for this study respects her wishes, but does not satisfy the stewardship criterion to refrain from low-value services.[35]

Scarce resources

Health care professionals in various settings routinely make decisions about resource use in one more set of circumstances. When a health care resource is scarce, that is, when the supply of that resource at a

[33] See Cassel and Guest (2012) and ABIM Foundation (2014).
[34] Emanuel and Fuchs (2008).   [35] See Ubel (2007) for discussion of a similar example.

particular time is insufficient to provide it to all of the patients who need it at that time, professionals are often charged to decide who will receive the scarce resource, and who will not. For example, Chapter 21, "Organ transplantation," describes the growing scarcity of transplant organs and the complex procedures used to determine which waiting patients will receive organs recovered from deceased donors. Scarcity of resources can be mild and temporary, as, for example, when a hospital ED triage nurse uses criteria of urgency of need and patient safety to decide which ED patients require immediate attention for an emergency condition and which patients can wait until an emergency physician is available to treat their non-urgent medical problem. Scarcity can also be extreme and enduring, as in a massive natural or man-made disaster that has produced thousands of injured survivors and also destroyed health facilities and injured or killed many health care providers.[36] In these situations of extreme scarcity, professionals may give priority to patients whose lives can be saved with the least investment of human and material resources.

Professionals face difficult allocation decisions when a specific resource becomes scarce in a specific setting. Consider the following example: In a crowded urban hospital, all but one mechanical ventilator is in use, and two new patients are in the ED with severe shortness of breath that has persisted despite initial drug treatment. The medical director of the intensive care unit (ICU) may bear the responsibility to determine which of these two patients should receive ventilator support, or whether ventilator support should be removed from a current patient to provide it to one of the new patients.[37] In many developing nations, there is a general scarcity of all financial, material, and human resources for health care, and that scarcity can be further exacerbated by war or by national health emergencies like the 2014 Ebola virus disease epidemic in West Africa.[38] In these resource-poor environments, the few physicians and other health care professionals who are on duty in clinics and hospitals face hourly decisions about how to distribute the very limited resources at their disposal among large numbers of patients in need.

---

[36] Examples include major hurricanes and destruction of urban areas in war.

[37] See Sprung et al. (2013) for a recent consensus statement regarding allocation criteria for ICU beds.

[38] Chan (2014).

Types and methods

The previous section reviewed different criteria that professionals may employ to allocate health care resources in different settings and circumstances. Another way to approach professional duties of resource stewardship is to review different types and methods of resource allocation. This section will consider two general types of allocation, rationing and triage, and two more specific methods for allocation, "gatekeeping" and "gaming the system."

Rationing

The obvious focus of the duty of stewardship is on decisions about the use of health care resources. The terms 'distribution,' 'allocation,' 'rationing,' and 'triage' are all in common use in this context. The broadest of these terms are 'distribution' and 'allocation' – these generic terms are roughly synonymous; they are used to refer to any choice to apportion some resource among members of a group. The resource distributed may or may not be either valuable or scarce; for example, a teacher may allocate desks among a group of students.

The term 'rationing' is somewhat more specific; it is used to describe allocation of a resource that is both valuable and at least relatively scarce. Rationing decisions occur at many different levels. For example, national legislatures decide how to allocate limited public funds among different public goods, including national security, education, and health care. Health care systems decide how to allocate their finite resources among different health services, including primary, secondary, and tertiary care. In other contexts described above, individual health care professionals decide how to allocate scarce resources, including ICU beds, drugs in short supply, and health insurance plan funds, among their patients. Notice that not all health care resource allocation decisions are rationing decisions; if a treatment is genuinely medically wasteful, that is, provides no medical benefit, the decision of a health insurance plan not to cover that treatment, or of a physician not to provide the treatment, is not a rationing decision, since it does not deprive patients of any benefit.[39]

Rationing decisions may be either explicit or implicit. In the context of organ transplantation, for example, a transplant program's decision to add

---

[39] Tilburt and Cassel (2013).

a patient to its waiting list may be primarily implicit, based perhaps on clinical judgments about the patient's ability to adhere to lifelong post-transplant immunosuppressive therapy. Once the patient is on a waiting list, however, access to a deceased donor transplant organ is based primarily on an explicit set of public criteria.

Rationing decisions made by individual health care professionals, especially implicit rationing decisions, are often referred to as 'bedside rationing.'[40] As noted earlier in this chapter, the prevailing opinion until the mid 1990s was that professionals should not engage in bedside rationing, leaving rationing decisions to public or institutional officials. Some commentators still maintain that resource stewardship should be limited to refraining from medically wasteful services, but as health care costs continue to increase, that position becomes harder to defend. As physicians, nurses, and other health care professionals are asked to care for larger numbers of patients in today's "leaner" and more productive health care systems, they make multiple daily implicit decisions to ration at least one valuable and increasingly scarce resource, that is, the time that they spend with each of their many patients.

Triage

Now used almost exclusively in health care contexts, the term 'triage' refers to a type of resource allocation decision that satisfies the following three conditions:

1. It is a rationing decision, that is, it distributes a valuable but scarce health care resource among multiple patients.
2. It is made by a health care professional, often called a "triage officer," and is usually based on a brief examination of the patient.
3. It relies on an established system, plan, or algorithm to allocate treatment among patients.[41]

Triage is thus one kind of explicit bedside rationing; in it, a clinician applies an established plan or algorithm to grant or deny a specific patient access to treatment. As noted above, triage is a routine practice in hospital emergency departments to determine priority for treatment among arriving patients.

[40] See, for example, Hall (1994), Ubel and Arnold (1995), and Ubel (2000).
[41] Iserson and Moskop (2007).

Multiple different triage systems have been developed and used in other contexts of resource scarcity, including sorting injured patients for treatment following airplane crashes, natural disasters, and military battles.[42]

Gatekeeping

In their heyday during the 1990s, managed care organizations (MCOs) relied heavily on a cost containment method called "gatekeeping." MCOs typically assigned each of their patients to one of the organization's primary care physicians and charged those physicians to serve as gatekeepers of the resources of the MCO. That is, primary care physicians would determine whether their patients should have access to a variety of expensive services, including referral to specialists for evaluation and treatment, and admission to the hospital.[43] Without authorization from its gatekeeper physicians, the MCO did not cover these services. To encourage gatekeepers to limit their authorization of these expensive services, MCOs offered either financial rewards for practice groups that kept their use of these services below an established threshold, or financial penalties for groups that exceeded that threshold.

Gatekeeping gives physicians explicit authority to be stewards of the resources of a health care organization – it asks them to determine whether use of those resources for a specific patient would be medically or economically wasteful. This method proved highly unpopular, however, for several reasons. Patients resented the clear limitation it placed on their access to services, as, for example, their freedom to consult a specialist without authorization from their primary care physician. Critics also expressed concerns that this method creates an unacceptable conflict of interest, since it gives organizations and physicians financial incentives to deny not only wasteful, but also clearly beneficial services to patients.[44]

Gaming the system

The primary goal of the duty of resource stewardship, however broadly or narrowly it is interpreted, is to limit the inappropriate *use* of health care

---

[42] Moskop and Iserson (2007).   [43] Reagan (1987).
[44] See, for example, Kassirer (1994).

resources. The final method of resource allocation I will discuss, however, is designed to overcome inappropriate *limitations* on patient access to treatment. Proponents recommend this method, commonly called "gaming the system," when a health system or health insurance plan refuses to provide or to cover a clearly beneficial or a necessary treatment.[45] In these situations, proponents argue, professionals may or should deceive the system or insurer by exaggerating or otherwise misrepresenting the patient's medical condition in such a way that the patient will be eligible for the treatment. This action is said to be justified by the physician's duty of beneficence, namely, the duty to act for the benefit of his or her patients.

In two surveys of US physicians conducted in the late 1990s, many respondents (39 percent in one study and 58 percent in the other) expressed their willingness to game the system, that is, to use deception to obtain coverage for services.[46] Notice that this practice constitutes a kind of health care fraud, since it obtains services under false premises. In gaming the system, the deception is not for the professional's own benefit, but rather for the benefit of the patient. Critics of gaming cite several problems with this practice, however.[47] First, falsification of medical records may secure a particular treatment for a patient, but it may also deceive other health care providers, resulting in misunderstanding of the patient's condition and unnecessary or harmful treatment. Second, gaming the system to secure treatment for one's patients may interfere with the ability of that system to provide even more beneficial treatment for other patients in the system. Finally, despite the good intention of benefiting one's patients, violating health system or plan rules to secure treatment is still a kind of theft from the owners of that resource. Its justification, therefore, may depend on a further claim that the health care system or insurance plan is not in fact the rightful owner of the resources it makes available to its patients.

Case analysis

Based on his review of research on sofosbuvir, the newly approved drug for treatment of hepatitis C infection, Dr. Moore is convinced that this

[45] See, for example, Tavaglione and Hurst (2012).
[46] Freeman et al. (1999) and Wynia et al. (2000).
[47] See Regis (2004) and Morreim (2012).

treatment would significantly benefit his patient Father Nolan. Dr. Moore recognizes that Father Nolan's liver disease is currently a chronic condition, but he also knows that hepatitis C infection can become fulminant at any time, that is, it can get much worse very suddenly and can cause liver failure and brain injury over a period of days or weeks. If that happened, Father Nolan would be critically ill and would urgently need a liver transplant to survive.

Dr. Moore also recognizes, however, that his treatment options for Father Nolan are limited. He knows that Father Nolan's health insurance plan currently limits access to the new drug treatment to patients with acute illness, and Father Nolan does not satisfy that condition. Dr. Moore may view the insurer's decision as unjustifiable and attempt to game the system to secure the treatment for his patient. He may, for example, exaggerate Father Nolan's symptoms, claiming that his fatigue, anorexia, and swelling are acute, life-threatening conditions. If the coding and billing staff in his practice, or insurance company reviewers, recognize that the medical record does not support this claim, however, they may reject the claim and report it as fraudulent.

Dr. Moore may accept the insurance plan's efforts to control its costs and to remain competitive, but view the drug manufacturer's pricing of its new drug as unacceptable. He may, therefore, contact the manufacturer, Gilead Sciences, and request that it provide sofosbuvir at low or no cost to Father Nolan. Gilead might honor such a request, and if it does, Dr. Moore will achieve his goal of securing this treatment for his patient. The company may, however, respond that it cannot make an exception for one patient among the thousands of patients who could benefit from its new drug. Gilead might defend its pricing by pointing out that it has spent $11 billion on research and development of the new drug, and that it has only a very short time period to recoup its investment and earn a profit before other HCV drugs currently in development enter the market.[48]

Even if he cannot convince the insurance company or the drug company to provide the new drug for Father Nolan, Dr. Moore may decide that he should inform his patient about this new and very promising treatment for his condition. Dr. Moore knows, however, that Father Nolan is a man of modest means and that he cannot easily afford the $140,000 cost of the

---

[48] Brennan and Shrank (2014).

treatment. He might, however, consider that Father Nolan may have retirement savings that he could use to fund the treatment. With information
about the treatment and its cost, Father Nolan might also solicit contributions from his parishioners to fund this treatment, but Father Nolan
may prefer not to reveal this personal medical information to his parishioners or to solicit money from them for this purpose, and the success of
such a solicitation would likely depend on the size and affluence of his
congregation.

Finally, Dr. Moore may decide not to mention the new drug to his patient,
but rather wait for expected changes in insurance coverage rules, in the
price of the new drug, or in the availability of other HCV drugs. He may
decide that he should not discuss a treatment that his patient cannot afford,
and should not suggest that Father Nolan deplete his retirement fund or
solicit contributions from church members to fund this treatment. Rather,
Dr. Moore may choose to continue symptomatic treatment of Father
Nolan's HCV infection and hope that his condition remains stable until
new treatment options become available.

Which course of action would you recommend to Dr. Moore? What,
if any, considerations of resource stewardship play a role in your
recommendation?

Part III

Controversies in health care ethics

Treatment choices at the beginning and at the end of life

Health care options at the "edges" of life, near the dramatic events of birth and death, can reveal deep value differences among us and provoke intense moral conflict. Contemporary health care offers unprecedented choices about whether, when, and how birth and death will occur. Part III of this volume is devoted to examination of these choices.

The beginning of life

For a variety of reasons, reproductive decisions are among the most significant and controversial of human choices. Reproduction is, after all, a life-altering event for most of us. It creates a new human life, and it enables the joys and imposes the responsibilities of parenthood on those who choose it. Reproduction is almost always the result of sexual intimacy, one of the most valued and intense of human experiences. It raises the question, therefore, whether couples should be able to share this experience without reproduction as a consequence. Reproduction requires two people, but the major burdens of pregnancy, labor, and delivery fall on women, and that raises questions about the rights of women to make reproductive decisions. Finally, reproduction sustains, but may also threaten human societies. Western European nations with shrinking populations, for example, offer special benefits for their citizens who choose to have children. China, in contrast, for many years imposed penalties on couples who had more than one child, in an effort to control overpopulation.

Human reproductive values and desires vary across a wide spectrum. Consider the following three attitudes toward reproduction, for example:

1. For many people, reproduction and parenthood are highly valued and sought-after experiences. If these people have difficulty reproducing, they may seek medical assistance. Should technological assistance in fulfilling reproductive goals be available to all who desire it? Chapter 12, "Assisted reproductive technologies," addresses this question, examining the scope and limits of reproductive freedom and the role of health care professionals and public policy in providing and controlling access to assisted reproductive technologies.

2. For many other people, reproduction is a highly undesirable event that they strive to avoid. Should abortion be available to all who desire it to prevent reproduction? Chapter 13, "Abortion," explores this controversial question through a review of two representative positions on the morality of abortion, one pro-life and one pro-choice.

3. For still others, reproduction may be a matter of relative indifference. These people may not avoid reproduction, but they may not alter preferred behaviors or accept medical treatment in order to prevent harm to their future children. Should the health-related choices and behaviors of pregnant women be constrained to protect their fetuses? Chapter 14, "Maternal-fetal conflict," addresses this question by describing the major types of conflict, reviewing various responses to these conflicts, and assessing arguments for and against coercive measures to protect the welfare of future children.

The end of life

Health care decisions near the end of life are no less complex and controversial than those at its beginning. The basic question whether death is a good, an evil, or a morally neutral event, remains a matter of considerable debate.[1] Whatever one's position on the general question of the moral significance of death, there is broad agreement that the timing and experience of dying can be either better or worse. We seek to avoid a death that is premature and a dying process that is marked by severe pain, mental anguish, or isolation. We have developed and implemented a variety of

---

[1] For opposing views on this question, see Engelhardt (1975) and Nagel (1979).

decision-making strategies and medical treatments to achieve our goals as we approach the end of life, but there is widespread disagreement about whether and when particular choices for end-of-life treatment are appropriate.

Chapter 15, "Advance care planning and advance directives," describes a strategy designed to prevent disagreements about medical treatment near the end of life. This strategy recognizes that patients are often unable to make or communicate treatment choices near the end of their lives, and so encourages people to formulate and communicate their preferences for end-of-life treatments in advance.

Advance care planning may avoid confusion and conflict over medical treatment decisions in many cases, but not in all. Chapter 16, therefore, is devoted to examination of these moral conflicts. It begins with an examination of major types of moral conflict in end-of-life care. The chapter then identifies common causes of conflict between health care professionals and patients or their representatives, including cognitive, affective, normative, and external causes. The chapter concludes with consideration of strategies for preventing and resolving these conflicts.

One proposed, but morally controversial strategy for choosing treatment near the end of life appeals to professional judgments that a particular treatment is medically futile. Chapter 17, "Medical futility," is devoted to evaluation of that strategy. The chapter identifies different criteria for futile treatment, reviews arguments for and against reliance on professional judgments about futility, and describes a shift from substantive futility criteria toward establishment of procedures for the resolution of futility disputes.

Another morally controversial issue is the use of medical means to control the manner and the time of death, via physician-assisted suicide or physician-administered euthanasia. Chapter 18, "Aid in dying," summarizes the recent history of these life-ending practices and examines arguments for and against the claim that these practices are morally permissible and so should not be prohibited by law.

12　Assisted reproductive technologies

Case example

Thirty-year-old Mr. Edward Dawson, an investment manager in a large bank, collapses one afternoon in his office. His assistant immediately calls 911. Emergency medical technicians respond rapidly, recognize that Mr. Dawson is in cardiac arrest, begin cardiopulmonary resuscitation, intubate Mr. Dawson, and transport him to nearby Downtown Medical Center, where he is placed on a ventilator and admitted to the medical intensive care unit. Physical examination and diagnostic imaging reveal that he has suffered a severe anoxic brain injury, and he does not regain consciousness. Eight weeks later, Mr. Dawson's medical condition is unchanged. A consulting neurologist informs his wife that, although he does not satisfy all of the neurologic criteria for the determination of death, his brain injury is extensive and irreversible. The neurologist explains that it is highly unlikely that Mr. Dawson will ever regain consciousness or the ability to breathe on his own.

Mr. Dawson had been married just four months before this accident. Dr. Milam, his attending physician, offers Mrs. Dawson the option that ventilator support be withdrawn and Mr. Dawson be allowed to die. Mrs. Dawson agrees with this treatment plan, but requests that, before the ventilator is withdrawn, her husband's sperm be recovered for artificial insemination at a later date. She reports that they had intended to have children in the course of the marriage, and that she would like to fulfill that goal. How should Dr. Milam respond?

Overcoming infertility

Reproduction is, of course, a natural process essential for the survival of any biological species, but not all individual organisms have the ability or the opportunity to reproduce. For most human beings, reproduction is also a life-changing event with great personal and moral significance. People who desire children and who experience difficulty reproducing may therefore seek medical assistance in achieving that goal. Human infertility is, in fact, a relatively common condition. According to a US National Survey of Family Growth conducted between 2006 and 2010, 6 percent of all married women aged 15–44 (1.5 million women) were infertile, where infertility was defined as having been sexually active without using contraceptive measures over the past twelve months and not having become pregnant. In the same survey, 11.5 percent of all men aged 25–44 who were not surgically sterile reported inability or difficulty fathering a child.[2]

For most of human history, reproduction was possible only through sexual intercourse. Basic biological mechanisms of reproduction in human beings and other animals were not well understood until the nineteenth century, and effective medical mechanisms to control human reproduction, through contraception and assisted reproductive techniques, did not appear until the latter half of the twentieth century.[3] The one exception to the recent origin of medically assisted reproduction techniques is the practice of artificial insemination, the introduction of sperm by a syringe or other instrument into the vagina or uterus of a woman. This practice dates back to the early nineteenth century, but it remained controversial well into the twentieth century, and sperm banks enabling artificial insemination with cryogenically preserved donor sperm emerged on a large scale only with the development of effective cryopreservation techniques in the 1970s.[4] A variety of other medical and surgical treatments have been developed and disseminated to correct infertility conditions within the past half century. These treatments include medications to stimulate ovulation in women and surgical procedures to repair or replace dysfunctional or diseased reproductive organs in both women and men.

An International Committee for Monitoring Assisted Reproductive Technology (ICMART), convened by the World Health Organization, recently recommended standardized terminology for medical interventions designed to assist reproduction. ICMART recommends the generic term 'medically assisted reproduction' (MAR) to refer to reproduction brought about through all of the above-described medical treatments. Also included among MAR techniques, according to the ICMART glossary, are "all procedures that include the *in vitro* handling of both human oocytes and sperm or of embryos for the

---

[2] Chandra et al. (2013).   [3] See Clarke (2006) and Djerassi (2002).
[4] See Clarke (2006) and Daniels and Golden (2004).

purpose of establishing a pregnancy."[5] ICMART reserves the term 'assisted reproductive technology' (ART) for the latter group of *in vitro* procedures.

Probably the most well-known ART is the practice of *in vitro* fertilization (IVF) followed by embryo transfer (ET). This practice involves four steps: recovery of mature ova from a woman, fertilization of these ova *in vitro*, culture of the resulting pre-implantation embryos, and placement of these embryos into a woman's uterus for implantation and gestation. Following decades of research on these steps in animal and human models, Patrick Steptoe and Robert Edwards announced the birth of Louise Brown, the first baby conceived via IVF, in Cambridge, England, in July 1978.[6] Although this research and the creation of "test tube babies" were highly controversial at the time of their announcement, IVF and ET are now offered world wide and have resulted in the birth of more than four million babies.[7] IVF and ET may be combined with several other medical procedures to enable reproduction in specific circumstances. The use of *donor sperm, ova, or embryos* in IVF and ET may, for example, allow women to bear children when they or their partners lack viable gametes. *Gestational surrogates* (also known as surrogate mothers) may bear a couple's genetic offspring when the female partner is unable to carry a child. *Intracytoplasmic sperm injection* (ICSI) is a method of *in vitro* fertilization that allows a male partner with very low sperm counts to father a child. *Pre-implantation genetic diagnosis* (PGD) of *in vitro* embryos enables couples at risk for producing a child with a serious genetic disease to select for transfer only embryos that do not carry the disease-producing genes.[8] The birth, in Scotland in 1996, of Dolly the sheep, the first mammal conceived by cloning of an adult somatic cell and transfer of the resulting embryo to a gestational surrogate, suggests that *reproductive cloning* is also a possible method of human reproduction.[9]

---

[5] Zegers-Hochschild et al. (2009).   [6] See Biggers (2012) and Steptoe and Edwards (1978).

[7] Biggers (2012).

[8] Couples may also request PGD for purposes other than preventing transmission of a genetic disease to their offspring. For example, some couples have sought PGD for identification and procreation of a "savior sibling." In this instance, PGD is used to select an embryo for transfer because its genetic make-up will allow the resulting child to serve as a compatible stem cell donor for an older sibling with a serious genetic illness whose only effective treatment is stem cell transplantation (see Pennings 2004).

[9] Wilmut et al. (1997). There are, however, no credible reports of human reproductive cloning, and multiple nations and US states have enacted legislation prohibiting this practice; see Matthews (2007).

Despite the wide availability of ARTs today, critics continue to pose moral questions about their use in a variety of situations. The most sensational recent example was the 2009 case of Nadya Suleman, nicknamed "Octomom" in the extensive international media coverage of her story.[10] Suleman, an unemployed single mother of six children conceived through IVF, requested transfer of twelve additional frozen embryos at one time, and Dr. Michael Kamrava, her fertility specialist in Beverly Hills, California, complied with that request. Suleman delivered octuplets in January 2009, the first recorded human case in which all eight octuplets survived the neonatal period. Media coverage of this "medical miracle" quickly gave way to sharp and sustained criticism of the choices and actions of this patient and her physician.[11] The American Society for Reproductive Medicine expelled Kamrava from its membership in 2009, and the Medical Board of California revoked his medical license in 2011, finding that he was guilty of gross negligence in his medical treatment of Suleman and of two other patients.[12]

This chapter will evaluate the use of ARTs by addressing the following three questions:

1. What should be the scope and limits of reproductive freedom?
2. Under what circumstances, if any, may health care professionals conscientiously refuse to provide assisted reproductive services requested by their patients?
3. How, if at all, should societies regulate or limit the use of ARTs?

Unless otherwise indicated, in the rest of this chapter I will use the term 'assisted reproductive technology,' or ART, in a broad sense to include all methods of medically assisted reproduction.

The scope and limits of reproductive freedom

As noted above, reproduction is both a basic biological process, and, for very many human beings, a pivotal and highly prized life experience. Having a child, whether planned or unplanned, desired or undesired, is typically a life-altering event. Control over reproduction is thus a central feature of human

---

[10] Brief summaries of the Suleman case may be found in Rosenthal (2010) and Rosenthal (2011).
[11] Ory (2010).   [12] Medical Board of California (2011).

autonomy, where autonomy is understood as the ability to make important life choices for oneself, based on one's own desires, goals, and values.

The reasons why many people choose to have children are well known and need little explanation; they include a recognition of the intrinsic value of human life, a desire to experience the distinctive parent–child relationship and to play a central role in nurturing and supporting one's children to adulthood, an interest in passing on one's genetic or cultural heritage, or one's religious or moral values, to one's children, and a hope for support from one's children in one's old age. For some people, reproduction may be accepted as a foreseen consequence of their primary desire for sexual and emotional intimacy with their partners.

There is significant evidence for the acceptance of reproduction as a fundamental human value. For example, the United Nations Universal Declaration of Human Rights, although it does not use the term 'right to reproduce,' does state that "Men and women of full age, without any limitation due to race, nationality, or religion, have the right to marry and to found a family."[13] The Declaration on Social Progress and Development, adopted by the UN General Assembly in 1969, is more specific; it asserts that "Parents have the exclusive right to determine freely and responsibly the number and spacing of their children."[14]

In the United States, a series of Supreme Court decisions have recognized a constitutional right to privacy in making reproductive decisions.[15] Writing for the majority in *Eisenstadt* v. *Baird,* Justice William J. Brennan articulated this right as follows: "If the right of privacy means anything, it is the right of the individual, married or single, to be free from unwarranted governmental intrusion into matters so fundamentally affecting a person as the decision whether to bear or beget a child."[16] Another kind of support for reproductive freedom as a fundamental human value or right can be found in the strong repudiation of public eugenics programs of forced sterilization carried out in Nazi Germany and in many US states for much of the twentieth century.[17]

For most human beings, fulfilling the desire to have children requires only that a heterosexual couple engage in sexual intercourse, that the partners are fertile, and that the female partner be willing to carry a fetus they conceive to delivery. For couples who satisfy these conditions,

---

[13] United Nations (1948).   [14] United Nations General Assembly (1969).

[15] See *Griswold* v. *Connecticut* (1965), *Eisenstadt* v. *Baird* (1972), and *Roe* v. *Wade* (1973).

[16] *Eisenstadt* v. *Baird* (1972).   [17] See Black (2003).

interfering with their freedom to reproduce would require the highly invasive actions of preventing sexual activity or of forced contraception or abortion. Because we are reluctant, at least in the case of adults, to take these invasive steps to prevent reproduction, the freedom of fertile adult heterosexual couples to reproduce is nearly unlimited.

In contrast, for individuals without sexual partners, and for couples who are infertile or who are gay, having children requires the assistance of third parties, such as health care professionals and gamete donors. For still other couples, sexual reproduction is possible, but it may impose significant burdens or risks on the couple or on their offspring, and so they may also seek assistance in reproduction to avoid these burdens or risks. Despite their inability or reluctance to reproduce without assistance, these individuals and couples may claim that their basic human right to reproductive freedom, including a right to bear children, should be recognized and respected. How should this claim be understood? Is the claim justified? Answers to these questions will be highly significant for decisions about the use of ARTs.

The claim that human beings have a basic right to reproductive freedom, that is, to choose whether or not to have children, can be interpreted in several ways. There is, for example, an important difference between negative and positive rights in this context.[18] In general terms, a negative right is understood as a right to freedom from interference with a decision or action. A negative right to reproductive freedom, therefore, would be a right to engage in reproduction-related actions (such as sexual intercourse, fertility treatments, contraception, and abortion) without interference from others. Negative rights create duties of forbearance in other people, that is, duties not to interfere with the actions of the rights-bearers. A positive right, in contrast, is understood as an entitlement to receive a particular good or service or to achieve a particular outcome. Positive rights create duties in others to provide specific services or promote specific outcomes.

To fulfill their desire to reproduce, *individual* human beings require the assistance of at least one other person, usually a heterosexual partner. Fertile heterosexual *couples* need only engage in sexual intercourse and carry a pregnancy to delivery, without interference by others, to achieve a desire to reproduce. For these couples, then, a negative right to freedom

---

[18] Beauchamp and Childress (2013): 370–371.

from interference with their reproductive activity is generally sufficient to achieve their goal (although successful reproduction may also depend on receiving at least basic prenatal health care).

Infertile couples, and individuals without sexual partners, require additional assistance in fulfilling a desire to reproduce. They may engage fertility specialists and gamete donors who are willing to provide ART services for them and claim only a negative right to freedom from outside interference with those activities. Or, they may claim that society should establish a positive right to receive ART services, regardless of their own ability to pay for those services.[19] In either case, imposing restrictions on the ability of these individuals and couples to reproduce does not require highly invasive interference with their sexual activity or with the bodily integrity of pregnant women. Rather, it involves imposing restrictions on their use of ARTs or deciding not to subsidize the costs of ARTs for people who cannot afford them. Are such limits justifiable? The answer to this question depends on an assessment of the moral significance of reproduction, including both its benefits and its burdens.

We have already reviewed some of the reasons why people desire to reproduce and the status of rights to reproductive freedom. The strongest advocates of a right to reproduce might argue that reproduction makes such a fundamental contribution to human fulfillment that everyone should enjoy an equal opportunity to have as many children as they desire, by whatever means are available, whether or not they are able to conceive or bear a child or to identify a willing reproductive partner. This assertion seems too strong, however, in the light of egregious examples like the Suleman case. What reasons can be offered for limitation of reproduction by means of ARTs?

At least four kinds of arguments are commonly offered for limiting access to ARTs. The first, and perhaps least persuasive, argument claims that ARTs should not be used because they are "unnatural." Proponents of this argument observe that ARTs are designed to correct problems in or to supplant the "normal" processes of human sexual reproduction, and they claim that reproduction should occur only by means of those unaided normal processes. On this view, the use of ARTs to enable people without sexual partners, infertile couples, or gay couples to reproduce is an unnatural and therefore immoral practice. This type of argument confronts two problems.

[19] Johnson and Gusmano (2013).

The first is defining what is meant by the term 'natural' or 'normal.' In one sense, for example, most if not all medical treatments, including drug therapy and surgery, correct or supplant natural physiologic processes, and so the boundary between the "natural" and the "unnatural" is not at all obvious. Even if that boundary were obvious, however, it is not clear why it should be morally significant. Suppose, for example, that the normal physiologic processes of aging in human beings include significant dementia beginning in the seventh or eighth decade of life. That fact should not, I submit, incline us to view dementia in the elderly as a morally beneficial or welcome condition; rather, we should pursue medical treatments to prevent or treat dementing conditions whenever they occur.

A second, and much more substantive, type of argument for limiting access to ARTs appeals to the fact that ARTs can endanger the health and welfare of pregnant women and children. Several different kinds of risks can be identified. One is that ART procedures can inflict significant physical injury on women and children. A clear risk of *in vitro* fertilization and embryo transfer, for example, is the fact that simultaneous transfer of multiple embryos often results in high-order multiple pregnancies, that is, pregnancies of triplets or higher numbers of fetuses. These high-order multiple pregnancies are much more likely to result in premature delivery, with greatly increased risks of maternal mortality and of infant death or severe impairment.[20] The Medical Board of California concluded that Dr. Kamrava was grossly negligent in transferring twelve embryos to Ms. Suleman because of the foreseeable consequence of a high-order multiple pregnancy and the resultant grave risk of harm such a pregnancy would pose to his patient and to the children she bore.[21]

Another potential risk of harm to children cited by some commentators is that of parental abuse or neglect. Like adoption agencies, fertility clinics have an opportunity to assess the ability of prospective parents seeking assisted reproductive services to provide a safe and nurturing environment for children.[22] If Ms. Suleman had sought to adopt another child, rather

---

[20] See Reddy et al. (2007), MacKay et al. (2006), and Schieve et al. (2002).

[21] Medical Board of California (2010). Although all eight of the Suleman octuplets survived, they were born nine weeks prematurely and with low birth weights; they are therefore at increased risk of significant disabilities (Kaiser Permanente 2009).

[22] See Ethics Committee of the American Society for Reproductive Medicine (2013a) and Johnson (2009).

than pursue IVF in 2008, for example, the fact that she was a single and unemployed mother of six minor children would almost certainly have resulted in rejection of her application for adoption. Since adoption agencies are required to screen prospective parents in order to protect the children in their care, it may be argued that fertility clinics should also be required, before they provide assisted reproductive services, to screen prospective parents and to refuse services to patients who would be unable to provide adequate parental care.

A third type of argument for limiting access to ARTs is based on a concern that patients can use ARTs to "hijack" social resources by producing multiple children, often in a single pregnancy, who will be dependent on social welfare programs for their well-being. This argument does not assert that children themselves will be endangered by the failure to meet basic needs like food or shelter, since they will receive public services to meet those needs, but rather that it is unjust for parents to bear children whom they cannot support and to rely on public resources for that purpose. Once again, the Suleman case is commonly cited as an example of this unjust reliance on public resources, since Suleman's fourteen children have received significant public welfare benefits from the state of California.[23]

Finally, some critics view the destruction of "leftover" embryos as a morally significant harm of IVF and ET.[24] In IVF, it is common practice to create more pre-implantation embryos than will be transferred at a single time. "Leftover" embryos are frozen and stored for possible transfer in the future, in the event that the first-transferred embryo or embryos fail to implant or abort spontaneously. If the first cycle of IVF and ET is successful, the couple may choose not to transfer the remaining embryos, and those embryos are usually destroyed. For those who view all living human organisms from the time of conception as having full and equal moral status, the annual destruction of thousands of leftover pre-implantation embryos is a grave moral transgression.

If any of the above arguments provides sufficient reason to limit access to ARTs, that conclusion raises at least two additional questions: *How* should access to ARTs be limited? *Who* should impose limitations on ARTs? The rest of this chapter will address those questions.

---

[23] January 2014 news reports announced that Suleman faces charges of welfare fraud for accepting $16,000 in welfare payments during the first six months of 2013, while failing to report $30,000 in personal income during that period. See Dave (2014).

[24] Congregation for the Doctrine of the Faith, Roman Catholic Church (2008).

ARTs and conscientious objection

In Chapter 10, "Professionalism," I examined the claim that health care professionals should be permitted to protect their own moral integrity by refusing to provide health care services that violate their moral convictions. This claim, usually described as a professional right to "conscientious objection" or "conscientious refusal," can also be invoked as a reason for limiting access to ARTs. Proponents of this strategy argue that physicians and other health care professionals should be granted the authority to decide whether or not to honor patient requests for assisted reproductive services. The concept of conscientious objection is often limited to situations in which a health care professional refuses to provide a requested service because that action would violate a personal moral belief, as, for example, a belief that induced abortion is an unjustified kind of killing. In the context of ARTs, the scope of conscientious objection might be extended to include refusals to provide requested services based on professional values or standards as well as personal moral convictions. Using such an extended sense of conscientious objection, for example, a physician might refuse a patient's request for transfer of six embryos at the same time on the grounds that the likely result, a high-order multiple pregnancy, poses too great a risk of harm to both the woman and the children who may be born as a result of that procedure. In such a situation, the physician's decision would be based on professional standards limiting the number of embryos transferred simultaneously, not on a personal moral conviction against embryo transfer.

Should professional conscientious objection be accepted as a mechanism for limiting access to ARTs? As in other areas of health care, permitting conscientious objection in reproductive health care respects the status of health care professionals as independent moral agents and enables them to protect their professional and moral integrity.[25] This respect for professional integrity can benefit patients and society as well as professionals. Realizing the benefits of health care depends significantly on recruiting and retaining professionals who embrace clear moral and professional values and are permitted to act on those values, rather than health care workers who are self-interested or unscrupulous. Reliance on professional decisions that are based on established standards of practice also promotes high-quality care and discourages substandard care.

[25] See Brock (2008) and Wicclair (2011).

Recognizing professional authority to refuse requests for ARTs has obvious benefits, but unlimited rights of conscientious refusal also pose obvious risks of harm to patients. Consider, for example, a fertility specialist who holds a strong moral conviction that homosexuality is a morally depraved lifestyle. A lesbian couple consults this physician and requests artificial insemination with donor sperm. Should the physician be permitted to refuse this request based on his belief that gay people should not be permitted to reproduce or raise children? Permitting conscientious refusal in this case would open the door to unjustified refusals based on prejudice or discrimination of many kinds, including racism and sexism as well as homophobia. An unlimited professional right to conscientious refusal may also impose an unjustified kind of paternalism on patients. Suppose, for example, that a married couple with two young children who were conceived via IVF consult their fertility specialist with a request to have a third child in the same way. The physician believes that two children is the optimal size for this family and so refuses their request for assistance. Although the physician claims that he has the best interests of the members of this family at heart in making this decision, the couple clearly have a different opinion and may assert that their judgment about the size of their family should be honored.

If at least some limits should be imposed on professional rights of conscientious objection, how should those limits be determined and enforced? Mechanisms for developing and implementing limits on professional conscientious objection can be identified along a spectrum from explicit and formal to implicit and informal. At one end of this spectrum, legislators may enact statutes permitting or prohibiting specific kinds of conscientious objection, as, for example, permitting refusal to perform abortions and prohibiting refusal to provide services based on racial prejudice. Such statutes and regulations may provide immunity from liability for protected conscientious refusals, and they may impose legal penalties for violation of prohibited refusals. Common law and professional licensure boards may establish standards of practice that permit or prohibit conscientious refusal of treatment in particular circumstances, and failure to adhere to those standards may expose professionals to liability for damages suffered by patients or to suspension or revocation of their license to practice. Health care professional associations may adopt explicit policies or guidelines that endorse or reject professional rights to conscientious objection in particular circumstances.[26] Individual institutions, such as hospitals or health care systems, may also adopt institutional polices to direct the decisions and actions of the professionals they employ. Finally, professional behavior may be influenced by informal discussion with colleagues and peers about what refusals of requests for treatment are appropriate and inappropriate.

Because they are the ones who provide assisted reproductive services to infertile patients, individual health care professionals are obvious candidates for deciding whether to provide or withhold access to ARTs. Relying solely on individual professionals to make these decisions, however, subjects patients seeking reproductive services to uncertainty and, in some cases, to unjustified discrimination or paternalism. In contrast, society-wide, public decisions about the use of ARTs would provide for more transparent and consistent practices. The next section will consider society's role in limiting access to ARTs.

Societal limitation of ARTs

Societies choose to regulate medical practice, including assisted reproductive services, in a variety of ways. Many nations and US states, for example, have enacted laws banning the practice of human reproduction by cloning, presumably on the grounds that there is no compelling reason for permitting reproduction in this way and that it would be susceptible to serious abuses.[27] With regard to "mainstream" assisted reproductive services like IVF and ET, the United Kingdom and the United States have chosen significantly different approaches to government regulation, not unlike the different roles government plays in the general provision of health care in those two nations. Let us consider these two approaches as models for the role of society in limiting access to ARTs.

In the United Kingdom, the Human Fertilisation and Embryology Authority (HFEA), a national government agency established by an act of Parliament in 1990, inspects and licenses all fertility clinics and issues and enforces human reproductive research and treatment regulations to

---

[26] See, for example, Committee on Ethics, American College of Obstetricians and Gynecologists (2007), and Committee on Bioethics, American Academy of Pediatrics (2009).

[27] Matthews (2007).

which all British clinics and individual professionals must adhere.[28] The HFEA maintains a central registry of data regarding the nature and outcomes of all treatments using stored or donated gametes and embryos conceived *in vitro*; it also evaluates new techniques before they can be offered at fertility clinics. Among the regulations enforced by the HFEA is a strict limit of three on the number of embryos that may be transferred in a single IVF cycle.

In the United States, in contrast, there is less federal regulation and no governmental agency devoted exclusively to oversight of fertility clinics or ARTs.[29] A 1992 federal law, the Fertility Clinic Success Rate and Certification Act, established a national system for reporting outcomes of IVF and other ARTs, but some ART clinics do not participate in this reporting system, and not all ART treatments are included in these reports.[30] The federal Food and Drug Administration approves and monitors the use of reproductive drugs and of donor sperm and ova. In addition to federal regulation, all US states require licensure of physicians and other health care professionals, and state medical and health care professional licensing boards are empowered to discipline or revoke the license of professionals who violate professional or legal standards. As in other areas of health care, the United States also relies heavily on professional self-regulation of ARTs. Examples of this self-regulation include accreditation of embryology laboratories, board certification of medical specialists, and publication of practice guidelines by professional associations like the American Society for Reproductive Medicine (ASRM) and its affiliate, the Society for Assisted Reproductive Technology (SART). ASRM and SART, for example, periodically publish updated guidelines regarding the number of embryos to be transferred in IVF cycles.[31] Although these societies may expel members for failing to follow their guidelines, they cannot compel professionals to adhere to them.

Which of these two approaches, that of the UK or the US, is the preferable model for societal regulation of ARTs? Gladys White proposes that the US adopt the British model.[32] She claims that the largely unregulated financial interests of US fertility clinics and professionals encourage substandard and risky treatments without fully informed consent. White argues that

---

[28] White (1998).   [29] Robertson (2009).   [30] Kushnir et al. (2013).

[31] Practice Committee of the American Society for Reproductive Medicine and Practice Committee of the Society for Assisted Reproductive Technology (2013).

[32] White (1998).

mandatory licensure and oversight of fertility clinics will more effectively promote the safety and quality of infertility services and control service costs. Although he acknowledges abuses in US fertility treatments, John Robertson claims that additional governmental regulation is not the best solution.[33] Robertson argues that legislation imposing limits on the size of families or denying reproductive services to couples with limited resources would interfere with basic reproductive freedoms and promote discrimination in access to those services. He claims that the law is "too blunt an instrument" to dictate specific fertility treatment decisions and prefers instead to rely on individual professionals and patients, with the assistance of professional guidelines, to make these decisions based on their anticipated benefits, risks, and costs. How one should strike the balance between government regulation and "free enterprise" in assisted reproductive services will likely depend on an assessment of how these two approaches affect the major outcomes of enabling reproduction, avoiding harmful complications, and controlling treatment costs.

Case analysis

Mr. Dawson has suffered a catastrophic brain injury, rendering him permanently unconscious and ventilator-dependent. His wife agrees to discontinue ventilator support and allow her husband to die, but she requests that this be done after his sperm have been recovered and stored for future artificial insemination, so that she may conceive and bear their biological child. How should Mr. Dawson's care team respond to her request?

Mrs. Dawson clearly requires professional assistance in this situation to achieve her reproductive goal. May Dr. Milam, the attending physician, rely on Mrs. Dawson's consent to these procedures on behalf of her husband? Assuming that Mr. Dawson had not previously designated another person to serve as his health care agent by means of a health care power of attorney, most jurisdictions recognize his wife as his authorized surrogate decision-maker, in the event that he lacks decision-making capacity. Mrs. Dawson articulates a clear and understandable reason for the procedures she

---

[33] Robertson (2009).

requests. If Dr. Milam asks Mrs. Dawson whether she believes that her husband would agree to these procedures, if he could make a decision about them, Mrs. Dawson is very likely to respond that he would agree, based on his interest in having children and on his loving concern for her and her wishes. Dr. Milam may request that Mrs. Dawson speak with a urologist who can describe sperm recovery and storage procedures and costs to her. Based on this information, Mrs. Dawson may reiterate her request for these services and express her willingness to assume the costs of the services and responsibility for the stored sperm. Dr. Milam may also seek additional information – he may, for example, ask Mr. Dawson's parents or siblings whether they can corroborate Mrs. Dawson's statement that Mr. Dawson wanted to have children and would agree to posthumous reproduction, and he might request an ethics consultation to help him evaluate options and reach a decision.

Dr. Milam may consider that he should honor Mrs. Dawson's request, based on her authority as his surrogate decision-maker and her assertion that her husband would consent to these procedures. He may, however, also consider that he should refuse her request, based on a conviction that reproduction by means of ART is a major life choice that requires the explicit consent of both reproductive partners. He may reflect that Mr. Dawson might not in fact wish to have a biological child with whom he will have no relationship, and might not want to undergo a somewhat invasive sperm recovery procedure that is unrelated to his medical condition and so does not offer any direct medical benefit to him. What response would you recommend to him?

If Dr. Milam consults the medical literature for guidance, he will discover that there is an ongoing debate about whether intimate partner requests for gamete recovery near or after death should be honored.[34] He will also learn that a number of hospitals have adopted policies to address these requests, and that some policies permit gamete recovery upon request by an intimate partner, and other policies permit gamete recovery only if the patient has given explicit permission for gamete recovery in advance, before losing decision-making capacity (a rare occurrence).[35]

[34] See, for example, Orr and Siegler (2002), Parker (2004), and Ethics Committee of the American Society for Reproductive Medicine (2013b).

[35] Bahm et al. (2013).

If Downtown Medical Center has such a policy, he may, of course, be guided by whatever position on gamete recovery requests the policy takes. Chances are, however, that Dr. Milam's hospital has not yet adopted a policy on this subject. Do you believe that it should implement such a policy? If so, what position should that policy take?

13   Abortion

Case example

Dr. Gold, an obstetrician-gynecologist, spends one day a week seeing patients at a rural clinic affiliated with the teaching hospital where she has admitting privileges. The clinic is about an hour drive from the city in which her teaching hospital is located. Mrs. Farmer, a 26-year-old mother of four, has made an appointment with Dr. Gold today at the rural clinic. Dr. Gold delivered Mrs. Farmer's youngest child two years ago, but has not seen her since then. Mrs. Farmer reports that she has missed a menstrual period and fears that she might be pregnant again. A pregnancy test is done; it confirms that Mrs. Farmer is pregnant, and the pregnancy is estimated at about seven weeks. Mrs. Farmer immediately states that she does not want to have another baby. She tells Dr. Gold that her husband will be furious when he finds out that she is pregnant and could pose a danger to her and her children – he was physically violent with her during her last pregnancy. She relates that she has been using birth control to prevent pregnancy, but it has obviously failed. The couple can barely afford to support their four children. Mrs. Farmer asks Dr. Gold to terminate the pregnancy.

The multi-institution health system in which Dr. Gold works has a firm policy about abortion. It states that, if an abortion is necessary for a therapeutic reason, that is, to protect the life or health of the pregnant woman, a physician may perform the procedure. Physicians are not, however, permitted to perform elective abortions in system facilities. Dr. Gold explains this to Mrs. Farmer and tells her that the nearest clinic that performs elective abortions is located about a three-hour drive away. Mrs. Farmer begins to weep and says that she cannot travel to have the procedure because she does not have access to a car and has no one to watch her children for more than a few hours. She pleads with Dr. Gold to consider her case to be one in which the pregnancy must be terminated to protect her health, and to perform the abortion. How should Dr. Gold respond?

Abortion: an intractable problem in health care ethics

Abortion has long been a high-profile ethical and public policy issue, and it is a standard topic in undergraduate, graduate, and professional school bioethics courses. Despite its high visibility, however, my students over the years have sometimes confessed that they dread discussion of this topic and have suggested that we just skip over it. When asked why they feel this way, students cite a number of reasons. Some point out that, because the issue is highly complicated, one or two class discussions can do little more than scratch the surface, and the risk of oversimplification is great. Others observe that abortion is an emotionally charged topic, and so discussions may generate more "heat" than "light," and more ill will than understanding. Still others argue that positions on abortion are both entrenched and deeply divided; people's minds are made up, and they are reluctant to subject their views to scrutiny or challenge. All of these concerns are highly plausible. Perhaps more than any other topic in bioethics, abortion seems to be an intractable conflict, with little progress toward public resolution over many decades.

This is not a complete account of the abortion issue, however, and there are also persuasive reasons why bioethics students should confront the issue directly. Precisely because abortion is such a highly visible and hotly debated topic, it demands our attention in order to appreciate why it is so difficult to resolve, if nothing else. Abortion is, after all, not a trivial or minor issue, but rather an issue with life and death implications for fetuses, and serious health and life consequences for pregnant women. Abortion is also an issue that is fraught with confusion and misunderstanding about key concepts, relevant factual information, and leading moral arguments. Discussion may thus at least dispel common misunderstandings and enable a better assessment of the arguments. Abortion is certainly a subject with deep disagreements, but it also offers some potential for common ground among those who disagree, and it is worth noting where there are areas of agreement and possible cooperation. Finally, abortion is an issue that health care professionals are likely to encounter in their practices, certainly if they work in obstetrics and gynecology, and also if they provide any type of primary health care for women. Professionals must be prepared, there-fore, to respond to questions about abortion that will arise in a wide variety of practice settings. For all of these reasons, the topic of abortion deserves our attention and should not be ignored.

The many dimensions of abortion

As befits a book on health care ethics, this chapter will focus on moral arguments regarding the practice of abortion. It is, however, important to acknowledge that there are many other kinds of questions about abortion and other ways to approach the issue. These different dimensions of abortion may inform moral conclusions in important ways.

Empirical dimensions

There are, for example, a variety of empirical questions about the practice of abortion. Among these are demographic questions, as, for example, how many abortions are performed, where they are performed, who performs them, on what patients, and at what stage of gestation.[1] There are also multiple and controversial questions about the medical and psychological consequences of both abortion and childbirth, as, for example, what risks these procedures pose to the physical and mental health of the women who undergo them.[2]

Religious dimensions

Many people adopt a position on the practice of abortion based on the doctrines of their faith community. Religious views on abortion vary widely, from strict condemnation to qualified acceptance of this practice, and there is lively theological debate both within and among religious traditions about abortion, both in general and in specific circumstances.[3]

---

[1] See, for example, Davis and Beasley (2009) for information about abortion in adolescents in the United States, and Shah and Ahman (2009) for a review of global data on safe and unsafe abortion.

[2] See, for example, Charles et al. (2008) for a review of research on long-term mental health outcomes of abortion, and Hammond (2009) for a review of second-trimester abortion methods.

[3] See Stephens et al. (2010) for a summary of the views on abortion of major world religions.

Members of different faith traditions may claim respect for their views on abortion as a matter of freedom of religion.[4]

Legal dimensions

Popular attitudes toward abortion are also strongly influenced by the laws governing this practice. As with religion, there is wide variation in national laws on abortion, from prohibition of virtually all abortions to acceptance of abortion on demand throughout pregnancy.[5] In the United States, the 1973 Supreme Court decision in *Roe* v. *Wade* recognized basic constitutional principles that remain in force.[6] In that decision, the Court ruled that a woman's choice of abortion is protected by a basic right of privacy, but that states may limit or prohibit abortion to protect the fetus after it has reached viability, unless an abortion is necessary to preserve the life or the health of the pregnant woman. This legal right to abortion in the United States is a negative right, that is, a right to freedom from interference by others in obtaining an abortion, not an entitlement to receive abortion services on demand, regardless of one's ability to pay for this service or to find a willing provider.

Within the broad framework of US federal law on abortion, there is significant variation among individual state abortion statutes. Some but not all states impose additional legal requirements on abortion procedures, including waiting periods of twenty-four to seventy-two hours, provision of specific types of information to patients seeking abortion, limits on which physicians and facilities may perform abortions, and parental consent for abortions on patients who are minors.[7]

Professional dimensions

Physicians and other health care providers recognize that questions regarding abortion may arise in their professional relationships with patients. They may, therefore, wonder whether there are specific professional responsibilities or privileges that should guide their response to

---

[4] See Wenz (1992).

[5] See Boland and Katzive (2008) for a recent overview of world abortion legislation.

[6] *Roe* v. *Wade* (1973).

[7] See Guttmacher Institute (2015) for a summary of state abortion laws.

questions about abortion. If professional principles do bear on these questions, how do these principles relate to any personal moral beliefs about abortion that particular professionals may hold? Laws and institutional policies in many jurisdictions recognize a professional right of conscientious refusal to participate in abortion procedures.[8] Chapter 10, "Professionalism," discusses the scope and limits of conscientious refusal as a protection for the moral integrity of health care professionals. The case analysis at the end of this chapter will also consider the relationship between professional responsibilities and personal beliefs.

The morality of abortion: examining two representative positions

For more than half a century, abortion has been both a highly significant and a deeply controversial topic in ethics and public policy. Not surprisingly, therefore, there is an abundance of nuanced positions and arguments on the morality of abortion in the bioethics literature, and I cannot do justice to the great variety of these positions and arguments in a single short chapter. I can, however, identify two general and opposed views on the morality of abortion. Most contributions to the literature can be grouped into one of these two general views. The "pro-choice" view asserts that women should be morally and legally permitted to choose abortion in most circumstances. The "pro-life" view asserts that abortion is, in most circumstances, an immoral life-ending practice that should be legally prohibited.

My intention in this section of the chapter is to examine two representative articles on abortion, one pro-choice and one pro-life. The articles I will examine are "The Wrong of Abortion," by Patrick Lee and Robert P. George, and "Abortion," by Mary Anne Warren.[9] I have chosen these two articles as examples of reasonably clear and well-developed philosophical positions on the morality of abortion. As their title suggests, Lee and George articulate and defend a pro-life position on abortion; Warren defends a pro-choice position. I will identify several areas of agreement between the two positions, followed by areas of disagreement. Then I will

---

[8] See, for example, Parr (2009) for a review of United States federal legislation establishing professional rights to conscientious refusal to participate in abortion procedures.

[9] Lee and George (2005); Warren (1998).

pose a concluding question for each position. My goal is not to propose and defend a solution to the abortion controversy (that is a much larger task!), but rather to show that there is at least some common ground on this issue, to focus on key claims that divide the two approaches, and thereby to help readers come to a clearer understanding of both their own position on abortion and of opposing positions.

Areas of agreement

Lee/George and Warren reach very similar conclusions about a number of important issues. Both articles recognize that becoming pregnant is not an entirely voluntary choice for many women and that unwanted pregnancy and procreation may have unwelcome consequences for women and others, including health risks, economic hardships, and social problems of overpopulation. Both articles also recognize, however, that these negative consequences do not provide sufficient reason to justify abortion, *if* the fetus[10] has the full complement of moral rights ascribed to human persons, including a robust right to life. One cannot, in other words, kill a person simply because that person's existence creates a hardship for oneself.[11]

Because they both acknowledge that claims based on the interests of women and others are not generally powerful enough by themselves to justify abortion, both Lee/George and Warren also agree that the key question in determining the morality of abortion is, "What is the moral status of the fetus?" If the fetus qualifies as a person with full moral rights, including a right to life, abortion will not be morally permissible, except perhaps in a few exceptional circumstances, such as a pregnancy that poses a clear threat to the life of the woman. If, in contrast, the fetus does not have a moral right to life, abortion may be justifiable in many or most circumstances in order to respect the self-determination or promote the welfare of the pregnant woman.

[10] Various medical terms are commonly used to refer to the developing human organism at different stages of gestation, including 'conceptus,' 'zygote,' 'embryo,' and 'fetus.' In this chapter, I will use 'fetus' as a generic term to refer to the developing organism at all of these stages, from conception until birth.

[11] In a widely anthologized article, however, Judith Jarvis Thomson (1971) offers a credible argument that abortion can be justified in certain specific circumstances, even if the fetus has a right to life. Thomson focuses on cases of pregnancy due to rape and cases in which continuing a pregnancy poses a serious threat to the life or health of the woman.

Other areas of agreement between the two articles have to do with the physical and developmental characteristics of the fetus. Both articles recognize that, after conception occurs, the fetus has all of the following characteristics:

1. It is a distinct organism, initially dependent on but not a part of the woman's body.
2. It is alive.
3. It is a human organism, and not a member of any other biological species.
4. It has a complete human genome that is inherited from its genetic parents but is distinct from the genome of either parent.
5. It has the potential, in the normal course of gestation, to develop into a viable human infant at birth, and thereafter into a mature human being.

Thus, these two articles agree on several key issues – both acknowledge that the moral status of the fetus is the central question in determining whether abortion is justifiable, and both affirm at least five significant empirical claims about the fetus. As we will see below, however, the articles differ sharply about the moral implications of those empirical claims.

Areas of disagreement

Despite the areas of agreement described above, Lee/George and Warren reach very different conclusions about the morality of abortion. Their different conclusions are based on strong disagreement about five key questions. For each of these, I will first state the question and then describe Lee/George and Warren's answers.

1. What kind of entity is a human person? These authors' answers to this basic metaphysical question are perhaps the most significant influence on their different conclusions about the morality of abortion. Lee and George offer a physicalist answer to this question; they assert that "we human persons are particular kinds of physical organisms."[12] They acknowledge that human organisms have nonphysical capacities, such as consciousness, but argue that what is essential to our existence is that we are living physical bodies with a complete and distinct human genome. For Lee and George, therefore, the terms 'human organism,' 'human being,' and

---

[12] Lee and George (2005): 15.

'person' refer to exactly the same set of entities, and they use these three terms interchangeably.

Warren, in contrast, proposes a basic distinction between human physical or "biological" life and human "biographical" life. She observes that the physical life of the early human fetus is very different from that of more developed human organisms:

> There are, to be sure, some striking physical resemblances: by the end of the first trimester a fetus has a face, hands, feet and many other physical features that are recognizably human. But in the mental and experiential realms there seem to be no resemblances at all. Prior to the latter part of the second trimester, and probably somewhat later ..., a fetus almost certainly lacks the neurophysiological structures and functions which are necessary for the occurrence of conscious experience, as well as for thought, self-awareness and other more complex mental capacities.[13]

Warren's implicit answer to the question "What kind of entity is a human person?" is, then, "a human organism capable of conscious experience."

Other commentators have proposed many other answers to this metaphysical question. A widely held religious view, for example, asserts that a human person is an entity with a spiritual soul.[14] Another view reserves the status of human person for self-conscious agents who can make moral decisions.[15] These different answers suggest different conclusions regarding the morality of abortion.

2. When does morally significant human life (or "human personhood") begin? For Lee and George, human life begins when a new and distinct human physical organism with a complete human genome appears, and that is at the moment of conception. Lee and George recognize that this initially one-celled organism will undergo many changes in the course of his or her lifetime, but observe that it will remain the same physical organism. They conclude, therefore, that morally significant human life begins at conception.

Warren acknowledges that a new and distinct human physical life begins at conception, but she asserts that morally significant human life, or human personhood, begins only later in the process of gestation, with the beginning of conscious experience, or of a "biographical life."

---

[13] Warren (1998): 130.

[14] See Disney and Poston (2010) for a description of this religious view.

[15] See Tooley (1972).

3. When does the fetus become conscious? This is an empirical question, but we do not have direct access to the conscious experience of others, and fetuses cannot report to us about their experience, so answers to this question depend on interpretation of information about fetal brain development and observed fetal behavior. Lee and George assert that, by eight or ten weeks of gestation, the fetus has "a complete brain" (but without complete synaptic connections) and feels pain, a type of conscious experience.[16] As noted above, Warren claims that the early fetus lacks the neurophysiological structures and functions necessary for consciousness and so "cannot suffer pain or be deprived of anything it wants."[17] This answer is especially significant for Warren, since she argues that the beginning of conscious experience marks a significant change in the moral status of the developing human organism.

4. What is the moral significance of fetal potential? One of the areas of agreement between the two articles noted above is the recognition that the fetus has, in the normal course of gestation, the potential to develop into a mature human person. The articles differ significantly, however, about the moral implications of fetal potential. Lee and George argue that the fact that fetal development is gradual, continuous, and inner-directed reinforces their view that morally significant human life begins at conception. They assert that the only difference in kind in procreation occurs at conception, and the subsequent changes in the fetus are only differences in degree along a continuum of development.

Warren, in contrast, discounts the moral significance of fetal potential. She observes that "we often treat a particular property as sufficient for the possession of a certain right, without treating the potential to develop that property as also sufficient." Warren offers the right to vote as an example of this moral difference between actual and potential properties. We grant 18-year-olds the right to vote; young children clearly have the potential to reach age 18, but this potential does not require that we grant them the right to vote before age 18. Similarly, she suggests, actual consciousness, or the immediate potential for consciousness of a sleeping person, justifies a different moral status than the potential of the fetus to become conscious at some future stage of its development. Warren also claims that fetal potential is not as robust as one might assume, citing

[16] Lee and George (2005): 14.   [17] Warren (1998): 130.

evidence from human reproductive biology that, even without induced abortion, most human zygotes do not survive to live birth.[18]

5. Is the developmental stage of the fetus morally significant? Lee and George answer this question in the negative, arguing that every fetus is a human person with a right to life from its beginning at conception and throughout its subsequent development. Warren responds that the stage of fetal development is morally significant, because fetuses achieve consciousness at a particular point in their development, and because abortion in the early stages of pregnancy is safer for the woman than in the later stages.

Two concluding questions

The above sections have described two specific positions on the morality of abortion. I have chosen these articles as representative examples of the pro-life and pro-choice views on abortion, but there are many variations on those two general views. By considering both areas of agreement and of disagreement between the two positions, readers may gain a better under-standing of both their own position on abortion and its supporting arguments, and the position and arguments of others. The two articles described each offer a sustained argument for their conclusions, but difficult moral questions can be posed about each position. I will conclude this section by raising two questions, one for each position.

For Lee and George. These authors base their rejection of abortion on the assertion that human persons are living physical organisms from the moment of their conception. Consciousness is not, therefore, an essential property for ascribing a right to life to human persons. Given this position, must Lee and George reject the use of neurologic (brain-oriented) criteria for the determination of human death? Neurologic criteria for death measure the irreversible loss of brain function in a human body whose physical life continues, with the assistance of "life support" technologies. Because the physical life of the body continues despite the loss of brain function, it appears that Lee and George would conclude that the human person is still alive. Every state in the United States and many nations around the world, however, accept neurologic criteria as a method for determining

[18] Warren (1998): 131.

the legal death of a human being.[19] This wide acceptance of neurologic criteria for death reflects a strong consensus belief that brain function, as the necessary substratum for mental activity, and not physical life alone, is essential for morally significant human life. If this is the case at the end of human life, shouldn't it also be the case at the beginning of human life?

For Warren. As we have seen, Warren would permit abortion, at least in the first half of pregnancy, on the grounds that during this period the fetus lacks the immediate capacity for conscious experience, which she views as an essential feature of a morally significant human life. Warren does not provide a detailed description of what kind of conscious experience she views as morally significant, but she affirms that fetuses in the latter stages of gestation have achieved "a rudimentary form of consciousness."[20] If this form of consciousness is sufficient to ascribe significant moral status, including a right to life, to human fetuses, is it also sufficient to ascribe a right to life to conscious *non-human* organisms? Though they apparently lack self-consciousness, many kinds of higher animals have conscious experience that is comparable to that of human fetuses. In this article, Warren does not examine the issue of the moral status of non-human animals that have conscious experience. Assuming that she would not ascribe the same moral status to all conscious organisms, both human and non-human, what reasons can she give for recognizing a higher moral status for conscious human life than for conscious non-human life?

I offer these questions as initial challenges to the positions defended by Lee and George and Warren, but those authors may well have ready responses. The moral arguments they provide, along with other moral arguments and empirical, religious, legal, and professional views, can all serve as guides for abortion decisions and practices. The case analysis below illustrates how various factors can influence decision-making about abortion in a specific situation.

Case analysis

Mrs. Farmer's pregnancy adds a major complication to her already difficult life situation. She clearly does not want another child. Is abortion a morally permissible option in this situation? Her emotional plea for assistance in

[19] Wijdicks (2002).   [20] Warren (1998): 132.

obtaining an abortion poses an obvious problem for Dr. Gold. May Dr. Gold perform an abortion for Mrs. Farmer under the rules of the health system that employs her? If so, should she perform the abortion?

Dr. Gold may seek information of several different kinds to guide her response to Mrs. Farmer. She may, for example, ask Mrs. Farmer if she has relatives or friends whom she can trust to support her with advice or material assistance. If so, they may be able to help Mrs. Farmer formulate and carry out a plan to obtain an abortion at a distant clinic. Dr. Gold may offer to meet with Mrs. Farmer and her husband to help her break the news to him and obtain his assistance. She may also inquire whether Mrs. Farmer is willing to explore options for protecting herself from the threat of domestic violence by her husband.

Dr. Gold may seek additional information about her health system's abortion policy. Does that policy, for example, include criteria for determining whether an abortion is necessary for therapeutic reasons? If so, are the criteria limited to physical risks of pregnancy, or do they include risks to the mental or emotional health of the woman? What are the likely consequences for Dr. Gold if she should decide to "stretch" or violate the policy to provide the requested abortion? She may seek the advice of obstetrician colleagues, or of her hospital's ethics committee, about the application of the institutional abortion policy to this case. Dr. Gold may, of course, also reflect on her own personal beliefs about the morality of abortion, and on her responsibilities to her patient in this situation.

Two obvious options suggest themselves: Dr. Gold may agree to perform the abortion, or she may refuse to do so. Let's consider each of these two options in turn.

Dr. Gold may choose to perform the abortion, for several reasons. She may believe that an abortion at this early stage of pregnancy is permissible because the fetus is not yet a person with a right to life. She may recognize that performing an abortion honors Mrs. Farmer's strong preference, and that it respects her interest in control over her body and over her life prospects. She may decide that abortion is the safest and most beneficial course of action for Mrs. Farmer and her four young children, in view of their limited means and her husband's violent behavior in the past. Finally, Dr. Gold may also ascertain that abortion in this case would be permitted under her health system's policy, or that, despite the policy, her performance of this procedure will not be questioned.

Dr. Gold may refuse to perform the abortion, for several other reasons. If Dr. Gold believes that abortion in this circumstance is an unjustified killing of a human person, she may decide that she cannot participate in this immoral course of action. She may also conclude that an abortion in this situation would violate health system policy and so subject her to major institutional sanctions. Dr. Gold may also recognize that, although she cannot in good conscience honor Mrs. Farmer's request, her patient may obtain an abortion elsewhere, although probably at increased cost and possibly at increased risk.

Are any other, less obvious responses available to Dr. Gold in this situation? Suppose, for example, that Dr. Gold concludes that an abortion is morally permissible in this circumstance, or that Mrs. Farmer's preference should be honored, but is barred by institutional policy from providing this service herself. We noted above that Dr. Gold may counsel her patient about possible sources of support and assistance from family members or friends. Mrs. Farmer may well respond that she is isolated from others in this rural area and so cannot count on anyone else's assistance. Dr. Gold might take additional time to seek out other sources of support, perhaps charitable institutions or churches that would be sympathetic to Mrs. Farmer's plight. In a rural and conservative setting, however, such institutions may not exist. Rather than continuing her likely unsuccessful efforts to find sources of support for Mrs. Farmer, Dr. Gold might offer her own personal financial support for Mrs. Farmer's transportation, or child care, or treatment needs. Would such an offer be a praiseworthy way for Dr. Gold to demonstrate her concern for Mrs. Farmer, or an impermissible violation of a professional boundary?

14 Maternal-fetal conflict

Case example

Thirty-seven-year-old Mrs. Grant is twenty-four weeks pregnant. She has been visiting her obstetrician, Dr. Perez, regularly for prenatal care. Her routine sixteen-week fetal ultrasound study revealed fetal anomalies that are consistent with trisomy 21, also known as Down syndrome. At that time, Mr. and Mrs. Grant refused amniocentesis (removal of fluid from the amniotic sac surrounding the fetus, for genetic testing). This testing would have confirmed or ruled out the suspected trisomy 21, but the Grants decided against it because they did not want to terminate the pregnancy, explaining that they would "go along with God's plan." Children with trisomy 21 have cognitive impairments of varying degrees, and they are at increased risk for cardiac anomalies and other physical impairments.

In her eighteenth week of pregnancy, Mrs. Grant developed polyhydramnios (excess accumulation of amniotic fluid), possibly as a result of the fetus's genetic condition or of Mrs. Grant's diabetes. After monitoring this condition for several weeks, Dr. Perez prescribed indomethacin, an oral medication that can decrease amniotic fluid volume. At her 24-week prenatal visit today, however, her amniotic fluid index (an ultrasonographic measure of amniotic fluid volume) was 36, well above the normal range of 10–22 for this gestational age. She is experiencing multiple symptoms, including shortness of breath when she is lying down, difficulty urinating, swelling of her legs and vulva, and abdominal pain. At her visit one week ago, Dr. Perez performed an amniocentesis to drain excess amniotic fluid, but that resulted in only a slight, temporary improvement in Mrs. Grant's symptoms. Dr. Perez recommends another amniocentesis to drain amniotic fluid, but Mr. and Mrs. Grant respond with a request that Dr. Perez induce labor now. They state that they understand that delivery at this stage of pregnancy will result in a very premature infant who may not survive, but they do not want to prolong Mrs. Grant's considerable pain and suffering or put her health at greater risk as a result of her condition. How should Dr. Perez respond?

What's special about health care for pregnant women?

Health care for pregnant women is distinctive in at least one morally significant way. With the rare exception of treatment for conjoined twins, it is the only type of health care that has a direct effect on two human beings, the pregnant woman and the fetus she carries. Although the fetus is a distinct organism with its own genome, it is physiologically dependent on the pregnant woman, and so its health, growth, and development are affected by her state of health, her health-related behaviors, including nutrition, use of tobacco, alcohol, and drugs, and her use of prenatal health care. With greater appreciation of the influence of these factors on children's health, and increased ability to monitor and treat the fetus in utero, contributors to the medical and bioethics literature in the 1980s began to call attention to the potential for "maternal-fetal conflict" during pregnancy, that is, circumstances in which the interests or desires of the pregnant woman appear to be contrary to the interests of her fetus.[1]

Some commentators object to use of the term 'conflict' in describing the maternal-fetal relationship.[2] They observe that the interests of pregnant women and their fetuses are nearly always aligned; prenatal care, for example, is beneficial for both. They also point out that pregnant women typically adopt healthy behaviors, such as eating nutritious food and getting plenty of rest, because of their strong interest in protecting and promoting the health of their fetuses. Certainly very many if not most women make deliberate decisions and act accordingly during pregnancy to promote both their own health and the health of their fetuses. In some situations, however, the choices and actions of pregnant women endanger the health or the life of their fetuses. In these latter situations, the woman's preferences and the interests of her fetus may indeed be in conflict. These situations are the subject of this chapter.

Are the moral issues posed by maternal-fetal conflict significantly different from those posed by the practice of abortion? A woman who chooses abortion generally does so because she judges that continuing a pregnancy, and thereby promoting the fetus's presumed interest in survival, is contrary to her own interests. This is clearly one type of maternal-fetal conflict, and it is the focus of Chapter 13. If the desired resolution of

[1] See, for example, Bowes and Selgestad (1981), Annas (1982), and Strong (1987).
[2] See, for example, Harris (2000) and Flagler et al. (1997).

a conflict between a pregnant woman and her fetus is abortion, moral analysis of that conflict can focus on whether abortion is permissible in that situation. But what if a woman continues her pregnancy, perhaps because she wants to bear and raise the child, or because she cannot secure the services of an abortion provider, or because the time period during which abortion is legally permitted has expired? Women who find themselves in these situations may make choices or engage in behaviors that endanger the health of their fetuses in the present, and of their children who will be born in the near future. If one concludes that both the fetus and the child after birth have the same strong right to life, that conclusion may provide sufficient reason both to prohibit most abortions and to constrain most actions of pregnant women that endanger their fetuses. If, however, the moral status of the fetus, during at least some part of its development, is judged to be significantly different from that of the newborn child, then the moral question of whether women's actions may be constrained to protect children who will be born is also different from the questions of whether and when abortion is permissible. Stated another way, these situations pose the following question: When, if ever, is *present* intervention justified to protect a being who, even if it does not (yet) have full human moral status, in all probability *will* have that status in the near future? The remainder of this chapter will focus on situations in which abortion is not a desired or an available option, and so the fetus will very probably survive to delivery. To make this focus clear, in what follows I will refer to the fetus who will, with high probability, become a live-born infant as "the future child."

Types of maternal-fetal conflict

Situations in which the interests of pregnant women and their future children come into conflict can be grouped into two broad categories. The first of these categories involves medical treatment decisions. Women may choose medical treatments that pose a risk of harm to their future children, or they may refuse treatments recommended in order to prevent harm to their future children. The second category involves pregnant women's activities that may cause harm to their future children. Activities in this second category include the use of tobacco, alcohol, and recreational drugs, and employment that may expose women and their future children to teratogenic workplace chemicals (that is, chemicals that cause birth defects).

Medical treatment decisions

A wide variety of medical treatment choices may have an effect on the health of future children. The most commonly discussed of these choices in the bioethics literature is a woman's *refusal* of treatments recommended to her either primarily or in part to benefit or to prevent harm to her future child. Examples include refusal of Cesarean section surgery for signs of fetal distress during delivery, refusal of intrauterine blood transfusions for severe fetal anemia that occurs when maternal antibodies destroy fetal blood cells, and refusal of intrauterine fetal surgery to correct severe congenital anomalies.[3] Pregnant women may also *choose* medical treatments that pose a risk of harm to their future children. A pregnant woman newly diagnosed with a severe form of cancer, for example, may decide to begin a course of chemotherapy despite its potential for injury to her future child, now in its thirtieth week of gestation. Finally, pregnant women *may not adhere* to medical treatment instructions provided to them, often both for their own health and for the health of their future children. For example, a woman with diabetes may not follow a prescribed diet or take insulin during her pregnancy, thereby threatening her own health and that of her future child.

Perhaps the most well-known and widely cited example of a medical intervention ordered for the benefit of a future child is the 1987 case of Mrs. Angela Carder.[4] Mrs. Carder was a 27-year-old woman with a long history of cancer who was pregnant with her first child. At twenty-six weeks gestation, she was admitted to the George Washington University Hospital with recurrence of cancer, and her medical condition rapidly worsened. Physicians informed her that she was near death, but that it might be possible to "intervene" to save her child. An emergency hearing was convened at the hospital, and a federal judge heard medical testimony that the fetus's chances of survival, if delivered immediately by Cesarean section, were perhaps 50–60 percent. Because Mrs. Carder was intubated and sedated, her own treatment choices were unclear. She had previously

---

[3] See, for example, Kolder et al. (1987) and Vrecenak and Flake (2013).

[4] *In re A.C.* (1990).

said that she wanted the baby, but later appeared to refuse Cesarean surgery. Citing uncertainty about the patient's wishes, the judge determined that the fetus's interests in survival outweighed Mrs. Carder's interests in bodily integrity and in avoiding a slightly hastened death, and he therefore ordered that the surgery be performed. The baby was delivered alive, but died within two and a half hours, and Mrs. Carder died two days later. An appellate decision three years later overturned the initial decision, ruling that the trial judge erred in not ascertaining whether Mrs. Carder had the capacity to make a decision about surgery. If she did have capacity, the appellate court asserted, her decision should prevail over any conflicting claims made on behalf of the future child.

Health-related behaviors

In addition to undergoing or refusing medical treatments, pregnant women may engage in a variety of other activities that adversely affect the health of their future children. Most notable among these activities are women's use of tobacco, alcohol, and other addictive drugs during pregnancy. Use of these substances during pregnancy can cause premature delivery, low birth weight, birth defects, and mental disabilities.[5] Because of their adverse health consequences for both the woman and her future child, health care professionals routinely advise women to abstain from use of these substances during pregnancy, but some do not follow this advice.

Women who are or may become pregnant may also engage in work or recreational activities that expose their future children to health risks. To prevent harm to future children of their employees, and potential liability for causing such harm, for example, some US companies in the 1980s adopted "fetal protection policies" that excluded fertile women from jobs involving exposure to toxic chemicals or to radiation. In its 1991 decision in *Automobile Workers* v. *Grant Controls, Inc.*, however, the US Supreme Court ruled that a company policy excluding women from jobs manufacturing lead batteries was an instance of sex discrimination that violated women's civil rights.[6] This ruling allows women to choose whether or not to accept employment that poses health risks to themselves and to their future children.

---

[5] See, for example, Wendell (2013).

[6] *Automobile Workers* v. *Grant Controls, Inc.* (1991).

Responses to conflict situations

When a health care professional encounters a situation in which the interests of a pregnant woman and of her future child appear to be opposed,
what alternative courses of action should he or she consider? What, if any,
courses of action should public officials or other third parties consider in
response to maternal-fetal conflict situations? Commentators have proposed and defended multiple options in these situations, including, in
rough order from less to more coercive actions:

1. Educating women about health-related choices and their consequences
2. Negotiating a mutually acceptable plan for self- and fetal care
3. Requiring public warnings about risky behaviors during pregnancy
4. Conscientiously refusing to provide health services that may harm the
   future child
5. Committing pregnant women involuntarily to prevent them from acting
   in ways that threaten the health of their future children
6. Forcing women to undergo treatment to prevent harm to their future
   children
7. Prosecuting women for engaging in prohibited behaviors during pregnancy that may have harmed their children

Let's review each of these responses in turn.

Education

The most benign and uncontroversial action health care professionals can
take in apparent maternal-fetal conflict situations is to help the woman to
understand the likely consequences of her medical and lifestyle choices for
her own health and the health of her future child. This education is, in fact,
a standard feature of prenatal care; it enables women to make informed
choices about their medical treatment and their health-related behaviors.
Armed with this information, most women will choose to accept treatment
for the benefit of their future children and to refrain from actions that may
harm those children, thus avoiding any conflict between their own interests
and those of their future children.

Education alone, however, will not persuade all pregnant women to
accept recommended treatments or alter their behavior for the sake of

their future children. Some women may not understand the information, despite professionals' best efforts to convey it, and others may not believe that the information is accurate. Still other women may understand and believe the information, but decide to continue activities they find rewarding, such as smoking or drinking. Some women may desire to alter risky behaviors, such as drug use, but due to addiction may be unable to conform their actions to this desire.

Negotiation

The above description of education by health care professionals suggests a one-way transmission of information from caregivers to their patients. An effective therapeutic relationship, however, requires a dialogue, in which each party shares information with the other, asks questions, and responds to those questions. Thus, professionals should encourage pregnant women to communicate their own preferences, experiences, hopes, and fears, both for themselves and for their future children. Based on this shared information, the parties can evaluate health care options and seek agreement on a prenatal care plan. In this process, each party may offer reasons for a particular course of action, in an effort to persuade the other of its importance. A woman might, for example, emphasize the importance to her of employment that exposes her and her future child to workplace toxins, and her physician may inquire whether there are additional precautions that she can take to minimize those exposures during her pregnancy. The negotiated plan might then be for the woman to take protective measures and for the physician to monitor blood levels of toxic chemicals regularly to determine whether those protective measures are effective.

Like patient education, dialogue and negotiation about treatment options are routine, expected, and morally significant activities within professional–patient relationships. Chervenak and McCullough, for example, recommend education, negotiation, and respectful persuasion as approaches that can prevent most disagreements between pregnant women and their physicians.[7] There is, however, no guarantee that these approaches will result in implementation of a mutually agreeable prenatal

[7] Chervenak and McCullough (1990).

care plan. Despite their best efforts at persuasion and negotiation, the parties may simply not be able to agree on a plan, or they may not be able to carry out the agreed-on plan. If negotiation is unsuccessful, what other options should be considered?

Public warnings

Legislators in many jurisdictions around the world have enacted statutes requiring posting of public warnings regarding the harmful effects on future children of in utero exposure to commonly used substances, especially tobacco and alcohol. These warnings take several forms, including messages on product containers, messages posted wherever products are bought and sold, and public service announcements on television and radio.[8] The obvious public health purpose of these warnings is to inform pregnant women, and others, of the potential adverse effects of these substances on future children and to encourage women to abstain from or to curtail the use of these substances during pregnancy. Other mandatory warning labels describe the harmful effects of these substances on those who use them.

Mandatory public health warnings like these have distinct advantages and disadvantages. Because they can be displayed on the products themselves and wherever the products are sold, they have the potential to reach virtually the entire population engaging in risky behaviors, including women in the earliest days of pregnancy and those who do not seek prenatal care. Studies suggest that these health warnings can influence behavior, especially when they are prominently displayed and contain graphic images.[9] Because they are necessarily very brief, however, warning notices can provide only very limited information, and so they are susceptible to misinterpretation. Because they are so widely distributed and are difficult to avoid, warnings override the preferences of those who do not want to receive this information. With repeated exposure, however, warnings may "fade into the background" and lose most of their effectiveness in changing behavior.

---

[8] See, for example, Agostinelli and Grube (2002), Hammond et al. (2007), and Thomas et al. (2014).

[9] Hammond et al. (2007).

Conscientious refusal

As noted above, pregnant women may request medical treatments that pose a recognized risk of harm to their future children. A physician may judge that the requested treatment will be highly beneficial for the woman, as, for example, a course of chemotherapy likely to be effective for a newly diagnosed aggressive cancer, and so agree to provide that treatment despite its potential to injure the future child. In another circumstance, however, the physician may conclude that the expected benefits for the woman of the requested treatment are not sufficient to justify the expected harms of that treatment to the future child. In the latter circumstance, the physician may decide that he or she must conscientiously refuse to provide the requested treatment. Chapter 10, "Professionalism," includes additional discussion of the scope and limits of professional rights to conscientious refusal to provide medical services.

One prominent example of a medical treatment denied to pregnant women is the anti-acne medication isotretinoin (also known by its trade name Accutane®).[10] Isotretinoin is a highly effective prescription medication for severe acne that has not responded to topical or other oral medications. It is, however, also a potent teratogen that poses a very high risk of severe birth defects, including skull and facial deformities and central nervous system, cardiovascular, and glandular abnormalities. To minimize fetal exposure to isotretinoin, the manufacturer makes the drug available only to physicians and patients who agree to adhere to a special distribution and monitoring program that includes patient registration, mandatory counseling, monthly pregnancy testing, and patient use of two forms of contraception. In this special case, physicians have no choice but to refuse requests for this drug by women who are pregnant or who are unwilling to comply with the required drug distribution program. In addition to isotretinoin, the US Food and Drug Administration has classified dozens of other drugs as Category X, contraindicated for use during pregnancy. Relying on that FDA assessment, physicians may choose to deny requests for these drugs by their patients who are pregnant. Refusal to provide Category X medications to pregnant women is, therefore, as much a result of manufacturer and FDA guidelines as it is of individual physician decisions.

---

[10] See Moskop et al. (1997) for an ethical and legal analysis of this issue.

Involuntary commitment

Most jurisdictions permit involuntary commitment and treatment of patients who pose a danger to themselves or to other persons as a result of mental illness or of substance abuse. Some commentators have proposed, and some jurisdictions have adopted, expansion of involuntary commitment to include pregnant women whose behaviors, especially the use of alcohol and illegal drugs, threaten the health of their future children. In Wisconsin, for example, legislation enacted in 1998 revised the state's child abuse statute to include protection of "unborn children," as well as children after birth.[11] This legislation expands the definition of abuse to include "serious physical harm inflicted on the unborn child, and the risk of serious physical harm to the child when born, caused by the habitual lack of self-control of the expectant mother of the unborn child in the use of alcoholic beverages, controlled substances, or controlled substance analogs, exhibited to a severe degree."[12] The legislation directs health care professionals to report suspicion of harm to unborn children to child protective services or law enforcement officials. In response to such reports, public officials are authorized to investigate and to take pregnant women into temporary custody. At a subsequent hearing, a judge may order involuntary commitment and treatment, in a private home, treatment facility, or hospital, for as long as is necessary to protect the unborn child.

It is worth noting that this approach to maternal-fetal conflict situations requires the cooperation of multiple health care professionals and public officials. Health care professionals must report their suspicion that a pregnant woman is abusing her future child and must supervise and provide treatment for women who are committed to hospitals or treatment facilities. Public officials must investigate reports of abuse of unborn children and take women into temporary custody, and judges must issue orders involuntarily committing women to prevent harm to their future children. De Ville and Kopelman describe several significant problems confronting the Wisconsin approach.[13] They point out that use of the terms 'unborn child' and 'expectant mother' rather than 'fetus' and

---

[11] De Ville and Kopelman (1999).   [12] Wis. Stat. § 48.02(1)(am) (1998).
[13] De Ville and Kopelman (1999).

'pregnant woman' confuses important legal and moral distinctions between fetuses that will not be brought to delivery, fetuses that will become children, and children after birth. They note that broadening the scope of child abuse to include future children enables the state to abrogate a fundamental personal right of freedom of movement. Finally, they note that the available evidence suggests that the harm to future children caused by these maternal behaviors varies dramatically from individual to individual. Resort to these protective measures, therefore, is likely to be both arbitrary and inconsistent.

Forced treatment

If medical treatment of a pregnant woman and her fetus is deemed necessary for the survival or health of a future child, and the woman refuses that treatment, one possible response is to override the woman's refusal and administer the treatment by force. Chapter 8, "Informed consent to treatment," defends informed consent and refusal of treatment as basic rights of patients, but it also describes several widely recognized exceptions to the duty to obtain a patient's informed consent to treatment. Should treatments recommended for the health of a future child be added to the list of recognized exceptions to informed consent?

In a 1986 US national survey of obstetrician directors of maternal-fetal medicine training programs, Kolder et al. identified twenty-one petitions for court orders for involuntary treatment of pregnant women and their fetuses submitted over the previous five years.[14] Court orders were issued, usually in a matter of hours, for eighteen of these petitions, including fourteen Cesarean sections, two hospital detentions for diabetes treatment, and two intrauterine transfusions. In their discussion of these findings, Kolder et al. acknowledge the difficulty of these situations for obstetricians and their patients, but they question the wisdom of forced invasion of women's bodies to promote the interests of their future children. The appellate court decision in the Angela Carder case described above reached a similar conclusion, holding that treatment refusal of a woman with decision-making capacity should not be overridden for the sake of her future child.

[14] Kolder et al. (1987).

Criminal prosecution

In addition to authorizing interventions to protect children from abuse and neglect, state laws typically define abuse and neglect as criminal offenses, subject to prosecution and punishment. As described above, Wisconsin and other states have expanded their child abuse statutes to permit involuntary commitment for the purpose of controlling women's behaviors that pose a risk of harm to their future or "unborn" children. Another state, South Carolina, pioneered the use of criminal child abuse sanctions against women who use illegal drugs during pregnancy. In 1989, the Medical University of South Carolina (MUSC) in Charleston, South Carolina, in cooperation with the Charleston police and prosecutor's office, implemented an "Interagency Policy on Management of Substance Abuse during Pregnancy."[15] Under this policy, pregnant women presenting for treatment at the MUSC obstetrics clinic were screened for illegal drugs. Women who tested positive were informed that they must obtain substance abuse treatment and prenatal care or face arrest and prosecution, and more than forty women who did not comply were arrested on drug possession or distribution charges.[16] This policy was later suspended, but in 1997, the South Carolina Supreme Court upheld a state child abuse and neglect statute provision that recognizes a viable fetus as a person under the law.[17] This decision authorizes the prosecution of pregnant women for actions that are likely to "endanger the life, health, or comfort" of their viable fetuses. The US Supreme Court in 1998 refused to hear an appeal of this decision, thus allowing it to stand. More recently, two other states have endorsed criminal prosecution of pregnant women for drug use. In 2013, the Alabama Supreme Court upheld the child endangerment convictions of two women for drug use during pregnancy, and in 2014, Tennessee enacted a statute authorizing prosecution, for assault, of women who use narcotics illegally during pregnancy.[18]

Unlike South Carolina, Alabama, and Tennessee, most US appellate courts have rejected the application to pregnant women of criminal laws designed to protect children. Nevertheless, Paltrow and Flavin documented 413 US cases between 1973 and 2005 in which pregnant women were deprived of physical liberty through arrest, incarceration, involuntary

[15] Jos et al. (1995).   [16] Jos et al. (2003).   [17] *Whitner* v. *State* (1997).
[18] See *Ankrom* v. *State of Alabama* (2013) and Tennessee Public Chapter No. 820.

detention, or forced treatment.[19] In 354 of these cases, or 86 percent, the women were charged with at least one crime, and in 295 cases, that crime was a felony. Specific criminal charges included child abuse, child endangerment, drug delivery to a minor, feticide, and homicide. Charles Condon, former Attorney General of South Carolina, defended the Charleston Interagency Policy as a "tough" but effective measure to deter irresponsible, drug-addicted pregnant women from behaviors that injure their future children.[20] Other prosecutors and judges appeal to state abortion and feticide statutes that give independent legal status to fetuses as grounds for criminal charges against pregnant women whose actions endanger the health of their future children.[21]

The case for coercive interventions

The responses to maternal-fetal conflict situations described in the preceding section range from generally accepted strategies for conflict resolution to highly controversial coercive measures. If patient education and negotiation between a pregnant woman and her caregivers can achieve a mutually agreeable care plan that reasonably accommodates the interests of both the pregnant woman and her future child, that is clearly a morally desirable outcome. Because these approaches do not always result in agreement on a care plan for the woman and her future child, other proposed measures would constrain the choices or actions of the pregnant woman in order to promote the health interests of her future child. When, if ever, are these coercive measures morally justified? This section will propose and defend an argument *for* the use of coercive interventions in conflict situations, and the following section will make a case *against* resort to coercive interventions.

Consider the following argument:

1. Women's behaviors and treatment choices during pregnancy can cause severe injuries to their children (and those injuries can impose high costs on society).
2. Coercive measures can be effective and are sometimes necessary to prevent severe injuries to children inflicted during pregnancy.

---

[19] Paltrow and Flavin (2013).   [20] Condon (1995).   [21] Paltrow and Flavin (2013).

3. Some injuries to children that can be prevented by coercive measures during pregnancy are much more harmful to those children than the harm inflicted on women by those coercive measures.

4. Health care professionals and society may intervene on behalf of children, when such interventions are necessary to prevent injuries that would have caused much greater harm to children than the harm they inflict on women.

5. Therefore, health care professionals and society may impose coercive measures on pregnant women, when those measures are necessary to prevent injuries that would have caused much greater harm to children than the harm they inflict on women.

What evidence can be offered to support this argument for coercive measures? The first premise makes an empirical claim about the effects on children of women's choices and actions during pregnancy. Support for this claim can be found in multiple studies that correlate various birth defects and disabilities with specific behaviors and treatment choices made by pregnant women. Maternal alcohol consumption during pregnancy, for example, can have a variety of adverse physical and cognitive effects on children, including fetal alcohol syndrome, a condition that is marked by growth restriction, facial deformities, and developmental disability.[22] In another situation, obstetricians caring for a woman in active labor may diagnose a condition in which vaginal delivery poses a grave risk of severe injury to the child, but the woman refuses a Cesarean section.

This premise also contains a parenthetical reference to the costs society will incur in subsidizing health care and other services required for children born with preventable disabilities. The rest of the argument is based on an appeal only to the value of preventing injury to children, but it could be expanded to include the value of preventing these significant costs to society.

The second premise asserts that coercive measures can be effective and are sometimes necessary to prevent harms to children. This is also an empirical premise. It has probably not been the subject of formal research, but nevertheless seems at least plausible. If, for example, a pregnant woman who is a heavy drinker is committed to a treatment facility in which she is under the close supervision of facility staff, she

---

[22] Bailey and Sokol (2008).

will probably be unable to continue drinking, thus protecting the child she will bear from injuries caused by alcohol exposure during that time period. Moreover, if this woman either refuses or is simply unable to abstain from alcohol, it may be necessary to commit her involuntarily to a controlled environment in order to change her drinking behavior. Similarly, obstetricians presumably can prevent foreseeable fetal injury during vaginal delivery by means of a forced Cesarean section, and this forced treatment may be necessary to achieve that goal if the woman persists in refusing this surgery.

The third premise compares the effects of coercive interventions on the child and on the pregnant woman; it asserts that the harms to children resulting from nonintervention are, in some cases, much greater than the harms to women of intervention. This premise assumes that we can identify the adverse effects on women and their children of nonintervention and of intervention and can determine the relative significance or magnitude of those effects. There is no single yardstick for measuring or comparing the significance of different consequences of an action, however, and opinions about what consequences are more harmful than others are sure to differ. The premise does not assert that a comparative judgment can be made in all cases, but only that we can, in some cases, determine that the harms to children of one course of action are much greater than the harms to women of the contrary course of action. Thus, we may conclude that the likely harms to a child of prenatal exposure to isotretinoin, namely, permanent and severe mental and physical disabilities, are much greater than the harms to a woman of denying her access to this effective treatment for her severe acne condition.

The fourth premise asserts that health care professionals and society may intervene in maternal-fetal conflict situations, when a course of action will prevent harms to children that are much greater than the harms they inflict on pregnant women. This premise can appeal to the moral value of protecting the interests of children and to the recognized roles of health care professionals as advocates for their pediatric patients and of society as an advocate for its members who are children. It presupposes that protection of children's interests is justifiable in these situations despite the fact it must occur before the children are born. In other words, this premise depends on the claim that actions to prevent harm to a person are permissible whenever they are necessary, including during the period before the person exists.[23] It also presupposes that protection of these interests of children is justifiable despite the fact that intervention also adversely affects the interests of the pregnant women. One might defend this presupposition by arguing that pregnant women assume moral obligations to the children they will bear, and so they should subordinate their own interests to the interests of those children.[24] Notice, however, that this premise restricts intervention by professionals and society to just those situations in which the adverse consequences for the child are much more severe than the consequences for the pregnant woman.

If these premises are true, I believe that the conclusion follows, namely, health care professionals may use coercive measures in some cases during pregnancy to prevent serious harm to children. Arguments like this one have presumably persuaded scholars, legislators, judges, and health care professionals to defend, authorize, and pursue these interventions in a number of the maternal-fetal conflict situations described in this chapter. But, are the premises of this argument true? The next section will review challenges to coercive intervention.

The case against coercive interventions

Multiple medical, legal, and ethics commentators have argued that involuntary commitment, forced medical treatment, and criminal sanctions should not be imposed on pregnant women for the sake of their future children.[25] A 2005 opinion of the Committee on Ethics of the American College of Obstetricians and Gynecologists (ACOG), entitled "Maternal Decision Making, Ethics, and the Law," provides a concise summary of six leading criticisms of coercive and punitive measures against pregnant women, namely:

1. These measures violate basic rights to informed refusal of treatment and to bodily integrity.
2. These measures fail to recognize significant limitations in physicians' ability to predict obstetric outcomes.

---

[23] See Murray (1987) for a defense of this claim.

[24] See Chervenak and McCullough (1985).

[25] See, for example, Annas (1982), Flagler et al. (1997), Harris (2000), Kolder et al. (1987), Nelson and Milliken (1988), and Paltrow and Flavin (2013).

3. These measures mistakenly view as moral failings actions that are the result of addictive or mental illness.

4. These measures will produce more harm than good for women and children, by discouraging women from seeking prenatal care.

5. These measures promote discrimination against poor and minority women.

6. These measures provide a rationale for much broader violations of women's privacy and freedom.[26]

Let's consider each of these criticisms in more detail. The first criticism emphasizes that coercive measures abrogate fundamental rights to refuse medical treatment and to protect one's body against unwanted invasion. Failure to respect these rights can cause grave harm to pregnant women. In defense of this claim, the ACOG Committee points out that US law does not permit involuntary treatment of one person for the benefit of a second person, as, for example, removal of organs or tissues without the consent of the donor for transplantation into another person, even if that other person needs the organ or tissue to survive. The appellate court in the Carder case described above also affirmed that pregnant women may not be subjected to involuntary treatment for the benefit of their future children. There are, however, recognized legal limits on pregnant women's rights to *receive* treatments that threaten the health of their future children, including limits on abortion after fetal viability and limits on access to teratogenic medications like isotretinoin.

The second criticism asserts that physicians' predictions of harm to future children during pregnancy are too uncertain to justify coercive measures against pregnant women. Kolder et al., for example, cite six published cases in which women had vaginal deliveries without injury to their children after court orders for Cesarean section were sought. Despite media reports of severely disabled "crack babies," a systematic review of published studies by Frank et al. found no consistent correlation between prenatal cocaine exposure and childhood growth retardation, developmental disability, language impairment, or any other adverse outcome.[27] Alcohol use during pregnancy is believed to be the most common cause of disability in children, but even in this instance the likelihood of injury from

---

[26] Committee on Ethics, American College of Obstetricians and Gynecologists (2005).

[27] Frank et al. (2001).

prenatal alcohol exposure is highly variable and may depend on additional factors, including diet and genetic susceptibility.[28] Uncertainty in the prediction of adverse outcomes for children undermines the argument that involuntary detention or treatment of pregnant women in any given situation is necessary to prevent those outcomes.

The third criticism challenges claims that punitive actions are justified either to deter irresponsible behavior by pregnant women or to punish women who act irresponsibly. These claims fail to recognize that pregnant women's behaviors are often not the result of free choice, but are rather compelled by their addictive or mental illness, or by social and familial constraints under which they live. The appropriate response to these conditions is medical attention or social support, not blame and punishment. If, however, women's behaviors in these situations are truly out of their control and dangerous to themselves or their future children, that would presumably strengthen the case for involuntary commitment and treatment, since these women lack autonomy, and they or their children need protection from the harmful consequences of their behavior.

The fourth criticism argues that coercive measures intended to prevent harm to children at risk for prenatal injury may be counterproductive. If pregnant women learn that getting prenatal care may subject them to coercion or criminal prosecution, they may decide not to seek prenatal care in order to protect themselves. Absence of prenatal care or medical assistance in childbirth, however, may result in more serious adverse health outcomes for children than receiving regular prenatal and delivery care, even if pregnant women do not adhere to all recommendations for treatment and health-related practices.

The fifth criticism cites evidence that coercive and punitive measures are applied in a discriminatory way that targets poor and minority women. In the Kolder study of court orders for involuntary treatment, for example, seventeen of the twenty-one women for whom court orders were sought were African-American, Asian, or Hispanic.[29] Of the more than forty women arrested under the Charleston Interagency Policy described above, all except one were African-American.[30] These findings raise the questions about whether coercive strategies can be implemented in ways that do not

---

[28] Pruett et al. (2013).   [29] Kolder et al. (1987).   [30] Jos et al. (2003).

impose additional burdens on women who are already among the most disadvantaged and vulnerable members of society.

The final criticism asserts that there is no bright line separating behaviors that do justify coercive control measures from those that do not. If forced treatment or detention to control pregnant women's use of alcohol, tobacco, or drugs is justified, a variety of other choices made by pregnant women might also be mandated, including choices about diet, physical activity, and control of chronic illnesses. Because the burdens of these coercive measures would fall only on women, they may constitute an unjust form of gender discrimination.

Based on its review of these six criticisms, the ACOG Committee on Ethics makes several recommendations, including the following:

- Pregnant women's autonomous decisions should be respected ... In the absence of extraordinary circumstances, circumstances that, in fact, the Committee on Ethics cannot currently imagine, judicial authority should not be used to implement treatment regimens aimed at protecting the fetus, for such actions violate the pregnant woman's autonomy.
- Pregnant women should not be punished for adverse perinatal outcomes.[31]

The Committee is thus not persuaded that coercive and punitive measures against pregnant women are either necessary or effective ways to prevent harm to children; rather, it emphasizes the seriousness of the adverse effects of these measures on women.

Case analysis

This situation confronts Dr. Perez with a difficult decision. Should he honor Mrs. Grant's request for induction of labor in order to relieve her distressing symptoms? Or, should he refuse that request, citing the danger to the child of severe complications associated with extreme prematurity?

Several kinds of information are obviously relevant to Dr. Perez's decision. He will, for example, want to assess the seriousness of Mrs. Grant's polyhydramnios and review options for treatment. Her amniotic fluid index of 36, and her reports of multiple symptoms, including shortness

---

[31] Committee on Ethics, American College of Obstetricians and Gynecologists (2005).

of breath, pain, and swelling, indicate a severe form of this condition.[32] Standard therapies, including oral medication and amniocentesis, have not resulted in significant improvement in her condition. He will also want to assess the likely consequences for the child of delivery at 24 weeks gestational age. If he consults the literature, he will find that survival rates for all infants born at twenty-four weeks gestation are in the 50–60 percent range, and 90 percent of the survivors have illness or injuries, including severe lung, circulatory, gastrointestinal, and eye conditions.[33] He will also find that premature infants with Down syndrome are at higher risk for death and for non-fatal complications than premature infants without this genetic condition.[34] The Grants have said that they know their infant may not survive, but they may not know that he or she has a greater than 50 percent risk of early death if delivered at this time, and they may also not know that, if delivered at twenty-four weeks, their infant is very likely to have multiple severe complications of prematurity.

Dr. Perez will want to share all of this information with Mr. and Mrs. Grant and inform them that delaying delivery for even a few weeks will significantly increase their child's probability of survival and of avoiding major complications. He may offer to arrange for them to receive more information by meeting with a neonatologist and taking a tour of a neonatal intensive care unit. He may also recommend giving Mrs. Grant two steroid injections to accelerate fetal lung maturity before delivery, to reduce the risk of death and disability. This information may persuade Mrs. Grant to accept another amniocentesis to relieve her symptoms, rather than to request immediate induction of labor. She may, however, respond that her symptoms of pain and breathlessness are becoming more severe and frightening, and urge Dr. Perez to induce labor now. If she persists in this request, how should he respond?

Dr. Perez may decide to honor her request for immediate delivery. He may judge that this is Mrs. Grant's informed and considered preference and conclude that complying with her decision should take preference over his concerns about the welfare of the child who will be born prematurely. He may also recognize that Mrs. Grant is experiencing severe symptoms and that proceeding to delivery will relieve those symptoms.

---

[32] Cunningham et al. (2010).   [33] Stoll et al. (2010).   [34] Boghossian et al. (2010).

Or, Dr. Perez may decide that he must refuse Mrs. Grant's request. He may believe that he can safely manage Mrs. Grant's polyhydramnios and may conclude that he cannot in good conscience carry out a treatment plan that will, in his judgment, lead to the death or the grave injury and disability of the child she will bear. If he chooses this response, Dr. Perez may offer to continue to monitor and treat Mrs. Grant's polyhydramnios and to proceed to delivery if it worsens significantly, or when the risks to the child are not so great. He may also offer to help the Grants obtain a second medical opinion from an obstetrician who may be willing to honor their request.

Dr. Perez may be uncertain how to handle this situation, and he may seek out an obstetrician colleague to ask for advice. If you were that colleague, how would you advise him?

15 Advance care planning and advance directives

Case example

Mr. Charles Bauer is a 75-year-old man with several illnesses, including chronic obstructive pulmonary disease (COPD) and congestive heart failure. He lives at home with his wife; they have been married for forty-seven years and have two adult children. He suddenly collapses late one evening, and Mrs. Bauer immediately calls for assistance. The emergency medical services team arrives very promptly, determines that Mr. Bauer is not breathing, begins cardiopulmonary resuscitation, and transports him to the ED of the nearby hospital. In the ED, physicians insert an endotracheal tube to provide artificial ventilation, and Mr. Bauer is admitted to the hospital's MICU.

One week later, Mr. Bauer is still a patient in the MICU; he has not regained consciousness, and he remains dependent on a mechanical ventilator to support his breathing. A neurologist has examined Mr. Bauer; she reports that he has suffered anoxic brain damage and may not regain consciousness. He has also acquired pneumonia and is receiving antibiotics. In view of his multiple and severe medical problems, Dr. Kane, Mr. Bauer's attending physician in the MICU, estimates that his chances of leaving the hospital alive are no better than 20 percent.

Dr. Kane explains the situation to Mr. Bauer's wife and his adult son and daughter, and he asks them what kind of treatment they believe Mr. Bauer would want. In response, Mrs. Bauer expresses her fervent hope for her husband's recovery and insists that Dr. Kane and his colleagues do whatever they can to keep her husband alive.

Mr. Bauer's son, however, disagrees with his mother. He says that his father recently confided to him that he would not want to be kept alive "on machines," and he gives Dr. Kane a copy of a living will, signed by Mr. Bauer, that states a desire not to receive life-prolonging treatments if he is in a "hopeless condition." Mrs. Bauer acknowledges that Mr. Bauer prepared this living will many years previously, but she adds that she doesn't believe that he meant it to apply to the current situation. When asked,

213

Mr. Bauer's daughter says that she is not sure what kind of treatment her father would want. How should Dr. Kane proceed?[1]

The moral significance of end-of-life care

With this chapter, our focus shifts from health care near the beginning of life to care near the end of life. Like the beginning-of-life issues discussed in the last three chapters, moral issues in end-of-life care are often complex and highly controversial. In the case described above, for example, Mr. Bauer's wife and son express strongly held but different views about what kind of medical treatment Mr. Bauer would want and should receive.

As human beings, we invest special significance in the dying process and the event of death. We hope for a "good death," we reach out to our loved ones in their last days of life, and we mourn their deaths. Professionals who care for patients near the end of life know that the dying process can take many different forms – it can be a time of suffering, or of peace; of regression, or growth; of isolation, or togetherness; of debasement, or dignity; of confusion, or insight; of despair, or hope. We strongly prefer the latter of each of the above alternatives, but we often do not agree about *how* to achieve the kind of death we want. Our strong and often divergent views about end-of-life medical treatment evoke frequent moral conflicts. In my experience as a clinical ethics consultant at two academic medical centers over two decades, for example, the large majority of requests for ethics consultation have involved treatment decisions near the end of life. The field of bioethics, therefore, has devoted major attention to the prevention and to the resolution of moral conflicts regarding end-of-life care. This chapter will examine advance care planning, a practice designed to *prevent* these conflicts, and the following three chapters will consider measures to *resolve* conflicts over treatment near the end of life.

A brief history

Although the manner and timing of one's death have always been important human concerns, significant moral controversy about medical treatments near the end of life did not arise until the last quarter of the twentieth

[1] Adapted from Moskop (2004).

century. Until the second half of the last century, physicians could do little to alter the time and manner of death. Rapidly increasing investment in biomedical research after World War II, however, produced a steady stream of new medical treatments and technologies able to prolong life, such as cardiopulmonary resuscitation, mechanical ventilation, intensive care units, artificial nutrition and hydration, renal dialysis, and organ transplantation, to name just a few. With medicine's increasing *ability* to prolong life came the question whether physicians and patients were *obligated* to prolong life whenever possible.

Moral questions about the use of life-prolonging treatments first came to prominent public attention in the United States with the case of Karen Ann Quinlan.[2] In April 1975, 21-year-old Karen suffered a cardiopulmonary arrest and was resuscitated and hospitalized. Months later, her physicians concluded that she was in a persistent vegetative state (that is, a state of irreversible unconsciousness) and was permanently dependent on a mechanical ventilator to support her breathing. Karen's parents requested removal of the ventilator to allow Karen to die, but her physicians refused this request, arguing that Karen depended on the ventilator for survival and that removing the ventilator would make them the agents of her death. A New Jersey trial court sided with the physicians and against Karen's parents. The New Jersey Supreme Court heard the case on appeal, however, and overturned the lower court decision.[3] The Supreme Court based its decision on recognition that Karen had a right to refuse life-prolonging treatment, and that Karen's parents were entitled to exercise that right on her behalf.

US national media avidly reported Karen's story, and the trial court decision evoked widespread public expressions of fear and concern about unwanted life-prolonging treatment. US state legislatures, beginning with California in 1976, responded with statutes recognizing a new kind of document called a "living will." Living wills, the first type of advance directive, were offered as a way to avoid unwanted life-prolonging medical treatment by stating one's desire not to receive such treatment in specific circumstances. Beginning about ten years later, state statutes began to recognize a second type of advance directive, called a "health care power

---

[2] Pence (2004); the case of Karen Quinlan is also discussed in Chapter 2.

[3] *In re Quinlan* (1976). (Contrary to their claims at trial, Karen's physicians were able to wean her from dependence on the mechanical ventilator, and she lived another ten years in a vegetative state.)

of attorney" (HCPOA) or "durable power of attorney for health care." In this kind of document, a person can appoint another person, often called a "health care agent," to make medical treatment decisions in the event that the first person has lost decision-making capacity.

By the year 2000, virtually every US state had enacted statutes formally recognizing both of these two types of advance directives. Despite their strong advocates and widespread adoption, however, advance directives also have outspoken critics. In a 2004 article entitled "Enough: The Failure of the Living Will," Angela Fagerlin and Carl Schneider argue that most people will not in fact complete living wills, that these documents do not give useful guidance, that they are often not available when needed, and that they are often ignored.[4] Proponents of advance directives acknowledge at least some of these problems, and they caution against an exclusive emphasis on completing written advance directive documents. Instead, these proponents recommend the use of advance directives as one component in a broader practice of planning in advance for medical treatment near the end of life, or advance care planning.[5]

Key concepts

A widely used training manual defines advance care planning as "an organized approach to initiating discussion, reflection, and understanding regarding an individual's current state of health, goals, values, and preferences for future treatment decisions."[6] The central idea here is that advance care planning is a *process* in which a person determines his or her preferred approach to future medical treatment based on reflection and discussion with others. An *advance directive* is the expected *product* or outcome of this planning process, a statement of the person's wishes regarding future health care.

A highly effective advance care planning process usually includes the following steps: First, people should be informed or reminded that frequently there are important treatment choices to be made near the end of life, and that one can plan ahead for these choices. Second, if a person expresses interest in this planning (I will refer to that person as "the

---

[4] Fagerlin and Schneider (2004).   [5] Singer et al. (1998), Moskop (2004).
[6] Hammes and Briggs (2000).

planner"), he or she should receive basic information about his or her own health condition and planning options. If the planner has a serious chronic or progressive illness, he or she should also be informed about what treatments are likely to be offered for that illness. Third, with that information in hand, the planner can discuss and reflect on what treatment goals and options he or she would prefer, given his or her own guiding beliefs and values. Fourth, based on this discussion and reflection, the planner can formulate plans for future health care, called advance directives. Fifth, because these plans cannot be honored unless others are aware of them, the planner must communicate his or her plans to those who can help to implement them at the appropriate time, especially loved ones and health care providers. Finally, as the planner's relationships or medical condition changes, his or her plans may well change, and so the planner should review, and, if desired, revise those plans periodically.

As noted above, the statement of one's plans for care near the end of life is called an advance directive. Advance directives can take several forms. They can be an oral statement made to a loved one or to one's physician, a written document, or a combination of oral and written instructions. Advance directives can be communicated informally, as, for example, in an open letter to one's relatives and caregivers, or they can be formal documents that satisfy statutory requirements and are witnessed and notarized. As described in the previous section, there are two main types of advance directives, living wills and HCPOAs. Living wills (sometimes called "instructional directives") describe what kinds of treatment a person would or would not want in particular medical conditions. HCPOAs (also called "proxy directives") appoint another person to make future treatment decisions on one's behalf. Both types of advance directives are intended to direct a planner's treatment decisions only *after* that person has lost decision-making capacity. If the planner still has the capacity to make his or her own medical decisions, health care professionals should obtain that person's informed consent to treatment, and there is no need or justification for reliance on an advance directive.

Another type of document designed to guide medical treatment near the end of life has attracted increasing attention in the United States over the past two decades. The general term for this type of document is a 'portable physician order for end-of-life care.' Like advance directives, these portable physician orders also communicate plans for medical treatment near the end of life, and some commentators view them as another type of advance directive. Most commentators, however, use the term 'advance directive' to apply to a statement prepared by a person to guide his or her own treatment; in contrast, a physician (or other health care professional authorized to write treatment orders) must write and sign these provider orders directing a patient's medical care. Unlike physician orders written and carried out in a hospital or other health care facility, however, these orders are *portable*, that is, they are intended to direct the treatment that a patient receives *wherever* the patient happens to be, including at home, in an ambulance, or anywhere else.

Like advance directives, there are two main types of portable physician orders. The first type of portable physician order to be widely adopted is the *portable do not resuscitate (DNR) order*. This order addresses one specific treatment option for one specific medical condition, namely, cardiopulmonary resuscitation (CPR) in the event of a cardiopulmonary arrest (cessation of heartbeat and breathing), and it instructs health care providers *not* to attempt CPR. This type of order was developed and implemented primarily to authorize emergency medical technicians to withhold CPR "in the field" for certain patients near the end of life. For these patients, cardiopulmonary arrest may be an expected event, and CPR efforts are likely to be ineffective or even harmful, therefore unwanted. Without a portable DNR order's clear authorization, however, emergency medical technicians are required to initiate CPR on all patients in cardiopulmonary arrest, unless clear signs of death are present.

A second type of portable physician order was first developed and implemented in the state of Oregon in the 1990s.[7] The title of this document is "Physician's Orders for Life-Sustaining Treatment," or POLST. Dozens of other US states have since adopted similar portable orders, but many have chosen slightly different names; for example, the title adopted in North Carolina is "Medical Orders for Scope of Treatment," or MOST.[8] POLST-type portable physician orders include instructions regarding CPR in the event of a cardiopulmonary arrest, but they also include physician orders regarding several other life-prolonging medical treatments, such as antibiotics and artificial nutrition and hydration, or "tube feeding." Figure 1 displays one type of portable physician order, namely, North Carolina's MOST form.

---

[7] Tolle and Tilden (2002).   [8] North Carolina General Statutes § 90–21.17.

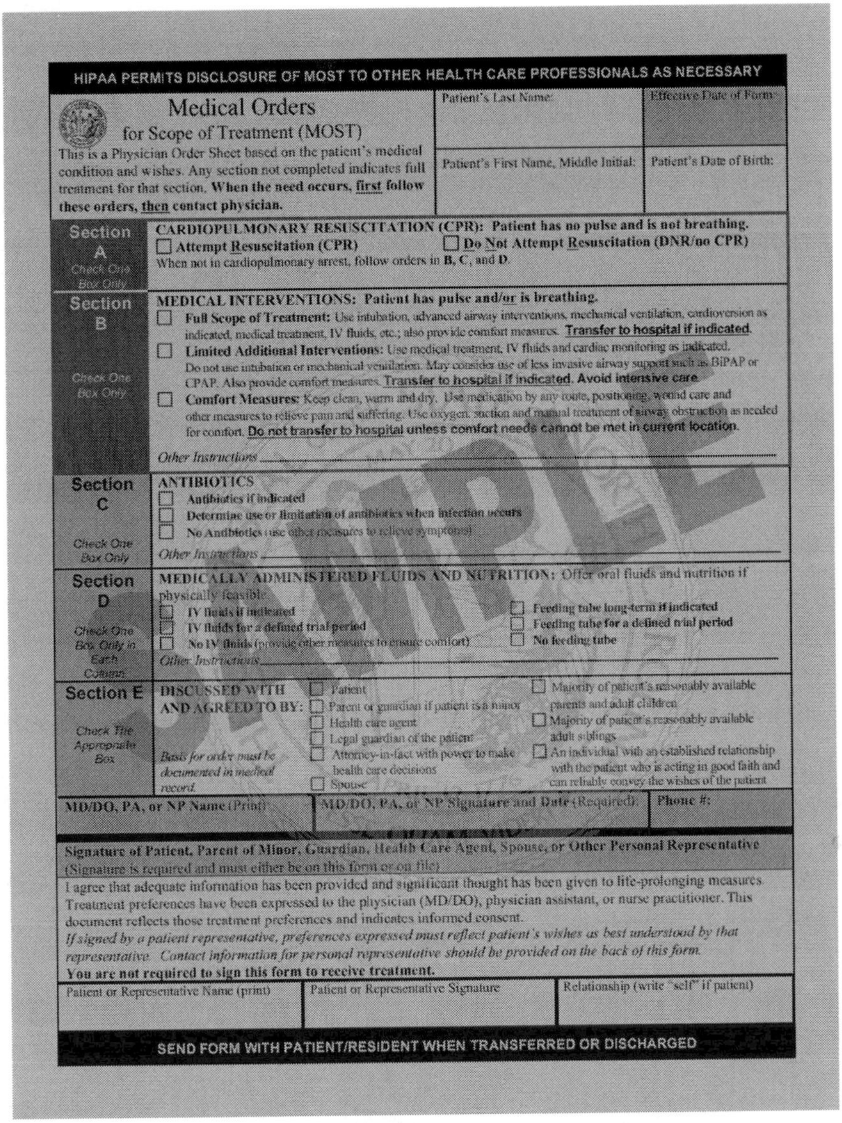

HIPAA PERMITS DISCLOSURE OF MOST TO OTHER HEALTH CARE PROFESSIONALS AS NECESSARY

Medical Orders for Scope of Treatment (MOST)

This is a Physician Order Sheet based on the patient's medical condition and wishes. Any section not completed indicates full treatment for that section. **When the need occurs, first follow these orders, then contact physician.**

Patient's Last Name:	Effective Date of Form:
Patient's First Name, Middle Initial:	Patient's Date of Birth:

Section A (Check One Box Only)
CARDIOPULMONARY RESUSCITATION (CPR): Patient has no pulse and is not breathing.
☐ Attempt Resuscitation (CPR) ☐ Do Not Attempt Resuscitation (DNR/no CPR)
When not in cardiopulmonary arrest, follow orders in **B, C**, and **D**.

Section B (Check One Box Only)
MEDICAL INTERVENTIONS: Patient has pulse and/or is breathing.
☐ **Full Scope of Treatment:** Use intubation, advanced airway interventions, mechanical ventilation, cardioversion as indicated, medical treatment, IV fluids, etc.; also provide comfort measures. **Transfer to hospital if indicated.**
☐ **Limited Additional Interventions:** Use medical treatment, IV fluids and cardiac monitoring as indicated. Do not use intubation or mechanical ventilation. May consider use of less invasive airway support such as BiPAP or CPAP. Also provide comfort measures. **Transfer to hospital if indicated. Avoid intensive care.**
☐ **Comfort Measures:** Keep clean, warm and dry. Use medication by any route, positioning, wound care and other measures to relieve pain and suffering. Use oxygen, suction and manual treatment of airway obstruction as needed for comfort. **Do not transfer to hospital unless comfort needs cannot be met in current location.**
Other Instructions ________

Section C (Check One Box Only)
ANTIBIOTICS
☐ Antibiotics if indicated
☐ Determine use or limitation of antibiotics when infection occurs
☐ No Antibiotics (use other measures to relieve symptoms)
Other Instructions ________

Section D (Check One Box Only in Each Column)
MEDICALLY ADMINISTERED FLUIDS AND NUTRITION: Offer oral fluids and nutrition if physically feasible.
☐ IV fluids if indicated ☐ Feeding tube long-term if indicated
☐ IV fluids for a defined trial period ☐ Feeding tube for a defined trial period
☐ No IV fluids (provide other measures to ensure comfort) ☐ No feeding tube
Other Instructions ________

Section E (Check The Appropriate Box)
DISCUSSED WITH AND AGREED TO BY:
☐ Patient
☐ Parent or guardian if patient is a minor
☐ Health care agent
☐ Legal guardian of the patient
☐ Attorney-in-fact with power to make health care decisions
☐ Spouse
☐ Majority of patient's reasonably available parents and adult children
☐ Majority of patient's reasonably available adult siblings
☐ An individual with an established relationship with the patient who is acting in good faith and can reliably convey the wishes of the patient
Basis for order must be documented in medical record.

MD/DO, PA, or NP Name (Print)	MD/DO, PA, or NP Signature and Date (Required)	Phone #:

Signature of Patient, Parent of Minor, Guardian, Health Care Agent, Spouse, or Other Personal Representative
(Signature is required and must either be on this form or on file)
I agree that adequate information has been provided and significant thought has been given to life-prolonging measures. Treatment preferences have been expressed to the physician (MD/DO), physician assistant, or nurse practitioner. This document reflects those treatment preferences and indicates informed consent.
If signed by a patient representative, preferences expressed must reflect patient's wishes as best understood by that representative. Contact information for personal representative should be provided on the back of this form.
You are not required to sign this form to receive treatment.

Patient or Representative Name (print)	Patient or Representative Signature	Relationship (write "self" if patient)

SEND FORM WITH PATIENT/RESIDENT WHEN TRANSFERRED OR DISCHARGED

Figure 1 Front page of North Carolina Medical Orders for Scope of Treatment (MOST) form

Since several different kinds of documents are widely available to record and communicate plans for treatment near the end of life, an obvious question arises, namely, "Which of these documents is best?" that is, "Which document is most likely to achieve its primary purpose of honoring a person's preferences for end-of-life care?" Not surprisingly, the correct response is: "It depends on a person's individual circumstances." Portable physician orders for end-of-life care, for example, will be of greatest value for people who are nearing the end of life, since these orders give clear direction regarding whether to provide or forgo specific life-prolonging treatments. Portable physician orders provide little or no additional benefit for healthy people, because the clear default option for healthy people will be to provide CPR and other life-prolonging treatments in the event of sudden illness or injury.

Of the two types of advance directives, however, I believe that HCPOAs have several distinct advantages over living wills for most people. First, they enable one to select and appoint a trusted relative or friend to make medical treatment decisions on one's behalf, and such an agent is most likely to make informed, careful choices. Appointing a health care agent enables one to share specific information with one's agent about one's medical condition, treatment options, and treatment preferences, and thus allows one's health care agent to make well informed treatment decisions based on that information. In contrast, living wills authorize a patient's attending physician, who often has no previous acquaintance with the patient, to interpret and apply the instructions contained in the living will. Moreover, HCPOAs can guide treatment choices in a much broader range of situations than living wills. Living wills usually state general treatment preferences only for a few medical conditions, while HCPOAs enable health care agents to make decisions on behalf of those who have appointed them whenever the people they represent have lost the ability to make decisions for themselves. Because a person who completes an HCPOA gives significant authority and responsibility to his or her health care agent, it is important both to choose one's agent carefully and to discuss one's treatment preferences with one's agent, so that the agent can understand and carry out those preferences.

The benefits of advance care planning (and barriers to achieving them)

Proponents assert that planning in advance for medical treatment near the end of life and completing advance directives can provide significant benefits for people who engage in these practices. What are these promised benefits? First and foremost, advance care planning can give patients greater control over the treatment they receive *after* they have lost the ability to make treatment choices. It therefore respects and expands the sphere of personal autonomy, and it promotes the goal of providing patient-centered care near the end of life. By enabling people to formulate and communicate clear plans for treatment near the end of life, advance care planning reduces uncertainty about what treatment to provide, and it avoids what is often the default decision under uncertainty, namely, provision of all treatment measures that may prolong life. Clear treatment directions from the person, as stated in a living will or communicated by the person's health care agent, can also prevent conflict regarding what treatment should be provided. Statutes in many US states provide immunity from liability for physicians who honor advance directives and portable physician orders; these statutes give physicians an additional incentive to respect patients' end-of-life treatment wishes. Finally, advance care planning can conserve health care resources, by honoring patient wishes to forgo life-prolonging treatment that is often both costly and ineffective.[9]

To achieve these significant benefits, advance care planning must be organized in systems or programs that inform and guide both the planners and the health care professionals who carry out the plans people make for their treatment near the end of life. Organized programs are essential in order to satisfy the following four necessary conditions for success. First, people must devote the time and effort required to engage in the planning process. Second, they must be able to formulate plans that are clear and clinically relevant. Third, they must communicate their plans so that the plans will be accessible when they are needed. Fourth, health care providers must carry out the plans in the appropriate circumstances.

There are considerable barriers to satisfying these necessary conditions for a successful advance care planning program. A 2007 review of the US medical literature cites estimates that only 18–30 percent of Americans have completed advance directives.[10] Some US states and communities have a much higher percentage of residents with advance directives, however. Thanks to a longstanding community-wide advance care planning program in the city of La Crosse, Wisconsin, for example, 90 percent of people who died in that community in 2007–2008 had an advance directive at the time of death.[11]

---

[9] Nicholas et al. (2011).   [10] Wilkinson et al. (2007).   [11] Hammes et al. (2010).

If advance directive forms are difficult to understand, and no one is available to provide knowledgeable assistance in completing them, people may abandon the process, or they may prepare forms that do not express their wishes correctly or clearly, and so do not serve their intended purpose. To overcome this barrier, health care systems and communities have trained both professionals and volunteers to serve as advance care planning facilitators. Communities have also championed the use of advance directive forms that give clear instructions and are easy to understand and complete.

Once people prepare advance directives, they must share their directives with others, especially family members and caregivers, so that the documents can be retained and retrieved when they are needed. Medical record systems can be designed or augmented to perform these functions effectively. And, when directives are available, physicians must learn to interpret them accurately and must commit to carry them out faithfully.

Finally, during the US national debate over health care reform legislation in 2009–2010, some politicians accused advance care planning programs of being "death panels" in disguise, designed to deny treatment to vulnerable patients.[12] This charge, however, clearly misrepresents the purpose of advance care planning. Rather than imposing treatment decisions on unwilling patients, advance care planning programs are designed to assist people in making their own plans for end-of-life care and to honor the plans people make.

A philosophical challenge

As mentioned earlier in this chapter, commentators have cited a number of practical problems confronting the practice of advance care planning, including people's reluctance to take the time to plan, the creation of plans that do not express a person's wishes clearly or accurately, difficulties in accessing plans when they are needed, and the unwillingness of some physicians to honor plans in the situations for which they were prepared. I have suggested that a well-structured system for encouraging and assisting people with advance care planning, and for accessing and honoring advance directives, can address these practical problems effectively.

---

[12] Kenny (2012).

Another group of critics, however, has posed a more fundamental philosophical challenge to the practice of advance care planning.[13] Rather than questioning the feasibility of advance care planning systems, these critics challenge the moral authority of advance directives. Here is their argument: When we honor advance directives, we allow a person's preferences expressed in the past (either in a living will or in oral instructions to one's health care agent) to govern present medical treatment decisions for that person after the person has lost decision-making capacity. The loss of decision-making capacity, along with other changes in the person's mental and physical condition, however, may cause a radical change in the best interests of that person. People preparing advance directives may not anticipate this change in their interests and so may not take it into account in the choices they make. They may not, for example, realize that life may contain value and enjoyment even after they have lost decision-making capacity (competence). Their advance directives may, therefore, not accurately reflect their later interests, and so should not be honored.

Even if people do recognize how their future situation and interests may change and prepare advance directives with that information in mind, these critics reject a duty to honor those advance directives. What is morally compelling, they argue, is providing treatment that promotes a person's current interests, not treatment that reflects the person's past preferences. This claim is sometimes defended by arguing that the present incompetent patient is so different from the "former self" who prepared the advance directive that they are, morally speaking, no longer the same person. Because the former self is, or was, a different person, his or her preferences should not govern the treatment of the now-incompetent patient. Rather, treatment decisions should be based on evaluation of the incompetent person's present best interests.

A significant difficulty for this approach is the vagueness and lack of agreement about best interests. As discussed in Chapter 9, "Surrogate decision-making," the patient's best interests is one of the standards used to guide and assess treatment decisions made by surrogates on behalf of incompetent patients. That standard includes a number of different considerations, however, including prolongation of life, preservation or restoration of mental and physical function, and relief of pain and suffering.

[13] See, for example, Dresser and Robertson (1989), The President's Council on Bioethics (2005).

Because people value and prioritize these different goals in very different ways, they often disagree about what treatment option is in a patient's best interests. If there is no agreement about what is in a particular patient's best interests, however, whose assessment should prevail? Defenders of advance directives maintain that the patient's own previously expressed preferences, or those expressed by his or her appointed health care agent, should prevail over those of health care providers or others who had no prior relationship with the patient.

Case analysis

In the case described at the beginning of this chapter, Mr. Charles Bauer is clearly gravely ill, and his wife and son disagree strongly about what kind of treatment he should receive. The situation poses an apparent moral dilemma for Dr. Kane and Mr. Bauer's family. There are two obvious treatment alternatives, and plausible reasons can be offered for each one. There are also unavoidable uncertainties about the outcomes of the treatment alternatives, and about what Mr. Bauer would want, if he were able to express an opinion. A decision is necessary, but there is no obvious treatment plan that all the interested parties will accept and that will prevent hard feelings. Chapter 16, "Moral conflicts in end-of-life care," will examine common causes of these conflict situations and strategies for resolving them.

For the purposes of this chapter on advance care planning, however, let's suppose that Mr. Bauer had engaged in an ongoing process of advance care planning prior to his hospital admission. Could this have prevented the dilemma that arose in this case? Mr. Bauer had apparently given some attention to end-of-life care in the past, since he had prepared a living will years earlier. Ongoing discussion about his medical condition, possible complications, and future treatment options may have given him a better understanding of his situation and helped him to express his treatment wishes more clearly to his loved ones. Additional information about advance directives may have prompted him to prepare a directive better suited to his situation, perhaps an HCPOA naming his son as his health care agent, since he had recently discussed his wishes with his son. Mr. Bauer might also have been encouraged to discuss his wishes with his wife and daughter, and that may have helped them to understand and accept his wishes. During a previous stay in the hospital or clinic visit, Mr. Bauer's

HCPOA or living will could have been made a part of his permanent medical record. If so, it could have been retrieved and made available to Dr. Kane when he was admitted to MICU. Dr. Kane would then have a better understanding of his patient's wishes, and, if Mr. Bauer had prepared an HCPOA, Dr. Kane would know who Mr. Bauer had appointed to make treatment decisions on his behalf.

How likely is it, do you think, that careful advance care planning would have prevented the moral conflict over treatment near the end of life in this case?

16 Moral conflicts in end-of-life care

Case example

Thirty-five-year-old Ted Jones is brought to the ED of a small rural hospital one after-noon by his partner, James Moore. Mr. Jones was diagnosed with HIV infection ten years ago, and with AIDS two years ago. He has had multiple medical problems over the past two years, including several opportunistic infections. His presenting symptoms today are shortness of breath, chest pain, cough, and fever. He appears tired and emaciated, and he reports a two-week history of fatigue and weight loss of 8 lbs.

Despite his discomfort and fatigue, Mr. Jones is alert and oriented. Dr. Turner, the emergency physician on duty, administers a brief mental status exam; he observes that Mr. Jones has difficulty counting backwards from one hundred by sevens, and cannot accurately copy a geometric design. Mr. Moore, his partner for the past five years, reports that Mr. Jones has become increasingly tired, forgetful, and unable to concentrate over the past six months. Dr. Turner strongly suspects that Mr. Jones has Pneumocystis pneumonia (PCP). Dr. Turner requests a sputum sample for testing and recommends immediate initiation of targeted therapy to treat the suspected infection. Mr. Jones responds, however, that he does not want specific drug treatment if he has pneumonia. He maintains that he is tired of living with AIDS and wants to be allowed to die. He adds that he agreed to come to the hospital only because the pain and difficulty breathing became too great, and asks that he be given only treatment to relieve his pain and make him comfortable.

Mr. Moore, however, urgently requests that his partner be given definitive therapy for his lung condition. If Mr. Jones has PCP, Dr. Turner believes that prompt initiation of IV antimicrobial treatment has a 70–80 percent chance of treating his infection successfully. If Mr. Jones has PCP and it is left untreated, he will have progressive respiratory symptoms that will lead to death in a few days. How should Dr. Turner proceed?[1]

---

[1] Adapted from Moskop (1999).

In this chapter, we continue the examination of moral issues in medical treatment near the end of life. Chapter 15 described advance care planning, a strategy designed to prevent moral conflicts over end-of-life care by identifying and honoring the patient's own treatment preferences. Despite its promise, however, advance care planning is no panacea; it cannot prevent all moral conflicts over what treatments to provide patients near the end of life. Many people do not plan ahead for these decisions; some who do plan ahead create plans that do not address particular situations, and some advance directives are challenged by family members or professional caregivers. Moral conflicts over treatment near the end of life will, therefore, remain a frequent occurrence in health care for the foreseeable future. This chapter will begin with a brief review of various types of end-of-life moral conflict. I will then focus on one major type of conflict, namely, conflict between patients or their representatives, on the one hand, and professional caregivers, on the other. I will identify major causes of this type of conflict and suggest strategies for conflict resolution.

Types of end-of-life moral conflict

It is important to recognize that conflict over care near the end of life can occur in several different settings. One way to organize three main types of this conflict is according to the locus of the conflict, as follows: *internal* conflicts occur within a single individual, *interpersonal* conflicts occur between two, or among three or more persons, and *public policy* conflicts pit groups of people against one another regarding the legal and social parameters for end-of-life care. Let's take a closer look at each of these types of conflict in turn.

Internal conflicts

People who are dying, their loved ones, and their caregivers may all experience internal moral or prudential conflicts about treatment near the end of life. Dying patients may confront the following conflicts, for example:

1. pursuit of the goal of prolonging life by means of a difficult course of treatment, versus enhancement of the quality of one's life by forgoing that course of treatment

2. enduring pain caused by advanced disease in order to remain alert and responsive to others, versus accepting sedation to manage pain

3. reliance on loved ones to provide needed assistance with treatment and activities of daily living, versus forgoing life-prolonging treatment in order to relieve loved ones of the burdens of caregiving

4. trust in the treatment recommendations of one's professional caregivers, versus suspicion of the intentions of those caregivers

Dying patients may find it difficult to reconcile conflicting beliefs, values, interests, and obligations in order to make morally defensible decisions in these choice situations. A comparable list of internal conflicts could be constructed for the relatives or professional caregivers of dying patients.

Interpersonal conflicts

Moral conflicts regarding treatment choices near the end of life may arise between or among any of the following: the dying person (if he or she is still conscious), family members and friends, and physicians and other health care professionals caring for the patient. Later in this chapter, we will review common causes of interpersonal conflicts between patients or their representatives and their professional caregivers, and consider strategies for their resolution.

Public policy conflicts

Public and institutional policies guide medical treatment decisions near the end of life in multiple ways. They may, for example, determine what treatment options are lawful and unlawful, who may provide various treatments, and what resources are available to pay for different treatment options. Three major public debates in the United States over the past four decades have shaped public policy and professional practice regarding medical treatment for patients nearing the end of life: the "natural death" debate, the physician-assisted suicide debate, and the "futility" debate. Because these debates have been so influential in the US, a brief review will set the stage for the discussion of interpersonal conflicts to follow.

As mentioned in Chapters 2 and 15, the case of Karen Ann Quinlan in 1975–1976 triggered the first sustained public attention to life-sustaining medical treatment in the US.[2] The ensuing "natural death" debate featured requests by patients and their representatives for release from unwanted life-prolonging medical treatment to enable a natural or peaceful death, and responses from physicians and health care institutions that forgoing life-prolonging treatment would amount to killing the patient and thus cannot be permitted. A series of court decisions from *Quinlan* through *Cruzan*,[3] the first US Supreme Court ruling on life-prolonging medical treatment, recognized and defined a basic patient right to refuse such treatment.[4] Despite formal acceptance of this right, however, research studies of the care of patients near the end of life have suggested that patient desires to forgo life-prolonging treatment are often not known or honored.[5] The Florida case of Terri Schiavo, which was the subject of multiple court rulings, state and federal statutes, and executive orders from 1998 through 2005, exposed deep divisions in US public opinion about the use of life-prolonging medical treatment.[6]

The second major US public policy debate addressed the practice of physician-assisted suicide. Proponents, most notably Dr. Jack Kevorkian, argued that physicians should be permitted to provide assistance in suicide at the request of their patients; opponents argued that this practice was both immoral and fraught with danger and should therefore be prohibited. A pair of seminal 1997 US Supreme Court decisions rejected the claim that assistance in suicide is a basic constitutional right and allowed individual states to decide its legal status within their borders.[7] By 2015, five states (Oregon, Washington, Montana, Vermont, and California) had legalized this practice. Chapter 18 will examine physician-assisted suicide in more detail.

The third notable US policy debate over end-of-life care revolves around the concept of futility. Beginning in the late 1980s, reports appeared in the medical literature that patients and their representatives were requesting or demanding life-prolonging treatments like cardiopulmonary resuscitation.[8] Some physicians resisted these demands on the grounds that the treatments requested would be futile. Other

---

[2] *In re Quinlan* (1976).   [3] *Cruzan v. Director, Missouri Department of Health* (1990).
[4] For a detailed review of this debate, see Meisel (1993).
[5] See, for example, The SUPPORT Principal Investigators (1995).   [6] See Gostin (2005).
[7] *Vacco v. Quill* (1997); *Washington v. Glucksberg* (1997).
[8] See, for example, Blackhall (1987).

commentators challenged this appeal to futility, arguing that it often did not provide a clear or adequate justification for denying requested treatments. Debate over the role of futility in decisions about providing life-prolonging treatment continues, and this issue is the topic of Chapter 17.

Though the three issues described above have been the most sustained and prominent public policy debates regarding end-of-life care in the United States, they are certainly not the only controversial policy issues in this area. Two other difficult policy issues regarding access to specific treatments deserve brief mention. One ongoing debate is over access to narcotic pain medications. These medications are highly effective for managing the severe pain of patients with advanced cancer and other serious illnesses, but they are also in great demand for recreational use, and are now among the most commonly misused prescription drugs. Placing restrictions on the use of these drugs and closely monitoring physician prescribing patterns may reduce their misuse, but may also make it more difficult for patients who need these drugs for effective pain management to receive them. Another ongoing issue has to do with access to very costly life-prolonging treatment modalities. Recently developed anticancer agents, for example, may extend life for patients with metastatic cancer for a median of three to five months, at a cost of $140,000 to more than $500,000 per quality-adjusted life year gained, depending on the type of cancer.[9] Must public and private health insurance carriers provide this modest benefit at this high cost, or may they deny coverage in an effort to control their costs and provide sustainable coverage for their insured population? This issue is likely to become more urgent in the United States as health care reform efforts attempt to expand coverage and simultaneously to control health system expenditures.[10]

Conflicts between patients or their representatives, and professional caregivers

We return now to an important type of interpersonal conflict, namely, conflict between health care professionals, on the one hand, and patients, or surrogate decision-makers representing patients who lack decision-making

---

[9] Emanuel (2013).

[10] See Chapter 11, "Resource stewardship," for further discussion of health care cost containment issues.

capacity, on the other hand. As we have already noted, these conflicts can be about different issues, but I believe that the vast majority of conflicts between these parties are variations on the following general theme. The parties in conflict cannot agree on what are appropriate goals of care or treatment priorities. One party believes that cure or life prolongation is the most appropriate goal of care, and thus curative or life-prolonging treatments should be initiated or continued. The other party believes that a natural or peaceful dying process is the most appropriate goal of care, and thus curative or life-sustaining treatments should be withheld or withdrawn. The rest of this chapter will consider why these conflicts occur and how they might be resolved.

Common causes of conflict about end-of-life care

Why do conflicts frequently arise between patients or their surrogates and health care professionals over treatment near the end of life? I suggest that the causes of these conflicts fall into four main categories, which I will call cognitive causes, affective causes, normative causes, and external causes. Let's review these four categories in sequence.

Cognitive (knowledge-based) causes

Conflicts of this type occur because the parties have different understandings of the facts of the situation at hand. To take an obvious example, if one party believes that a particular treatment offers a realistic chance to cure a serious illness, and the other party does not, they are very likely to disagree about whether to provide or receive that treatment.

Either party to a conflict can be ignorant (that is, have no information) or can have a misunderstanding (that is, a false belief) about any of the following relevant items:

1. Who has the authority to make a treatment decision?
2. What is the patient's illness or injury?
3. What is the patient's prognosis?
4. What are realistic goals of care?
5. What are available treatment options and their expected benefits and burdens?
6. What are the patient's wishes?

When the parties' beliefs about any of these items are significantly different, they are likely to disagree about what treatment to pursue.

Affective (feeling-based) causes

Conflicts of this type occur because one or both of the parties are influenced by strong emotions that impede their ability to reason, make decisions, or take action. For example, parents whose child has recently suffered a catastrophic injury may be so distraught that they are not able to contemplate any limitation of life-prolonging measures, no matter how poor the child's prognosis for survival or what treatment plan the child's physicians recommend.

Emotions that can influence either party's decisions include the following:

1. fear (of powerlessness, of experiencing or causing suffering, of abandonment, of death)
2. grief (over the loss of function, of relationships, of a future)
3. guilt (over past or present failings)
4. denial (based on fear, grief, or guilt)
5. mistrust or suspicion (of another person's motives or good will)
6. dislike or hatred (based on prejudice, or on past injuries suffered)

When either or both parties to a conflict are experiencing these or other powerful emotions, they may be unwilling or unable to evaluate treatment options and reach a reasonable conclusion about how to proceed.

Normative (value-based) causes

Conflicts of this type occur because the parties base their decisions on different value commitments. To cite a well-known example, health care professionals may recommend immediate blood transfusion in order to save the life of an unconscious patient who is bleeding profusely from injuries suffered in an automobile accident, but the patient's surrogate may refuse transfusion based on the patient's belief, as a Jehovah's Witness, that accepting blood products is a serious violation of divine law.[11]

---

[11] For a review of this issue, see Smith (1997).

The interested parties may rely on a number of different kinds of values, including:

1. religious values (for example, the sanctity of human life)
2. cultural values
3. professional values (for example, reliance on scientific evidence)
4. moral values
5. self-interest

If the parties hold different values, or prioritize values in different ways, and if different treatment options are expected to realize those different values, then the parties will not be able to agree on what treatment to pursue.

External causes

Conflicts of this type occur because the decisions of one or both of the parties are constrained by external circumstances beyond their control. A patient with a painful terminal illness may, for example, request assistance in suicide from her physician in order to obtain relief from her suffering, but the physician may refuse this request because assistance in suicide is a criminal offense in that jurisdiction.

The parties may be bound by a number of external factors, including:

1. time constraints
2. financial constraints
3. legal constraints
4. liability risks
5. employment-related constraints (for example, institutional policies)

Any one or more of these constraints on the decisions or actions of the parties to a conflict may make it difficult or impossible for them to reach agreement on a treatment plan.

Strategies for conflict prevention and resolution

Medical treatment decisions near the end of a patient's life are typically matters of great importance to the stakeholders – patients, loved ones, and health care professionals alike. Conflict over these decisions, and especially intractable conflict, can itself be a source of great moral distress. We seek, therefore, to prevent or resolve these conflicts in morally defensible ways. The remainder of this chapter will review strategies to accomplish that goal. To be effective, these strategies must be able to identify and respond to the underlying cause of the conflict. I will, therefore, review different prevention and resolution strategies designed for the four different types of causes of conflict described above.

Responding to cognitive causes of conflict

As noted above, the cause of conflict in this category is a disparity in the parties' knowledge of significant information about the situation. To address conflicts of this kind, therefore, it will be important to identify what information is significant and to communicate that information accurately to the parties.

Previous chapters in this book have already examined several kinds of information that should guide treatment decisions. In Chapter 8, "Informed consent," we noted that patients who have decision-making capacity have moral and legal authority to make treatment choices for themselves. In Chapter 9, "Surrogate decision-making," we saw that surrogates are authorized to make treatment decisions on behalf of patients who lack decision-making authority. Professionals' ability to identify the appropriate decision-makers can enable them to share relevant information and seek agreement about treatment with those decision-makers. Chapter 15, "Advance care planning," described a strategy for making, communicating, and honoring treatment preferences expressed in advance. Advance care planning enables professionals to know and to act on patient preferences and to minimize uncertainty or conflict about what treatment a person would have wanted near the end of life.

Once the appropriate decision-maker is identified, professionals have a responsibility to communicate accurate, significant, and timely information to that person about the patient's condition and treatment options. This communication process can be deficient in a variety of ways, including the following:

1. failure to meet and talk with the patient or surrogate
2. not asking the patient or surrogate what he or she understands, or what he or she wants to know

3. use of technical medical language that the patient or surrogate does not understand

4. disclosing more information at one time than the patient or surrogate can assimilate

5. provision of conflicting information by different caregivers

6. offering an overoptimistic prognosis to "preserve hope"

7. use of misleading language, for example: "Do you want us to do everything?" (Does this mean everything possible? everything appropriate?); "There is nothing more we can do" (Palliative care to relieve patient symptoms is always an option, and so this statement is always false!); "Will you agree to withdraw care?" (Is this question asking a surrogate to stop caring for, or about, a loved one?!)

Recognizing these common pitfalls is an important step toward more effective and sensitive communication about treatment near the end of life. What positive strategies can professionals use to share information with patients and their representatives? Here are some recommendations from expert clinicians:[12]

1. Take sufficient time to gather, prepare, and present significant information.

2. Begin by asking the patient or surrogate what he or she understands or has been told; responses can reveal what he or she does and doesn't understand and can provide cues for further discussion.

3. Use simple, non-technical, non-euphemistic language.

4. Ask questions to assess understanding, and encourage questions from the patient or surrogate.

5. Offer information about prognosis, but acknowledge the limits of prediction.

6. Use open-ended questions to elicit the patient's or surrogate's goals of care, for example, "What are you hoping for?" "What do you fear most?"

7. Begin with broad goals of care, and then recommend specific treatments that serve those goals.

8. Suggest realistic goals for patients near the end of life, for example, improving quality of life and enjoying relationships, and tell how these can be achieved.

---

[12] See, for example, von Gunten et al. (2000), and Buckman (1992).

9. In discussions with surrogates, focus on what goals and treatments the patient would want.

Insofar as these strategies, and the communication skills needed to implement them, are successful in giving patients or their representatives a clear understanding of significant information about the patient's situation and treatment choices, they can prevent or resolve conflicts about treatment that are the result of absent or false information.

Responding to affective causes of conflict

Recall that this kind of conflict is due to powerful emotional responses to life-threatening illness or injury. To "diagnose" conflicts of this kind, health care professionals must first recognize the emotions that the stakeholders in a situation (including the professionals themselves) are experiencing. With this recognition, professionals can address these emotions in a variety of ways:

1. When breaking bad news, as, for example, the diagnosis of a terminal illness, professionals can allow time for the patient and loved ones to express emotions.
2. Professionals can express awareness of and concern for the patient's feelings, as, for example, in the following words: "This must be very difficult for you," or "I wish the news were different."
3. Professionals can provide non-verbal support to patients or loved ones who are afraid or sorrowful, by, for example, maintaining eye contact, holding a patient's hand, helping a tearful spouse to compose himself or herself.
4. Professionals can reassure the fearful patient that he or she will not be abandoned, that much can be done to allow him or her to live well during this stage of life.
5. In discussing treatment choices near the end of life with a surrogate, professionals can make clear that the surrogate is not responsible for the patient's death, and so should not feel guilty for accepting a recommendation to forgo life-prolonging measures.
6. If a patient appears suspicious of his or her health care providers, professionals can express their commitment to providing excellent care, sharing information, and respecting the patient's wishes. They

can also offer to assist the patient in obtaining a second opinion about what treatment to pursue.

In *On Death and Dying*, her classic 1969 description of the dying process, Elizabeth Kübler-Ross argues that dying patients typically progress through five psychological stages – denial, anger, bargaining, depression, and acceptance.[13] Three of these stages, denial, anger, and depression, are obvious emotional responses to the prospect of death. Professionals may help patients recognize and work through these emotions, and they should allow time for these processes to unfold. If a patient is in denial about a terminal illness, for example, offering information and listening to the patient's concerns is likely to be more productive than repeated efforts to persuade him or her to forgo curative therapy.

Responding to normative causes of conflict

Conflicts of this kind occur when the decisions of the parties are the result of divergent moral beliefs or values. To achieve a conclusive and final resolution of these normative conflicts, one would have to establish the truth of an ethical theory and show how that theory dictates a unique, morally correct course of action in the situation at hand. Because we lack consensus on both fundamental ethical theories and their application in our morally pluralistic societies, conflicts based on fundamental differences in values can be intractable.

There are, however, several strategies health care professionals can employ to seek resolution of normative causes of conflict, including the following:

1. Professionals can elicit and explicitly acknowledge the values or moral beliefs on which the patient or representative is relying. Encouraging the patient or surrogate to articulate the reasons for his or her choice lets that person know that he or she is being heard and understood.
2. Professionals can, in turn, clearly explain the reasons for their own treatment recommendations, so that the patient or surrogate knows and can assess those reasons.
3. With knowledge of each other's values and goals, the parties can seek common ground and explore the potential for compromise on a

[13] Kübler-Ross (1969).

treatment plan that both can accept. Such a compromise solution may not satisfy all of the competing values held by the parties, but it may promise enough benefit to secure the parties' agreement to proceed.

4. Professionals and patients can enlist the assistance of other advisors, including ministers, hospital chaplains, and ethics consultants. These advisors may help the parties to interpret and apply their beliefs and values to the situation at hand, and to promote communication and trust between the parties. (Advisors may also, however, reinforce the value differences between the parties, making resolution of conflict less likely.)

5. Professionals can keep the patient or his or her surrogate informed about changes in the patient's condition, prognosis, and treatment options. If, for example, a patient with a serious illness takes a significant turn for the worse, it may be easier for all parties to agree that the primary goal of treatment should shift from cure to palliation of suffering.

These strategies can improve the prospects for resolving disputes over treatment near the end of life, but conflicts based on fundamentally different value commitments may persist despite the best efforts of the parties to resolve them. In situations of persistent disagreement, the treatment plan may ultimately depend on who has the final authority to make this decision and who has the responsibility to implement it.

Responses to external causes of conflict

Conflicts of this type occur when the decisions or actions of one or both of the parties are constrained by external forces that are largely beyond their control. Strategies to resolve these conflicts must, therefore, address the particular factors that are restricting the choices of the parties. The following are examples of specific strategies for conflicts of this kind:

1. When the time available to a physician to pursue resolution of a conflict about treatment near the end of life is severely limited, it may be possible to identify and use available efficiencies to compensate for that time constraint. Many hospitals, for example, have established palliative care consultation services to assist in planning and providing care for these patients. Palliative care consultants with special expertise

in discussing goals of care and treatment options may be able to prevent or resolve conflicts in this area.

2. Financial constraints may prevent health care professionals or institutions from providing beneficial treatments requested by patients who lack the ability to pay for those treatments. Prevention of conflicts about treatment based on this kind of constraint was the primary motivation for the provisions designed to increase access to health insurance in the Affordable Care Act, the US federal health care reform law enacted in 2010.

3. Where laws, regulations, or institutional rules prevent professionals from agreeing to a course of treatment sought by a patient, professionals may advocate for appropriate changes in those policies to enable them to carry out the patient's wishes.

4. Physicians may consider the risk of a professional liability judgment against them in their clinical judgments, but they should be careful not to overestimate that risk to the detriment of their patients.[14] "Can I be sued for this action?" is generally not a useful question in making decisions about liability. Much more important are these questions: "How important is this action for my patient?" "Is a suit against me likely?" and "If a suit is brought, what are its chances of success?"

These strategies illustrate how health care professionals, patients, and society at large can take action to understand how their options regarding treatment near the end of life may be constrained, and to remove those constraints or find alternative ways to achieve common goals.

Case analysis

In the case described at the beginning of this chapter, Mr. Jones expresses a desire not to receive a potentially life-preserving treatment for what appears to be a serious infection. Failure to treat this condition will likely result in his death within the next few days. Should Dr. Turner honor this refusal of treatment?

A key question is whether Mr. Jones has sufficient mental capacity to make this treatment decision. Mr. Jones's ability to understand his

---

[14] Chapter 4, "Law and ethics in health care," examines the relationship between legal and moral grounds for action in greater detail.

condition and evaluate treatment options may be compromised by multiple factors, including pain, anxiety, confusion, and depression. His partner Mr. Moore reports that Mr. Jones has become forgetful and has lost the ability to concentrate over the past six months. Dr. Turner administers a brief mental status exam to assess his patient's cognitive function. Although Mr. Jones knows who he is, where he is, and what time it is, he has deficits in other reasoning functions.

Perhaps Mr. Jones's refusal of the recommended drug therapy for pneumonia has a cognitive cause. Mr. Jones may not realize that the drug therapy can very likely cure his infection and relieve the symptoms he is experiencing. Dr. Turner can review this information and ask Mr. Jones questions to assess his understanding. Let's suppose that Mr. Jones does appear to understand his medical condition and the likely outcome of the recommended treatment, however, and he offers a clear reason why he does not what the treatment.

Mr. Jones's stated reason for refusing treatment is that he is tired of living with AIDS. Is this a reasonable decision in light of the burdens of his disease, or is it the result of a profound depression? If it is the latter, the disagreement about whether to begin drug therapy may be due to an affective cause. Mr. Jones may feel that his life can no longer have any meaning or pleasure. Dr. Turner might seek a psychiatric consultation to assess whether depression has rendered Mr. Jones unable to make this treatment decision. If the psychiatrist reaches that conclusion, Dr. Turner might then choose to initiate PCP therapy, with the agreement of Mr. Moore.

The psychiatric consultant might, however, report that Mr. Jones is not depressed and does have sufficient capacity to refuse treatment. As an emergency physician, Dr. Turner may nevertheless feel a strong professional responsibility to act promptly to preserve his life. If so, the conflict in this situation may have a normative cause. Mr. Jones and Dr. Turner may reach different conclusions based on their different value commitments. Dr. Turner may explain his recommendation and seek to persuade Mr. Jones to accept therapy, but if he cannot, he should recognize his patient's right to refuse this treatment.

Mr. Jones does request treatment to relieve his pain and make him comfortable. Dr. Turner may wish to honor this request, but not believe that he has the requisite knowledge to initiate this palliative care plan in the ED. Moreover, this small hospital lacks a palliative care specialist or palliative care unit able to manage this care for Mr. Jones. If this is the case, failure to provide highly effective palliative care for Mr. Jones may have an external cause, that is, the limited resources of the hospital. Is this an unfortunate but unavoidable limitation of hospital services, or should every hospital have the resources and professional staff expertise to provide the palliative care Mr. Jones requests?

17   Medical futility

Case example

Dr. Tyson is a general pediatrician in private practice. He is caring for Gail, a 5-week-old infant who presented to his office three weeks ago when her parents became concerned about her decreased feeding and apparent weakness. The parents reported that they were told that Gail was normal and healthy when they took her home from the hospital. Gail is a pretty baby girl, but Dr. Tyson's initial physical examination three weeks ago revealed that she was seriously ill. She had an elevated respiratory rate and very poor muscle tone.

Dr. Tyson was concerned about a life-threatening infection and so began a course of antibiotics immediately and admitted Gail to the hospital. While in the hospital, her respiratory condition worsened, and she was intubated and placed on a ventilator. No infection was discovered, but a muscle biopsy revealed tragic news: Gail has a rare and incurable genetic disease called fatal infantile myopathy. This condition is caused by a genetic mutation in the mitochondria of the muscles that leads to progressive weakness and death, usually within six months. Dr. Tyson shared this diagnosis with Gail's parents and grandparents and grieved with them.

At a subsequent family meeting, Gail's parents and grandfather (who is a pastor at a local church) told Dr. Tyson that they were praying for Gail's recovery and believed that God would not allow her to die. Dr. Tyson replied that he wished that Gail could be cured, but that he believed that Gail's illness was incurable and that she would die soon, with or without the current treatment measures. He voiced his concern about the pain and suffering associated with artificial ventilation, needle sticks, feeding tubes, and other interventions required to keep Gail alive. Dr. Tyson recommended removing the ventilator, but the family rejected this recommendation. The family did seek the advice of a theologian from a nearby Bible college. The theologian listened to Dr. Tyson's and the family's views, and acknowledged the difficulty of the situation, but offered no solution. How should Dr. Tyson proceed?

The rise of the futility debate

As described in Chapters 15 and 16, a series of US court decisions in the 1970s and 1980s established patient rights to *refuse* life-prolonging medical treatment. During this period, states also enacted statutes that enabled patients to express their desire to forgo life-prolonging treatment by means of advance directives and encouraged or required physicians to honor those directives.

A new controversy regarding treatment near the end of life emerged in the late 1980s. Reports began to appear in the medical literature that some patients and families were *demanding access* to aggressive treatments, even though their physicians recommended against those treatments on the grounds that they would not be successful.[1] In response to these demands, commentators asserted a right of physicians to withhold or withdraw treatment because it would be futile, regardless of patient or surrogate wishes. In an early article entitled "Must We Always Use CPR?" for example, physician Leslie Blackhall makes the following assertion: "The issue of patient autonomy is irrelevant, however, when CPR has no potential benefit. Here the physician's duty to provide responsible medical care precludes CPR, either as a routine process in the absence of a decision by the patient, or a response to a patient's misguided request for such treatment."[2]

Other commentators quickly challenged these appeals to futility as a justification for denying requests for life-prolonging treatment.[3] Physicians Robert Truog, Allan Brett, and Joel Frader conclude their 1992 article "The Problem with Futility" with the claim that "the rapid advance of the language of futility into the jargon of bioethics should be followed by an equally rapid retreat."[4] The ensuing intense debate has been the subject of more than 2000 medical journal articles over the past two decades, including contributions from most of the leading scholars in the field of bioethics.

---

[1] See, for example, Blackhall (1987), Tomlinson and Brody (1988), and Schneiderman et al. (1990).

[2] Blackhall (1987).

[3] For early critiques of the concept of futility, see Lantos et al. (1989), Truog et al. (1992), and Veatch and Spicer (1992).

[4] Truog et al. (1992).

What is futility?

Many of the early contributions to the literature on medical futility proposed definitions of the term and then applied those definitions to various medical treatments. The etymology of the term offers an instructive example: 'futile' is derived from the Latin term *futilis*, meaning "leaky." According to Greek mythology, the daughters of King Danaus were condemned by the gods to carry water forever in jars that were riddled with holes.[5] Because the jars were leaky, their task was futile. As this example illustrates, we judge a task to be futile when we are highly confident that it cannot achieve its goal. Arthur Caplan points out that futility judgments are about "odds and ends" – that is, a futile effort must have very low *odds* of achieving its desired *ends*.[6] Each futility judgment, then, has both a quantitative and a qualitative aspect. Quantitatively, we must determine how unlikely it is that an effort will achieve its end, and qualitatively, we must identify what is the intended end or goal of the effort.

How does this general concept of futility apply to medical treatments? If the primary goal of medicine is to benefit patients, then a medical treatment is presumably futile when it cannot benefit a particular patient. The concept of patient benefit is very broad and at least somewhat vague, however. Various authors have, therefore, proposed more specific quantitative and qualitative criteria for futile medical treatment. Baruch Brody and Amir Halevy offer a helpful description of the following four types of medical futility:[7]

1. Physiological futility. A treatment is physiologically futile when it cannot have the intended physiological effect. CPR example: If the immediate goal of CPR is to keep blood flowing to the brain and other vital organs, CPR is physiologically futile when rupture of the aorta prevents blood from reaching those organs despite chest compressions.
2. Imminent demise futility. A treatment is futile in this way when it cannot prevent the patient's death in the very near future. CPR example: Even if it can perfuse vital organs and restore spontaneous heartbeat and respiration, CPR is futile in this sense when evidence demonstrates that the patient will arrest again very soon and will not survive for more than a few hours or days.

---

[5] Hamilton (1942).   [6] Caplan (1996).   [7] Brody and Halevy (1995).

3. Lethal condition futility. A treatment is futile in this way when it cannot affect an underlying lethal condition that will cause death in the not-too-far future. CPR example: Although it can restore spontaneous heartbeat and respiration, CPR is futile in this sense when a patient has late stage terminal cancer that will result in death within weeks to several months.

4. Qualitative futility. A treatment is qualitatively futile if it cannot result in an acceptable quality of life. CPR example: Although it can enable prolongation of physical life for a long period, CPR on a patient in a permanent vegetative state may be judged to be qualitatively futile because it cannot change the patient's unacceptable quality of life.

These four types of medical futility are listed in order from less to more inclusive and from less to more controversial. That is, few scholars would deny that a treatment that clearly cannot achieve its physiological end is futile, but only a few treatments in specific situations are likely to satisfy that description. Many more treatments may be judged to be futile because they prolong a life that has an unacceptable quality, but views about what constitutes an acceptable quality of life are highly variable and debatable. It is worth emphasizing, however, that not all futility judgments are controversial. In every medical specialty, there are examples of treatments that have been clearly demonstrated to be ineffective. One prominent example is the use of laetrile, a chemical extracted from apricot and peach pits, as an alternative cancer therapy, despite multiple scientific studies concluding that it provides no benefit and can be harmful.[8] Should patients nevertheless request such an ineffective treatment, there is general consensus that physicians may justifiably refuse to honor that request. The moral debate over futility has centered on more controversial appeals to the broader types of futility described above to justify unilateral physician decisions to withhold or withdraw life-prolonging treatments like CPR, mechanical ventilation, and artificial nutrition and hydration. These morally controversial appeals to futility involve medical interventions that are effective in some situations, but are said to be futile for a particular patient or class of patients.

---

[8] Milazzo et al. (2011).

Key arguments in the futility debate

Both proponents and opponents of the appeal to medical futility can marshal persuasive arguments to support their positions. We turn now to consideration of leading arguments in the debate. I will begin with three arguments offered by proponents of medical futility (the "futilitarians"), and then offer three arguments made by opponents of futility (the "anti-futilitarians").

Futilitarian arguments

1. Professional integrity. This argument asserts that physicians must be recognized as moral agents in their own right, not merely technicians carrying out the will of others. Forcing physicians to provide treatments that they judge to be useless or harmful and thus contrary to professional standards of care violates their professional integrity and autonomy. Physicians should not, in the words of John Paris and Frank Reardon, be "transformed into an extension of the patient's (or family's) whim, fantasy, or unrealizable hopes and desires."[9] Physicians may, therefore, refuse patient requests for treatments they deem futile.

2. Professional expertise. This argument points out that patients rely on the expertise of their physicians to determine what are reasonable treatment options, based on established standards of care, and to present those options to the patient. Options judged by physicians to be futile are not reasonable, and thus are more likely to confuse patients than to enhance their ability to make effective treatment choices. Therefore, physicians should not offer treatment options to their patients that they deem to be futile.

3. Responsible stewardship of scarce resources. As discussed in Chapter 11, physicians have a duty to be responsible stewards of the health care resources entrusted to them. Providing futile treatment wastes resources, since it cannot achieve its desired end of benefiting the patient. Physicians should therefore not provide treatments that they deem futile, but should rather conserve resources for use when they can have beneficial consequences.

---

[9] Paris and Reardon (1992).

Anti-futilitarian arguments

1. Patient autonomy. This argument observes that patients and physicians may have different views about what length or quality of life is worth preserving, or what odds of a successful outcome are worth pursuing. When this is the case, the argument continues, physicians should not be allowed simply to impose their views on patients in the name of futility. Unilateral withdrawal of life-prolonging treatment would be a kind of abandonment of the patient. Instead, physicians should discuss a broad range of treatment options with their patients and help them to achieve the patients' own goals.

2. Uncertainties of prognosis. This argument asserts that, in order to reach a treatment decision based on futility, physicians must be highly confident that the intended goal of treatment, be it extending life or improving quality of life, cannot be achieved. Studies of available prognostic measures, however, indicate that such measures cannot predict outcomes such as short-term mortality with a high degree of probability in individual situations, even for very seriously ill patients.[10] Thus, physicians often lack the necessary scientific basis to make unilateral treatment decisions based on futility.

3. Lack of social consensus. This argument claims that acceptance and implementation of criteria for forgoing treatment based on futility should be based, not on individual physician judgments, but on a broad social consensus. Some kinds of futile treatment (like laetrile for cancer, or attempting CPR on a patient with obvious signs of death) are supported by a clear consensus of scientific and public opinion, but the ongoing debate over appeals to futility in more controversial cases provides strong evidence of the lack of social consensus about treatment decisions in these cases. In the absence of consensus about these latter situations, physicians should not impose unilateral judgments about futility on unwilling patients.

Notice that these arguments turn on both empirical and moral claims. Futilitarian arguments depend on strong empirical evidence about the inefficacy of the treatments in question, and anti-futilitarian arguments challenge the strength of that empirical evidence. Futilitarian arguments

---

[10] See, for example, Halevy et al. (1996) and Lynn et al. (1997).

appeal to the professional prerogatives of physicians, and anti-futilitarians appeal to patient rights and more general social and moral norms.

A shift to procedures

Despite intense debate and many hundreds of scholarly articles during the 1990s, the dispute over medical futility seemed little closer to resolution by the end of the decade. Three events around this time signaled a shift in approach to the topic. The first of these was the publication in 1999 of a report by the Council on Ethical and Judicial Affairs of the AMA entitled "Medical Futility in End-of-Life Care."[11] In this report, the Council reviews various proposed definitions and standards of medical futility and asserts its conclusion that "a fully objective and concrete definition of futility is unattainable." In place of a substantive definition of futility, the Council proposes a "fair process approach" to resolving futility disputes. The Council outlines a multi-step process, including planning in advance of critical illness, joint deliberation and decision-making by physicians and patients or their representatives at the bedside, seeking advice from consultants and institutional ethics committees, arranging transfer to another physician or institution, and, if none of these steps resolves the dispute, forgoing the disputed treatment despite patient or surrogate requests to continue it.

The second of these events was the enactment by the state of Texas in 1999 of a statute that establishes a legally endorsed process whereby health care facilities can settle disputes about treatment near the end of life.[12] The process includes review of a dispute about treatment between physicians and patients or their representatives by an institutional "ethics or medical committee." If that committee agrees with the physician that continuing life-sustaining treatment is inappropriate, the physician and facility must make reasonable efforts to transfer the patient to another physician or another facility willing to provide the requested treatment. If no transfer can be arranged within ten days, the life-sustaining treatment may be discontinued. If this procedure is followed, the statute grants physicians and facilities immunity from criminal and civil liability for their actions in

---

[11] Council on Ethical and Judicial Affairs, American Medical Association (1999).
[12] Texas Health and Safety Code § 166.046.

withdrawing life-sustaining treatment without the consent of the patient or the patient's surrogate. Although many hospitals had developed procedures to address disputes about life-sustaining procedures, this Texas statute was the first to provide immunity from liability for providers who forgo treatment after following the statutory procedure.

The Texas futile care statute remains in force, but no other state has followed Texas's example by establishing a similar legal safe harbor to protect physicians and facilities that follow a procedure culminating in unilateral withdrawal of life-prolonging treatment. Proponents of the Texas model argue that providers need and should receive legal protection for their considered decisions to forgo futile life-prolonging treatments.[13] Critics maintain that so-called "fair process approaches" like the Texas procedure favor providers over patients and may discriminate against minority patients.[14]

The third of these events was the publication in 2000 of a *New England Journal of Medicine* article entitled "The Rise and Fall of the Futility Movement." In this article, authors Paul Helft, Mark Siegler, and John Lantos echo the AMA Council's conclusion that efforts to find a consensus definition of futile treatment have failed. They go on to observe that empirical measures, based on physician judgments or prognostic scoring systems, are too variable or too imprecise to justify futility judgments. They also point out that disputes about futility typically involve a clash between the autonomy claims of physicians and patients, with no consensus about whose claims should prevail. Finally, these authors acknowledge the growing emphasis on procedures like that proposed in the AMA Council report and enacted by statute in Texas, and they emphasize the importance of ongoing physician discussion with patients and families about treatments and their outcomes.

Since 2000, the debate over appeal to medical futility has focused on the content of procedures for resolving futility disputes and on the question whether procedures that allow unilateral physician withdrawal of disputed life-prolonging treatment should receive legal protection. Although the focus has shifted, the appeal of the concept of futility for many physicians and the suspicion of futility judgments by patients and others both remain, and so the debate over medical futility rages on.

---

[13] See, for example, Kopelman et al. (2005).   [14] See, for example, Wojtasiewicz (2006).

Case analysis

In the case described at the beginning of this chapter, Dr. Tyson and the family of baby Gail disagree about whether to continue life-prolonging measures for Gail. Dr. Tyson has informed the family about the diagnosis of an incurable and fatal genetic disease and recommended that life-support measures be discontinued. Gail's parents and extended family are unwilling to accept this information and recommendation, however. They inform Dr. Tyson that they and their religious community have hope that God will cure Gail, and they insist that Dr. Tyson continue the mechanical ventilation, nutritional support, and other treatments that are keeping her alive.

Is continuation of these treatments an example of medically futile treatment? Dr. Tyson may well conclude that it is. His rationale would presumably be that neither the treatments in use nor any other available treatments are able to cure or control this progressive disease. With or without treatment, therefore, Gail will likely die within the next six months, and her survival during those months will be marked primarily by physical deterioration and discomfort. Dr. Tyson may, in other words, be making an appeal to concepts of lethal condition futility and qualitative futility.

Relying on their religious faith rather than the available scientific evidence, Gail's family appears to have a very different view about the potential outcome of her illness and the futility of continuing treatment. They may, therefore, want to continue treatment in the hope that prolongation of Gail's life will allow time for a miraculous cure to occur. Even if they accept Dr. Tyson's prediction that Gail will die relatively soon, they may place great value on her survival for the next several months and believe that this is a goal worth pursuing.

As Gail's illness progresses, Dr. Tyson and his parents may eventually be able to reach agreement on a treatment plan for her continuing care. If their disagreement persists, however, whose view about the proper goals of treatment and the prospects for achieving them should prevail in this case? We are morally reluctant simply to force one party to the dispute to accept the other's decision, but what is the alternative? We may look for guidance to another source of moral or legal authority, such as a legislative body or court. The Texas statute endorses a procedure that ultimately allows health care facilities to forgo futile or inappropriate life-prolonging treatment, but the few US court decisions on disputes about medically futile treatment have generally sided with families who request continuation of treatment.[15] Thus, there is no general consensus about who should be authorized to make these decisions. Whose decision about treatment for baby Gail do you believe should prevail?

[15] For a review of these decisions, see Daar (1995).

18   Aid in dying

Case example

Dr. Quill has recently given his patient Diane some very bad news; a bone marrow biopsy shows that she has acute myelomonocytic leukemia. Diane owns a successful business, is married, and has a college-aged son. An oncologist informs her that treatment for her leukemia involves two courses of chemotherapy followed by whole body irradiation and stem cell transplantation, with a projected five-year survival rate of about 25 percent. Without treatment, life expectancy is less than six months. The oncologist recommends that she begin the chemotherapy immediately. To the surprise and dismay of her physicians, Diane refuses aggressive therapy for her condition, saying that the one-in-four chance of five-year survival is not good enough for her to undergo so difficult a course of therapy. Despite their efforts to persuade her to begin chemotherapy, she persists in her decision to live the rest of her life outside the hospital and to accept only palliative and hospice care.

Shortly thereafter, Diane tells Dr. Quill, who has been her primary care physician for the past eight years, that she dreads the thought of a lingering and painful death and very much wants to maintain control and dignity in her final days. She says that, when her condition gets worse, she wants to take her own life in the least painful way possible. She adds that she has discussed this at length with her husband and son, and they believe that they should respect her choice. Diane then asks Dr. Quill if he will help her take her life when her discomfort, physical deterioration, and dependence become too great. She tells him that having the means to end her life will free her from the fear of a lingering death and enable her to enjoy the time she has left.

How should Dr. Quill respond?[1]

---

[1] Quill (1991).

Key concepts

For more than half a century, the potential role of physicians in aiding the death of their patients has been one of the most controversial issues of health care ethics. Because "aid in dying" includes several different practices, and because commentators do not always use the terms that describe these practices in the same way, it is important to begin with definitions of suicide, physician-assisted suicide, and euthanasia. I define these concepts as follows: *Suicide* is the act of taking one's own life voluntarily and intentionally. *Physician-assisted suicide* is the act of taking one's own life voluntarily and intentionally, using means provided or prescribed by a physician, or with the advice of a physician. *Euthanasia* is the act of killing a gravely ill or injured person (but not oneself) in a relatively painless or humane way, for reasons of mercy.

In early discussions of euthanasia, some commentators defined euthanasia in a broader sense that included both killing and allowing the death of a suffering person for beneficent reasons.[2] Relying on this broader definition, these commentators offered a distinction between active and passive euthanasia. In active euthanasia, a physician (or other person) directly kills a patient, as, for example, by injecting a lethal drug, while in passive euthanasia, a physician withholds or withdraws a life-sustaining treatment, allowing the patient to die. As decisions to allow a patient to die by withholding or withdrawing life-sustaining treatment became more and more common, the term 'passive euthanasia' fell into disuse, and most contemporary scholars use the term 'euthanasia' to refer exclusively to the active killing of a patient for that patient's own good. Chapter 16, "Moral conflicts in end-of-life care," examines decisions to limit life-sustaining treatment in more detail.

Another distinction is often made between voluntary and non-voluntary euthanasia. In voluntary euthanasia, a patient is killed for beneficent reasons at his or her own request, or with his or her consent. In non-voluntary euthanasia, a patient who lacks decision-making capacity, and therefore cannot give consent, is killed for beneficent reasons.

A brief recent history

'Mercy killing' (*Gnadentod*) and 'euthanasia' (*Euthanasie*) were the terms used to describe physician-administered programs that killed thousands

---

[2] Rachels (1975) and Kuhse (1986).

of mentally and physically disabled patients in Nazi Germany between 1939 and 1945.[3] These programs served as a training and proving ground for the Holocaust, the Nazi genocide of European Jews.[4] Though the use of the term 'euthanasia' to describe these extermination programs is highly questionable, the moral outrage they evoked also cast grave doubt on the concept and practice of euthanasia in the years following World War II.

In a series of court decisions beginning the 1970s, the Netherlands became the first country in the world to permit physicians to practice euthanasia and physician-assisted suicide without significant risk of criminal prosecution.[5] National legislation in the Netherlands enacted in 2002 formally legalized the practices of euthanasia and physician-assisted suicide, and a nationwide survey estimated that 1.7 percent (or about 2300) of all deaths in the Netherlands in 2005 were the result of euthanasia (defined as "medication that is administered by a physician with the explicit intention of hastening death at the explicit request of the patient"), and another 0.1 percent (or about 113) of deaths in 2005 were the result of physician-assisted suicide.[6] Benelux neighbors Belgium, in 2002, and Luxembourg, in 2008, joined the Netherlands in legalizing euthanasia and assisted suicide.[7] Swiss law has, for many decades, permitted assistance in suicide for altruistic reasons, by both physicians and non-physicians.[8] In February 2015, the Supreme Court of Canada issued a decision legalizing physician-assisted suicide, following a year-long transition period for development of guidelines and procedures.[9] Despite ongoing public debate and news reports featuring patient appeals for aid in dying, the United Kingdom has retained its legal prohibition of euthanasia and physician-assisted suicide.[10]

In the United States, Dr. Jack Kevorkian, a retired pathologist, captured wide public attention when he announced, in June 1990, that he had used a "suicide machine" to assist the death of Janet Adkins, an Alzheimer's disease patient from Portland, Oregon.[11] Despite harsh criticism, Kevorkian assisted the suicides of more than one hundred patients over the next decade. In 1999, Kevorkian was convicted of murder after the popular US TV news program "60 Minutes" broadcast a videotape in

---

[3] Proctor (1988).   [4] Lifton (1986).   [5] Angell (1996).   [6] Van der Heide et al. (2007).
[7] Smets et al. (2010) and Watson (2009).   [8] Hurst and Mauron (2003).
[9] Attaran (2015).   [10] Biggs and Ost (2010).   [11] Kevorkian (1991).

which he administered a lethal injection to Thomas Youk, a patient with amyotrophic lateral sclerosis.[12]

Physician-assisted suicide was also a topic of major attention in US courts and at the ballot box during the 1990s. After failed voter initiatives in Washington in 1991 and in California in 1992, Oregon voters approved an initiative legalizing physician-assisted suicide in 1994, and reaffirmed their support for this practice in 1997.[13] Seventeen years after enactment of the law, the Oregon Public Health Division reported that 859 patients had completed physician-assisted suicide under the law (about 0.3 percent of all deaths in that state).[14] Voters in the state of Washington followed Oregon's lead in approving an initiative legalizing physician-assisted suicide in 2008, and the Vermont legislature enacted a state statute legalizing physician-assisted suicide in 2013.[15] A Montana Supreme Court decision legalized physician-assisted suicide in that state in 2009, and a 2014 New Mexico district court decision, now under appeal, legalized physician-assisted suicide in that court's jurisdiction, Bernalillo County.[16]

In the mid-1990s, US federal courts addressed the question whether assistance in suicide is a basic right under the US Constitution. In the spring of 1996, two federal Circuit Courts of Appeals ruled that terminally ill patients have a constitutional right to physician-assisted suicide, striking down state statutes in Washington and New York that prohibited this practice.[17] The US Supreme Court's announcement later that year that it would hear appeals of these two decisions stimulated an intense national debate about the morality of this practice. In its 1997 opinions, the Supreme Court rejected the Circuit Courts' assertions of a constitutional right to physician-assisted suicide.[18] Instead, the High Court reaffirmed the legal distinction between forgoing life-sustaining treatment and receiving assistance in suicide, and the authority of states to enact legislation either permitting or prohibiting this practice. As of 2012, some thirty-seven US states had statutes that explicitly prohibit assistance in suicide, and other states prohibited this practice under the common law.[19]

---

[12] Brody (1999).   [13] Moskop and Iserson (2001).

[14] Oregon Public Health Division (2015).   [15] Steinbrook (2008) and Davies (2013).

[16] Johnson (2009) and Eckholm (2014).

[17] *Compassion in Dying* v. *Washington* (1996) and *Quill* v. *Vacco* (1996).

[18] *Vacco* v. *Quill* (1997) and *Washington* v. *Glucksberg* (1997).

[19] Patient Rights Council (2012).

The case *for* aid in dying

The many contributors to the worldwide debate over aid-in-dying practices have marshaled a variety of moral and legal arguments for and against these practices. In this and the next section of this chapter, I will offer concise statements of leading arguments in this debate.

The argument from autonomy

Probably the most prominent argument in support of physician aid in dying relies on the moral principle of respect for individual autonomy. To respect individual autonomy is to allow a person to make important life decisions and to act on those decisions. Some persons with decision-making capacity express a strong desire to control the timing and manner of their own deaths, in order to avoid foreseen suffering, loss of mental and physical function, indignity, and dependence. These persons may request the assistance of a physician to end their lives in an effective, painless, and non-disfiguring way. To respect personal autonomy, this argument concludes, physicians who are willing to provide euthanasia or assistance in suicide should be permitted to do so.

The argument from consistency

A second argument for physician aid in dying emphasizes the similarities between these and other medical practices. This argument begins by pointing out the general moral consensus that patients should be permitted to refuse unwanted life-sustaining medical treatments. Patients approaching the end of life do frequently refuse these treatments in order to avoid prolongation of suffering, thereby hastening their deaths. Decisions to forgo life-sustaining treatment thus commonly have the same rationale (avoiding suffering) and the same result (an earlier death) as decisions for euthanasia or physician-assisted suicide. The means are different in these practices, but, this argument contends, these differences in means are not, in themselves, morally significant. Therefore, if forgoing life-sustaining treatment is morally and legally permissible, euthanasia and physician-assisted suicide should be permissible as well.

The argument from suffering

A third argument in support of physician aid in dying appeals to the moral significance of preventing suffering. This argument points out that allowing a terminal illness or a lethal injury to progress, despite medical treatment, to the foreseen failure of a vital function and subsequent death of a patient can cause significant suffering. That suffering can be prevented, however, if the patient is permitted to choose euthanasia or physician-assisted suicide. Because aid in dying can prevent that significant suffering, this argument concludes, it should be permitted for those who desire it.

The case *against* aid in dying

The argument from theology

For many opponents of physician aid in dying, the most compelling argument against these practices is theological. Several leading religious traditions assert that human authority does not extend to choosing the time and manner of one's death by means of euthanasia or suicide, and that control over life and death belongs instead to God. From this doctrine follows the conclusion that the practices of euthanasia and physician-assisted suicide are morally wrong. Those who hold this religious belief are also likely to support legal prohibition of these practices.

The argument from abuse

Another leading argument against physician aid in dying does not assert that these practices are intrinsically wrong, but rather that legalizing them is likely to cause significant abuses and harms. According to this argument, legalization of euthanasia and physician-assisted suicide would enable physicians and other caregivers to end the lives of vulnerable patients, as, for example, frail elderly patients or patients with severe depression, by pressuring or coercing them to receive these lethal interventions. These actions, it is claimed, would often be taken not to benefit the patients, but rather to relieve others of the burden of caring for them. This argument concludes that physician aid in dying should be prohibited in order to protect these vulnerable patients from harm.

The argument from medical integrity

A third argument against physician aid in dying appeals to the moral foundations of the medical profession. This argument asserts that physicians accept a basic professional commitment to healing and to the preservation of life. Physician participation in euthanasia and assisted suicide, the argument continues, would violate that commitment and would undermine patient trust in their physicians' intentions. This argument concludes that prohibition of physician aid in dying is necessary in order to preserve the identity and integrity of medicine as a healing and life-affirming profession.

Responses

Each of the above arguments has many proponents and opponents, and readers are very likely to find some arguments more persuasive than others. In the long and intense moral debate over physician aid in dying, each argument has received sustained scrutiny and multiple responses. To take the discussion one step further, let's consider some of these responses.

The argument from autonomy: This argument applies only to competent requests for assistance in suicide and to voluntary euthanasia, and so provides no justification of life-ending actions for patients who cannot make their wishes known. Furthermore, autonomous decisions and actions that threaten others may not merit respect, and so aid in dying may be prohibited if prohibition is necessary to prevent serious harms due to abuse of these practices.

The argument from consistency: This argument asserts that the different means used to relieve suffering and to hasten death (that is, forgoing life-prolonging treatment, physician-assisted suicide, and euthanasia) are not significantly different from one another on moral grounds. Is this assertion correct? Some critics respond that the primary cause of death is different in these three different practices, and that that difference is morally significant. When life-prolonging treatment is withheld or withdrawn in a terminal illness, the illness is the primary cause of death, while in physician-assisted suicide, the patient's own action is the cause of death, and in euthanasia, the physician's action is the cause of death. Other critics point out differences in the "finality" of these means of ending life. When life-sustaining treatments are withheld or withdrawn, patients sometimes unexpectedly survive without these treatments. When physicians prescribe lethal medications, patients sometimes choose not to use those medications to end their lives. In contrast, when physicians inject a lethal drug, the rapid death of the patient is virtually assured. Is "finality" a morally significant feature of an intervention, and, if so, should it count for or against that intervention?

The argument from suffering: This argument concludes that physician aid in dying should be permitted to enable patients to avoid the substantial suffering caused by terminal illness. But is substantial suffering an inevitable feature of terminal illness? Critics argue that, although such suffering may once have been unavoidable, recent developments in palliative care now make it possible to provide effective relief for physical pain, and psychological and spiritual support can relieve the mental suffering associated with terminal illness. If this is the case, then access to physician aid in dying is not necessary in order to relieve suffering, and it may distract health care professionals from providing optimal palliative care for their patients.

The argument from theology: This argument relies on specific religious beliefs. Although many people do embrace a theology-based prohibition of suicide and euthanasia, many others endorse these practices, on both religious and secular moral grounds. Critics of this argument maintain that religious convictions alone cannot justify prohibition of physician aid in dying in a secular, religiously pluralistic society.

The argument from abuse: This argument asserts that legalization of physician aid-in-dying practices will lead to widespread abuse, in particular the premature death of vulnerable patients. Critics may respond that any medical practice, including the limitation of life-sustaining treatment, is subject to abuse, and that regulations can be implemented to reduce the risk of abuse. What is the evidence that physician aid in dying is especially susceptible to widespread or serious abuse? There is now many years of experience with a regulated legal practice of euthanasia and physician-assisted suicide in the Netherlands and of physician-assisted suicide in the state of Oregon. Both jurisdictions require reporting of these actions, and review of this data provides evidence about the potential for abuse. In the most recent report from the Netherlands, based on 2005 death records, investigators found a moderate decrease in rates of euthanasia and physician-assisted suicide from previous reports in 1995 and 2001; they attribute this decrease to physicians' increased use of continuous deep sedation near the end of life and their increased recognition that opioid pain medication near the end of life does not hasten death.[20] The state of Oregon publishes annual reports about the characteristics of patients who complete physician-assisted suicide under that state's law.[21] One study of these data concludes that they provide no evidence for claims that physician aid in dying leads to abuse of vulnerable patients, and that patients with higher social, economic, educational, and professional status are in fact more likely to end their lives with physician assistance.[22]

The argument from medical integrity: This argument asserts that aid-in-dying practices pose an unacceptable threat to the integrity of medicine as a healing and a life-preserving profession. Critics respond that healing and the preservation of life are important, but not the only important professional responsibilities of physicians. Other essential professional responsibilities of physicians are respect for patient autonomy and relief of patient suffering. In the situation of terminal illness, these critics argue, healing is no longer possible, and the value of preserving life is significantly diminished. When that is the case, they conclude, the responsibilities of respect for patient wishes and relief of suffering should come to the fore and should permit physicians to provide assistance in dying upon patient request.

Case analysis

Diane's request obviously poses a serious moral question for Dr. Quill. He knows that she has decided to forgo aggressive treatment for her leukemia and to concentrate instead on living fully and comfortably in the time she has left. She clearly has the capacity to understand her situation and make a treatment decision, and, given the severe side effects of the proposed curative treatments and their high risk of failure, her choice is an understandable one. Dr. Quill can treat her pain and other physical symptoms, but he recognizes that, as her disease

---

[20] Van der Heide et al. (2007).   [21] Oregon Public Health Division (2015).
[22] Battin et al. (2007).

progresses, discomfort, weakness, and disability will eventually become more persistent and severe.

Her quality of life in these final weeks and months is obviously of the greatest importance for Diane, but this situation may also have significant consequences for Dr. Quill. He may, for example, have strong moral reservations about the propriety of assisting a patient in suicide. If assisting a suicide is a criminal offence in his jurisdiction, agreeing to help Diane may also expose him to criminal prosecution.

Dr. Quill has at least two clear alternatives. On the one hand, he can pledge to provide excellent palliative care for Diane, but refuse to provide assistance in suicide, perhaps citing professional standards or a duty to obey a law prohibiting assistance in suicide. On the other hand, he may decide to assist her by prescribing a lethal medication, perhaps reasoning that this action will give her the best chance to live well in the days ahead and to end her life before it becomes too burdensome.

If Dr. Quill chooses the latter alternative, should the law permit him to assist Diane in suicide without fear of criminal sanctions? Or is this situation, in which a patient makes an apparently reasonable request of an apparently sympathetic physician, an "outlier," and so not a representative example of the overall benefits and harms likely to follow from legalization of the practice of physician-assisted suicide?

For the record, Dr. Quill recounted Diane's story in a 1991 article in the *New England Journal of Medicine*.[23] After an initial refusal, Dr. Quill reconsidered Diane's request and agreed to prescribe barbiturates and to tell her the amount needed to commit suicide. Diane informed him when she decided to end her life, and her husband called him after she had done so. Dr. Quill decided to report the cause of Diane's death as acute leukemia, not suicide, to protect the family (and himself) from an investigation and from possible criminal prosecution.

Unlike the overwhelmingly negative response to Dr. Kevorkian's announcement in 1990 that he had assisted a patient's suicide, professional and public reaction to Dr. Quill's story was more subdued and ambivalent.[24] Some physicians praised Dr. Quill's compassion, courage, and loyalty to Diane. Others expressed fear about the abuses of a legal practice of physician aid in dying and criticized Dr. Quill's

---

[23] Quill (1991).   [24] Death and dignity (1991).

misrepresentation of the cause of death on Diane's death certificate. New York authorities investigated the situation, but could not find enough evidence to prosecute Dr. Quill for assisting a suicide.[25]

Was Dr. Quill's decision to assist Diane's suicide morally defensible? Should other jurisdictions follow Oregon's lead in legalizing this practice?

[25] Gianelli (1991).

Part IV

Ethics in special contexts

Biomedical research, genetics, and organ transplantation

Parts I, II, and III of this volume have examined the roles, history, and methods of health care ethics, the moral foundations of therapeutic relationships, and moral issues at the beginning and at the end of life. Part IV will consider complex moral questions encountered in three specific health care contexts: biomedical research on human subjects, health care for genetic conditions, and organ transplantation.

Chapter 19, "Research on human subjects," begins by recognizing the importance of biomedical research for achieving the beneficent goals of health care. It also recognizes the potential for grave harm to research subjects, illustrated in the Nazi medical research on concentration camp inmates and the Tuskegee syphilis study conducted by the US Public Health Service. The chapter goes on to examine basic criteria for morally defensible research on human subjects: informed consent, assessment of risks and benefits of the research, confidentiality, and equitable selection of subjects. It concludes with a discussion of who bears what responsibilities for the protection of human research subjects.

Chapter 20, "The genetic revolution," describes both the great promise of the emerging practice of "personalized genomic medicine" and the great peril of misunderstanding and misuse of genetic information evidenced in the morally abhorrent eugenic sterilization and extermination programs of the twentieth century. The chapter examines moral questions in three domains of genetics activity: biomedical research, health policy, and clinical medical care. The discussions in this chapter focus on the use of genetic testing and the disclosure of genetic test results in various settings, including prenatal care, care for newborn infants, pediatrics, and adult medicine.

The volume's final chapter is Chapter 21, "Organ transplantation." This chapter describes the emergence and growth of transplantation as a life-extending intervention for patients with a catastrophic medical condition, end-stage organ failure. The success of transplantation has stimulated great demand for this treatment, and the available supply of transplant organs has not kept pace with the increasing demand. Faced with the growing scarcity of transplant organs, transplantation advocates have proposed, and societies have implemented, a variety of strategies to increase organ supply. The chapter reviews and evaluates several of these proposed strategies, including presumed consent to organ donation, financial incentives for organ donation, revision of neurologic criteria for the determination of death, abandonment of the "dead donor rule," animal-to-human organ transplantation, and bioengineering of human organs. Given the current scarcity of transplant organs, transplantation systems confront difficult questions of who among the many waiting transplant candidates should receive each transplant organ as it becomes available. The chapter concludes with examination of the US approach to transplant organ distribution, including the role of individual transplant programs in adding patients to their transplant waiting lists, and the role of a national system of algorithms for ranking waiting list patients for access to transplant organs. These algorithms attempt to balance considerations of utility, maximizing the benefits of transplantation, with considerations of equity, ensuring fair access to this treatment.

19   Research on human subjects

Case example

Mr. Simpson, a high school biology teacher, is a community member of the Institutional Review Board (IRB) at University Medical Center (UMC), the nearby academic medical center. (US federal regulations require that health care institutions establish IRBs to review and approve all publicly funded biomedical research on human subjects conducted at the institution.) At today's meeting of the UMC IRB, members are considering a research proposal entitled "Angina Pain Relief and Outcome Network Study," or APRONS. Dr. Russell, Professor of Cardiology, explains that APRONS is a proposed multi-institution clinical trial of treatments for patients with stable coronary artery disease (narrowing of the arteries of the heart), and that he will be the lead investigator of this study at UMC. The study intends to enroll as research subjects more than 2000 patients with this condition over a period of three years. Patient-subjects will be randomly assigned to receive one of the following three interventions:

1. *Optimal medical (drug) therapy to relieve angina (severe chest pain caused by inadequate blood supply to the heart) and to control progression of the disease.*
2. *Percutaneous coronary intervention (PCI), also called coronary angioplasty – a procedure in which a clinician feeds a catheter (a flexible tubular instrument) from an artery in the patient's leg through the blood vessels into an artery of the heart, then inflates a balloon to dilate that artery. When the balloon inflates, it implants an expandable wire mesh tubular device, called a stent, inside the artery. The expanded stent remains in the artery to keep it open. Subjects in this group will receive optimal drug therapy after PCI.*
3. *Sham PCI – a similar procedure in which a clinician feeds a catheter from an artery in the patient's leg through the blood vessels into an artery of the heart, but then removes the catheter without any additional intervention. Subjects in this group will receive optimal drug therapy after the sham procedure.*

Patient-subjects in groups two and three will not be told which of the two procedures they have received until the study is completed. All study subjects will receive identical counseling and support for lifestyle changes to prevent disease progression, including smoking cessation, exercise, and diet. The investigators will follow these patient-subjects over the next four years and will compare the effect of the three interventions on three outcomes: chest pain, myocardial infarction (heart attack), and patient death from cardiac or vascular causes.

Mr. Simpson has several reservations about this proposed research. He knows that the first two treatments are already in wide use for patients with heart disease, and so he wonders why they need further investigation. He is especially concerned about the third intervention. How, he wonders, can the investigators justify an invasive procedure that has clear risks, but does nothing to treat a patient's partially obstructed coronary artery? Given these concerns, Mr. Simpson is unsure whether he should vote to approve or reject the APRONS study proposal.

An obvious and fundamental goal of health care professionals is the provision of beneficial treatment to patients suffering from illness, injury, or disability. This is not their only goal, however. Consider, for example, this statement from the fifth principle of the "Principles of Medical Ethics" of the AMA: "A physician shall continue to study, apply, and advance scientific knowledge ..."[1] This principle asserts a duty to advance scientific knowledge, and it makes no mention of patients. Contemporary physicians, and most other health care professionals, receive extensive training in the biomedical and behavioral sciences. Acting as scientists, they contribute to knowledge by engaging in research, defined as "a systematic investigation including research development, testing and evaluation, designed to develop or contribute to generalizable knowledge."[2]

Why does the AMA assert a fundamental responsibility of physicians to advance scientific knowledge, presumably through biomedical research? One rationale might be the intrinsic value of knowledge, based on our innate curiosity about ourselves and the world around us. This rationale supports basic research in all of the sciences – physical, biological, behavioral, and social. A second, and perhaps more compelling, rationale for research by physicians and biomedical scientists links research to the fundamental medical goal of providing beneficial treatment for patients.

[1] American Medical Association (2001b).
[2] US Department of Health and Human Services (2009), at §46.102.

Research in the biomedical sciences is essential to understanding the structure and function of our bodies and the causes and effects of disease and injury. That understanding, in turn, can enable the development and evaluation of new and more effective treatments to cure or ameliorate disease and injury. Because research plays an essential role in achieving the goals of health care, the AMA recognizes participation in advancing scientific knowledge through research as a fundamental professional responsibility of physicians.

Investigators engage in biomedical research in several different settings. Laboratory, or "bench," research examines biochemical and physiological processes in living cells and tissues "*in vitro*," that is, "in glass," in a controlled laboratory environment outside of the organism. Animal research examines biological processes and the effects of drugs and other interventions on animal subjects, usually housed in a protected environment. Finally, human subjects research examines biological processes and therapeutic interventions in human beings, including both healthy research subjects and patients with illness or injury. Each of these types of research makes essential contributions to scientific knowledge, and each raises significant ethical questions. Bench and animal research serve the therapeutic goals of health care by increasing our understanding of basic biological processes and by identifying promising candidates for effective treatment of disease and injury. Tissues *in vitro* and animal subjects are significantly different in their structure and function from living human beings, however, and therefore promising experimental treatments must also be tested on human subjects.

Bench scientists, animal researchers, and investigators performing studies on human subjects have multiple moral responsibilities in common. These responsibilities include honesty in the collection and reporting of research results and in the disclosure of errors, appropriate management of potential conflicts between scientific integrity and financial self-interest, and fairness in the allocation of credit for research contributions.[3] Because health care professionals practicing in clinical settings most often engage in research on human subjects, and because this research poses especially serious ethical issues, the rest of this chapter will focus on human subjects research.

---

[3] For a review of these moral responsibilities of scientists, see Committee on Science, Engineering, and Public Policy et al. (2009).

Two historical examples

As noted above, without biomedical research, including research on human subjects, to determine what treatments are effective, health care professionals cannot achieve their central goal of providing beneficial therapy for their patients. It seems obvious, therefore, that human subjects research is a morally permissible and indeed a morally praiseworthy activity. What, then, are the morally serious or controversial issues posed by this research? Two notorious twentieth-century examples, research on concentration camp inmates in Nazi Germany during World War II, and US Public Health Service research on black patients with syphilis in Alabama, provide compelling evidence of unethical practice in research on human subjects. A brief review of these examples shows how research on human subjects can violate fundamental moral norms.

Nazi medical research

During World War II, Nazi military physicians stationed at concentration camps in Germany and its occupied territories carried out a wide variety of research studies on inmates of those camps.[4] Medical research was one function of the camps, along with forced labor and their primary function of extermination of so-called "inferior races" under the Nazi racist ideology, a morally repugnant event now identified as the Holocaust. Many of these research studies had overtly eugenic or military purposes that were highly morally suspect – they included studies of new methods for sterilization and execution, studies of conditions affecting military personnel, such as rapid decompression from high altitude, immersion in cold water, and exposure to infectious diseases, and studies of the relative role of genetics and environment in identical twins. The physician-investigators conducted this research on prisoners without their consent. Most of the studies inflicted severe injury and great suffering, and many included the intentional killing of the subjects.

The Nuremberg "Doctors' Trial," conducted by a US Military Tribunal in 1946–1947, prosecuted twenty physicians and three other defendants for murder and other war crimes, based on their roles in medical research

---

[4] See, for example, Alexander (1949) and Barondess (1996).

conducted at Nazi concentration camps.[5] At this trial, US prosecutors presented detailed evidence about these experiments, emphasizing the grave injuries, severe suffering, and death intentionally inflicted on thousands of the research subjects. Sixteen of the defendants were convicted, and seven were sentenced to death. In their published judgment, the Doctors' Trial judges articulated a set of ten principles for the protection of human research subjects.[6] That declaration, called the Nuremberg Code, asserts the rights of subjects to consent to and to withdraw from research studies, and the duties of investigators to insure that their research has appropriate goals and a scientifically valid design and that it protects subjects from grave or unnecessary harms.

Tuskegee syphilis study

In 1932, the US Public Health Service initiated a long-term study of the natural history of untreated syphilis, a common and serious sexually transmitted infection.[7] The study subjects were poor black sharecroppers and laborers with latent syphilis in Macon County, Alabama. Subjects were deceived about the purpose of the study. Told that they were being treated for "bad blood," the subjects were in fact deliberately denied treatment for syphilis, and were prevented from receiving treatment elsewhere, even after a highly effective treatment, the antibiotic penicillin, became widely available in the early 1950s. Subjects agreed to participate in the study in exchange for free meals, free medical examinations and treatment for minor conditions at the Tuskegee Veterans Hospital, and burial insurance. Investigators examined the subjects annually to observe the progression of the disease and conducted autopsies to determine the cause of their deaths.

The study continued until 1972, when *The New York Times* published a front-page article, "Syphilis Victims in U.S. Study Went Untreated for 40 Years," by investigative reporter Jean Heller.[8] Public revelation of the Tuskegee Study evoked a storm of criticism and condemnation, a formal investigation by the US Department of Health, Education, and Welfare, and congressional hearings conducted by Senator Edward Kennedy. In 1974, the federal government awarded more than nine million dollars to

[5] See, for example, Shuster (1997) and Marrus (1999).
[6] See Shuster (1997) for a reprint of the text of the Nuremberg Code.
[7] For a detailed account of this study, see Jones (1981).   [8] Heller (1972).

the surviving study subjects in an out-of-court settlement.[9] Also in 1974, Congress created a National Commission for the Protection of Human Subjects of Biomedical and Behavioral Research to recommend moral and legal guidelines for research on human subjects.[10] In the four years of its existence, the National Commission published ten reports with recommendations on the protection of research subjects. In 1997, twenty-five years after the Tuskegee Study was halted, President Bill Clinton issued a formal apology to the study subjects and their families on behalf of the US government.[11]

Although the Nazi concentration camp research and the Tuskegee syphilis study are perhaps the most infamous cases of abuse of human research subjects, they are only two of multiple examples in the medical and bioethics literature.[12] How, then, can the substantial benefits of research on human subjects be achieved while also respecting the interests and rights of the subjects? The next sections will examine criteria and procedures for the protection of human research subjects.

Criteria for human subjects research

The years since the publication of the Nuremberg Code in 1947 have seen the adoption of multiple codes of human subjects research ethics, including the Declaration of Helsinki of the World Medical Association (adopted 1964, last revised 2013) and the International Ethical Guidelines for Biomedical Research Involving Human Subjects of the Council for International Organizations of Medical Sciences (adopted 1982, last revised 2002).[13] The United States and many other nations have enacted multiple regulations for the protection of human subjects; the set of basic US regulations has the informal title "The Common Rule."[14] These codes and regulations identify a number of basic criteria for morally permissible research on human subjects, including informed consent, risk-benefit assessment,

---

[9] Jones (1981).

[10] For more information on the National Commission for the Protection of Human Subjects of Biomedical and Behavioral Research, see Bioethics Research Library, Kennedy Institute of Ethics, Georgetown University (2013).

[11] Clinton (1997).   [12] For other US examples, see Coleman et al. (2005): 37–50.

[13] World Medical Association (2013); Council for International Organizations of Medical Sciences (CIOMS) (2002).

[14] US Department of Health and Human Services (2009).

confidentiality, and equitable selection of subjects. Let's examine each of these criteria in turn.

Informed consent

As described above, Nazi researchers forced concentration camp prisoners to participate in harmful and often lethal experiments. The first principle of the Nuremberg Code asserts a clear response; it states that "the voluntary consent of the human subject is absolutely essential." As in the case of clinical care (see Chapter 8, "Informed consent to treatment"), informed consent has become a moral and legal cornerstone of research on human subjects. Because the major goal of research, namely, acquiring new knowledge, is significantly different from the primary goal of treatment, namely, benefiting the patient, requirements for informed consent in the two contexts are also different. The US Common Rule, for example, requires that investigators provide the following eight specific types of information to potential research subjects as part of the informed consent process:

1. a statement that the study involves research, an explanation of the purposes of the research and the expected duration of the subject's participation, a description of the procedures to be followed, and identification of any procedures which are experimental;
2. a description of any reasonably foreseeable risks or discomforts to the subject;
3. a description of any benefits to the subject or to others which may reasonably be expected from the research;
4. a disclosure of appropriate alternative procedures or courses of treatment, if any, that might be advantageous to the subject;
5. a statement describing the extent, if any, to which confidentiality of records identifying the subject will be maintained;
6. for research involving more than minimal risk, an explanation as to whether any compensation and an explanation as to whether any medical treatment are available if injury occurs and, if so, what they consist of, or where further information may be obtained;
7. an explanation of whom to contact for answers to pertinent questions about the research and research subjects' rights, and whom to contact in the event of a research-related injury to the subject; and

8. a statement that participation is voluntary, refusal to participate will involve no penalty or loss of benefits to which the subject is otherwise entitled, and the subject may discontinue participation at any time without penalty or loss of benefits to which the subject is otherwise entitled.[15]

With this information, potential subjects can make their own voluntary and informed decisions about whether to participate in research, based on their evaluation of the purposes of the research, the expected risks and benefits of the research to them, and alternative treatment options. Just as there are generally recognized exceptions to the duty to obtain patient informed consent to treatment, however, there are also exceptions to the duty to obtain subject informed consent to participation in research. Some potential subjects, including fetuses, children, and adults who lack decision-making capacity, cannot give informed consent. Prohibiting all research on these subjects would protect them from research-related harms, but it would also make them "therapeutic orphans," that is, it would deny them the benefits of research to develop and provide new treatments designed specifically for them. Research codes and regulations, therefore, generally permit informed consent by authorized surrogate decision-makers for patient-subjects who lack decision-making capacity, often with additional restrictions to protect these more vulnerable subjects from exploitation or harm.

The Common Rule also recognizes that some types of morally justifiable research could not be conducted without alteration or waiver of some of the elements of informed consent. One prominent example is research on new techniques in the emergency treatment of sudden illness or injury. In this circumstance, the eligible patient-subjects have usually lost decision-making capacity, surrogates are generally not available, and interventions must be initiated very quickly. New regulations were adopted in 1996 to permit waiver of informed consent in emergency medicine research, provided that investigators satisfy multiple other conditions designed to protect the interests of the subjects of this research.[16]

An ongoing problem in obtaining informed consent to participation in research is a phenomenon called 'the therapeutic misconception.' This

---

[15] US Department of Health and Human Services (2009), at §46.116.
[16] US Department of Health and Human Services (1996).

term was coined to describe the persistent belief of patient-subjects that the primary purpose of the treatment they will receive in a research study is to benefit them individually, as would ordinarily be the case in clinical care outside a research study.[17] This belief often persists despite investigators' efforts to explain that one major purpose of research is to generate new knowledge and that research methods, including randomized assignment to different treatment groups, the use of control groups that will receive a placebo or a sham therapy, and double-blind procedures in which neither the investigator nor the patient-subject knows which treatment the subject is receiving, are not designed to benefit subjects and may not in fact serve their best interests. Appelbaum and colleagues suggest that one explanation for the strength of the therapeutic misconception is the implicit expectation of patients that their physicians will always act in their best interests.[18] To overcome this expectation, investigators must convince their patient-subjects that the goals and procedures used in a proposed research study are significantly different from those of clinical care. Study information should clearly identify the risks of participation, in addition to any potential benefits. To distinguish the research endeavor from clinical care, this information could be provided by a person other than the patient's physician, and the patient-subject's understanding of the information could be assessed by posing questions about research goals and methodology. Insofar as the therapeutic misconception may increase the number of patients willing to enroll in a research study, however, physician-investigators may be reluctant to make great efforts to overcome it and thereby undermine their own interest in recruiting research subjects.

Risk–benefit assessment

The informed consent requirement is a central protection of the interests of human research subjects. Consent of an involved person does not always make an action morally permissible, however – to cite an obvious example, consent of the victim is not a defense for murder. Similarly, consent of the subjects is not, by itself, sufficient to justify a research study. The Nuremberg Code, for example, identifies a number of

---

[17] See Appelbaum et al. (1987) and Dresser (2002).   [18] Appelbaum et al. (1987).

additional criteria for research on human subjects, including morally valuable research goals, sound research design, avoidance of grave or unnecessary risks to subjects, and a positive ratio of expected benefits to risks.[19] All of these criteria require evaluation of the foreseeable outcomes of the research study, both for the subjects themselves and for others who may be affected by the knowledge gained through the study. The US Common Rule addresses outcomes in the following two of its basic criteria for research on human subjects:

1. Risks to subjects are minimized: (i) by using procedures which are consistent with sound research design and which do not unnecessarily expose subjects to risk, and (ii) whenever appropriate, by using procedures already being performed on the subjects for diagnostic or therapeutic purposes.
2. Risks to subjects are reasonable in relation to anticipated benefits, if any, to subjects, and the importance of the knowledge that may reasonably be expected to result ...[20]

Satisfying these two criteria requires identification of risks of harm and benefits of a research study, assessment of the magnitude and probability of the identified risks and benefits, determination that the identified risks have been minimized, and comparison of the risks and benefits to determine whether the risks are reasonable in comparison to the benefits.

The concepts of risk and benefit thus play key roles in evaluating research on human subjects. These concepts have both qualitative and quantitative dimensions; that is, they include recognition of a possible harmful or a beneficial consequence, and estimation of the likelihood of that consequence. Commentators identify multiple types of research risk, including physical risk, such as pain, injury, or death; psychological risk, such as depression or guilt; social risk, such as discrimination or stigmatization; and economic risk, such as medical costs or loss of earnings.[21] There are also multiple types of research benefit, including direct health-related benefit to subjects from receiving a research intervention, indirect benefit to subjects, such as free medical care and feelings of personal satisfaction from contributing to research, and benefit to society and to

---

[19] Shuster (1997).   [20] US Department of Health and Human Services (2009), at §46.111.
[21] Prentice and Gordon (2001).

future patients from the results of the research.[22] Research that offers direct health-related benefits to patient-subjects is commonly referred to as "therapeutic research." In contrast, "non-therapeutic research" offers no direct benefit to individual subjects, who are often healthy volunteers; its sole purpose is the generation of new knowledge that may benefit future patients or society at large.

To assess the significance of research risks and expected benefits, one must consider both the nature of the outcome and its likelihood. Some risks and benefits may be relatively easy to identify and quantify; for example, venipuncture of a subject to measure blood levels of an investigational drug is known to cause some pain, some risk of bruising, and slight risks of fainting and infection. Other risks and benefits may be much more difficult to identify or quantify; for example, the chance that a new investigational drug will have a harmful or a beneficial effect on human subjects may not be predictable with any confidence on the basis of *in vitro* or animal studies alone. Even if the nature and likelihood of a research risk or expected benefit is known, research subjects and external evaluators may vary in their assessment of the significance of that risk or benefit in different circumstances. An adult patient-subject, for example, may find the risks associated with two additional venipunctures for research purposes to be negligible, but a six-year-old patient-subject may object very strongly to the prospect of monthly venipunctures over an entire year.

Another central concept for risk assessment in the Common Rule regulations is that of "minimal risk." The regulations offer the following criterion for determining that a research study has no more than minimal risk: "the probability and magnitude of harm or discomfort anticipated in the research are not greater in and of themselves than those ordinarily encountered in daily life or during the performance of routine physical or psychological examinations or tests."[23] US research regulations use the criterion of minimal risk in several ways to determine the

---

[22] King (2000). Although it is not directly addressed in US federal research regulations, payment to subjects for participation in research is another common but controversial type of economic benefit. Proponents claim that payment is a permissible and effective method for recruiting subjects; critics argue that it may constitute an undue inducement that undermines informed consent.

[23] US Department of Health and Human Services (2009), at §46.102.

justifiability of proposed studies. Minimal risk studies receive less extensive scrutiny, and their informed consent requirements may be modified or waived. Studies using vulnerable subjects (e.g., children, prisoners, and fetuses) must satisfy additional criteria for approval if they pose a greater than minimal risk. There is, however, considerable debate about how the minimal risk criterion should be interpreted and applied. Some commentators interpret the criterion's reference to "daily life" to mean the daily life of a normal healthy person, while others argue that "daily life" in the context of research should be understood as the daily life of a potential biomedical research subject with an identified illness or injury.[24] These two interpretations set significantly different thresholds for determining that a study poses no more than a minimal risk to subjects, and they therefore make approval of that study either more or less likely.

As noted above, the Common Rule requires that risks to research subjects be minimized, and it appeals specifically to the use of "sound research design" and to avoidance of unnecessary risks. The relationship of sound research design to minimization of risk may not be obvious, but it is nevertheless significant. Unless a research study has a scientifically sound design, it cannot achieve its goal of generating valuable new knowledge. Without the prospect of new knowledge, however, *any* increased risk imposed on subjects by participation in the study is unnecessary and cannot be justified. In addition to requiring a scientifically sound research design, risks to subjects can be reduced by requiring that qualified clinical staff perform research procedures and by selecting the least invasive and safest of alternative procedures for collection of study data.

The Common Rule also requires that "risks to subjects are reasonable in relation to anticipated benefits ..." What, we might ask, constitutes a "reasonable" relationship of risks to expected benefits? Presumably this means, at least, that the expected benefits of the research are greater than the risks, and so the research should, all things considered, do more good than harm. A significant obstacle to direct comparison of research risks and expected benefits is that these risks and benefits are often of very different kinds, and so are said to be "incommensurable."[25] How, for example, should an evaluator compare the potential benefit of a subject's

---

[24] See Prentice and Gordon (2001) and Kopelman (2004).   [25] Martin et al. (1995).

satisfaction in making a contribution to scientific advancement against the risk of a subject suffering a painful complication of a research procedure? How should an evaluator weigh the risk of specific harms to one group, the study subjects, against the prospect of specific benefits to a different group, future patients with the disease being investigated? There is no single measure for comparison of these different research outcomes.

The concept of clinical equipoise offers a specific approach to assessing whether the risk–benefit ratio of a therapeutic research study is reasonable.[26] According to this approach, research comparing different treatments for a particular medical condition is justified only if a state of clinical equipoise exists, that is, if there is no established consensus within the community of clinical experts regarding which of several alternative treatments is superior. If one treatment is generally agreed to be better than others for a particular condition, then it is unreasonable to deny the superior treatment to patients with that condition. If clinical equipoise among treatments does exist, however, a clinical trial can serve the valuable purpose of determining whether one of the alternative treatments is in fact superior to the others.

Confidentiality

Like informed consent, protection of the confidentiality of personal health information is a moral responsibility that applies to both clinical care and research on human subjects (see Chapter 6, "Privacy and confidentiality"). In clinical care, patients disclose personal information to health care professionals for the purpose of accurate diagnosis and effective treatment of their medical conditions. In therapeutic clinical research, patient-subjects disclose personal information to investigators for the purpose of answering a research question, as well as for their own medical treatment. In both settings, patients and subjects expect that this personal information will be protected from disclosures unrelated to these purposes. This protection is especially important for treatment or study of sensitive conditions such as mental illness, substance abuse, and sexually transmitted disease, where disclosure to unauthorized persons could result in stigmatization, discrimination, and feelings of shame

---

[26] Freedman (1987).

and embarrassment. The Common Rule identifies protection of subject privacy and confidentiality as a basic criterion for human research: "When appropriate, there are adequate provisions to protect the privacy of subjects and to maintain the confidentiality of data."[27]

The federal privacy regulations implemented in 2003 under the Health Insurance Portability and Accountability Act (HIPAA) contain additional provisions regarding confidentiality protection in research.[28] In order to use or disclose personal health information in research, investigators must satisfy one of the following three conditions:

1. the investigator obtains the subjects' specific authorization for obtaining and using their personal health information; or
2. the investigator obtains a waiver of authorization from an authorized IRB or privacy board, if the research meets certain requirements; or
3. the investigator reaches an agreement with a health care institution in which the institution agrees to provide to the investigator only a "limited data set" of patient information that excludes sixteen specific types of information that could enable identification of patients.[29]

Equitable selection of subjects

The Nazi medical research exploited thousands of political prisoners of that regime, and the Tuskegee syphilis study took advantage of indigent and uneducated minority patients. The outcomes of those studies were not designed or intended to benefit the research subjects. These notorious examples suggest an important question, namely, "Who should be recruited and selected to serve as human subjects of research?" The Common Rule identifies equitable subject selection as one of its basic criteria for human research, in these words:

> Selection of subjects is equitable. In making this assessment the IRB should take into account the purposes of the research and the setting in which the research will be conducted and should be particularly cognizant of the special problems of research involving vulnerable populations, such as

---

[27] US Department of Health and Human Services (2009), at §46.111.
[28] US Department of Health and Human Services, Office for Civil Rights (2003).
[29] See Moskop et al. (2005).

children, prisoners, pregnant women, mentally disabled persons, or economically or educationally disadvantaged persons.[30]

How do the "special problems" of research involving vulnerable populations affect subject selection? One potential problem is that investigators might be tempted to focus their subject recruitment efforts on vulnerable groups, because they are already under the control of others and they cannot protect their own interests. These vulnerable groups may then bear a disproportionate share of research risks, while the population at large enjoys the benefits of the research results. A fairer system would distribute the risks of participation in research more widely among all of those who will benefit from the research.

To address this problem, US regulations impose additional requirements on research involving pregnant women and fetuses, prisoners, and children, beyond the general research protections included in the Common Rule.[31] These additional requirements are specific to each of the vulnerable groups, but they are similar in many respects. The regulations limit most research on these groups to interventions that hold out the prospect of direct benefit to individual subjects, or that investigate conditions specific to that particular group, as, for example, studies of criminal behavior using prisoners as subjects. The regulations impose stricter limits on studies that pose a greater than minimal risk to these vulnerable subjects including, in some cases, review and approval of the study by the Secretary of the Department of Health and Human Services.

The regulations described above are designed to protect vulnerable groups from too great an exposure to the risks of participation in research. A different problem for equitable selection of subjects is insuring that different population groups are not *underrepresented* in research studies, and thereby deprived of the benefits of those studies. For example, women and racial minorities were routinely excluded from many large

---

[30] US Department of Health and Human Services (2009), at §46.111.

[31] US Department of Health and Human Services (2009), Subparts B, C, and D. These regulations for research on pregnant women and fetuses, prisoners, and children were adopted based on reports and recommendations of the National Commission for the Protection of Human Subjects of Biomedical and Behavioral Research. The National Commission also issued a report recommending regulations for the protection of patients institutionalized as mentally infirm, but those recommendations were not adopted as regulations.

US biomedical research studies conducted before 1990.[32] Investigators defended these exclusions on several grounds. They argued that the hormonal changes of the female menstrual cycle would complicate study of the physiological effects of research interventions, that exclusion of women of childbearing potential would avoid risks of miscarriage and birth defects caused by investigational drugs, and that too few women and minorities were willing to participate in research. Critics responded that this practice required clinicians to extrapolate research findings on white male subjects to women and minority patients who are physiologically different in demonstrable ways. These critics concluded that failure to include women and minorities in research studies increases the risks and decreases the expected benefits of research for those groups, and thus amounts to unjust discrimination. New US federal guidelines issued in the 1990s require inclusion of women and minorities in research funded by the National Institutes of Health and the Food and Drug Administration.[33]

Protection of human subjects – whose responsibility?

The preceding section identified and described multiple criteria for determining whether a research study on human subjects is morally justifiable. It did not, however, directly address two other essential questions for the protection of human research subjects, namely, "Who bears the responsibility to apply these criteria?" and "How should that responsibility be carried out?" In this section, I will suggest that protection of human subjects is a shared responsibility that is carried out in different ways by governments, IRBs, individual investigators, and research subjects themselves.

Human beings depend on their governments in various ways to promote their welfare and to protect their security. In this chapter, we have noted that research on human subjects provides substantial benefits for human health and well-being, but that it can also inflict grave harm on subjects. Because we do not have the ability as individuals to secure the benefits of research and protect ourselves from its harms, we authorize our governments both to promote research and to protect research subjects from its potential abuses. Thus, as we have seen, the United States has enacted legislation and adopted multiple regulations to encourage

---

[32] Dresser (1992).

[33] For summaries of these guidelines, see Coleman et al. (2005): 430–433.

research and to protect human subjects. Multiple governmental agencies and their officials have responsibilities of various kinds to implement these research regulations.

In the United States, however, the primary responsibility for implementing federal research regulations is delegated not to public officials, but rather to IRBs at health care facilities, universities, and other institutions that engage in research on human subjects supported by federal funds.[34] These institutions must establish and maintain IRBs to review research that investigators propose to perform at their institution with federal funding. In addition, most institutions agree, in the contract establishing their IRB system, to apply federal regulations and IRB review to all research conducted on human subjects at their institution. IRBs, therefore, assume the task of reviewing research proposals and determining whether they satisfy the criteria for protection of human subjects described above; IRB review includes examination of procedures for obtaining informed consent of subjects, assessment of study risks and expected benefits, review of measures to protect subject confidentiality, and consideration of methods for subject recruitment and selection. Based on their review, IRBs are authorized to approve, require modifications for approval, or disapprove research proposals. The Common Rule establishes general requirements for IRB membership, procedures, and reports.[35] For example, each IRB must have at least five members of different backgrounds and qualifications, including at least one scientist and one non-scientist and one member who is not employed by the institution. IRBs must also assume responsibility for periodic review of ongoing research studies that they have approved. If an institution fails to carry out its responsibilities under this system, its eligibility to receive federal research funding may be suspended or revoked.

In the US research review system, IRBs bear major responsibility for evaluating the moral justifiability of research studies on human subjects. Once a research proposal is approved and funding is secured, responsibility shifts to the investigators to conduct the study according to the approved proposal, and that responsibility includes implementation of

---

[34] Other nations with similar systems use different terms to refer to institutional research ethics review committees. In Canada, for example, these committees are called Research Ethics Boards (Martin et al. 1995).

[35] US Department of Health and Human Services (2009), at §46.103 and §46.107–46.110.

the protections for human research subjects described in the research proposal. The research enterprise thus depends heavily on the moral integrity of investigators, since they are the ones who interact directly with the subjects of their research, and there is little or no direct scrutiny of those interactions. There may, moreover, be significant potential for investigator conflict of interest if, for example, pharmaceutical industry funding of an investigational drug study is based on the number of subjects the investigator is able to enroll in the study. If an investigator's failure to satisfy responsibilities to subjects is discovered, responses may include cancellation of the study, public censure, a ban on future research funding, and other penalties.

Finally, the subjects themselves, and the authorized representatives of subjects who lack decision-making capacity, play a significant role in protecting their own interests as subjects and the interests of the subjects they represent. Because participation as a subject in research is a decision that can have important beneficial and adverse consequences, potential research subjects have a clear interest in learning about the purpose of the research and its expected consequences, evaluating that information in light of their own goals, values, and desires, and making an informed decision about whether they will participate. For potential subjects who can decide for themselves about participation in research, this is primarily a matter of prudence or of responsibility to oneself, even though others may be affected by their decisions. For representatives authorized to make choices on behalf of a person who lacks decision-making capacity, active participation in the informed consent process is required by their broader responsibility to protect the interests of the person they represent.

My conclusion is that each of the actors in the US system – governments, IRBs, investigators, subjects, and the representatives of subjects who lack decision-making capacity – has substantial and inter-related responsibilities in the protection of research subjects. Because the research enterprise depends on the trust and cooperation of its subjects, an effective system of subject protection is essential to its success.

Case analysis

As a volunteer community member of an IRB at University Medical Center (UMC), Mr. Simpson has accepted a responsibility to contribute to the protection of research subjects at that institution. His thoughtful review of the APRONS research proposal under consideration by the IRB suggests that he takes this responsibility seriously.

The case description does not indicate that Mr. Simpson has any misgivings about the study consent process, confidentiality protections, or subject selection process. Presumably, therefore, Mr. Simpson is satisfied that the APRONS consent and confidentiality procedures are appropriate and that the study consent form clearly indicates that the study involves research and explains the purpose of the study, the three different treatments and their risks and expected benefits, and the process for assignment of subjects to the three treatment groups. He is presumably also satisfied that the subject eligibility criteria for APRONS are clearly defined and appropriate, that the study will include major population groups that stand to benefit from its results, including both men and women and members of different racial groups, and that the study will not rely unduly on indigent patients or another vulnerable group.

Mr. Simpson does, however, have serious concerns about the risk–benefit ratio of this study. He recognizes that medical (drug) treatment and PCI are both commonly used therapies for coronary artery disease. One rationale for comparing them in this study, therefore, might be to compare the overall benefits and risks of these very different treatments to determine whether one is superior to the other. Mr. Simpson consults the cardiology literature, and he discovers that a large clinical study, the COURAGE trial, did in fact compare drug therapy and PCI for patients with stable coronary artery disease. The COURAGE trial found that PCI was more successful in relieving angina, but that there was no difference between the two therapies in either death or heart attack rates.[36] Because both drug treatments and intravascular cardiac procedures have evolved in the years since the COURAGE trial was conducted, one purpose of the proposed APRONS study would be to confirm or disconfirm the results of the previous study. That result would provide potentially valuable information for the ongoing treatment of patients with this condition.

Mr. Simpson's primary concern is about the third study group, the group that will receive a sham PCI. Patient-subjects in this group will undergo cardiac catheterization, an invasive procedure that has multiple possible

[36] Boden et al. (2007).

complications, including heart attack, stroke, irregular heartbeat, perfora-
tion or tearing of an artery, bleeding, infection, and (rarely) death. Because
this is a sham procedure, however, it will do nothing to eliminate or relieve
the obstruction of blood flow in the diseased coronary arteries. Since this
procedure poses clear risks but offers no added benefit to patient-subjects,
how can inclusion of this treatment group be justified? What is its purpose?

If Mr. Simpson poses these questions to Dr. Russell, the UMC lead investigator of the proposed study, Dr. Russell might offer the following
explanation:

> We believe that inclusion of a sham procedure group in research on invasive
> procedures like PCI is essential in order to determine whether that procedure
> is truly beneficial. There is good evidence that medical procedures like PCI
> have a strong placebo effect, especially on subjective outcomes like pain
> control. Our study will be blinded; that is, patient-subjects will not know
> whether they are receiving PCI or sham PCI. Previous studies show that a high
> percentage of patients who receive invasive procedures, including a sham
> procedure, report significant pain relief. In order, therefore, to determine
> whether PCI has a specific effect on relieving angina, rather than just a
> placebo effect, our study will compare it with a sham procedure. Although
> PCI is a very widely used procedure, it has never been investigated in a
> blinded trial like this one. We recognize that our study will expose patients in
> the sham procedure group to some additional risks of the catheterization
> procedure, with no added benefits to those subjects, but all subjects will
> receive optimal drug treatment. If APRONS demonstrates that PCI has only a
> placebo effect, it may save many thousands of future patients from a risky,
> costly, and unnecessary procedure. That would be a highly beneficial
> result.[37]

Does this explanation provide a sufficient justification for the proposed
study? How would you advise Mr. Simpson to vote on the APRONS proposal?

---

[37] See Redberg (2014) for a defense of sham procedure controls in research on medical
procedures and medical devices.

20 The genetic revolution

Case example

Twenty-three-year-old Ms. Alice Kemper seeks treatment in the ED of University Hospital for abdominal pain and bloating that has gotten progressively worse over the past week. Ms. Kemper reports that she had abnormal liver function tests during an uncomplicated pregnancy one year previously and that several members of her family have had cirrhosis or hepatitis. This information, along with her physical examination and the results of initial blood tests and urinalysis, suggests severe liver disease, and she is admitted to the hospital for further diagnostic testing. Based on a liver biopsy, eye examination, and genetic testing, Ms. Kemper is diagnosed with an advanced case of Wilson disease, a rare inherited disease in which excess copper accumulates in the liver, brain, eyes, and other organs. Because her liver damage is severe, Ms. Kemper is evaluated for a liver transplant. She meets the criteria for transplantation and is placed on the hospital transplant program's waiting list for a liver transplant.

While Ms. Kemper is waiting for a transplant liver to become available, she is referred to Mr. Quinn, a genetic counselor, to give her more information about her condition. Mr. Quinn explains to her that Wilson disease is caused by multiple mutations in a gene that enables production of a protein that transports copper within the body. Without this protein, excess copper accumulates in and damages multiple organs. Because Wilson disease is an autosomal recessive disorder, patients with this condition have inherited gene mutations from both of their parents. If both parents are carriers of this gene, each of their children has a one-in-four chance of inheriting the mutations from both parents and developing the disease. Mr. Quinn explains that Ms. Kemper's siblings are also at risk for this life-threatening genetic disease. Ms. Kemper informs him that she has two younger siblings, a 16-year-old brother and a 14-year-old sister, but that she does not want to inform them about her condition or communicate with them in any way. She explains that she was abandoned by her parents and her family years ago, and she refuses to have anything to do with them. She does, however, ask whether her 1-year-old daughter can be tested for the genetic markers for Wilson disease, so that she can be on the lookout for signs of the disease. Mr. Quinn replies that early signs of the disease do not generally appear until at least 5 years of age, and that it is very unlikely that her daughter has the condition, since transmission of the disease requires that both parents are carriers of the mutated genes. Ms. Kemper responds that her child's father has moved away from the area and they are no longer in touch. She adds that, even though she understands that the chance that her child has the condition is small, she wants that information. How should Mr. Quinn and the medical team caring for Ms. Kemper proceed?

Promise and peril: the checkered history of human genetics

In 2003, scientists announced the successful completion of the Human Genome Project, the high-profile, fourteen-year-long, multi-billion-dollar international research initiative to produce a comprehensive map and chemical sequencing of the entire human genome.[1] Proponents hailed this event as a monumental accomplishment in biomedical research, the achievement of what one researcher called "the Holy Grail" of human biology![2] The mapping and sequencing data of the Human Genome Project enabled a rapid acceleration in the pace of discovery of genes responsible for human diseases, from fewer than 200 disease-associated genes discovered in 1990 to more than 1800 such genes discovered in 2005.[3] Francis Collins, Director for fifteen years of the US National Human Genome Research Institute, described the expected medical benefits of contemporary genomic science in these glowing terms:

> We are on the leading edge of a true revolution in medicine, one that promises to transform the traditional "one-size-fits-all" approach into a much more powerful strategy that considers each individual as unique and as having special characteristics that should guide an approach to staying healthy.[4]

'Personalized genomic medicine' (PGM) and 'precision medicine' are terms widely used to refer to this "revolutionary" and "much more powerful" strategy for health care. PGM advocates envision the feasibility and routine use of detailed individual genomic profiles for large patient populations. This information, they maintain, will provide significant benefits in four

---

[1] Collins et al. (2003).   [2] Gilbert (1992).
[3] US National Human Genome Research Institute, no date (a).   [4] Collins (2010).

major areas: prediction, prevention, personalization, and participation. First, PGM will enable *prediction* of future health risks for individual patients by identifying genes that are associated with various health conditions. Second, PGM's early identification of these risks will enable professionals and patients to employ targeted *preventive* measures to minimize those specific health risks. Third, PGM will enable professionals to *personalize* their treatment of each individual patient. Physicians can, for example, focus their attention on the patient's most significant health risks, and they can tailor drug treatments for the patient's existing conditions based on "pharmacogenomic" information about specific gene variants that increase or decrease the effectiveness of specific medications. Finally, by giving patients important information about their own individual genetic health risks, PGM will enable patients to understand their individual health conditions and risks more fully, to *participate* more actively in health care decisions, and to take a more active role in health-promoting behaviors.[5]

PGM thus offers the prospect of significant benefits to patients, but it is surely not an unmixed blessing. Even very strong proponents of PGM like Collins acknowledge that genetic information can pose complex moral problems and can cause significant harm as well as benefit.[6] Recognition of the potential risks of new genetic information prompted the architects of the Human Genome Project, from the inception of the Project, to commit a portion of its annual budget (initially 3 percent, and later 5 percent) to study of its ethical, legal, and social implications.[7] This concern about the broader implications of genetic science was doubtlessly inspired in part by the history of grave abuses committed in the name of genetics.

The modern science of genetics emerged at the turn of the twentieth century with the rediscovery of the plant hybridization experiments of Gregor Mendel. Mendel's theory of inheritance of genetic traits soon found application to human beings in British physician Archibald Garrod's explanation of patterns of human inheritance of "inborn errors of metabolism" in 1908.[8] The early history of human genetic science was closely linked, in both America and Europe, with the eugenics movement, a social campaign dedicated to improvement of the human race by education and policies designed to guide and control human reproduction.[9] In addition to the new science of

---

[5] Juengst et al. (2012).   [6] See, for example, Guyer and Collins (1995).

[7] US National Human Genome Research Institute, no date (b).

[8] Bearn and Miller (1979).   [9] Ludmerer (1972) and Kevles (1999).

genetics, the eugenics movement of this era was heavily influenced by Darwin's theory of evolution by natural selection and by racist anthropologies that emphasized racial differences and posited a hierarchical order in the "fitness" of the several races of human beings. Based in part on genetic theories explaining the inheritance of inborn traits from one's parents, eugenicists sought to encourage the reproduction of those considered to have desirable traits (that is, "superior" races and upper social classes) and to discourage or prohibit the reproduction of the "unfit" ("inferior" races and the poor).

Major policy initiatives of the eugenics movement in the United States during the first half of the twentieth century included laws restricting immigration by southern and eastern Europeans and by Asians, laws prohibiting interracial marriage, and laws creating state programs for the involuntary sterilization of persons with a variety of conditions thought to be inherited, including "feeble-mindedness," mental illness, and epilepsy.[10] Proclaiming that their policies were "nothing but applied biology," the leaders of the Nazi regime in Germany, with the active assistance of German physicians and medical scientists, enacted a systematic program of "racial hygiene," including prohibition of marriage between Jews and "Aryans," involuntary sterilization and eventual extermination of institutionalized patients, and persecution and later genocide of Jews, gypsies, and other "inferior races."[11]

Post-war revelation of the grim details and the massive scope of these Nazi programs evoked worldwide moral revulsion and condemnation of the practice of eugenics (though state-authorized involuntary sterilization programs continued in a number of US states into the 1970s).[12] The grave harm inflicted by these programs on millions of victims cast strong and enduring suspicion on any perceived use of genetic information for eugenic purposes. The US state practices of involuntary sterilization of patients with conditions believed to be hereditary were eventually prohibited, and new laws were enacted to protect reproductive freedom.

Despite the clear potential for abuse of genetic information, other post-World War II events focused attention on the potential value of human genetics. The use of nuclear weapons on Japan, the post-war acceleration of

[10] Ludmerer (1972).   [11] Lifton (1986) and Proctor (1988).

[12] Schoen, for example, reports that the North Carolina Eugenics Board authorized sterilizations from 1929 until 1975 (Schoen 2001).

the nuclear arms race, and the rise of the atomic energy industry all called increasing attention to the need for protection from the genetic hazards of exposure to radiation.[13] In 1953, James Watson and Francis Crick announced their discovery of the double helix structure of deoxyribonucleic acid (DNA), paving the way for understanding of the biochemical mechanisms of the genetic code.[14] Subsequent discovery of the genes responsible for specific diseases enabled the development of tests for conditions like phenylketonuria (PKU) and Down syndrome. These developments had mixed consequences, however. Diagnosis enabled dietary treatment for PKU, but strongly negative attitudes about people with Down syndrome complicated the lives of those people and their families.[15] The decision to allow "Baby Doe," a newborn infant with Down syndrome, to die by forgoing life-saving surgery provoked a major ethics and public policy debate in the US in the 1980s and resulted in regulations designed to protect infants from denial of life-prolonging treatment.[16]

As this brief summary indicates, the history of modern human genetics is marked by both great promise and great peril. It is, therefore, no surprise that the Human Genome Project, a massive international research initiative with apparent potential to revolutionize health care, devoted sustained attention to the ethical, legal, and social implications of these revolutionary changes. This chapter will identify and examine major ethical questions prompted by the increasing role of genetics in health care.

Multiple issues, multiple players

The above outline of the history of human genetics indicates that genetic information poses a variety of ethical and social questions in several different domains, including biomedical research, health and social policy, and clinical medical care. This section will examine major issues in each of these three domains.

Biomedical research

Clinical genetics investigators assume all of the basic professional responsibilities for protection of human research subjects described in Chapter 19,

---

[13] Ludmerer (1972): 193–201.   [14] Watson and Crick (1953).   [15] Rapp (2000).
[16] Moskop and Saldanha (1986).

"Research on human subjects," including informing prospective subjects of the purpose and any expected benefits and risks of harm of genetic studies, obtaining their voluntary consent to participation in a research study, and protecting them from research-related harms. In addition to these basic responsibilities, genetic researchers also confront ethical issues that are distinctive to this type of research. Two issues, in particular, have been the subject of sustained attention and debate, the disclosure to subjects of "incidental findings" of genetics research, and the use of social categories in population-based genetics research.

Disclosing incidental findings. In both clinical and research contexts, professional caregivers and investigators may acquire specific information about the medical condition of a patient or subject that is not related to the health care sought by the patient or the research question under investigation. The likelihood of identifying potentially significant incidental information is especially high in genetic research that involves sequencing part or all of the genome of study subjects, and so multiple commentators, including the US Presidential Commission for the Study of Bioethical Issues, have addressed this topic and offered recommendations.[17] A range of responses to this situation are possible. Investigators, for example, may argue that their purpose is to produce generalizable knowledge, not to provide personal health care, and so they have no responsibility to inform subjects about incidental findings. Other commentators maintain that investigators' responsibilities should extend to disclosing incidental findings to their subjects if those findings are "clinically useful" or "medically actionable," that is, if that information would enable subjects to take specific measures (adopt health behaviors or receive treatments) to prevent or treat a significant health condition. These commentators propose several different criteria for what should count as medically actionable information that investigators must disclose.[18] Some patients and patient advocates, commonly called "citizen scientists," assert that they should receive all information about themselves, whether or not it has obvious clinical significance at the present time; investigators respond that this would impose too heavy a burden on them and would inhibit valuable research.[19] In light

---

[17] See Presidential Commission for the Study of Bioethical Issues (2013a) and Presidential Commission for the Study of Bioethical Issues (2013b).

[18] Parens et al. (2013) cite three different conceptions of clinically useful results.

[19] Knoppers (2013).

of the increasing ability to sequence whole genomes accurately and inexpensively, scholars have begun to consider whether genetic testing in both research and clinical contexts should look for all known genetic variants that are medically actionable and report any variants discovered.[20] If this requirement were implemented, finding medically significant individual genetic variants would no longer be an "incidental" occurrence, but rather a routine part of any genetic workup. This approach would presumably appeal to patients who want complete information about their genetic risks, but would not be welcomed by patients who prefer not to have that information. Later in this chapter, I will suggest that the value of whole genome sequencing in the clinical setting is still very limited.

Population-based comparative research. With the completion of the Human Genome Project's goals of mapping and sequencing the complete human genome, the attention of genetic investigators turned to *comparing* human genomes to understand their similarities and differences. These comparisons are essential for identifying the thousands of medically significant gene variants that will enable the genomic medicine of the future to personalize health care based on individual genetic profiles. This comparative research involves collecting tissue samples from members of different human populations, genotyping those samples, linking specific gene variants with medical conditions affecting those populations, and comparing the results. Obvious questions for this research are, "Which human groups should be chosen for comparison?" and "How will members of these groups be identified?" Groups and individuals chosen for comparative genetic studies might benefit from identification of significant genetic variants they have in common, enabling earlier and more accurate diagnosis, prevention, and treatment of gene-associated diseases. Research comparing African-American and European-American patients, for example, has identified gene variants that are associated with significantly different rates of kidney disease and prostate cancer in these populations.[21]

Genetic research comparing racial, ethnic, national, or tribal groups also poses significant risks of harm to those groups, however. Genetic research indicates that human beings are a relatively young and genetically homogeneous species, and so the DNA sequences of any two humans are about 99.5 percent identical, regardless of racial, ethnic, or other differences.[22]

---

[20] See Gliwa and Berkman (2013) and Green et al. (2013).   [21] Rotimi and Jorde (2010).
[22] Rotimi and Jorde (2010).

Research that focuses on genetic differences between groups, therefore, may reinforce and exaggerate the significance of groupings that are biologically and socially questionable. Identification of differences in disease susceptibility might encourage racial or ethnic stereotyping and discrimination, and might overshadow the major environmental and social factors, including poverty and racism, that contribute to health disparities. Eric Juengst poses the ethical challenge for comparative genomic research and practice in these terms: "How can we preserve our commitment to human moral equality in the face of our growing understanding of human biological diversity?"[23]

Health policy

As noted in the historical outline above, the United States, Germany, and many other nations implemented a variety of public eugenic policies and programs during the first half of the twentieth century, based in part on the genetic science of that era, with morally repugnant consequences. Despite that sordid history, and sometimes in reaction to it, legislators and government officials have also played central roles in promoting and guiding the "reformed" human genetics of the post-World War II era. In the United States, for example, National Institutes of Health officials sought, and Congress appropriated, several billion dollars to fund the major US contribution to the Human Genome Project.[24] With the discovery of specific genes responsible for multiple diseases and the development of screening tests for those diseases, state public health officials have recommended and obtained public funding to implement screening programs, including mandatory newborn screening for multiple genetic conditions.[25] In 2008, Congress enacted the Genetic Information Nondiscrimination Act (GINA), a federal statute designed to protect individuals from discrimination based

---

[23] Juengst (2007).   [24] Collins et al. (2003).

[25] 'Screening' is the term used to refer to the administration of a diagnostic test to a large group of people. Tests used for screening populations are typically highly sensitive, that is, they identify almost all of the people who have the condition the test is designed to find, but they are not as highly specific, that is, they also identify some people who do not have the condition in question. If a person has a positive screening test, therefore, a different confirmatory test is needed to determine whether the patient actually has the condition. The confirmatory test is typically highly specific, that is, it excludes almost all people who do not have the condition in question.

on their genetic information in health insurance and in employment.[26] I will examine in more detail just one of the complex policy questions posed by genetics, namely, the proper scope of routine newborn genetic screening.

Newborn genetic screening. For more than half a century, routine genetic screening of newborn infants has been a standard practice in the United States. This practice began in the 1960s, following the development of a simple and inexpensive test using dried blood spots for PKU. PKU is caused by an inherited gene defect that prevents the body from metabolizing the amino acid phenylalanine. If PKU is not detected in infancy, excess phenylalanine accumulation causes severe intellectual disability, seizures, and other disorders. Early detection enables treatment with a special diet of phenylalanine-free foods that can prevent or greatly reduce the harmful consequences of PKU. Although PKU is a rare condition (it affects about one in 10,000 infants), the great benefit to affected infants of early detection and effective dietary treatment was widely viewed as sufficient justification for state-based programs of mandatory screening of all newborns, and so PKU screening programs became an early "success story" of medical genetics.

In subsequent years, states expanded their newborn screening programs, as new conditions were identified and new tests were developed. State public health officers based decisions to add screening tests in part on advocacy campaigns by parents of children with particular disorders.[27] Screening for each additional disorder added considerable costs, not only for the screening test, but also for confirmatory testing, counseling of parents with affected infants, and treatment for the condition. In order to justify these costs, and the testing of newborns without the informed consent of their parents, public health scholars argued that screening tests must provide substantial benefits to infants by identifying serious conditions for which prompt treatment is both essential and effective. By the mid 1990s, some states screened for more than thirty genetic disorders, and others for fewer than five.[28] During that decade, a new screening technology, tandem mass spectrometry, became widely available; this technology enabled "multiplex" testing for many genetic conditions at the same time.[29] A working group of the American College of Medical Genetics (ACMG)

---

[26] Genetic Information Nondiscrimination Act 2008.   [27] Baily and Murray (2008).
[28] Committee on Assessing Genetic Risks, Institute of Medicine (1994).
[29] Baily and Murray (2008).

received federal funding in 2002 to evaluate candidate genetic conditions and recommend a uniform panel of conditions for adoption by all state newborn screening programs. Relying heavily on the capabilities of mass spectrometry, the ACMG working group recommended that states screen newborns for twenty-nine "primary" disorders and twenty-five "secondary" disorders; the secondary disorders would be detected incidentally while screening for the primary disorders.[30] To justify expansion of state mandatory newborn screening programs to include all of these disorders, the ACMG report offered a new and broader interpretation of the benefits of newborn screening. In addition to the traditional criterion of direct and significant benefit to children with these conditions, the report included consideration of the benefits of screening to families and to society. Families could benefit, for example, by receiving information that would be significant for future reproductive decisions and that would enable them to avoid a "diagnostic odyssey," a long process of evaluation and of therapeutic trials for a sick child before successful diagnosis of the child's rare genetic condition. Society could benefit from early identification of infants with rare and poorly understood conditions for which no treatments exist. If a sufficient number of infants with these rare conditions were identified and enrolled in research studies, investigators could understand the conditions better and develop effective treatments for them.

The ACMG-recommended uniform panel of newborn screening disorders was endorsed by multiple organizations, including an advisory committee of the US Department of Health and Human Services, the American Academy of Pediatrics, and the March of Dimes.[31] Ross et al. reported in 2013 that all fifty states had adopted the ACMG panel.[32] This result might suggest that there was little or no opposition to expansion of state newborn screening programs as recommended by the ACMG. In fact, however, several other prominent organizations, including the United States Preventive Services Task Force and the President's Council on Bioethics, and a number of individual commentators, voiced strong criticism of the ACMG newborn screening working group's study process, evaluation criteria, and screening recommendations.[33] These critics argued that the ACMG group placed too

---

[30] American College of Medical Genetics Newborn Screening Expert Group (2006).
[31] Baily and Murray (2008).   [32] Ross et al. (2013).
[33] Botkin et al. (2006), Moyer et al. (2008), Baily and Murray (2008), President's Council on Bioethics (2008).

much emphasis on the technological capabilities of tandem mass spectrometry and on the opinions of disease and screening specialists and of lay screening advocates, and it did not consult experts in the systematic review of evidence and in public health.[34] As a result, they argued, the evidence cited for the benefit of screening for many of the recommended conditions is weak, and the significant potential for harms of screening to children and families, including unnecessary worry, misdiagnosis, labeling, and discrimination, was neglected. The additional costs of expanded screening, including follow-up testing, education, family counseling, and treatment, critics claimed, would divert scarce resources from other worthy public health programs.[35] The President's Council on Bioethics concluded that *mandatory* newborn screening be limited to a small number of conditions that meet the traditional criteria of providing substantial medical benefit to affected children. For conditions that do not yet meet this strict criterion, the Council recommends that screening be provided via research studies that obtain the informed consent of parents, until the clear benefit to children of screening for those conditions has been demonstrated.[36]

The development and decreasing cost of new technologies for whole genome sequencing may soon enable an exponential increase in the number of genetic conditions identified in newborns, if state screening programs choose to adopt and employ those technologies.[37] This prospect will likely intensify the ongoing debate about the proper scope of screening programs and about whether the screening of newborn infants for a variety of different genetic conditions should be mandatory, voluntary, or even prohibited.

Medical care

As described above, proponents of personalized genomic medicine (PGM) proclaim that the information obtained through detailed individual genomic profiles will revolutionize the health care of the future. A few of the benefits envisioned by the champions of PGM have already found their way into clinical practice, but many others will depend on future genetic research and on the translation of research findings into diagnostic and therapeutic interventions that are effective, affordable, and morally

---

[34] Moyer et al. (2008).   [35] Baily and Murray (2008).
[36] President's Council on Bioethics (2008).   [37] Goldenberg and Sharp (2012).

justifiable.[38] Although the celebrated genetic revolution in health care is still more a promise than a reality, genetic information has enabled and guided medical treatment of a few diseases for some fifty years, as the description of newborn genetic screening in the preceding section illustrates. In this section, I will consider moral issues in present and future clinical applications of genetics in three areas: prenatal care, pediatrics, and adult medicine.

Prenatal care. Like newborn screening, testing for several fetal genetic conditions has been in wide use for four decades. Early guidelines recommended that pregnant women over 35 years old be offered amniocentesis, a procedure in which a small sample of amniotic fluid is removed, using a fine needle inserted through the woman's abdomen and into the uterus, followed by genetic testing of fetal cells in that sample.[39] Testing enabled diagnosis of Down syndrome and several other major chromosomal anomalies in the fetus, giving women with affected fetuses the option of terminating the pregnancy. With the development in the 1990s of screening tests for these conditions using maternal blood samples, obstetricians offered screening for these conditions to all pregnant women, followed by amniocentesis or chorionic villus sampling, another method for obtaining fetal cells for testing, to confirm the diagnosis after a positive screening test.

The longstanding practice of prenatal genetic screening and testing for major chromosomal anomalies raises several central bioethical issues that are shared with other treatment choices. Unlike mandatory state newborn screening programs, pregnant women are not required to undergo prenatal genetic screening, but commentators question whether clinicians give women enough information about the purpose, benefits, and risks of these screening and confirmatory tests to enable them to make an informed decision for or against testing.[40] Positive screening test results may put pressure on women to be "responsible reproducers" by accepting confirmatory testing and abortion of an affected fetus.[41] Prenatal genetic screening and testing also raise questions about resource use and access to care. The cost of these services may prevent many low-income women who lack

---

[38] See Green and Guyer (2011) and Marshall (2011).

[39] US National Institutes of Health (1979).

[40] Kuppermann et al. (2014). See also Chapter 8, "Informed consent to treatment."

[41] Juengst (1999).

health insurance from receiving them. Should this testing be available to all pregnant women, and if so, how should it be financed?[42]

One might argue that newborn screening gives women important choices about the prevention of genetic illness in their children, and so it should be universally available. Notice, however, that the type of prevention made possible by prenatal screening is significantly different from the prevention enabled by newborn screening for PKU. Early PKU identification and dietary treatment prevents the development of disabilities in people with this genetic condition, while prenatal genetic screening prevents genetic diseases by enabling decisions to abort affected fetuses. Prenatal screening is thus closely linked with the contentious issue of abortion.[43] Most abortion opponents reject the claim that the presence of a genetic condition is sufficient justification for killing a human being who, they argue, merits full moral status, including a right to life. Disability rights advocates decry the practice of routine screening for fetal Down syndrome and other conditions, followed by abortion of affected fetuses, as a kind of "back-door" eugenics that is fueled by and perpetuates unjustified stereotypes about people with these conditions.[44]

In addition to these mainstream bioethical issues, new options for prenatal genetic testing raise novel ethical questions. Standard prenatal screening is currently limited to identification of a few chromosomal anomalies that cause disability or early death. With the continuing discovery of genetic markers for thousands of diseases and other traits, and the availability of whole genome sequencing that can identify those genetic markers, should prenatal screening be routinely offered for additional genetic diseases? Expectant mothers (and fathers) may request testing for specific genetic markers of special interest to them, or they may request a comprehensive profile of all of the significant genetic traits of their fetus. Should obstetricians honor these requests? If not, where should they draw the line between appropriate and inappropriate prenatal testing? Responses to these questions will require careful assessment of the interests and rights of parents, fetuses, children, health care professionals, and society. Parents, for example, have a clear interest in the health of their children and the makeup of their families. Donley et al. argue that the massive amount of information generated by prenatal whole genome sequencing is more likely to frighten

---

[42] See also Chapter 11, "Resource stewardship."   [43] See also Chapter 13, "Abortion."
[44] Dresser (2009).

and confuse prospective parents than to help them make reproductive decisions.[45]

Some parental requests for prenatal genetic information may be very simple, however. Consider the following situation: 35-year-old Mrs. Mary Taylor has just learned that she is pregnant for the fifth time. She and her husband Richard have four boys, and Mrs. Taylor tells Dr. Sanders, her obstetrician, that it is their most fervent desire to complete their family with a daughter. They request prenatal testing at the earliest possible stage of pregnancy for the purpose of determining the sex of the fetus, and they state their intention to terminate the pregnancy if the fetus is a male. The Taylors' desire is understandable, if not particularly praiseworthy. Suppose Dr. Sanders responds that he views this as an unacceptable reason for choosing abortion and denies their request as a matter of conscience.[46] Fetal ultrasound imaging is a routine prenatal practice later in pregnancy, and ultrasound images often give clear evidence of the sex of the fetus.[47] May, or should, he also deny Mrs. Taylor access to this technology?

Pediatrics. In addition to the state-based newborn screening and testing programs described above, testing of children for genetic conditions is a routine practice in several different situations. When a pediatric or adult patient is diagnosed with a genetic condition, for example, physicians may recommend that other family members, including parents, siblings, and children, also undergo testing to determine whether they are at risk for developing the condition, especially if early treatment can prevent or ameliorate symptoms of that condition. When a child shows signs of illness or disability that are suggestive of a genetic disease, or when no obvious cause or diagnosis of the child's illness can be found, physicians may also recommend testing to identify a genetic cause of the child's condition. Because

---

[45] See Donley et al. (2012).

[46] See the discussion of professional rights to conscientious objection in Chapter 10, "Professionalism."

[47] The Taylors might also adopt a less forthright approach to achieving their desired outcome. They could express strong interest in a new genetic testing technology to detect chromosomal anomalies, due to Mrs. Taylor's advanced age, and also simply express a great interest in knowing the sex of the fetus. This more recently developed and now widely available technology, called cell-free DNA analysis, analyzes fetal DNA fragments circulating in the pregnant woman's blood, and it can provide information about chromosomal anomalies and about the sex of the fetus (see Greenfieldboyce 2015). If the Taylors take this approach to learning the sex of the fetus, should Dr. Sanders order the test and tell the Taylors the results, including fetal sex?

genetic testing in these situations can provide valuable information for the diagnosis and treatment of childhood illness and disability, there is clear justification for its use.

Genetic testing of children in other circumstances, however, poses morally controversial questions. One widely discussed issue is the testing of children for "late-onset" genetic diseases.[48] The genes responsible for these late-onset diseases can be identified by testing at any age, but symptoms of the diseases do not appear until adulthood. The most well-known late-onset genetic disease is Huntington disease, an incurable condition that causes progressive symptoms, including loss of motor function, cognitive impairment, and depression, beginning at about age 40. When parents discover that they have or are at risk for one of these late-onset diseases, they may request testing of their children, who are also at risk. Parents may argue that this information will be of great value for them and their children, helping them to understand better what the future holds for their family and to plan and prepare together for their children's long-term welfare. They may also explain that they intend in any case to explain to their children that everyone in the family is at risk for this disease. Should physicians honor these requests?

Several reasons have been offered for resisting parental requests for testing for late-onset genetic diseases. For many of these diseases, early diagnosis does not enable effective prevention or treatment, because there is no medical intervention that can prevent or ameliorate the disease. A positive diagnosis may cause harms of several kinds, including anxiety, depression, loss of privacy (if others learn of the child's condition), and possible stigmatization and discrimination. Even knowledge that the child does not have the genetic disease may result in "survivor guilt," a feeling of guilt or sadness that one has escaped a catastrophic disease that does or will afflict one's parents or siblings. Dena Davis argues that pediatric testing for late-onset disease violates children's "right to an open future," because it deprives them of the opportunity to decide for themselves as adults whether they want to have this information or not.[49] Citing reports that only 10–15 percent of *adults* who are at risk for Huntington disease choose to have pre-symptomatic testing,[50] Davis concludes that a person's option not to have this information should not be pre-empted by a testing decision

---

[48] Mand et al. (2012).   [49] Davis (2010).
[50] Working Party of the Clinical Genetics Society (UK) (1994).

made for the person in childhood. A 2006 review of professional policy statements and guidelines found a consensus in favor of denying parental requests to test children for late-onset genetic diseases.[51] A 2012 analysis, however, reported that arguments in favor of testing have gained momentum and called for empirical study of the actual benefits and harms of decisions to test or not to test for these late-onset conditions in childhood.[52]

A related issue is the testing of children for carrier status of genetic diseases with an autosomal recessive pattern of inheritance. If both parents are carriers, that is, have one gene for this kind of disease, their children have a one-in-four chance of developing the disease and a one-in-two chance of themselves being carriers. Parents in this situation may request testing to know both the disease status and the carrier status of their children. Should physicians honor these requests? Carriers will not develop the genetic disease, but they are at risk of bearing children with the disease, if their reproductive partner is also a carrier. Learning that one is a carrier, therefore, can enable a person to make marital and reproductive decisions that minimize the risk of transmitting a genetic disease to one's children. Because marital and reproductive decisions are both serious and private life choices, Davis argues that carrier status should generally not be disclosed to parents, but only to the child him or herself when he or she is preparing to make marital and reproductive choices.[53]

Adult medicine. Like the previously discussed areas of health care, the role of genetics in adult medicine raises both longstanding and novel ethical issues. In this section, I will discuss three prominent issues in genetics for adult patients, namely, information disclosure and confidentiality, access to expanded genetic testing, and prospects for gene therapy.

Disclosure and confidentiality. Since the development of tests for genetic conditions like cystic fibrosis and sickle cell disease, clinicians and scholars have raised questions about the ownership and control of the genetic information provided by those tests. That information is of great importance to the individuals tested, but, as Juengst points out, "genetics is, by definition, a science of family connections."[54] Understanding the significance of one's own medical condition may depend on one's family members' willingness to accept testing and to share genetic information about themselves, and one's own genetic information may be of great importance

---

[51] Borry et al. (2006).   [52] Mand et al. (2012).   [53] Davis (2010).   [54] Juengst (1999).

for one's relatives. How, then, should patients and physicians strike a balance between disclosing important genetic information and protecting the confidentiality of that information?

One early discussion about the confidentiality and disclosure of genetic information focused on an incidental finding in clinical genetics.[55] When an infant is diagnosed with an unexpected genetic condition, parents may seek genetic testing and counseling to understand their risk of transmitting the disease to future children. If the condition in question is autosomal recessive, and the father's (accurate) test results show that he is not a carrier of the condition, then he is almost certainly not the biological father of the child. That is, presumably, not information sought by the couple, but it is relevant to their concern about the risk of disease in future children. How, then, should genetic counselors deal with this sensitive information? Most commentators on this issue concluded that counselors did have a duty to disclose this finding to the father, despite its potentially adverse consequences for the couple's relationship.

A finding of misattributed paternity requires the comparison of genetic information from two individuals. Diagnosis of a serious genetic condition in a single patient may also be highly significant for that patient's relatives, since they may be at risk for the same disease. What, if any, responsibilities does the possession of this information impose on patients and health care professionals? Because we ascribe moral, and sometimes legal, duties to family members for the care of their children and other dependent family members, perhaps we should also recognize a familial duty to inform one's close relatives when they are at risk for a serious genetic disease. Members of close-knit families will likely offer this information to loved ones voluntarily, out of concern for their welfare, but members of broken families, as in the introductory case for this chapter, may strongly prefer to keep this information confidential. If the patient is unwilling to disclose genetic information to family members at risk, must health care professionals respect that decision?

Davis reports that the profession of genetic counseling has long embraced a strong commitment to respect for patient autonomy and to "value neutrality" and "non-directiveness" in its services.[56] In other words,

---

[55] See, for example, President's Commission for the Study of Ethical Problems in Medicine and Biomedical and Behavioral Research (1983c).

[56] Davis (2010): 12–17.

genetic counselors strive to educate patients about their genetic condition and treatment alternatives, but refrain from recommending or attempting to persuade patients to make specific choices. Adherence to this commitment to patient autonomy would require counselors to honor patient decisions to keep genetic information confidential and not disclose it to relatives. Several commentators, however, have questioned this near-absolute deference to patient autonomy in genetic counseling. In other contexts, including dangers posed by infectious disease and mental illness, we recognize that a duty to warn third parties at risk may override patients' claims to confidentiality.[57] The rationale for those duties to warn would seem to apply with similar force to situations in which genetic information about one patient identifies clear risks of preventable harm to that patient's close relatives. Some have argued that genes and genetic information should be viewed as the shared or collective property of families, not of individuals, and therefore families should make joint decisions about genetic testing and information disclosure.[58]

Access to expanded genetic testing. Preceding sections of this chapter discussed ethical issues raised by expansion of prenatal and newborn genetic screening and testing. As we have also observed, many of the hoped-for benefits of personalized genomic medicine are predicated on obtaining detailed genomic profiles for individual patients. With the introduction of "next generation" DNA sequencing technologies in 2008, the cost of whole genome sequencing dropped precipitously, from ten *million* dollars per genome in 2007 to less than $1000 in 2014![59] Whole genome sequencing is thus affordable for many people in developed nations, if not for most of the rest of the world's population. Whole genome sequencing has not, however, become a routine part of personal health care, primarily because its practical value for guiding treatment or improving health remains uncertain. In a few contexts, such as treatment of aggressive and treatment-resistant malignant tumors, genomic sequencing of the tumor can identify specific mutations that make tumor cells susceptible to narrowly targeted therapy using specific antibody medications, with dramatic positive results.[60] For most people, however, individual genomic sequencing

---

[57] See Chapter 6, "Privacy and confidentiality," for further discussion of these limits to confidentiality.

[58] See Wachbroit (1993) and Parker and Lucassen (2004).   [59] Wetterstrand (2014).

[60] See Kris et al. (2014) and Pasche and Grant (2014).

will not identify a single gene that causes a specific disease and that will enable measures to prevent or treat that disease. Rather, sequencing will likely yield a result more like this: "Your genome contains 100 gene variants that have been associated with some increased risk for ten different common diseases, including cancer, heart disease, and dementia. Due to the large number of these gene variants and their uncertain significance, however, these findings do not suggest any obvious options for prevention or treatment of future illness." Until the clinical significance of genomic profiling is more clearly established, there is insufficient reason to incorporate this practice into most health care settings.

Despite the limited clinical value of genomic profiles, multiple companies have in recent years taken advantage of lower-cost sequencing technologies to offer DNA testing and interpretation of results directly to consumers, and many customers have purchased their services. Marketing for these services was designed to appeal to curiosity about one's ancestry and personal identity as well as one's health risks. Nordgren and Juengst argue that genomic science is still too weak to enable these direct-to-consumer genetic testing companies to provide consistently reliable and significant health information to their customers.[61] In 2013, the US Food and Drug Administration (FDA) warned "23andMe," a leading direct-to-consumer testing company, that its "Personal Genome Service," including reporting of health risks to customers, was an inaccurate and unapproved use of a medical device, and that it must be discontinued.[62] The company responded by discontinuing its reporting of health-related results and limiting its services to ancestry-related genetic information.[63]

Prospects for gene therapy. This chapter has discussed a variety of issues raised by the collection of genetic information and the use of that information to diagnosis disease, to make reproductive decisions, and to control the symptoms of genetic diseases. In addition to genetic diagnosis and efforts to control the effects of genetic disease, scientists are also engaged in research efforts to make direct alterations in the structure of the genome for therapeutic purposes. 'Gene therapy' is the term used to describe treatments that target the genome directly, either by inactivating a disease-causing gene, inserting a "healthy" gene, or inserting a new gene engineered to perform a therapeutic function.[64]

---

[61] See Nordgren and Juengst (2009).   [62] US Food and Drug Administration (2013).
[63] Wojcicki (2013).   [64] US National Library of Medicine (2015).

Gene therapy holds out the promise of highly desirable results – the cure of genetic diseases, and effective treatment for other major illnesses. To be successful, however, a gene therapy intervention must be able to isolate or construct the genes to be inserted, to deliver those genes to the appropriate cells (for example, bone marrow cells in a leukemia patient), to incorporate the new genes into the patient's DNA, to stimulate the new genes to carry out the desired function, and to avoid complications or side effects of this alteration in the patient's genome. These are formidable scientific hurdles, and despite hundreds of past and ongoing clinical trials, the FDA has not yet approved any gene therapy products for general use.[65] The recent discovery of a new genome engineering method may, however, pave the way for clinically effective human gene therapy. This method, known as clustered regularly interspaced short palindromic repeats (CRISPR)-Cas9, gives researchers a simple, inexpensive, and efficient way to make specific modifications to a genome.[66]

If successful techniques for the delivery and expression of genetic alterations are developed, they could be used for a variety of purposes. Current research is focused on genetic alterations to human organs and tissues to treat pathologic processes in those body parts; this is called somatic cell gene therapy. Gene therapy could also target mutations in a person's egg or sperm cells, enabling genetic changes to be passed on to one's offspring; this more controversial application is called germline gene therapy.[67] An even more controversial future use of gene therapy techniques might be to enhance genes that contribute to non-medical traits like intelligence, height, longevity, or muscle strength.

Given the continuing high level of research activity, I believe that gene therapy techniques will eventually be approved for clinical use. As gene therapies become available, health care professionals, patients, and policy makers will face a number of significant moral choices. Professionals will have to decide when to recommend gene therapy to their patients and how to respond to patient requests for this novel approach to treatment for their illnesses. Patients, if they have decision-making capacity, or their surrogate

---

[65] US National Library of Medicine (2015).   [66] Doudna and Charpentier (2014).

[67] An interdisciplinary group of US scientists, bioethicists, and legal scholars meeting in January 2015 recommended a moratorium on attempts at human germline genome modification to allow for further study and discussion of the merits and risks of the CRISPR-Cas9 genome engineering technology (Baltimore et al. 2015).

decision-makers, if patients lack capacity, will have to evaluate the potential benefits and harms of these therapies, in the light of their values, hopes, and fears. Policymakers will have to decide which gene therapies should be available, which should be covered by health insurance, and whether certain uses of gene therapy should be prohibited.

Case analysis

Based on her symptoms, family history, physical examination, and multiple diagnostic tests, physicians at University Hospital have determined that Wilson disease, a rare genetic disorder, is the cause of Ms. Kemper's severe illness. This diagnosis is too late to prevent her acute liver failure, but her physicians give her the good news that liver transplantation (if a donor liver becomes available) will likely result in disease-free, long-term survival.

While Ms. Kemper is waiting for a donor liver, genetic counselor Mr. Quinn gives her more information about Wilson disease. He explains that, in addition to liver damage, patients with this condition often develop severe neurologic or psychiatric symptoms, including speech impairment, movement disorders, and depression, and Ms. Kemper is relieved that she has not yet developed those symptoms. Mr. Quinn also explains that Ms. Kemper's siblings have a one-in-four chance of having inherited from their parents the gene mutations that cause the disease. Symptoms of the disease usually appear between the ages of 5 and 35, but organ damage from excess copper accumulation is gradual and cumulative. Early diagnosis of the condition enables highly effective treatment with medications that enable the body to excrete excess copper and prevent its accumulation, thereby preventing organ damage. Thus, if any of Ms. Kemper's siblings have Wilson disease, early diagnosis and drug treatment can prevent debilitating or life-threatening complications like those she has experienced.

After informing Ms. Kemper about the potential benefits of informing her siblings about their risk for Wilson disease, Mr. Quinn could proceed in several ways. He could simply allow her to make her own decision about informing them, and say no more about the matter. He could offer to help Ms. Kemper explain the information to them. He could ask Ms. Kemper whether she intends to inform them. He could explicitly recommend that she provide this information to them. Which of these options would be most consistent with a value-neutral, non-directive approach to genetic counseling? Is strict value-neutrality the best approach to counseling in this situation?

When Mr. Quinn explains the risk of disease to the siblings, Ms. Kemper volunteers the information that she has two younger siblings, but adds that she is estranged from her family and does not wish to communicate with them in any way. Although this would be clearly incompatible with a non-directive approach to counseling, Mr. Quinn may view the situation as an opportunity to prevent great harm and so want to try to persuade Ms. Kemper to share this valuable information with her siblings. May he make that attempt?

Whatever approach Mr. Quinn decides to take, Ms. Kemper may not waver in her decision not to inform her siblings about their risk for Wilson disease. Mr. Quinn and his colleagues might consider whether they may override her decision in order to provide this information to her siblings. Despite its potentially great value for the siblings, disclosure would violate Ms. Kemper's strong interest in confidentiality about her medical condition. Would disclosure of this information to the siblings without her permission nevertheless be morally permissible?

In contrast to her desire not to inform her siblings about their risk for Wilson disease, Ms. Kemper expresses a great desire to pursue genetic testing in order to learn whether her infant daughter has this genetic condition. Ms. Kemper has Wilson disease, but her daughter must also inherit mutations for this condition from her father in order to manifest the disease, a risk estimated at less than 0.6 percent.[68] Genetic diagnosis of Wilson disease in the daughter would enable dietary and drug treatment to prevent organ damage, and determination that she does not have the disease would relieve Ms. Kemper's anxiety. Presumably due to the low risk and to the availability of other indirect methods to screen older children for Wilson disease, genetic testing for infant children of Wilson disease patients is not a routine practice.[69] Should the medical team nevertheless honor Mrs. Kemper's request for immediate genetic testing of her daughter, or should they refuse that request and instead reassure her that they will monitor her daughter's health and perform non-genetic screening tests later to rule out the remote chance that she has Wilson disease?

[68] Dufernez et al. (2013).   [69] Dufernez et al. (2013).

21 Organ transplantation

Case example

The clinical staff of the liver transplantation program at a major US academic medical center is having its monthly meeting to determine which of the candidates recently evaluated by the program will be added to the program's waiting list for liver transplantation. Among the patients under consideration today are the following three:

Mr. Hale is an 18-year-old university student who suffered acute liver failure as the result of an overdose of acetaminophen (thirty-seven tablets within one hour). He states that he took the tablets for an unrelenting headache and had no suicidal intent. He has a history of attention deficit disorder, depression, and cannabis use. His parents appear to be quite willing to support his medical care.

Mr. Irving is a 32-year-old inmate of Central Prison. He was convicted on a murder charge at age 19 and has eight more years to serve on his sentence. He has liver failure due to cirrhosis, and his cirrhosis is a result of juvenile hemochromatosis, a rare genetic condition causing severe iron overload in the liver and other organs. Mr. Irving also has ascites (fluid accumulation in his abdomen) and encephalopathy (loss of brain function due to liver failure). He has a history of drug abuse prior to his incarceration. His father has petitioned the Governor for early release due to his illness.

Mrs. Nguyen is a 73-year-old Vietnamese immigrant with cirrhosis caused by chronic hepatitis C infection. Her condition was stable until she took a Chinese herbal remedy that resulted in acute liver failure. She has no other illnesses and, until the present acute illness, worked full-time in a clothing store. She is a widow, but has a large and supportive family.

Which of these patients, if any, should be added to the program's waiting list for a liver transplant?[1]

---

[1] Cases adapted from Paul H. Hayashi, "Ethical Issues in Liver Transplantation," presentation at Ethical Dilemmas in Health Care conference, University of North Carolina at Chapel Hill, Chapel Hill, North Carolina, November 6, 2009.

Success and scarcity

Success

On December 23, 1954, surgeons in Boston performed the first successful human organ transplant, transplanting a kidney from a healthy identical twin into his dying twin brother.[2] Since that time, surgeons have developed techniques for transplantation of multiple organs, and investigators have discovered effective therapies to prevent immune system rejection of transplant organs. Many nations have developed sophisticated systems for recovering transplant organs from patients after death and distributing those organs to waiting patients. More than a half century after that first success, organ transplantation has become an established medical treatment and a symbol of the success of heroic, technologically sophisticated medicine. The practice of organ transplantation raises complex moral and public policy questions regarding the procurement of transplant organs and the distribution of those organs among patients in need. This chapter will consider responses to those questions.

29,531 organ transplants were performed in the United States in 2014, and many thousands more were performed world wide.[3] Current survival rates for liver transplantation patients in the United States are 82 percent at one year after transplantation, 72 percent at two years, and 65 percent at three years. Survival rates for kidney transplant patients are significantly higher – 96 percent at one year after transplantation, 91 percent at two years, and 85 percent at three years, due in part to dialysis as a fallback therapy in the event of failure of a graft kidney.[4] Organ transplantation enables many patients with debilitating, often terminal illnesses to return to a relatively normal, active lifestyle. Transplantation thus offers a longer life and a better quality of life for patients with end-stage organ failure.

Despite its success, it is important to recognize that organ transplantation is not a panacea for patients with these catastrophic medical conditions. Transplantation does not cure the underlying disease that caused the original organ failure, and so the transplant organ may also fail. Some

---

[2] Merrill et al. (1956).

[3] Data from the Organ Procurement and Transplantation Network, US Department of Health and Human Services (2015).

[4] Organ Procurement and Transplantation Network, US Department of Health and Human Services (2015).

transplant organs never function, and most do fail eventually. Transplant patients must adhere to a life-long regimen of immunosuppressive drugs to prevent rejection of the transplant organ, and those drugs have various side-effects and complications. Finally, transplantation and its associated supportive therapies are relatively costly. Nevertheless, transplantation does significantly prolong survival and improve the quality of life for patients with failure of a vital organ.

Scarcity

The significant benefits of organ transplantation have stimulated increasing demand for this treatment, and that demand now poses a major problem for the transplantation enterprise. The problem is a large and growing scarcity of organs available for transplantation. In the United States and most other developed nations, the majority of transplant organs come from newly deceased donors. Most of these deceased donors have been pronounced dead on the basis of neurologic (brain-oriented) criteria, but their organs are suitable for transplantation because mechanical ventilation and other technologies continue to support basic physiologic function. In the decade 2005–2014, the number of deceased donors in the United States grew at a rate of less than 2 percent annually, from 7593 in 2005 to 8594 in 2014. During that same decade, the annual number of living donors in the US decreased, from 6904 in 2005 to 5818 in 2014. Over the same time period, the number of US patients on transplant waiting lists has increased by almost 5 percent annually, from 86,355 at the beginning of 2004 to 123,283 in April 2015.[5]

As the number of patients waiting for an organ continues to outstrip the number of available transplant organs, and by a wider margin each year, patient waiting time for an organ has increased significantly. For example, the median waiting time for a kidney for patients of black, Hispanic, or Asian ethnicity added to the transplant waiting list in 2003–2004 was more than five years. As more patients wait longer for an organ to become available, a significant number of these waiting patients die or become too sick to undergo a transplant procedure each year. Every year since 2000, between 6600 and 7600 patients on US transplant waiting lists have died

[5] Organ Procurement and Transplantation Network, US Department of Health and Human Services (2015).

while waiting for a transplant, and between 1500 and 6000 more patients were removed from transplant waiting lists because they were too sick to receive a transplant.[6]

In summary, physicians are identifying more patients who could benefit from an organ transplant each year, but more and more often no organ is available for these waiting patients. If our goal is to provide the benefits of organ transplantation to as many of those in need as possible, the most obvious response to this situation of scarcity is to seek ways to increase the number of organs for transplantation.

Increasing organ supply

In its early development during the 1960s, organ transplantation was hampered by uncertainty about when death could be pronounced, a necessary condition for recovery of a dead patient's organs for transplantation. A landmark 1968 report from Harvard Medical School addressed this problem by proposing novel criteria for the determination of human death based on the irreversible loss of brain function, and US state legislatures quickly recognized new neurologic criteria for the determination of death, popularly called 'brain death.'[7] This change gave organ transplantation programs a new and valuable source of transplant organs, that is, patients pronounced dead by neurologic criteria whose organ function was preserved by continuing circulation of blood and mechanical ventilation. This new source of donor organs, composed primarily of healthy young people who suffered catastrophic brain injury, enabled transplantation programs to expand, but the number of patients who met neurologic criteria for death eventually reached a plateau, while the number of new candidates for organ transplants continued its steady increase.

In response to the longstanding and increasing shortfall in the number of organs available for transplantation, transplantation advocates have

---

[6] Organ Procurement and Transplantation Network, US Department of Health and Human Services (2015).

[7] Ad Hoc Committee of the Harvard Medical School to Examine the Definition of Brain Death (1968). The term 'brain death' is still widely used. Many commentators avoid this term, however, because it misleadingly suggests that "brain death" is something different from death of the person, rather than a criterion for determining that the person has died.

proposed a variety of strategies for increasing the organ supply. Many of these strategies were adopted and are now standard features of the organ procurement system in the United States. Federal legislation enacted in 1986, for example, requires that hospitals refer all potential organ donors to their regional organ procurement organization (OPO) for evaluation and follow-up by trained organ procurement coordinators.[8] This legislation was designed to ensure that all potential deceased donors are identified and that families of donors are approached by professionals specially trained to discuss this sensitive issue and to obtain consent for donation. In the 1980s, OPOs and organ transplant programs also expanded their criteria of eligibility for organ donation, accepting organs from older donors and from donors with medical conditions that had previously made them ineligible for donation.[9] With the increase in patients waiting for donor kidneys, transplantation programs have also placed greater emphasis on recruitment of living kidney donors. Programs that previously accepted kidney donation only from biologically related family members (that is, parents, children, and siblings) now began to encourage donation from biologically unrelated persons, including spouses and altruistic strangers. Kidneys from these unrelated donors have high graft survival rates, but critics voice concern about the possible coercion of living donors and about the health risks to them of kidney donation.[10]

A 2005 US national conference encouraged hospitals to implement new protocols to recover organs from patients after determination of death by the traditional heart-lung criteria.[11] These protocols are designed for patients who do not meet neurologic criteria for death, but whose lives are being sustained by mechanical ventilation, and for whom a decision has been made to withdraw that life-sustaining treatment. The protocols establish a process for treatment withdrawal in a surgical setting, followed by cessation of respiration and circulation, a short waiting period, pronouncement of death, and immediate recovery of organs for transplantation. Another recent US policy initiative has encouraged prospective first-person consent to organ donation.[12] In the state of North Carolina, for example, 2007 legislation recognized an expression of willingness to be an organ donor made when obtaining or renewing a driver's license as legal consent

[8] Andersen and Fox (1988).   [9] Ratner et al. (1996).   [10] Terasaki et al. (1995).
[11] Bernat et al. (2006).   [12] Wynn and Alexander (2011).

for organ donation after death.[13] First-person consent to organ donation allows US OPOs to recover organs without seeking permission from family members at the time of organ recovery, but OPOs still inform family members about organ recovery from a deceased relative, and many honor family requests that organs not be recovered.

Each of these measures has had some effect on increasing the number of available transplant organs. The number of organ donors after circulatory determination of death, for example, increased from 2 percent of all deceased donors in 2000 to 10 percent of deceased donors in 2010.[14] Despite all of these initiatives, however, the gap between organ demand and supply has widened, due primarily to the steady and significant annual increase in the number of patients added to transplant waiting lists. Multiple additional strategies for increasing organ supply, therefore, have been proposed, including presumed consent to organ donation, financial incentives for donation, revision of neurologic criteria for the determination of death, abandonment of the "dead-donor rule," animal-to-human organ transplantation, and development of bioengineered transplant organs. These strategies would make more fundamental, and more controversial, changes to the US organ procurement and transplantation system. Let's briefly consider each of the strategies mentioned above in turn.

Presumed consent to organ donation

The United States, the United Kingdom, and most other English-speaking nations require informed consent to organ donation after death, either first-person prospective consent or consent by a surrogate at the time of donation. These "opt-in" systems thus require an explicit decision to donate organs. Most European countries, in contrast, *presume* consent to organ donation after death. In these presumed consent or "opt-out" systems, organs may be recovered unless an individual has formally stated in advance a desire not to be an organ donor.[15] Because roughly half of

---

[13] North Carolina General Statutes § 20–43.2.

[14] Wynn and Alexander (2011). 'Circulatory determination of death' is the currently preferred term for determination of death using the traditional criteria of irreversible cessation of heart and lung function.

[15] Bilgel (2012). This author explains that some European nations, like Austria and the Czech Republic, enforce presumed consent to donation strictly, while others allow family members to veto donation.

American driver's license holders choose not to be organ donors, and probably only a small percentage of these would make a special effort to register as organ donation refusers, adoption of a presumed consent system would likely increase the number of organs recovered. The fact that so many Americans choose not to designate themselves as organ donors when they obtain or renew a driver's license, however, is strong support for the view that consent to organ donation cannot and should not be presumed, but rather explicitly obtained. Given this significant rate of refusal and the established presumption that persons and their families should control disposition of the body after death, change to a presumed consent system is not likely to be a politically feasible option in the United States.

Financial incentives for organ donation

A 1984 US federal statute, the National Organ Transplant Act, laid the groundwork for the current US organ procurement and transplantation system.[16] That statute also banned the sale or purchase of human organs. Critics of a market in human organs offer multiple reasons for this ban, including the following: (1) Viewing the human body and its parts as a commodity that can be bought and sold undermines the special dignity and moral worth of human life. (2) Allowing organ sales will exploit or coerce indigent people who see the sale of an organ as the only way to improve their desperate financial situation. (3) People who are repelled by a legal practice of organ sales may choose not to become organ donors, and the number of altruistic organ donors may therefore decrease.[17] Most other nations have similar laws banning organ sales, but black markets for organs and "transplant tourism" have been active in several nations, including India, Pakistan, Egypt, the Philippines, and China.[18]

Financial incentives for organ donation have always had proponents as well as critics, and, with the growing scarcity of transplant organs, there has been increasing support for relaxing the ban on financial incentives.[19] Among the arguments offered by those who favor remuneration for organs are the following: (1) Because all of the other participants in the organ

---

[16] National Organ Transplant Act (1984).   [17] See, for example, Cohen (2013).

[18] Shimazono (2007).

[19] See, for example, Working Group on Incentives for Living Donation (2012).

transplantation enterprise, including those who recover and transplant organs, are paid for their contributions, those who donate the organs should also receive remuneration for that essential contribution. (2) Those who agree to sell their own or a loved one's organs can make this decision freely, and a legal and well-regulated organ recovery system can prevent exploitation of these organ vendors. (3) Financial incentives can motivate more people to agree to organ recovery, thereby increasing the number of organs available for transplantation and achieving the beneficent goal of extending the lives of more patients with organ failure. The US federal ban on organ sales remains in effect, but several states have adopted policies to reimburse families of deceased organ donors for a portion of their funeral expenses, and to give tax deductions for expenses incurred by living organ donors.[20] In one nation, Iran, a regulated legal system of compensating organ donors by government and by organ recipients has been in place since 1997.[21]

Revision of neurologic criteria for the determination of death

As noted above, most transplant organs in developed nations are recovered from deceased donors after neurologic determination of death. For this category of donors, a necessary step in the organ recovery process is the determination that the patient satisfies neurological criteria for death. In the United States, expert panels appointed by medical professional societies have developed and revised separate neurologic criteria for death in adults and in children.[22] These clinical criteria are based on the standard brain-oriented legal definition of death, namely, "irreversible cessation of all functions of the entire brain, including the brain stem."[23]

Some commentators have argued that this definition of death, and the clinical criteria based on it, are too narrow.[24] These commentators maintain that the potential for conscious experience is essential for human personal life, and death should be pronounced when that potential is irreversibly lost. Criteria for death, they argue, should focus on the loss of the higher brain functions that support consciousness, not the loss of all brain

---

[20] See Stolberg (1999), Paulson (2004).   [21] Mahdavi-Mazdeh (2012).

[22] See Wijdicks et al. (2010) and Nakagawa et al. (2011).

[23] National Conference of Commissioners on Uniform State Laws (1980).

[24] See, for example, Veatch (1993).

function. Expanded criteria of this kind for determining death would create new categories of deceased, but heart-beating potential organ donors, including anencephalic infants[25] and individuals in permanent vegetative states, and these new donors could provide thousands of transplant organs annually. This proposed expansion of the definition and neurologic criteria for death faces several major obstacles, however. First, there is likely to be strong disagreement by some with the claim that irreversible loss of the potential for consciousness is the key element in the definition of human death. This definition, for example, would allow pronouncement of death of some patients who are breathing spontaneously, a result that seems strongly counterintuitive. Second, even if there is agreement about defining human death in this way, physicians may lack diagnostic criteria that can identify loss of the specific higher brain functions necessary for consciousness with the high degree of accuracy needed to prevent false positive determinations of death.

Abandonment of the "dead-donor rule"

In sharp contrast to the above-described position that neurologic criteria for the determination of death should be modified in ways that would increase the number of deceased donors, other commentators argue that the established whole-brain criteria for neurologic determination of death do not accurately diagnose the complete absence of brain function, and so should be rejected.[26] These commentators recommend a return to traditional heart-lung based criteria as the sole criteria for the determination of death.

Recall that a major impetus for the recognition of neurologic criteria for the determination of death was the desire to recover organs from patients with irreversible loss of brain function whose respiration and circulation were supported by medical technologies. Unless these patients were first declared dead, their organs could not be recovered, because the removal of vital organs for transplantation would otherwise be the cause of their death, and the surgeons removing those organs would be committing a form of homicide. This legal rule that organ recovery cannot be the cause of a patient's death is commonly called "the dead-donor rule."

---

[25] Anencephalic infants are born with a congenital absence of most of the brain, including the higher brain centers necessary for consciousness.

[26] See, for example, Truog et al. (2013).

Those who recommend rejection of neurologic criteria for the determination of death recognize that this change would severely limit the number of organs recovered for transplantation as long as the dead-donor rule remains in effect. To prevent that unwanted consequence, these commentators propose that the dead-donor rule also be abandoned. That is, recovery of vital organs from living patients should be permitted, when patients or their surrogate decision-makers consent and when that recovery does not harm the patient. They argue that this approach would permit recovery of organs from patients who are now declared dead by whole-brain oriented criteria, as well as from anencephalic infants, other terminally ill patients dependent on life support technologies, and patients in permanent vegetative states.

In fact, no jurisdiction has yet decided to abandon or relax the dead-donor rule. Given concerns voiced by some about premature pronouncement of death to promote organ recovery, there is likely to be strong opposition to allowing organ recovery to be the immediate cause of death. The practice of euthanasia offers a partial analogy here; except in the Netherlands, Belgium, and Luxembourg, patient consent is not recognized as a justification for physician administration of a lethal drug.[27]

Animal-to-human organ transplantation

All of the strategies discussed above have some potential for increasing the supply of available transplant organs, but that supply is still unavoidably limited by the absolute number of potential deceased donors and willing living donors. Some scientists and clinicians, therefore, are investigating the transplantation of animal organs and tissues into human patients, also known as "xenotransplantation." Early US attempts at xenotransplantation, including the highly publicized heart transplant of "Baby Fae" in 1984, used baboon organs.[28] These transplants did not succeed, and non-human primates are no longer the preferred source of xenograft organs for several reasons, including the risk of cross-species disease transmission and a desire to protect these intelligent and social primates. Current research is focused on pig models, including the creation of genetically modified pigs whose

[27] See Chapter 18, "Aid in dying," for further discussion of the practice of euthanasia in these nations.
[28] Bailey et al. (1985).

organs are less susceptible to immune rejection by human recipients, and alteration of the transplant recipient's immune system to enable it to tolerate a pig organ.[29] Transplantation of porcine organs also poses some risk of zoonosis, the transmission of an infectious disease from pig organ donors to human recipients, and perhaps further to other humans.

Because pigs are already bred in very large numbers for food, large-scale breeding of genetically modified pigs for transplant organs seems feasible. Whether xenotransplantation using porcine organs can be successful, however, will likely depend on the results of continuing animal research and of clinical trials on human subjects at some indefinite future time. Xenotransplantation is, therefore, a possible long-term response to the problem of organ scarcity, but not a short-term solution.

Bioengineered transplant organs

The emerging field of regenerative medicine offers another potential future source of organs for transplantation. Over the past two decades, investigators have developed techniques to engineer body parts in the laboratory, using cells grown in culture and supporting "scaffolds," and to implant these bioengineered body parts into living patients. Bioengineering techniques have produced functioning human bladders, urethras, blood vessels, skin grafts, and tracheas.[30] These investigators are also engaged in research on the engineering of more complex solid human organs like kidneys, livers, and hearts, and they have developed small scale animal models of these organs that show some organ-specific function.

Bioengineered organs have two major advantages over organs recovered from human or animal donors. They are, first of all, not dependent on the availability and compatibility of an organ donor, but rather on stem cells and other biological materials and on technicians able to engineer the organs in "bioreactors" or other production facilities. Second, if the patient's own stem cells are recovered and used to engineer a transplant organ, the patient's immune system should accept the organ as its own, without a need for immunosuppressive therapy or risk of rejection of the organ. Leaders in the field of regenerative medicine acknowledge, however, that multiple scientific hurdles still stand in the way of development of

[29] Pierson (2009).   [30] Orlando et al. (2011).

successful bioengineered solid organs and of the large-scale production of such organs. Like xenotransplantation, therefore, bioengineered human transplant organs will not solve the problem of organ scarcity in the foreseeable future.

What general conclusions can be drawn from this review of strategies designed to increase the supply of organs for transplantation? Multiple organ procurement initiatives have been implemented over the past few decades, with some success, but the demand for organs has grown much more quickly than the available supply. Additional strategies have been proposed and debated, but each faces significant hurdles, some moral, some political, and some scientific. For the foreseeable future, therefore, I expect the scarcity of transplant organs to persist and increase. In the face of this increasing scarcity of a resource with life-and-death consequences for thousands of patients, the distribution of organs among waiting patients is an issue of profound moral significance.

Distributing a scarce resource

Over the past three decades, the United States has developed a complex national system for the recovery, allocation, and transplantation of human organs. In mid-2014, that system included fifty-eight OPOs that carry out organ recovery activities, each in its own designated service area, and 248 transplant centers, with more than 800 organ-specific transplant programs. These organ transplant programs evaluate potential transplant patients and living donors for transplant and donation eligibility, and they perform organ recovery and transplant procedures. A national Organ Procurement and Transplantation Network (OPTN), maintained under contract with the federal government by the United Network for Organ Sharing (UNOS), coordinates the activities of OPOs and transplant programs, maintains national transplant waiting lists for each organ, establishes, revises, and implements organ-specific allocation systems, and collects national, regional, and local data on organ donation and transplantation.[31]

Access to organ transplantation in the United States is a process that includes four necessary steps. First, a physician must identify his or her

---

[31] Organ Procurement and Transplantation Network, US Department of Health and Human Services (2015).

patient as a potential organ transplant candidate and offer to refer the patient to a transplant program, and the patient must accept that referral. Second, the transplant program must evaluate the patient to determine whether he or she is an appropriate candidate for transplantation. Third, on the basis of its evaluation, the program must determine that the patient is in fact an appropriate candidate for transplantation. If the program does decide that the patient is a transplant candidate, it may seek and find a suitable and willing living organ donor, or it may add that patient to the program's waiting list for transplantation with a deceased donor organ.[32] Finally, if the patient is placed on the program's transplant waiting list, each time a deceased donor organ becomes available, the patient will be ranked by UNOS, using the national organ allocation system for that organ, along with the other patients on the local, regional, and national waiting lists. When that patient is ranked first by the national allocation system for that organ, the organ will be offered to the local transplant program and to that patient. If they accept the offered organ, it will be promptly transported to the program for transplantation within the relatively brief period in which the organ remains viable outside a living body. There are, therefore, two sets of criteria used to determine access to transplantation, criteria for addition to a transplant waiting list, and criteria for allocation of available organs among patients on waiting lists. Let's consider each set of criteria in turn.

Criteria for addition to a transplant waiting list

Each US transplant program establishes and uses its own criteria for deciding which patients to add to its transplantation waiting list. These criteria may be explicit and formal, or implicit and informal. Commonly used criteria include the following:

1. a diagnosis of end-stage organ failure (to establish the need for transplantation)
2. absence of active infection, malignancy, or other major illness (because these conditions would make surgery too risky or would limit patient survival after transplantation)

---

[32] Because kidneys are paired organs, people may choose to donate a kidney with a relatively low level of health risk to themselves. Some people also choose to donate a lobe of their liver or lung for transplantation, although these procedures pose a greater risk to themselves. For more information on risks in living donation, see Gordon (2013).

3. ability to adhere to post-transplant immunosuppressive therapy (because that therapy is essential for transplant organ survival and function)

4. ability to abstain from unhealthy behaviors (because smoking and alcohol or drug abuse would threaten organ and patient survival after transplantation)

5. health insurance coverage or other ability to pay for transplantation (required for the continuing operation of the transplant program)

Objective measures exist for some of these criteria, but others obviously depend on the judgment of transplant program staff, based on review of patients' medical records, physical examination, diagnostic testing, and interviews. Consultant psychiatrists, for example, may be asked to assess whether a patient's motivation, mental health, cognitive capacity, and family support will enable him or her to abstain from alcohol or to adhere to a daily schedule of medications for the rest of his or her life. The stakes are high – a decision not to list the patient may foreclose his or her access to the benefits of transplantation, and a decision to list and transplant a patient unsuccessfully will deprive another waiting patient of the benefits of a successful transplant.

Criteria for ranking waiting list patients

Once a patient is placed on a transplant program's waiting list in the United States, that patient's access to deceased donor organs is governed largely by specific algorithms for each type of organ. As the organization that administers the national OPTN, UNOS develops, evaluates, revises, and applies these algorithms to rank order waiting patients for each deceased donor organ as it becomes available.[33] These algorithms have become increasingly complex over the past three decades, as national data collection has enabled the identification, measurement, and comparison of various factors that affect transplant access and outcomes. Current algorithms use multiple criteria to assign waiting patients to priority categories, or "bins," with additional criteria for ranking patients within the same bin; see Figures 1 and 2 for graphic representations of two current allocation systems, for

---

[33] For summaries of these algorithms, see Smith et al. (2012) and Colvin-Adams et al. (2012).

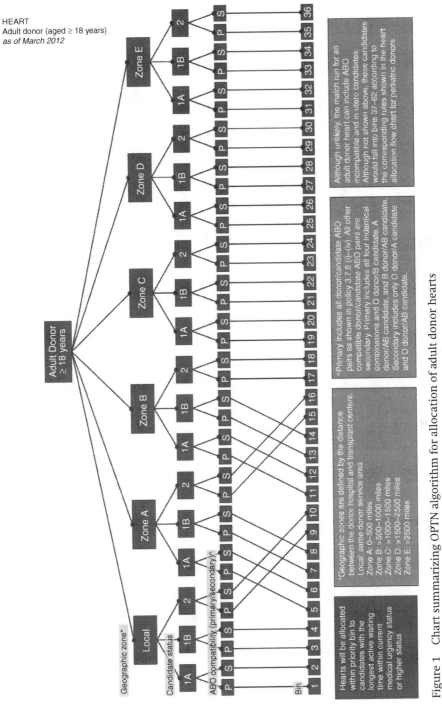

Figure 1　Chart summarizing OPTN algorithm for allocation of adult donor hearts

Available at: www.srtr.org/allocationcharts/files/Heart_adult_donor.pdf

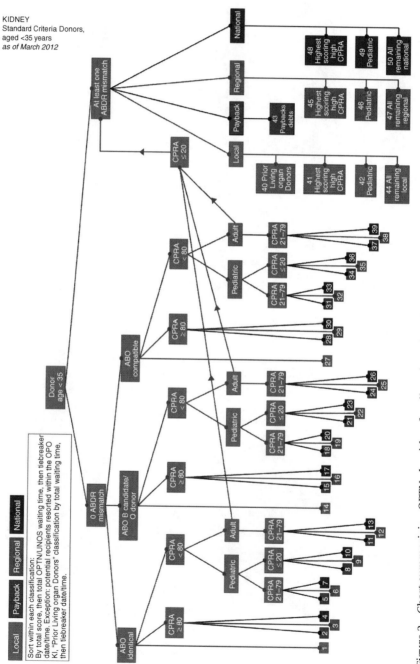

Figure 2 Chart summarizing OPTN algorithm for allocation of kidneys from standard criteria donors aged younger than 35 years
Available at: www.srtr.org/allocationcharts/files/Kidney_SCD_age_less_than_35.pdf

hearts and for "standard criteria" kidneys (that is, kidneys from younger donors without significant comorbid conditions).

What moral considerations are these algorithms designed to address? According to one recent review, "the goal of deceased donor organ allocation policy in the US has been to balance utility and equity in the distribution of deceased donor organs. The policy has changed incrementally over time in efforts to optimize allocation to meet these often competing goals."[34] Because organs are scarce, and because the goals of utility and equity are "often competing," allocation systems must "balance" these general goals, by assigning relative priorities or weights to different factors in order to arrive at a discrete ranking for each candidate for each specific organ. What exactly is meant by these general goals of utility and equity? How do specific allocation criteria serve each goal? Let's consider each of these goals and their corresponding criteria.

Utility and its criteria. Generally speaking, utility refers to assessment of the consequences of an action. In this context, we promote utility by selecting patients for transplantation who are most likely to benefit, and least likely to be harmed, by this procedure. Notice that one can assess the utility of transplantation for an individual patient, and also for a group of patients, as, for example, the local or national waiting list for a particular organ. Transplantation may promise significant benefit for a particular patient, such as an extension of life and significant improvement in the quality of life, but even greater benefit for another patient, because the latter patient may live longer and have even more improvement in his or her quality of life. In this case, if all other factors are equal, the overall utility for a group that includes both patients is increased by allocating the organ to the latter patient. Utility-based criteria in allocation algorithms include the following:

1 blood type compatibility (because organs of an incompatible blood type are rejected)
2 negative cross-match testing (performed in kidney transplantation to determine that the potential recipient does not have pre-formed antibodies that will reject the organ)
3 human leukocyte antigen (HLA) matching (used in kidney and pancreas transplantation to reduce the likelihood of organ rejection when these antigens do not match)

[34] Smith et al. (2012).

4 organ size matching (because adult organs may be too large to transplant into pediatric recipients, and pediatric organs may be too small to provide adequate organ function in adult recipients)

Each of these criteria is used to rule out candidates who are unlikely to benefit and likely to be harmed by transplantation with a particular donor organ.

Equity and its criteria. Generally speaking, equity refers to the concern to provide fair access to a valued good or service. In this context, we promote equity by giving all those who need and can benefit from transplantation a fair opportunity to receive it. Unlike utility, equity is not primarily concerned with producing good individual or overall consequences of the practice of transplantation, but rather with giving patients access to transplantation based on their need, desert, or some other morally significant consideration. Equity-based criteria in organ allocation systems include the following:

1 urgency (heart, liver, and lung allocation algorithms give priority to the sickest patients, those most likely to die in the near future without a transplant)
2 waiting time (because patients waiting longer for an organ have a stronger claim than those waiting a shorter time)
3 prior living donors (because those who have given an organ to another should have priority if they later suffer organ failure, in part because of their donation)
4 degree of immune system pre-sensitization (to give certain kidney transplant candidates an increased chance for transplantation)[35]

Incorporating these criteria into allocation algorithms gives some patients access to transplantation despite the fact that another waiting patient is likely to benefit more from receiving that organ.

---

[35] The immune systems of some kidney patients who have received multiple blood transfusions or previous transplants or who have had multiple pregnancies are highly pre-sensitized against foreign tissue, and so cannot accept most deceased donor organs. The degree of pre-sensitization can be measured and represented by a value called the Calculated Panel Reactive Antibodies (CPRA). Kidney allocation algorithms give priority to these highly pre-sensitized patients when cross-matching testing with blood from a donor is negative, indicating that they do not have pre-formed antibodies that would reject that particular organ.

Mixed criteria. Additional organ allocation criteria can be defended using both utility and equity arguments. These "mixed" criteria include the following:

1 geographic proximity. Allocation criteria give priority to waiting patients who are closer to where the deceased donor organ was recovered. In the early days of transplantation, there was a strong utility argument for this criterion, since organs needed to be transplanted as soon as possible after their recovery in order to function properly. Better organ preservation and transportation systems now allow organs to remain viable longer, and so this utility argument is less persuasive. An equity argument can also be made for geographic proximity, namely, local community and organizational efforts to donate and recover organs should be rewarded by enabling patients in the same community or region to receive those organs.

2 age. Allocation algorithms commonly give priority to pediatric over adult patients. This priority can be defended on utility grounds, since end-stage organ failure in children can stunt growth and have other severe quality of life consequences, and children are likely to live longer than elderly organ recipients. It may also be defended on equity grounds, appealing to an argument that children deserve priority because they have not yet had the opportunities and experiences that we should strive to provide to all people as parts of a full life.

As these different criteria suggest, we recognize the moral significance of both utility and equity considerations in allocating organs, and so are unwilling to give one of these goals absolute priority over the other. We are faced, therefore, with the difficult question of how to strike an appropriate balance between these general goals, and among multiple specific allocation criteria. Which criteria should be weighted more heavily, and which less? These issues provoke ongoing debate and frequent revision of UNOS allocation algorithms. Consider, for example, the following two representative questions:

1 Should the kidney allocation system permit large differences in access to transplantation for patients of different races?[36] The initial UNOS kidney allocation system put great weight on HLA antigen matching between the donor and recipient. Because most kidney donors are white, and antigens

---

[36] For further discussion of this question, see Young and Gaston (2000).

are more often shared within than across racial groupings, white patients were more likely to be ranked ahead of minority patients, and minority patients had much longer waiting times. The system was revised to de-emphasize antigen matching, giving minority patients a better chance to receive a kidney, but more antigen mismatches between donor and recipient can result in earlier rejection of the organ, reducing its overall benefit. This risk of rejection may be offset, however, by improved post-transplant immunosuppressive therapies.

2 Should local transplant patients receive priority over more distant patients?[37] OPOs and transplant programs in the same service area must communicate and collaborate closely with one another to recover and transplant organs effectively. Giving priority to local sharing encourages and rewards this collaboration by allowing organs recovered in one area to be transplanted in that same area. This priority may also disadvantage other patients based solely on where they live, preventing sicker patients in some areas from receiving a transplant more quickly, despite their more urgent need.

Case analysis

The staff of the liver transplant program must decide whether it will add three new patients to its waiting list for transplantation. Evaluation of the patients confirms that all meet several of their established criteria for transplant eligibility. All three patients have end-stage liver failure, and none has evidence of an active infection or malignancy. Mr. Irving, the state prison inmate, does have ascites and hepatic encephalopathy, but those conditions may be at least partly reversible if he receives a transplant.

The three patients differ significantly in several other ways, however. A transplant may give Mr. Hale, the young university student, an indefinite number of additional years of life. His medical history and recent actions, however, raise several questions. Despite his denial, his massive acetaminophen overdose may well have been a suicide attempt, and his depression and drug use may interfere with his ability to adhere to post-transplant drug therapy and to avoid self-destructive behavior. He does, however, appear to

---

[37] For further discussion of this question, see Ubel and Caplan (1998).

have strong support from his anxious parents, and his transplant would be covered by their medical insurance.

Mr. Irving's liver failure is the result of a rare genetic disease. Would that disease also damage a transplanted liver, and if so, how long would the new organ function before it failed? Assuming that he remains incarcerated, would that interfere with his ability to receive necessary post-transplant care and to adhere to a daily medication schedule? If he is released on parole, would he resume his prior drug use, and so damage the transplant organ? The state prison system is responsible for Mr. Irving's health care, and it has not indicated whether it would pay for a liver transplant and all of the associated medical care.

Mrs. Nguyen is 73 years old, with both a chronic liver infection and acute liver failure. She is, however, otherwise healthy and has the support of a large extended family. The small clothing store in which she works does not provide health insurance for its employees, but her four children and their families say that they will be responsible for the costs of her transplant procedure and her continuing care.

The transplant program may add any, all, or none of these three patients to its waiting list. What decisions would you recommend to it? How would you justify your decisions? Would you put greater weight on giving every patient in need a chance to receive a liver transplant, or on giving transplants to those patients who are likely to benefit from them the most?

Further reading

Chapter 1, The role of ethics in health care

Aulisio, Mark P. 2003. Meeting the need: ethics consultation in health care today. In Aulisio, Mark P., Arnold, Robert M., and Youngner, Stuart J. (eds.) *Ethics Consultation: From Theory to Practice*. Baltimore, MD: Johns Hopkins University Press.

Clouser, K. Danner. 1975. Medical ethics: some uses, abuses, and limitations. *New England Journal of Medicine* 293: 384–387.

Hester, D. Micah and Schonfeld, Toby (eds.) 2012. *Guidance for Healthcare Ethics Committees*. Cambridge: Cambridge University Press.

Weston, Anthony. 1997. *A Practical Companion to Ethics*. New York: Oxford University Press.

Chapter 2, A brief history of health care ethics and clinical ethics consultation in the United States

Aulisio, Mark P., Arnold, Robert M., and Stuart J., Youngner. (eds.) 2003. *Ethics Consultation: From Theory to Practice*. Baltimore, MD: Johns Hopkins University Press.

Baker, Robert. 2013. *Before Bioethics: A History of American Medical Ethics from the Colonial Period to the Bioethics Revolution*. New York: Oxford University Press.

Baker, Robert B. and McCullough, Laurence B. (eds.) 2008. *The Cambridge World History of Medical Ethics*. Cambridge: Cambridge University Press.

Jonsen, Albert R. 1998. *The Birth of Bioethics*. New York: Oxford University Press.

Pence, Gregory E. 2004. *Classic Cases in Medical Ethics*. Fourth edition. New York: McGraw-Hill.

Rothman, David J. 1992. *Strangers at the Bedside: A History of How Law and Bioethics Transformed Medical Decision Making*. New York: Basic Books.

Chapter 3, Methods of health care ethics

Beauchamp, Tom L. and Childress, James F. 2013. *Principles of Biomedical Ethics*. Seventh edition. New York: Oxford University Press.

Engelhardt, H. Tristram, Jr. 1996. *The Foundations of Bioethics*. Second edition. New York: Oxford University Press.

Gert, Bernard, Culver, Charles M., and Danner, Clouser, K. 2006. *Bioethics: A Systematic Approach*. Second edition. New York: Oxford University Press.

Jonsen, Albert R. and Toulmin, Stephen. 1988. *The Abuse of Casuistry*. Berkeley, CA: University of California Press.

Pellegrino, Edmund D. and Thomasma, David C. 1993. *The Virtues in Medical Practice*. New York: Oxford University Press.

Chapter 4, Law and ethics in health care

De Ville, Kenneth. 1994. "What does the law say?" law, ethics, and medical decision making. *Western Journal of Medicine* 160: 478–480.

Hall, Mark A., Ellman, Ira M., and Orentlicher, David. 2011. *Health Care Law and Ethics in a Nutshell*. St. Paul, MN: West Publishing Company.

Liang, Bryan A. 2000. *Health Law & Policy: A Survival Guide to Medicolegal Issues for Practitioners*. Boston, MA: Butterworth-Heinemann.

McCrary, S. Van, Swanson, Jeffrey W., Perkins, Henry S., et al. 1992. Treatment decisions for terminally ill patients: physicians' legal defensiveness and knowledge of medical law. *Law Medicine and Health Care* 20: 364–376.

Chapter 5, Culture and ethics in health care

Carrese, Joseph A. and Rhodes, Lorna A. 2000. Bridging cultural differences in medical practice: the case of discussing negative information with Navajo patients. *Journal of General Internal Medicine* 15: 92–96.

Kagawa-Singer, Marjorie and Blackhall, Leslie J. 2001. Negotiating cross-cultural issues at the end of life: "you got to go where he lives." *JAMA* 286: 2993–3001.

Kopelman, Loretta M. 1997. Medicine's challenge to relativism: the case of female genital mutilation. In Carson, Ronald A. and Burns, Chester R. (eds.) *Philosophy of Medicine and Bioethics*. Dordrecht: Kluwer Academic Publishers: 221–237.

Macklin, Ruth. 1998. Ethical relativism in a multicultural society. *Kennedy Institute of Ethics Journal* 8: 1–22.

Tervalon, Melanie and Murray-Garcia, Jann. 1998. Cultural humility versus cultural competence: a critical distinction in defining physician training outcomes in multicultural education. *Journal of Health Care for the Poor and Underserved* 9: 117–125.

Chapter 6, Privacy and confidentiality

Council on Scientific Affairs, American Medical Association. 1993. Confidential health services for adolescents. *JAMA* 269: 1420–1424.

Moskop, John C., Marco, Catherine A., Larkin, Gregory Luke, et al. 2005. From Hippocrates to HIPAA: privacy and confidentiality in emergency medicine – part I: conceptual, moral, and legal foundations. *Annals of Emergency Medicine* 45: 53–59.

Moskop, John C., Marco, Catherine A., Larkin, Gregory Luke, et al. 2005. From Hippocrates to HIPAA: privacy and confidentiality in emergency medicine – part II: challenges in the emergency department. *Annals of Emergency Medicine* 45: 60–67.

Thomson, Judith Jarvis. 1975. The right to privacy. *Philosophy and Public Affairs* 4: 295–314.

Ubel, Peter A., Zell, Margaret M., Miller, David J., et al. 1995. Elevator talk: observational study of inappropriate comments in a public space. *American Journal of Medicine* 99: 190–194.

Chapter 7, Truthfulness

Bonhoeffer, Dietrich. 1965. What is meant by "telling the truth"? In *Ethics*. New York: Macmillan: 363–372.

Cabot, Richard. 1903. The use of truth and falsehood in medicine: an experimental study. *American Medicine* 5: 344–349. Reprinted in Reiser, Stanley J., Dyck, Arthur J., and Curran, William J. (eds.) 1977. *Ethics in Medicine: Historical Perspectives and Contemporary Concerns*. Cambridge, MA: The MIT Press: 213–220.

Freedman, Benjamin. 1993. Offering truth: one ethical approach to the uninformed cancer patient. *Archives of Internal Medicine* 153: 572–576.

Novack, Dennis H., Detering, Barbara J., Arnold, Robert, et al. 1989. Physicians' attitudes toward using deception to resolve difficult ethical problems. *JAMA* 261: 2980–2985.

Chapter 8, Informed consent to treatment

Brock, Dan W. 1987. Informed consent. In Van DeVeer, Donald and Regan, Tom (eds.) *Health Care Ethics: An Introduction*. Philadelphia, PA: Temple University Press: 98–126.

Faden, Ruth R., Beauchamp, Tom L., and King, Nancy M.P. 1986. *A History and Theory of Informed Consent*. New York: Oxford University Press.

Grisso, Thomas and Appelbaum, Paul S. 1998. *Assessing Competence to Consent to Treatment*. New York: Oxford University Press: 31–60.

Moskop, John C. 2006. Informed consent and refusal of treatment: challenges for emergency physicians. *Emergency Medicine Clinics of North America* 24: 605–618.

Wicclair, Mark R. 1991. Patient decision-making capacity and risk. *Bioethics* 5: 91–104.

Chapter 9, Surrogate decision-making

Berger, Jeffrey T., DeRenzo, Evan G., and Schwartz, Jack. 2008. Surrogate decision making: reconciling ethical theory and clinical practice. *Annals of Internal Medicine* 149: 48–53.

Buchanan, Allen E. and Brock, Dan W. 1989. *Deciding for Others: The Ethics of Surrogate Decision Making*. Cambridge: Cambridge University Press.

Pope, Thaddeus Mason. 2013. Making medical decisions for patients without surrogates. *New England Journal of Medicine* 369: 1976–1977.

Rhodes, Rosamond and Holzman, Ian R. 2004. The *not unreasonable* standard for assessment of surrogates and surrogate decisions. *Theoretical Medicine and Bioethics* 25: 367–385.

Chapter 10, Professionalism: responsibilities and privileges

ABIM Foundation, ACP-ASIM Foundation, and European Federation of Internal Medicine. 2002. Medical professionalism in the new millennium: a physician charter. *Annals of Internal Medicine* 136: 243–246.

Hafferty, Frederic W. 2006. Definitions of professionalism: a search for meaning and identity. *Clinical Orthopaedics and Related Research, Number* 449: 193–204.

Pellegrino, Edmund D. 1983. What is a profession? *Journal of Allied Health* 12: 168–175.

Spandorfer, John, Pohl, Charles A., and Rattner, Susan L. (eds.) 2010. *Professionalism in Medicine: A Case-Based Guide for Medical Students*. Cambridge: Cambridge University Press.

Wicclair, Mark R. 2011. *Conscientious Objection in Health Care: An Ethical Analysis*. Cambridge: Cambridge University Press.

Chapter 11, Resource stewardship

Brody, Howard. 2010. Medicine's ethical responsibility for health care reform – the top five list. *New England Journal of Medicine* 362: 283–285.

Hall, Mark A. 1997. *Making Medical Spending Decisions*. New York: Oxford University Press.

Larkin, Gregory Luke, Weber, James E., and Moskop, John C. 1998. Resource utilization in the emergency department: the duty of stewardship. *The Journal of Emergency Medicine* 16: 499–503.

Morreim, E. Haavi. 1995. *Balancing Act: The New Medical Ethics of Medicine's New Economics*. Washington, DC: Georgetown University Press.

Ubel, Peter A. 2000. *Pricing Life: Why It's Time for Health Care Rationing*. Cambridge, MA: The MIT Press.

Chapter 12, Assisted reproductive technologies

Arras, John D. 2003. Reproductive technology. In Frey, R.G. and Wellman, Christopher Heath (eds.) *A Companion to Applied Ethics*. Malden, MA: Blackwell Publishing: 342–355.

Caplan, Arthur L. 1997. And baby makes – moral muddles. In *Am I My Brother's Keeper?* Bloomington, IN: Indiana University Press: 3–21.

Furger, Franco and Fukuyama, Francis. 2007. A proposal for modernizing the regulation of human biotechnologies. *Hastings Center Report* 37(4): 16–20.

Robertson, John A. 2007. The virtues of muddling through. *Hastings Center Report* 37(4): 26–28.

White, Gladys B. 1998. Crisis in assisted conception: the British approach to an American dilemma. *Journal of Women's Health* 7: 321–327.

Chapter 13, Abortion

Chervenak, Frank A. and McCullough, Laurence B. 1990. Does obstetric ethics have any role in the obstetrician's response to the abortion controversy? *American Journal of Obstetrics and Gynecology* 163: 1425–1429.

Lee, Patrick and George, Robert P. 2005. The wrong of abortion. In Cohen, Andrew I. and Wellman, Christopher Heath (eds.) *Contemporary Debates in Applied Ethics*. Oxford: Blackwell: 13–26.

Thomson, Judith Jarvis. 1971. A defense of abortion. *Philosophy and Public Affairs* 1: 47–66.

Warren, Mary Anne. 1998. Abortion. In Kuhse, Helga and Singer, Peter (eds.) *A Companion to Bioethics*. Oxford: Blackwell: 127–134.

Chapter 14, Maternal-fetal conflict

Committee on Ethics, American College of Obstetricians and Gynecologists. 2005. ACOG Committee opinion no. 321: maternal decision making, ethics, and the law. *Obstetrics and Gynecology* 106: 1127–1137.

Murray, Thomas H. 1987. Moral obligations to the not-yet born: the fetus as patient. *Clinics in Perinatology* 14: 329–343.

Paltrow, Lynn M. and Flavin, Jeanne. 2013. Arrests of and forced interventions on pregnant women in the United States, 1973–2005: implications for women's legal status and public health. *Journal of Health Politics, Policy, and Law* 38: 299–343.

Strong, Carson. 1987. Ethical conflicts between mother and fetus in obstetrics. *Clinics in Perinatology* 14: 313–328.

Chapter 15, Advance care planning and advance directives

Fagerlin, Angela and Schneider, Carl E. 2004. Enough: the failure of the living will. *Hastings Center Report* 34(2): 30–42.

Hammes, Bernard J., Rooney, Brenda L., and Gundrum, Jacob D. 2010. A comparative, retrospective, observational study of the prevalence, availability, and specificity of advance care plans in a county that implemented an advance care planning microsystem. *Journal of the American Geriatrics Society* 58: 1249–1255.

King, Nancy M.P. and Moskop, John C. 2012. Advance care planning and end-of-life decision-making. In Hester, D. Micah and Schonfeld, Toby (eds.) 2012. *Guidance for Healthcare Ethics Committees*. Cambridge: Cambridge University Press: 80–87.

Moskop, John C. 2004. Improving care at the end of life: how advance care planning can help. *Palliative and Supportive Care* 2: 191–197.

Chapter 16, Moral conflicts in end-of-life care

Gawande, Atul. 2014. *Being Mortal*. New York: Metropolitan Books.

Hardwig, John. 1997. Is there a duty to die? *Hastings Center Report* 27(2): 34–42.

Nuland, Sherwin B. 1993. *How We Die: Reflections on Life's Final Chapter*. New York: Vintage Books.

The SUPPORT Principal Investigators. 1995. A controlled trial to improve care for seriously ill hospitalized patients. *JAMA* 274: 1591–1598.

Von Gunten, Charles F., Ferris, Frank D., and Emanuel, Linda L. 2000. Ensuring competency in end-of-life care: communication and relational skills. *JAMA* 284: 3051–3057.

Chapter 17, Medical futility

Council on Ethical and Judicial Affairs, American Medical Association. 1999. Medical futility in end-of-life care. *JAMA* 281: 937–941.

Helft, Paul R., Siegler, Mark, and Lantos, John. 2000. The rise and fall of the futility movement. *New England Journal of Medicine* 343: 293–296.

Schneiderman, Lawrence J., Jecker, Nancy S., and Jonsen, Albert R. 1990. Medical futility: its meaning and ethical implications. *Annals of Internal Medicine* 112: 949–954.

Truog, Robert D., Brett, Allan S., and Frader, Joel. 1992. The trouble with futility. *New England Journal of Medicine* 326: 1560–1564.

Chapter 18, Aid in dying

Battin, Margaret P. 2005. *Ending Life: Ethics and the Way We Die*. Oxford University Press.

Foley, Kathleen and Hendin, Herbert (eds.) 2002. *The Case against Assisted Suicide: For the Right to End-of-Life Care*. Baltimore, MD: Johns Hopkins University Press.

Quill, Timothy and Battin, Margaret P. (eds.) 2004. *Physician-Assisted Dying: The Case for Palliative Care & Patient Choice*. Baltimore, MD: Johns Hopkins University Press.

Rachels, James. 1975. Active and passive euthanasia. *New England Journal of Medicine* 292: 78–80.

Chapter 19, Research on human subjects

Beecher, Henry K. 1966. Ethics and clinical research. *New England Journal of Medicine* 274: 1354–1360.

Emanuel, Ezekiel J., Grady, Christine C., Crouch, Robert A., et al. (eds.) 2008. *The Oxford Textbook of Clinical Research Ethics*. Oxford University Press.

Katz, Jay, Capron, Alexander, and Glass, Eleanor Swift (eds.) 1972. *Experimentation with Human Beings*. New York: Russell Sage Foundation.

Levine, Robert J. 1988. *Ethics and Regulation of Clinical Research*. Second edition. New Haven, CT: Yale University Press.

National Commission for the Protection of Human Subjects of Biomedical and Behavioral Research. 1978. *The Belmont Report: Ethical Principles and Guidelines for the Protection of Human Subjects of Research*. Washington, DC: US Department of Health, Education, and Welfare.

Chapter 20, The genetic revolution

Buchanan, Allen, Brock, Dan W., Daniels, Norman, et al. 2000. *From Chance to Choice: Genetics and Justice*. Cambridge University Press.

Collins, Francis S. 2010. *The Language of Life: DNA and the Revolution in Personalized Medicine*. New York: HarperCollins Publishers.

Davis, Dena S. 2010. *Genetic Dilemmas: Reproductive Technology, Parental Choices, and Children's Futures*. Oxford University Press.

Juengst, Eric T. 2007. Population genetic research and screening: conceptual and ethical issues. In Steinbock, Bonnie (ed.) *The Oxford Handbook of Bioethics*. Oxford University Press: 471–490.

Chapter 21, Organ transplantation

Ad Hoc Committee of the Harvard Medical School to Examine the Definition of Brain Death. 1968. A definition of irreversible coma. *JAMA* 205: 337–340.

Cherry, Mark J. *Kidney for Sale by Owner: Human Organs, Transplantation, and the Market*. Washington, DC: Georgetown University Press.

Fox, Renee C. and Swazey, Judith P. 1992. *Spare Parts: Organ Replacement in American Society*. Oxford University Press.

Veatch, Robert M. and Ross, Lainie Friedman. 2015. *Transplantation Ethics*. Second edition. Washington, DC: Georgetown University Press.

References

Legal sources

Statutes

Genetic Information Nondiscrimination Act of 2008. Public Law 110–233. 42 U. S.C. 2000ff.

National Organ Transplant Act. 1984. Public Law 98–507. 42 U.S.C. § 273.

National Research Act. 1974. Public Law 93–948. 88 Stat. 342–354.

Natural Death Act, 1976 Cal. Stat., Chapter 1439, Code of Health and Safety, §§ 7185 through 7195 (September 30, 1976).

North Carolina General Statutes § 20–9.1. Physicians and psychologists providing medical information on drivers with physical and mental disabilities.

North Carolina General Statutes § 20–43.2. Internet access to organ donation records by organ procurement organizations.

North Carolina General Statutes § 90–21.13. Informed consent to health care treatment or procedure.

North Carolina General Statutes § 90–21.17. Portable do not resuscitate order and medical order for scope of treatment.

Tennessee Public Chapter No. 820. 2014. Available at: http://state.tn.us/sos/acts/108/pub/pc0820.pdf. Accessed August 9, 2014.

Texas Health and Safety Code § 166.046. Procedure if not effectuating a directive or treatment decision.

Case law

Ankrom v. Alabama; Kimbrough v. Alabama, 2013 Ala.LEXIS 8 (Ala. 2013).

Automobile Workers v. Grant Controls, Inc., 499 U.S. 187 (1991).

Bouvia v. Superior Court, 179 Cal.App.3d 1127,225 Cal. Rptr. 297 (1986).

Compassion in Dying v. Washington, 79 F3d 790 (9th Cir 1996).

Cruzan v. Director, Missouri Department of Health, 110 S. Ct. 2841 (1990).

Eisenstadt v. *Baird*, 405 U.S. 438 (1972).

Griswold v. *Connecticut*, 381 U.S. 479 (1965).

In re A.C., 573 A.2d. 1235 (D.C. 1990).

In re Quinlan, 70 N.J. 10, 355 A2d 647, 429 U.S. 922 (1976).

Jacobellis v. *Ohio*, 378 U.S. 184 (1964).

Quill v. *Vacco*, 80 F3d 716 (2d Cir 1996).

Roe v. *Wade*, 410 U.S. 113 (1973).

Schloendorff v. *Society of New York Hospital*, 211 N.Y. 125, 105 N.E. 92 (1914).

Vacco v. *Quill*, 117 S Ct 2293 (1997).

Washington v. *Glucksberg*, 117 S Ct 2302 (1997).

Whitner v. *State*, 492 S.E.2d 777 (S.C. 1997).

General sources

Aaron, Henry J. 2008. Waste, we know you are out there. *New England Journal of Medicine* 359: 1865–1867.

ABIM Foundation. 2014. Choosing Wisely (website). Available at: http://www.choosingwisely.org/. Accessed April 1, 2015.

ABIM Foundation, ACP-ASIM Foundation, and European Federation of Internal Medicine. 2002. Medical professionalism in the new millennium: a physician charter. *Annals of Internal Medicine* 136: 243–246.

Abrams, Frederick R. 1986. Patient advocate or secret agent? *JAMA* 256: 1784–1785.

Accreditation Council for Graduate Medical Education. 2013. ACGME program requirements for graduate medical education in internal medicine. Available at: http://www.acgme.org/acgmeweb/Portals/0/PFAssets/2013-PR-FAQ-PIF/140_internal_medicine_07012013.pdf. Accessed March 21, 2015.

Ad Hoc Committee of the Harvard Medical School to Examine the Definition of Brain Death. 1968. A definition of irreversible coma. *JAMA* 205: 337–340.

Agostinelli, Gina and Grube, Joel W. 2002. Alcohol counter-advertising and the media: a review of recent research. *Alcohol Research and Health* 26: 15–21.

Alexander, Leo. 1949. Medical science under dictatorship. *New England Journal of Medicine* 241: 39–47.

Alexander, Shana. 1962. They decide who lives, who dies. *LIFE Magazine* 53: 102–125.

Allen, Anita. 1995. Privacy in health care. In Reich, Warren T. (ed.) *Encyclopedia of Bioethics*. Revised edition. Volume 4. New York: Macmillan: 2064–2073.

Altman, Drew E. and Levitt, Larry. 2002. The sad history of health care cost containment as told in one chart. *Health Affairs* (Web Exclusive, January 23,

2002): W83–W84. Available at: http://content.healthaffairs.org/content/early/ 2002/02/23/hlthaff.w2.83.citation. Accessed April 1, 2015.

American Bar Association. 2014. Default surrogate consent statutes as of June 2014 (table). Available at: http://www.americanbar.org/content/dam/aba/ administrative/law_aging/2014_default_surrogate_consent_statutes.auth checkdam.pdf. Accessed March 30, 2015.

American Cancer Society. 2014. Laetrile. Available at: http://www.cancer.org/ treatment/treatmentsandsideeffects/complementaryandalternativemedi cine/pharmacologicalandbiologicaltreatment/laetrile. Accessed April 1, 2015.

American College of Emergency Physicians. 1997. Code of ethics for emergency physicians. *Annals of Emergency Medicine* 30: 365–372.

American College of Medical Genetics Newborn Screening Expert Group. 2006. Newborn screening: toward a uniform screening panel and system: executive summary and main report. *Genetics in Medicine* 8(5), supplement: 1S–252S.

American College of Physicians. 1998. Ethics manual: fourth edition. *Annals of Internal Medicine* 128: 576–594.

American Medical Association. 1847. First code of medical ethics. Reprinted in Reiser, Stanley J., Dyck, Arthur J., and Curran, William J. (eds.) *Ethics in Medicine: Historical Perspectives and Contemporary Concerns*. Cambridge, MA: MIT Press, 1977: 26–34.

American Medical Association. 1957. Principles of medical ethics. In Reich, Warren T. (ed.) *Encyclopedia of Bioethics*. Revised edition. Volume 5. New York: Macmillan: 2648–2649.

American Medical Association. 1980. Principles of medical ethics. In Reich, Warren T. (ed.) *Encyclopedia of Bioethics*. Revised edition. Volume 5. New York: Macmillan: 2649–2650.

American Medical Association. 1990. Opinion 8.14 – sexual misconduct in the practice of medicine. In *AMA Code of Medical Ethics*. Available at: http://www .ama-assn.org/ama/pub/physician-resources/medical-ethics/code-medical-ethics/opinion814.page. Accessed January 13, 2013.

American Medical Association. 2000. Opinion 9.045 – physicians with disruptive behavior. In *AMA Code of Medical Ethics*. Available at: http://www.ama-assn .org/ama/pub/physician-resources/medical-ethics/code-medical-ethics/opi nion9045.page. Accessed January 14, 2013.

American Medical Association. 2001a. Opinion 8.081 – surrogate decision making. In *AMA Code of Medical Ethics*. Available at: http://www.ama-assn.org/ama/ pub/physician-resources/medical-ethics/code-medical-ethics/opinion8081 .page. Accessed March 30, 2015.

American Medical Association. 2001b. Principles of medical ethics. In *AMA Code of Medical Ethics*. Available at http://www.ama-assn.org/ama/pub/physician-resources/medical-ethics/code-medical-ethics/principles-medical-ethics.page. Accessed March 21, 2015.

American Medical Association. 2012. Opinion 9.0652 – physician stewardship of health care resources. In *AMA Code of Medical Ethics*. Available at: http://www.ama-assn.org/ama/pub/physician-resources/medical-ethics/code-medical-ethics/opinion90652.page. Accessed April 1, 2015.

American Society for Bioethics and Humanities. 2011. *Core Competencies for Healthcare Ethics Consultation*. Second edition. Glenview, IL: American Society for Bioethics and Humanities.

American Society for Bioethics and Humanities. 2014. *Code of Ethics and Professional Responsibilities for Healthcare Ethics Consultants*. Available at: http://www.asbh.org/uploads/files/pubs/pdfs/asbh_code_of_ethics.pdf. Accessed December 8, 2014.

American Society for Bioethics and Humanities Clinical Ethics Task Force. 2009. *Improving Competencies in Clinical Ethics Consultation: An Education Guide*. Glenview, IL: American Society for Bioethics and Humanities.

Andersen, Kathleen S. and Fox, Daniel M. 1988. The impact of routine inquiry laws on organ donation. *Health Affairs* 7(5): 65–78.

Angell, Marcia. 1996. Euthanasia in the Netherlands – good news or bad? *New England Journal of Medicine* 335: 1676–1678.

Annas, George J. 1982. Forced Cesareans: the most unkindest cut of all. *Hastings Center Report* 12(3): 16–17, 45.

Anonymous. 1981. The lie. *JAMA* 245: 173.

Anonymous. 1983. How can medical-moral committees function effectively in Catholic health facilities? *Hospital Progress* 64(4): 77–78.

Anonymous. 1985. Ethics committees double since '83: survey. *Hospitals* 59(21): 60, 64.

Appel, Jacob M. 2012. "How hard it is that we have to die": rethinking suicide liability for psychiatrists. *Cambridge Quarterly of Healthcare Ethics* 21: 527–536.

Appelbaum, Paul S. 2007. Assessment of patients' competence to consent to treatment. *New England Journal of Medicine* 357: 1834–1840.

Appelbaum, Paul S., Roth, Loren H., Lidz, Charles W., et al. 1987. False hopes and best data: consent to research and the therapeutic misconception. *Hastings Center Report* 17(2): 20–24.

Aristotle. 1999. *Nicomachean Ethics*. Indianapolis, IN: Hackett Publishing: 71–72.

Arras, John D. 1991. Getting down to cases: the revival of casuistry in bioethics. *Journal of Medicine and Philosophy* 16: 29–51.

Arras, John D. 2009. The hedgehog and the Borg: common morality in bioethics. *Theoretical Medicine and Bioethics* 30: 11–30.

Ashley, Benedict M. and O'Rourke, Kevin D. 1978. *Health Care Ethics: A Theological Analysis*. St. Louis, MO: The Catholic Hospital Association.

Attaran, Amir. 2015. Unanimity on death with dignity – legalizing physician-assisted dying in Canada. *New England Journal of Medicine* 372: 2080–2082.

Aulisio, Mark P., Arnold, Robert M., and Youngner Stuart J. (eds.) 2003. *Ethics Consultation: From Theory to Practice*. Baltimore, MD: Johns Hopkins University Press.

Bahm, Sarah M., Karkazis, Katrina, and Magnus, David. 2013. A content analysis of posthumous sperm procurement protocols with considerations for developing an institutional policy. *Fertility and Sterility* 100: 839–843.

Bailey, Beth A. and Sokol, Robert J. 2008. Pregnancy and alcohol use: evidence and recommendations for prenatal care. *Clinical Obstetrics and Gynecology* 51: 436–444.

Bailey, Leonard L., Cannarella, Sandra L., Concepcion, Waldo, et al. 1985. Baboon-to-human cardiac xenotransplantation in a neonate. *JAMA* 254: 3321–3329

Baily, Mary Ann and Murray, Thomas H. 2008. Ethics, evidence, and cost in newborn screening. *Hastings Center Report* 38(3): 23–31.

Baltimore, David, Berg, Paul, Botchan, Michael, et al. 2015. A prudent way forward for genomic engineering and germline gene modification. *Science* 348: 36–38.

Barnard, David. 1992. Reflections of a reluctant clinical ethicist: ethics consultation and the collapse of clinical distance. *Theoretical Medicine* 13: 15–22.

Barondess, Jeremiah A. 1996. Medicine against society: lessons from the Third Reich. *New England Journal of Medicine* 276: 1657–1661.

Battin, Margaret P., van der Heide, Agnes, Ganzini, Linda, et al. 2007. Legal physician-assisted dying in Oregon and the Netherlands: evidence concerning the impact on patients in "vulnerable" groups. *Journal of Medical Ethics* 33: 591–597.

Bearn, A. G. and Miller, E. D. 1979. Archibald Garrod and the development of inborn errors of metabolism. *Bulletin of the History of Medicine* 53: 315–328.

Beauchamp, Tom L. 2007. The "four principles" approach to health care ethics. In Ashcroft, R. E., Dawson, A., Draper, H., et al. (eds.) *Principles of Health Care Ethics*. Second edition. Chichester: John Wiley and Sons: 3–10.

Beauchamp, Tom L. and Childress, James F. 1979. *Principles of Biomedical Ethics*. New York: Oxford University Press.

Beauchamp, Tom L. and Childress, James F. 2013. *Principles of Biomedical Ethics*. Seventh edition. New York: Oxford University Press.

Beauchamp, Tom L. and Walters, LeRoy (eds.) 1978. *Contemporary Issues in Bioethics*. Encino, CA: Dickenson Publishing Co.

Bebinger, Martha. 2012. How much for an MRI? $500? $5,000? A reporter struggles to find out. *Kaiser Health News*. December 9. Available at: http://www.kaiserhealthnews.org/stories/2012/december/09/mri-cost-price-comparison-health-insurance.aspx. Accessed April 1, 2015.

Berger, Jeffery T. 2005. Ignorance is bliss? Ethical considerations in therapeutic nondisclosure. *Cancer Investigation* 23: 94–98.

Bernat, J. L., D'Alessandro, A. M., Port, F. K., et al. 2006. Report of a national conference on donation after cardiac death. *American Journal of Transplantation* 6: 281–291.

Berwick, Donald M. and Hackbarth, Andrew D. 2012. Eliminating waste in US health care. *JAMA* 307: 1513–1516.

Biggers, John D. 2012. IVF and embryo transfer: historical origin and development. *Reproductive Biomedicine Online* 25: 118–127.

Biggs, Hazel and Ost, Suzanne. 2010. As it is at the end so it is at the beginning: legal challenges and new horizons for medicalized death and dying. *Medical Law Review* 18: 437–441.

Bilgel, Firat. 2012. The impact of presumed consent laws and institutions on deceased organ donation. *European Journal of Health Economics* 13: 29–38.

Bioethics Research Library, Kennedy Institute of Ethics, Georgetown University. 2013. A guide to the archival collection of The National Commission for the Protection of Human Subjects of Biomedical and Behavioral Research. Available at: https://repository.library.georgetown.edu/handle/10822/708752. Accessed April 14, 2015.

Black, Edwin. 2003. *War Against the Weak: Eugenics and America's Campaign to Create a Master Race*. New York: Basic Books.

Blackhall, Leslie J. 1987. Must we always use CPR? *New England Journal of Medicine* 317: 1281–1285.

Block, A. Jay, Block, Linda C., and Jaffe, Allison B. 1996. The barbarism of managed care. *Chest* 110: 1–2.

Boden, William E., O'Rourke, Robert A., Teo, Koon K., et al. 2007. Optimal medical therapy with or without PCI for stable coronary disease. *New England Journal of Medicine* 356: 1503–1516.

Boghossian, Nansi S., Hansen, Nellie I., Bell, Edward F., et al. 2010. Survival and morbidity outcomes for very low birth weight infants with Down syndrome. *Pediatrics* 126: 1132–1140.

Boland, Reed and Katzive, Laura. 2008. Developments in laws on induced abortion: 1998–2007. *International Family Planning Perspectives* 34: 110–120.

Bonhoeffer, Dietrich. 1965. What is meant by 'telling the truth'? In Bonhoeffer, Dietrich. *Ethics*. New York: Macmillan: 363–372.

Borry, Pascal, Stultiens, L., Nys, H., et al. 2006. Presymptomatic and predictive genetic testing in minors: a systemic review of guidelines and position papers. *Clinical Genetics* 70: 374–381.

Botkin, Jeffrey R., Clayton, Ellen Wright, Fost, Norman C., et al. 2006. Newborn screening technology: proceed with caution. *Pediatrics* 117: 1793–1799.

Bowes, Watson A. Jr. and Selgestad, Brad. 1981. Fetal versus maternal rights: medical and legal perspectives. *Obstetrics & Gynecology* 58: 209–214.

Brennan, Troyen and Shrank, William. 2014. New expensive treatments for hepatitis C infection. *JAMA* 312: 593–594.

Brock, Dan W. 1987. Informed consent. In Van DeVeer, Donald and Regan, Tom (eds.) *Health Care Ethics: An Introduction*. Philadelphia, PA: Temple University Press: 98–126.

Brock, Dan W. 1991. Surrogate decision making for incompetent adults: an ethical framework. *Mount Sinai Journal of Medicine* 58: 388–392.

Brock, Dan W. 2008. Conscientious refusal by physicians and pharmacists: who is obligated to do what, and why? *Theoretical Medicine and Bioethics*. 29: 187–200.

Brody, Baruch A. 1988. *Life and Death Decision Making*. New York: Oxford University Press.

Brody, Baruch A. and Halevy, Amir. 1995. Is futility a futile concept? *Journal of Medicine and Philosophy* 20: 123–144.

Brody, Howard. 1999. Kevorkian and assisted death in the United States. *BMJ* 7189: 953–954.

Brody, Howard. 2010. Medicine's ethical responsibility for health care reform – the top five lists. *New England Journal of Medicine* 362: 283–285.

Buchanan, Allen E. and Brock, Dan W. 1989. *Deciding for Others: The Ethics of Surrogate Decision Making*. Cambridge: Cambridge University Press: 51–57.

Buckman, Robert. 1992. *How to Break Bad News: A Guide for Health Care Professionals*. Baltimore, MD: Johns Hopkins University Press.

Cabot, Richard. 1903. The use of truth and falsehood in medicine: an experimental study. *American Medicine* 5: 344–349.

Caplan, Arthur L. 1996. Odds and ends: trust and the debate over medical futility. *Annals of Internal Medicine* 125: 688–689.

Carrese, Joseph A. and Rhodes, Lorna A. 1995. Western bioethics on the Navajo reservation: benefit or harm? *JAMA* 274: 826–829.

Cassel, Christine K. and Guest, James A. 2012. Choosing wisely: helping physicians and patients make smart decisions about their care. *JAMA* 307: 1801–1802.

Chan, Margaret. 2014. Ebola virus disease in West Africa – no early end to the outbreak. *New England Journal of Medicine* 371: 1183–1185.

Chandra, Anjani, Copen, Casey E., Stephen, Elizabeth H. 2013. Infertility and impaired fecundity in the United States, 1982–2010: data from the national survey of family growth. *National Health Statistics Reports*, Number 67, August 14: 1–18.

Charles, Vignetta E., Polis, Chelsea B., Sridhara, Srinivas K., et al. 2008. Abortion and long-term mental health outcomes: a systematic review of the evidence. *Contraception* 78: 436–450.

Charo, R. Alta. 2005. The celestial fire of conscience – refusing to deliver medical care. *New England Journal of Medicine* 352: 2471–2473.

Charon, Rita, and Montello, Martha (eds.) 2002. *Stories Matter: The Role of Narrative in Medical Ethics*. New York: Routledge.

Cherry, Mark J. 2012. Conscience clauses, the refusal to treat, and civil disobedience – practicing medicine as a Christian in a hostile secular space. *Christian Bioethics* 18: 1–14.

Chervenak, Frank A. and McCullough, Laurence B. 1985. Perinatal ethics: a practical method of analysis of obligations to mother and fetus. *Obstetrics & Gynecology* 66: 442–446.

Chervenak, Frank A. and McCullough, Laurence B. 1990. Clinical guides to preventing ethical conflicts between pregnant women and their physicians. *American Journal of Obstetrics and Gynecology* 162: 303–307.

Church, George J. 1997. Backlash against HMOs. *Time* April 14: 32–39.

Clarke, Gary N. 2006. A.R.T. and history, 1678–1978. *Human Reproduction* 21: 1645–1650.

Clinton, Bill. 1992. The Clinton health care plan. *New England Journal of Medicine* 327: 804–807.

Clinton, Bill. 1997. Presidential apology. Available at: http://www.cdc.gov/tuske gee/clintonp.htm. Accessed April 14, 2015.

Cohen, I. Glenn. 2013. Transplant tourism: the ethics and regulation of international markets for organs. *Journal of Law, Medicine, and Ethics* 41: 269–285.

Coleman, Carl H., Menikoff, Jerry A., Goldner, Jesse A., et al. 2005. *The Ethics and Regulation of Research with Human Subjects*. Newark, NJ: LexisNexis.

Collins, Allan J., Foley, Robert N., Chavers, Blanche, et al. 2013. Incidence, prevalence, patient characteristics, & treatment modalities. In US Renal Data System 2013 annual data report. *American Journal of Kidney Diseases* 63 (Supplement): e215–e228.

Collins, Francis S. 2010. *The Language of Life: DNA and the Revolution in Personalized Medicine*. New York: HarperCollins.

Collins, Francis S., Morgan, Michael, and Patrinos, Arisitides. 2003. The Human Genome Project: lessons from large-scale biology. *Science* 300: 286–290.

Colvin-Adams, M., Valapour, M., Hertz, M., et al. 2012. Lung and heart allocation in the United States. *American Journal of Transplantation* 12: 3213–3234.

Committee on Assessing Genetic Risks, Institute of Medicine. 1994. *Assessing Genetic Risks: Implications for Health and Social Policy.* Washington, DC: National Academies Press.

Committee on Bioethics, American Academy of Pediatrics. 2009. Physician refusal to provide information or treatment on the basis of claims of conscience. *Pediatrics* 124: 1689–1693.

Committee on Ethics, American College of Obstetricians and Gynecologists. 2005. ACOG Committee opinion no. 321: maternal decision making, ethics, and the law. *Obstetrics and Gynecology* 106: 1127–1137.

Committee on Ethics, American College of Obstetricians and Gynecologists. 2007. ACOG Committee Opinion no. 385: the limits of conscientious refusal in reproductive medicine. *Obstetrics and Gynecology* 110: 1203–1208.

Committee on Science, Engineering, and Public Policy, National Academy of Sciences, National Academy of Engineering, and Institute of Medicine. 2009. *On Being a Scientist: A Guide to Responsible Conduct in Research.* Third edition. Washington, DC: National Academy Press.

Condon, Charles M. 1995. Clinton's cocaine babies: why won't the administration let us save our children? *Policy Review* 72 (Spring): 12–15.

Cong, Yali. 2004. Doctor-family-patient relationship: the Chinese paradigm of informed consent. *Journal of Medicine and Philosophy* 29: 149–178.

Congregation for the Doctrine of the Faith, Roman Catholic Church. 2008. *Instruction Dignitas Personae on Certain Bioethical Questions.* Available at: http://www.vatican.va/roman_curia/congregations/cfaith/documents/rc_con_cfaith_doc_20081208_dignitas-personae_en.html. Accessed April 2, 2015.

Council for International Organizations of Medical Sciences (CIOMS). 2002. *International Ethical Guidelines for Biomedical Research Involving Human Subjects.* Available at: http://cioms.ch/publications/layout_guide2002.pdf. Accessed September 25, 2015.

Council on Ethical and Judicial Affairs, American Medical Association. 1999. Medical futility in end-of-life care. *JAMA* 281: 937–941.

Council on Scientific Affairs, American Medical Association. 1995. Female genital mutilation. *JAMA* 274: 1714–1716.

Crandall, Sonia J., George, Geeta, Marion, Gail S., et al. 2003. Applying theory to the design of cultural competency training for medical students: a case study. *Academic Medicine* 78: 588–594.

Cunningham, F. Gary, Leveno, Kenneth J., Bloom, Steven L., et al. 2010. Chapter 21. Disorders of amnionic fluid volume. In Cunningham, F., Leveno Kenneth J., Bloom Steven, L., et al. *Williams Obstetrics*. Twenty-third edition. New York, NY: McGraw-Hill: 490–499.

Daar, Judith F. 1995. Medical futility and implications for physician autonomy. *American Journal of Law and Medicine* 21: 221–240.

Daniels, Cynthia R. and Golden, Janet. 2004. Procreative compounds: artificial insemination and the rise of the American sperm banking industry. *Journal of Social History* 38: 5–27.

Dave, Paresh. 2014. 'Octomom' Nadya Suleman faces 5-year sentence in welfare fraud case. *Los Angeles Times*. January 14. Available at: http://www.latimes.com/local/lanow/la-me-ln-octomom-welfare-fraud-case-20140114,0,3365379,print.story. Accessed April 2, 2015.

Davies, Edward. 2013. Assisted dying: what happens after Vermont? *BMJ* 346: f4041.

Davis, Anne R. and Beasley, Anitra D. 2009. Abortion in adolescents: epidemiology, confidentiality, and methods. *Current Opinion in Obstetrics and Gynecology* 21: 390–395.

Davis, Dena S. 2010. *Genetic Dilemmas: Reproductive Technology, Parental Choices, and Children's Futures*. New York: Oxford University Press.

De Ville, Kenneth. 1994. "What does the law say?" Law, ethics, and medical decision making. *Western Journal of Medicine* 160: 478–480.

De Ville, Kenneth A. and Kopelman, Loretta M. 1999. Fetal protection in Wisconsin's revised child abuse law: right goal, wrong remedy. *Journal of Law, Medicine, and Ethics* 27: 332–342.

Death and dignity: the case of Diane (correspondence). 1991. *New England Journal of Medicine* 325: 658–660.

DiMaio, J. Michael, Salerno, Tomas A., Bernstein, Ron, et al. 2009. Ethical obligation of surgeons to noncompliant patients: can a surgeon refuse to operate on an intravenous drug-abusing patient with recurrent aortic valve prosthesis infection? *Annals of Thoracic Surgery* 88: 1–8.

Disney, Lindsey and Poston, Larry. 2010. The breath of life: Christian perspectives on conception and ensoulment. *Anglican Theological Review* 92: 271–295.

Dixon, J. Lowell and Smalley, M. Gene. 1981. Jehovah's Witnesses: the surgical/ethical challenge. *JAMA* 246: 2471–2472.

Djerassi, Carl. 2002. Technology and human reproduction: 1950–2050. *Journal of Molecular Biology* 319: 979–984.

Donley, Greer, Hull, Sara Chandros, and Berkman, Benjamin E. 2012. Prenatal whole genome sequencing: just because we can, should we? *Hastings Center Report* 42(4): 28–40.

Doudna, Jennifer A. and Charpentier, Emmanuelle. 2014. The new frontier of genome engineering with CRISPR-Cas9. *Science* 346: 1258096.

Dresser, Rebecca. 1992. Wanted: single, white male for medical research. *Hastings Center Report* 22(1): 24–29.

Dresser, Rebecca. 2002. The ubiquity and utility of the therapeutic misconception. *Social Philosophy and Policy* 19: 271–294.

Dresser, Rebecca. 2009. Prenatal testing and disability: a truce in the culture wars? *Hastings Center Report* 39(3): 7–8.

Dresser, Rebecca S. and Robertson, John A. 1989. Quality of life and non-treatment decisions for incompetent persons: a critique of the orthodox approach. *Law, Medicine & Health Care* 17: 234–244.

Dubler, Nancy N., Webber, Mayris P., Swiderski, Deborah M., et al. 2009. Charting the future: credentialing, privileging, quality, and evaluation in clinical ethics consultation. *Hastings Center Report* 39(6): 23–33.

Dufernez, Fabienne, Lachaux, Alain, Chappuis, Philippe, et al. 2013. Wilson disease in offspring of affected patients: report of four French families. *Clinics and Research in Hepatology and Gastroenterology* 37: 240–245.

Dworkin, Gerald. 2014. Paternalism. In *Stanford Encyclopedia of Philosophy*. Available at: http://plato.stanford.edu/entries/paternalism/. Accessed June 7, 2015.

Eckholm, Erik. 2014. New Mexico judge affirms right to "aid in dying." *New York Times*, January 13: A16. Available at: http://www.nytimes.com/2014/01/14/us/new-mexico-judge-affirms-right-to-aid-in-dying.html?_r=2. Accessed June 9, 2015.

Emanuel, Ezekiel. 2013. The future of biomedical research. *JAMA* 309: 1589–1590.

Emanuel, Ezekiel J. and Fuchs, Victor R. 2008. The perfect storm of overutilization. *JAMA* 299: 2789–2791.

Engelhardt, H. Tristram, Jr. 1975. The counsels of finitude. *Hastings Center Report* 5(2): 29–36.

Engelhardt, H. Tristram, Jr. 1996. *The Foundations of Bioethics*. Second edition. New York: Oxford University Press.

Engelhardt, H. Tristram, Jr. 2000. *The Foundations of Christian Bioethics*. Lisse: Swets & Zeitlinger.

Engelhardt, H. Tristram, Jr. 2009. Credentialling strategically ambiguous and heterogeneous social skills: the emperor without clothes. *HEC Forum* 21: 293–306.

Epstein, Ronald M., Korones, David N., and Quill, Timothy E. 2010. Withholding information from patients – when less is more. *New England Journal of Medicine* 362: 380–381.

Ethics Committee of the American Society for Reproductive Medicine. 2013a. Child-rearing ability and the provision of fertility services: a committee opinion. *Fertility and Sterility* 100: 50–53.

Ethics Committee of the American Society for Reproductive Medicine. 2013b. Posthumous collection and use of reproductive tissue: a committee opinion. *Fertility and Sterility* 99: 1842–1845.

Faden, Ruth R., Beauchamp, Tom L., and King, Nancy M. P. 1986. *A History and Theory of Informed Consent.* New York: Oxford University Press.

Fagerlin, Angela and Schneider, Carl E. 2004. Enough: the failure of the living will. *Hastings Center Report* 34(2): 30–42.

Fan, Ruiping and Li, Benfu. 2004. Truth telling in medicine: the Confucian view. *Journal of Medicine and Philosophy* 29: 179–193.

Flagler, Elizabeth, Baylis, Francoise, and Rodgers, Sanda. 1997. Bioethics for clinicians: 12. Ethical dilemmas that arise in the care of pregnant women: rethinking "maternal-fetal conflicts." *Canadian Medical Association Journal* 156: 1729–1732.

Fleetwood, Janet E., Arnold, Robert M., and Baron, Richard J. 1989. Giving answers or raising questions? The problematic role of institutional ethics committees. *Journal of Medical Ethics* 15: 137–142.

Fox, Ellen, Myers, Sarah, and Pearlman, Robert A. 2007. Ethics consultation in United States hospitals: a national survey. *American Journal of Bioethics* 7: 13–25.

Frank, Arthur W. 2013. *The Wounded Storyteller: Body, Illness, and Ethics.* Second edition. Chicago, IL: University of Chicago Press.

Frank, Deborah A., Augustyn, Marilyn, Knight, Wanda Grant, et al. 2001. Growth, development, and behavior in early childhood following prenatal cocaine exposure. *JAMA* 285: 1613–1625.

Freedman, Benjamin. 1987. Equipoise and the ethics of clinical research. *New England Journal of Medicine* 317: 141–145.

Freedman, Benjamin. 1993. Offering truth: one ethical approach to the uninformed cancer patient. *Archives of Internal Medicine* 153: 572–576.

Freeman, Victor G., Rathore, Saif S., Weinfurt, Kevin P., et al. 1999. Lying for patients: physician deception of third-party payers. *Archives of Internal Medicine* 159: 2263–2270.

Fried, Charles. 1976. Terminating life support: out of the closet. *New England Journal of Medicine* 295: 390–391.

Fuchs, Victor. 2009. Eliminating "waste" in health care. *JAMA* 302: 2481–2482.

Gert, Bernard. 1970. *The Moral Rules: A New Rational Foundation for Morality.* New York: Oxford University Press.

Gert, Bernard, Culver, Charles M., and Clouser, K. Danner. 2006. *Bioethics: A Systematic Approach*. Second edition. New York: Oxford University Press.

Getzendanner, Susan. 1988. Permanent injunction order against AMA. *JAMA* 259: 81–82.

Gianelli, Diane M. 1991. Doctor who aided suicide not to be prosecuted. *American Medical News* May 6: 8.

Gilbert, W. 1992. A vision of the grail. In Kevles, Daniel and Hood, L. (eds.) *The Code of Codes: Scientific and Social Issues in the Human Genome Project*. Cambridge, MA: Harvard University Press: 83–92.

Gilligan, Carol. 1982. *In a Different Voice*. Cambridge, MA: Harvard University Press.

Gliwa, Catherine and Berkman, Benjamin E. 2013. Do researchers have an obligation to actively look for genetic incidental findings? *American Journal of Bioethics* 13: 32–42.

Goldenberg, Aaron J. and Sharp, Richard R. 2012. The ethical hazards and programmatic challenges of genomic newborn screening. *JAMA* 307: 461–462.

Gordon, Elisa J. 2013. Ethical considerations in live donor transplantation: should complications be tolerated? *Current Opinion in Organ Transplantation* 18: 235–240.

Gorovitz, Samuel, Jameton, Andrew L., Macklin, Ruth et al. (eds.) 1976. *Moral Problems in Medicine*. Englewood Cliffs, NJ: Prentice-Hall.

Gostin, Lawrence O. 2005. Ethics, the Constitution, and the dying process: the case of Theresa Marie Schiavo. *JAMA* 293: 2403–2407.

Green, Eric D. and Guyer, Mark S. 2011. Charting a course for genomic medicine from base pairs to bedside. *Nature* 470: 204–213.

Green, Robert C., Berg, J., Grody, W., et al. 2013. ACMG recommendations for reporting of incidental findings in clinical exome and genome sequencing. *Genetics in Medicine* 15: 565–574.

Greene, Sandra B. 2003. The rise and decline of managed care: what comes next? *North Carolina Medical Journal* 64: 21–29.

Greenfieldboyce, Nell. 2015. DNA blood test gives women a new option for prenatal screening. In *KCUR Radio Report*. Available at: http://kcur.org/post/dna-blood-test-gives-women-new-option-prenatal-screening. Accessed April 14, 2015.

Grisso, Thomas and Appelbaum, Paul S. 1998. *Assessing Competence to Consent to Treatment*. New York: Oxford University Press: 31–60.

Guseh, J. S. II, Brendel, R. W., and Brendel, D. H. 2009. Medical professionalism in the age of online social networking. *Journal of Medical Ethics* 35: 584–586.

Guttmacher Institute. 2015. *An Overview of Abortion Laws*. Available at: http://www.guttmacher.org/statecenter/spibs/spib_OAL.pdf. Accessed June 8, 2015.

Guyer, Mark S. and Collins, Francis S. 1995. How is the Human Genome Project doing, and what have we learned so far? *Proceedings of the National Academy of Sciences of the United States of America* 92: 10841–10848.

Hafemeister, Thomas L. and Hannaford, Paula L. 1996a. Which decision and why? In *Resolving Disputes Over Life-Sustaining Treatment*. Williamsburg, VA: National Center for State Courts: 17–20.

Hafemeister, Thomas L. and Hannaford, Paula L. 1996b. Who should be the surrogate? In *Resolving Disputes Over Life-Sustaining Treatment*. Williamsburg, VA: National Center for State Courts: 16–17.

Halevy, Amir, Neal, Ryan C., and Brody, Baruch A. 1996. The low frequency of futility in an adult intensive care unit setting. *Archives of Internal Medicine* 156: 100–104.

Hall, Mark A. 1994. The ethics of health care rationing. *Public Affairs Quarterly* 8: 33–50.

Hamilton, Edith. 1942. New York: Grand Central Publishing: 415–416.

Hammes, Bernard J. and Briggs, Linda. 2000. *Respecting Choices Facilitator's Manual*. Second edition. La Crosse, WI: Gundersen Lutheran Medical Foundation: 2.1.

Hammes, Bernard J., Rooney, Brenda L., and Gundrum, Jacob D. 2010. A comparative, retrospective, observational study of the prevalence, availability, and specificity of advance care plans in a county that implemented an advance care planning microsystem. *Journal of the American Geriatrics Society* 58: 1249–1255.

Hammond, Cassing. 2009. Recent advances in second-trimester abortion: an evidence-based review. *American Journal of Obstetrics and Gynecology* 200: 347–356.

Hammond, David, Fong, Geoffrey T., Borland, Ron, et al. 2007. Communicating risk to smokers: the impact of health warnings on cigarette packages. *American Journal of Preventive Medicine* 32: 202–209.

Harris, Lisa H. 2000. Rethinking maternal-fetal conflict: gender and equality in perinatal ethics. *Obstetrics and Gynecology* 96: 786–791.

Heitman, Elizabeth and Bulger, Robert E. 1998. The healthcare ethics committee in the structural transformation of health care: administrative and organizational ethics in changing times. *HEC Forum* 10: 152–176.

Heller, Jean. 1972. Syphilis victims in U.S. study went untreated for 40 years. *New York Times*, July 26: 1, 8.

Hippocrates. 1923. *Hippocrates, Volume I: Ancient Medicine.* Jones, W. H. S. (trans.) Loeb Classical Library, no. 147. Cambridge, MA: Harvard University Press.

Hull, Sarah C., and Jadbabaie, Farid. 2014. When is enough enough? The dilemma of valve replacement in a recidivist intravenous drug user. *Annals of Thoracic Surgery* 97: 1486–1487.

Hunt, Linda M. 2001. Beyond cultural competence: applying humility to clinical settings. *The Park Ridge Center Bulletin* Issue 24: 3–4.

Hunter, Kathryn Montgomery. 1991. *Doctors' Stories.* Princeton, NJ: Princeton University Press.

Hurst, Samia A., and Mauron, Alex. 2003. Assisted suicide and euthanasia in Switzerland: allowing a role for non-physicians. *BMJ* 326: 271–273.

Inskip, H. M., Harris, E. C., and Barraclough, B. 1998. Lifetime risk of suicide for affective disorder, alcoholism and schizophrenia. *British Journal of Psychiatry* 172: 35–37.

International Council of Nurses. 2012. ICN Code of Ethics for Nurses. Available at: http://www.icn.ch/images/stories/documents/about/icncode_english.pdf. Accessed March 28, 2015.

Iserson, Kenneth V. and Moskop, John C. 2007. Triage in medicine, part I: concept, history, and types. *Annals of Emergency Medicine* 49: 275–281.

Jacobovitz, Immanuel. 1975. *Jewish Medical Ethics: A Comparative and Historical Study of the Jewish Religious Attitude to Medicine and Its Practice.* New York: Bloch Publishing.

Jameton, Andrew. 1984. *Nursing Practice: The Ethical Issues.* Englewood Cliffs, NJ: Prentice-Hall.

Jansen, Lynn A. 2013. Between beneficence and justice: the ethics of stewardship in medicine. *Journal of Medicine and Philosophy* 38: 50–63.

Jennings, Bruce. 2014. *Bioethics.* Six volumes. Fourth edition. New York: Macmillan.

Johnson, Josephine. 2009. Judging octomom. *Hastings Center Report* 39(3): 23–25.

Johnson, Josephine and Gusmano, Michael. 2013. Why we should all pay for fertility treatment: an argument from ethics and policy. *Hastings Center Report* 43(2): 18–21.

Johnson, Kirk. 2009. Montana ruling bolsters doctor-assisted suicide. *New York Times* December 31. Available at: http://www.nytimes.com/2010/01/01/us/01suicide.html. Accessed April 13, 2015.

Jones, James H. 1981. *Bad Blood: The Tuskegee Syphilis Experiment.* New York: The Free Press.

Jonsen, Albert R. 1977. Do no harm: axiom of medical ethics. In Spicker, Stuart F. and Engelhardt, H. Tristram, Jr. (eds.) *Philosophical Medical Ethics: Its Nature and Significance.* Dordrecht, Netherlands: D. Reidel: 27–41.

Jonsen, Albert R. 1986. Casuistry and clinical ethics. *Theoretical Medicine* 7: 65–74.

Jonsen, Albert R. 1998. *The Birth of Bioethics*. New York: Oxford University Press.

Jonsen, Albert R., Siegler, Mark, and Winslade, William J. 2006. *Clinical Ethics*. New York: McGraw-Hill.

Jonsen, Albert R. and Toulmin, Stephen. 1988. *The Abuse of Casuistry*. Berkeley, CA: University of California Press.

Jos, Philip H., Marshall, Mary Faith, and Perlmutter, Martin. 1995. The Charleston policy on cocaine use during pregnancy: a cautionary tale. *Journal of Law, Medicine, and Ethics* 23: 120–128.

Jos, Philip H., Perlmutter, Martin, and Marshall, Mary Faith. 2003. Substance abuse during pregnancy: clinical and public health approaches. *Journal of Law, Medicine, and Ethics* 31: 340–350.

Juengst, Eric T. 1999. Genetic testing and the moral dynamics of family life. *Public Understanding of Science* 8: 193–205.

Juengst, Eric T. 2007. Population genetic research and screening: conceptual and ethical issues. In Steinbock, Bonnie (ed.) *The Oxford Handbook of Bioethics*. Oxford University Press: 471–490.

Juengst, Eric T., Settersten, Richard A., Fishman, Jennifer R., et al. 2012. After the revolution? Ethical and social challenges in "personalized genomic medicine." *Personalized Medicine* 9: 429–439.

Kaiser Permanente. 2009. Octuplets born at Kaiser Permanente Medical Center in Bellflower, Calif. Available at: http://share.kaiserpermanente.org/article/octu plets-born-at-kaiser-permanente-medical-center-in-bellflower-calif/. Accessed April 2, 2015.

Kant, Immanuel. 1959. *Foundations of the Metaphysics of Morals*. Indianapolis, IN: Bobbs-Merrill.

Karopadi, Akash N., Mason, Giacomo, Rettore, Enrico, et al. 2013. Cost of peritoneal dialysis and haemodialysis across the world. *Nephrology, Dialysis, and Transplantation* 28: 2553–2569.

Kassier, Jerome P. 1994. Access to specialty care. *New England Journal of Medicine* 331: 1151–1152.

Kassirer, Jerome P. 2000. Financial indigestion. *JAMA* 284: 2156–2157.

Kelly, Gerald A. 1958. *Medico-Moral Problems*. St. Louis, MO: Catholic Hospital Association.

Kenny, Sister Nuala P. 2012. Debunking "death panels": unfounded assumptions undercut planning for a "good death." *Health Progress* 93(1): 48–56.

Kevles, Daniel J. 1999. Eugenics and human rights. *BMJ* 319: 435–438.

Kevorkian, Jack. 1991. *Prescription Medicide: The Goodness of Planned Death*. Buffalo, NY: Prometheus Books.

Kilo, Charles M. and Larson, Eric B. 2009. Exploring the harmful effects of health care. *JAMA* 302: 89–91.

King, Nancy M. P. 1993. Patient waiver of informed consent. *North Carolina Medical Journal* 54: 399–403.

King, Nancy M. P. 2000. Defining and describing benefit appropriately in clinical trials. *Journal of Law, Medicine, and Ethics* 28: 332–343.

Knoppers, Bartha M. 2013. Genomics: from persons to populations and back again. *Genome* 2013: 537–539.

Kolder, Veronika E. B., Gallagher, Janet, and Parsons, Michael T. 1987. Court-ordered obstetrical interventions. *New England Journal of Medicine* 316: 1192–1196.

Kopelman, Arthur E., Parker, J. Clinton, Ho, George, Jr., et al. 2005. The benefits of a North Carolina policy for determining inappropriate or futile care. *North Carolina Medical Journal* 66: 392–394.

Kopelman, Loretta M. 2004. Minimal risk as an international ethical standard in research. *Journal of Medicine and Philosophy* 29: 351–378.

Kopelman, Loretta M., Irons, Thomas G., and Kopelman, Arthur E. 1988. Neonatologists judge the "Baby Doe" regulations. *New England Journal of Medicine* 318: 677–683.

Kopelman, Loretta M. and Kopelman, Arthur E. 2007. Using a new analysis of the best interests standard to address cultural disputes: whose data, which values? *Theoretical Medicine and Bioethics* 28: 373–391.

Kosnik, A. R. 1974. Developing a health facility medical-moral committee. *Hospital Progress* 55(8): 40–44.

Kris, Mark G., Johnson, Bruce E., Berry, Lynne D., et al. 2014. Using multiplexed asseys of oncogenic drivers in lung cancers to select targeted drugs. *JAMA* 311: 1998–2006.

Kübler-Ross, Elizabeth. 1969. *On Death and Dying*. New York: Macmillan Publishing.

Kuhse, Helga. 1986. The case for active voluntary euthanasia. *Law, Medicine & Health Care* 14: 145–148.

Kuppermann, Miriam, Pena, Sherri, Bishop, Judith T., et al. 2014. Effect of enhanced information, values clarification, and removal of financial barriers on use of prenatal genetic testing. *JAMA* 312: 1210–1217.

Kushnir, Vitaly A., Vidali, Andrea, Barad, David H., et al. 2013. The status of public reporting of clinical outcomes in assisted reproductive technology. *Fertility and Sterility* 100: 736–741.

La Puma, John and Schiedermayer, David L. 1991. Ethics consultation: skills, roles, and training. *Annals of Internal Medicine* 114: 155–160.

Lantos, John D., Singer, Peter A., Walker, Robert M., et al. 1989. The illusion of futility in clinical practice. *American Journal of Medicine* 87: 81–84.

Lappetito, J. and Thompson, P. 1993. Today's ethics committees face varied issues. *Health Progress* 74(11): 34–39, 52.

Larkin, Gregory Luke, Weber, James E., and Moskop, John C. 1998. Resource utilization in the emergency department: the duty of stewardship. *The Journal of Emergency Medicine* 16: 499–503.

Lee, Patrick and George, Robert P. 2005. The wrong of abortion. In Cohen, Andrew I. and Wellman, Christopher Heath (eds.) *Contemporary Debates in Applied Ethics*. Oxford: Blackwell: 13–26.

Levinsky, Norman G. 1984. The doctor's master. *New England Journal of Medicine* 311: 1573–1575.

Lifton, Robert J. 1986. *The Nazi Doctors*. New York: Basic Books.

Ludmerer, Kenneth M. 1972. *Genetics and American Society*. Baltimore, MD: Johns Hopkins University Press.

Ludmerer, Kenneth M. 1999. Instilling professionalism in medical education. *JAMA* 282: 881–882.

Lundberg, George. 1990. Countdown to millennium – balancing the professionalism and business of medicine. *JAMA* 263: 86–87.

Lynn, Joanne, Harrell, Frank, Jr., Cohn, Felicia, et al. 1997. Prognosis of seriously ill hospitalized patients on the days before death: implications for patient care and public policy. *New Horizons* 5: 56–61.

MacKay, Andrea P., Berg, Cynthia J., King, Jeffrey C., et al. 2006. Pregnancy-related mortality among women with multifetal pregnancies. *Obstetrics & Gynecology* 107: 563–568.

Mahdavi-Mazdeh, Mitra. 2012. The Iranian model of living renal transplantation. *Kidney International* 82: 627–634.

Mand, Cara, Gillam, Lynn, Delatycki, Martin, B., et al. 2012. Predictive genetic testing in minors for late-onset conditions: a chronological and analytical review of the ethical arguments. *Journal of Medical Ethics* 38: 519–524.

Marrus, Michael E. 1999. The Nuremberg doctors' trial in historical context. *Bulletin of the History of Medicine* 73: 106–123.

Marshall, Eliot. 2011. Waiting for the revolution. *Science* 331: 526–529.

Martin, Douglas K., Meslin, Eric M., Kohut, Nitsa, et al. 1995. The incommensurability of research risks and benefits: practical help for research ethics committees. *IRB* 17: 8–10.

Matthews, Kirstin. 2007. Overview of world human cloning policies. Available at: http://cnx.org/content/m14834/latest/. Accessed April 2, 2015.

McCrary, S. Van, Swanson, Jeffrey W., Perkins, Henry S., et al. 1992. Treatment decisions for terminally ill patients: physicians' legal defensiveness and knowledge of medical law. *Law Medicine and Health Care* 20: 364–376.

Medical Board of California. 2010. In the matter of Michael Kamrava, M.D. Available at: http://documents.latimes.com/michael-kamrava-disciplinary-decision/. Accessed April 2, 2015.

Medical Board of California. 2011. Medical Board of California Revokes License of Former Beverly Hills Physician. News Release, June 2. Available at: http://www.mbc.ca.gov/About_Us/Media_Room/2011/news_releases_2011 .pdf#page=15. Accessed January 29, 2014.

Medical Society of New Jersey, Association of Osteopathic Physicians and Surgeons, and New Jersey Hospital Association. 1977. New Jersey guidelines for health care facilities to implement procedures concerning the care of comatose non-cognitive patients. Reprinted in President's Commission for the Study of Ethical Problems in Medicine and Biomedical and Behavioral Research. 1983. *Deciding to Forego Life-Sustaining Treatment*. Washington, DC: President's Commission: 463–466.

Meisel, Alan. 1993. The legal consensus about forgoing life-sustaining treatment: its status and its prospects. *Kennedy Institute of Ethics Journal* 2: 309–345.

Merrill, J., Murray, J. E., Harrison, J. H., et al. 1956. Successful homotransplantation of the human kidney between identical twins. *JAMA* 160: 277–282.

Milazzo, Stephania, Ernst, Edzard, Lejeune, Stephane, et al. 2011. Laetrile treatment for cancer. *Cochrane Database of Systematic Reviews*. Issue 11. Article Number CD005476.

Morreim, Haavi. 2012. Dodging the rules, ruling the dodgers. *American Journal of Bioethics* 12(3): 1–3.

Moskop, John C. 1999. Informed consent in the emergency department. *Emergency Medicine Clinics of North America* 17: 327–340.

Moskop, John C. 2004. Improving care at the end of life: how advance care planning can help. *Palliative and Supportive Care* 2: 191–197.

Moskop, John C. and Iserson, Kenneth V. 2001. Emergency physicians and physician-assisted suicide, part I: a review of the physician-assisted suicide debate. *Annals of Emergency Medicine* 38: 570–574.

Moskop, John C. and Iserson, Kenneth V. 2007. Triage in medicine, part II: underlying values and principles. *Annals of Emergency Medicine* 49: 282–287.

Moskop, John C., Marco, Catherine A., Larkin, Gregory Luke, et al. 2005. From Hippocrates to HIPAA: privacy and confidentiality in emergency medicine – part II: challenges in the emergency department. *Annals of Emergency Medicine* 45: 60–67.

Moskop, John C. and Saldanha, Rita L. 1986. The Baby Doe rule: still a threat. *Hastings Center Report* 16(2): 8–14.

Moskop, John C., Smith, Michael L., and de Ville, Kenneth. 1997. Ethical and legal aspects of teratogenic medications: the case of isotretinoin. *The Journal of Clinical Ethics* 8: 264–278.

Moyer, Virginia A., Calonge, Ned, Teutsch, Steven M., et al. 2008. Expanding newborn screening: process, policy, and priorities. *Hastings Center Report* 38(3): 32–39.

Murray, Thomas H. 1987. Moral obligations to the not-yet born: the fetus as patient. *Clinics in Perinatology* 14: 329–343.

Nadelson, Carol and Notman, Malkah T. 2002. Boundaries in the doctor-patient relationship. *Theoretical Medicine* 23: 191–201.

Nagel, Thomas. 1979. Death. In *Mortal Questions*. Cambridge: Cambridge University Press: 1–10.

Nakagawa, Thomas A., Ashwal, Stephen, Mathur, Mudit, et al. 2011. Guidelines for the determination of death in infants and children: an update of the 1987 Task Force recommendations. *Critical Care Medicine* 39: 2139–2155.

National Commission for the Protection of Human Subjects of Biomedical and Behavioral Research. 1978. *The Belmont Report: Ethical Principles and Guidelines for the Protection of Human Subjects of Research*. Washington, DC: US Department of Health, Education, and Welfare.

National Conference of Commissioners on Uniform State Laws. 1980. Uniform Determination of Death Act. Available at: http://pntb.org/wordpress/wp-content/uploads/Uniform-Determination-of-Death-1980_5c.pdf. Accessed April 14, 2015.

Nelson, Lawrence J. and Milliken, Nancy. 1988. Compelled treatment of pregnant women. *JAMA* 259: 1060–1066.

Neumann, Peter J., Cohen, Joshua T., and Weinstein, Milton C. 2014. Updating cost-effectiveness – the curious resilience of the $50,000-per-QALY threshold. *New England Journal of Medicine* 371: 796–797.

Nicholas, Lauren H., Langa, Kenneth M., Iwashyna, Theodore J., et al. 2011. Regional variation in the association between advance directives and end-of-life Medicare expenditures. *JAMA* 306: 1447–1453.

Nordgren, Anders and Juengst, Eric T. 2009. Can genomics tell me who I am? Essentialistic rhetoric in direct-to-consumer DNA testing. *New Genetics and Society* 28: 157–172.

Novack, Dennis H., Plumer, Robin, Smith, Raymond L., et al. 1979. Changes in physicians' attitudes toward telling the cancer patient. *JAMA* 241: 897–900.

Oath of Hippocrates. 1995. In Reich, Warren T. (ed.) *Encyclopedia of Bioethics*. Revised edition. Volume 5. New York: Macmillan: 2632.

Oken, Donald. 1961. What to tell cancer patients: a study of medical attitudes. *JAMA* 175: 1120–1128.

Oregon Public Health Division. 2015. Oregon's Death with Dignity Act – 2014. Available at: http://public.health.oregon.gov/ProviderPartnerResources/ EvaluationResearch/DeathwithDignityAct/Documents/year17.pdf. Accessed April 13, 2015.

Organ Procurement and Transplantation Network, US Department of Health and Human Services. 2015. National data. Available at: http://optn.transplant .hrsa.gov/converge/latestData/step2.asp. Accessed April 14, 2015.

Orlando, Giuseppe, Wood, Kathryn, Stratta, Robert J., et al. 2011. Regenerative medicine and organ transplantation: past, present, and future. *Transplantation* 91: 1310–1317.

Orr, Robert D. and Siegler, Mark. 2002. Is posthumous semen retrieval ethically permissible? *Journal of Medical Ethics* 28: 299–303.

Ory, Steven. 2010. The American octuplet experience: a transformative event. *Fertility and Sterility* 93: 337–338.

Paltrow, Lynn M. and Flavin, Jeanne. 2013. Arrests of and forced interventions on pregnant women in the United States, 1973–2005: implications for women's legal status and public health. *Journal of Health Politics, Policy, and Law* 38: 299–343.

Parens, Erik, Appelbaum, Paul, and Chung, Wendy. 2013. Incidental findings in the era of whole genome sequencing? *Hastings Center Report* 43(4): 16–19.

Paris, John J. and Reardon, Frank E. 1992. Physician refusal of requests for futile or ineffective interventions. *Cambridge Quarterly of Healthcare Ethics* 2: 127–134.

Parker, M. 2004. Response to Orr and Siegler – collective intentionality and procreative desires: the permissible view on consent to posthumous conception. *Journal of Medical Ethics* 30: 389–392.

Parker, Michael and Lucassen, Anneke M. 2004. Genetic information: a joint account? *BMJ* 329: 165–167.

Parr, Kimberly A. 2009. Beyond politics: a social and cultural history of federal healthcare conscience protections. *American Journal of Law and Medicine* 35: 620–646.

Pasche, Boris and Grant, Stefan C. 2014. Non-small cell lung cancer and precision medicine. *JAMA* 311: 1975–1976.

Patient Rights Council. 2012. Assisted suicide laws in the United States. Available at: http://www.patientsrightscouncil.org/site/assisted-suicide-state-laws/. Accessed April 13, 2015.

Paulson, Amanda. 2004. More states explore tax breaks to benefit organ donors. *The Christian Science Monitor* October 19: 2.

Pellegrino, Edmund D. 1983. What is a profession? *Journal of Allied Health* 12: 168–175.

Pellegrino, Edmund D. 2006. Toward a reconstruction of medical morality. *American Journal of Bioethics* 6: 65–71.

Pellegrino, Edmund D., and Thomasma, David C. 1993. *The Virtues in Medical Practice*. New York: Oxford University Press.

Pence, Gregory E. 2004. The Quinlan case. In *Classic Cases in Medical Ethics*. Fourth edition. New York: McGraw-Hill: 29–39.

Pennings, Guido. 2004. Saviour siblings: using preimplantation genetic diagnosis for tissue typing. *International Congress Series* 1266: 311–317.

Pierson, Richard N. 2009. Current status of xenotransplantation. *JAMA* 301: 967–969.

Post, Stephen G., Puchalski, Christina M., and Larson, David B. 2000. Physician and patient spirituality: professional boundaries, competency, and ethics. *Annals of Internal Medicine* 132: 578–583.

Practice Committee of the American Society for Reproductive Medicine and Practice Committee of the Society for Assisted Reproductive Technology. 2013. Criteria for number of embryos to transfer: a committee opinion. *Fertility and Sterility* 99: 44–46.

Prentice, Ernest D. and Gordon, Bruce G. 2001. Institutional review board assessment of risks and benefits associated with research. In National Bioethics Advisory Commission. *Ethical and Policy Issues in Research Involving Human Participants*. Volume II. Bethesda, MD: L-1–L-16. Available at: https://bioethicsarchive.georgetown.edu/nbac/human/overvol2.pdf. Accessed April 14, 2015.

President's Commission for the Study of Ethical Problems in Medicine and Biomedical and Behavioral Research. 1983a. Identification of a surrogate. In *Deciding to Forego Life-Sustaining Treatment*. Washington, DC: President's Commission for the Study of Ethical Problems in Medicine and Biomedical and Behavioral Research: 126–132.

President's Commission for the Study of Ethical Problems in Medicine and Biomedical and Behavioral Research. 1983b. Intrainstitutional review and the role of ethics committees. In *Deciding to Forego Life-Sustaining Treatment*. Washington, DC: President's Commission for the Study of Ethical Problems in Medicine and Biomedical and Behavioral Research: 160–170.

President's Commission for the Study of Ethical Problems in Medicine and Biomedical and Behavioral Research. 1983c. *Screening and Counseling for Genetic Conditions*. Washington, DC: President's Commission for the Study of Ethical Problems in Medicine and Biomedical and Behavioral Research: 59–62.

The President's Council on Bioethics. 2005. Chapter 2: the limited wisdom of advance directives. In *Taking Care: Ethical Caregiving in our Aging Society*. Available at: http://bioethics.georgetown.edu/pcbe/reports/taking_care/chapter2.html. Accessed April 12, 2015.

The President's Council on Bioethics. 2008. *The Changing Moral Focus of Newborn Screening*. Washington, DC: The President's Council on Bioethics.

Presidential Commission for the Study of Bioethical Issues. 2013a. *Privacy and Progress in Whole Genome Sequencing*. Washington, DC: Presidential Commission for the Study of Bioethical Issues.

Presidential Commission for the Study of Bioethical Issues. 2013b. *Anticipate and Communicate: Ethical Management of Incidental and Secondary Findings in the Clinical, Research, and Direct-to-Consumer Contexts*. Washington, DC: Presidential Commission for the Study of Bioethical Issues.

Proctor, Robert N. 1988. *Racial Hygiene: Medicine under the Nazis*. Cambridge, MA: Harvard University Press.

Professionalism. 1969. *Webster's Seventh New Collegiate Dictionary*. Springfield, MA: G. & C. Merriam: 680.

Pruett, Dawn, Waterman, Emily Hubbard, and Caughey, Aaron B. 2013. Fetal alcohol exposure: consequences, diagnosis, and treatment. *Obstetrical and Gynecological Survey* 68: 62–69.

Quill, Timothy E. 1991. Death and dignity: a case of individualized decision making. *New England Journal of Medicine* 324: 691–694.

Quinlan, Joseph and Quinlan, Julia. 1977. *Karen Ann: The Quinlans Tell Their Story*. New York: Doubleday Anchor.

Rachels, James. 1975. Active and passive euthanasia. *New England Journal of Medicine* 292: 78–80.

Ramsey, Paul. 1970. *The Patient as Person*. New Haven, CT: Yale University Press.

Rapp, Reyna. 2000. Extra chromosomes and blue tulips: medico-familial interpretations. In Lock, Margaret, Young, Alan, and Cambrosio, Alberto (eds.) *Living and Working with the New Medical Technologies*. Cambridge: Cambridge University Press: 184–207.

Ratner, L. E., Kraus, E., Magnuson, T., et al. 1996. Transplantation of kidneys from expanded criteria donors. *Surgery* 119: 372–377.

Reagan, Michael D. 1987. Physicians as gatekeepers: a complex challenge. *New England Journal of Medicine* 317: 1731–1734.

Redberg, Rita F. 2014. Sham controls in medical device trials. *New England Journal of Medicine* 371: 892–893.

Reddy, Uma M., Wapner, Ronald J., Rebar, Robert W., et al. 2007. Infertility, assisted reproductive technology, and adverse pregnancy outcomes: executive summary of a National Institute of Child Health and Human Development workshop. *Obstetrics & Gynecology* 109: 967–977.

Regis, Catherine. 2004. Physicians gaming the system: modern-day Robin Hood? *Health Law Review* 13:19–24.

Reich, Warren T. (ed. in chief). 1978. *Encyclopedia of Bioethics*. New York: Macmillan.

Reiser, Stanley J., Dyck, Arthur J., and Curran, William J. (eds.) 1977. *Ethics in Medicine: Historical Perspectives and Contemporary Concerns*. Cambridge, MA: MIT Press.

Relman, Arnold S. 1980. The new medical-industrial complex. *New England Journal of Medicine* 303: 963–970.

Rhodes, Rosamond and Holzman, Ian R. 2004. The *not unreasonable* standard for assessment of surrogates and surrogate decisions. *Theoretical Medicine and Bioethics* 25: 367–385.

Robertson, John A. 2009. The octuplet case – why more regulation is not likely. *Hastings Center Report* 39(3): 26–28.

Rosenthal, Sara. 2010. The Suleman octuplet case: an analysis of multiple ethical issues. *Women's Health Issues* 20: 260–265.

Rosenthal, Sara. 2011. The Suleman octuplet case and egregious ethical breaches. *Women's Health Issues* 21: 98.

Ross, Judith W., Bayley, Corrine, Michel, Vicki, et al. 1986. *Handbook for Hospital Ethics Committees*. Chicago, IL: American Hospital Publishing.

Ross, Lainie Friedman, Saal, Howard M., David, Karen L., et al. 2013. Technical report: ethical and policy issues in genetic testing and screening of children. *Genetics in Medicine* 15: 234–245.

Rothman, David J. 1992. *Strangers at the Bedside: A History of How Law and Bioethics Transformed Medical Decision Making*. New York: Basic Books.

Rothman, David J. 2000. Medical professionalism – focusing on the real issues. *New England Journal of Medicine* 342: 1284–1286.

Rotimi, Charles N. and Jorde, Lynn B. 2010. Ancestry and disease in the age of genomic medicine. *New England Journal of Medicine* 363: 1551–1558.

Rudinow, Joel. 1978. Manipulation. *Ethics* 88: 338–347.

Ruhnke, Gregory W., Wilson, Sandra R., Akamatsu, Takahashi, et al. 2000. Ethical decision making and patient autonomy: a comparison of physicians and patients in Japan and the United States. *Chest* 118: 172–182.

Rybak, E. A. 2009. Hippocratic ideal, Faustian bargain and Damocles' sword: erosion of patient autonomy in obstetrics. *Journal of Perinatology* 29: 721–725.

Sabo, Jennifer L. 2001. Survey of developments in North Carolina law and the Fourth Circuit, 2000: limiting a surrogate's authority to terminate life-support for an incompetent adult. *North Carolina Law Review* 79: 1815–1827.

Sanders, David and Dukeminier, Jessie. 1968. Medical advance and legal lag: hemodialysis and kidney transplantation. *UCLA Law Review* 15: 366–380.

Savulescu, Julian. 2006. Conscientious objection in medicine. *BMJ* 332: 294–297.

Schieve, Laura A., Meikle, Susan F., Ferre, Cynthia, et al. 2002. Low and very low birth weight in infants conceived with use of assisted reproductive technology. *New England Journal of Medicine* 346: 731–737.

Schneiderman, Lawrence J., Jecker, Nancy S., and Jonsen, Albert R. 1990. Medical futility: its meaning and ethical implications. *Annals of Internal Medicine* 112: 949–954.

Schoen, Johanna. 2001. Between choice and coercion: women and the politics of sterilization in North Carolina, 1929–1975. *Journal of Women's History* 13: 132–156.

Schroeder, Steven A. 2001. Prospects for expanding health insurance coverage. *New England Journal of Medicine* 344: 847–852.

Sessums, Laura L., Zembruska, Hanna, and Jackson, Jeffrey L. 2011. Does this patient have medical decision-making capacity? *JAMA* 306: 420–427.

Shah, Iqbal and Ahman, Elizabeth. 2009. Unsafe abortion: global and regional incidence, trends, consequences, and challenges. *Journal of Obstetrics and Gynaecology Canada* 31: 1149–1158.

Shimazono, Yosuke. 2007. The state of the international organ trade: a provisional picture based on integration of available information. *Bulletin of the World Health Organization* 85: 955–962.

Shuster, Evelyne. 1997. Fifty years later: the significance of the Nuremberg Code. *New England Journal of Medicine* 337: 1436–1440.

Siegler, Mark. 1979. Clinical ethics and clinical medicine. *Archives of Internal Medicine* 139: 914–915.

Singer, Peter A., Martin, Douglas K., Lavery, James V., et al. 1998. Reconceptualizing advance care planning from the patient's perspective. *Archives of Internal Medicine* 158: 879–884.

Sisko, Andrea M., Keehan, Sean P., Cuckler, Gigi A., et al. 2014. National health expenditure projections, 2103–23: faster growth expected with expanded coverage and improving economy. *Health Affairs* 33: 1841–1850.

Smets, Tinne, Bilsen, Johan, Cohen, Joachim, et al. 2010. Legal euthanasia in Belgium: characteristics of all reported cases. *Medical Care* 48: 187–192.

Smith, J. M., Biggins, S. W., Haselby, D. G., et al. 2012. Kidney, pancreas, and liver allocation and distribution in the United States. *American Journal of Transplantation* 12: 3191–3212.

Smith, Martin L. 1997. Ethical perspectives on Jehovah Witnesses' refusal of blood. *Cleveland Clinic Journal of Medicine* 64: 475–481.

Snyder, Lois and Leffler, Cathy. 2005. Ethics manual: fifth edition. *Annals of Internal Medicine* 142: 560–582.

Society for Health and Human Values – Society for Bioethics Consultation Task Force on Standards for Bioethics Consultation. 1998. *Core Competencies for Health Care Ethics Consultation*. Glenview, IL: American Society for Bioethics and Humanities.

Sprung, Charles L., Danis, Marion, Iapichino, Gaetano, et al. 2013. Triage of intensive care patients: identifying agreement and controversy. *Intensive Care Medicine* 39: 1916–1924.

Starr, Paul. 1982. *The Social Transformation of American Medicine*. New York: Basic Books.

Steinbrook, Robert. 2008. Physician-assisted death – from Oregon to Washington state. *New England Journal of Medicine* 359: 2513–2515.

Stell, Lance. 2001. Disabled patients still have rights. *The News and Observer* (Raleigh, NC) January 12.

Stephany, Kathleen. 2012. *The Ethic of Care: A Moral Compass for Canadian Nursing Practice*. Bentham E Books. Available at: http://ebooks.benthamsciencepubl isher.org/book/9781608053049/. Accessed March 13, 2015.

Stephens, Moira, Jordens, Christopher, F. C., Kerridge, Ian H., et al. 2010. Religious perspectives on abortion and a secular response. *Journal of Religion and Health* 49: 513–535.

Steptoe, Patrick C. and Edwards, Robert G. 1978. Birth after the reimplantation of a human embryo. *Lancet* 2(8085): 366.

Stolberg, Sheryl G. 1999. Pennsylvania set to break taboo on reward for organ donations. *The New York Times* May 6: 1.

Stoll, Barbara J., Hansen, Nellie I., Bell, Edward F., et al. 2010. Neonatal outcomes of extremely preterm infants from the NICHD neonatal research network. *Pediatrics* 126: 443–455.

Strong, Carson. 1987. Ethical conflicts between mother and fetus in obstetrics. *Clinics in Perinatology* 14: 313–328.

Studdert, David M., Mello, Michelle M., DesRoches, William M., et al. 2005. Defensive medicine among high-risk specialist physicians in a volatile malpractice environment. *JAMA* 293: 2609–2617.

Sullivan, William M. 1999. What is left of professionalism after managed care? *Hastings Center Report* 29(2): 7–13.

Sulmasy, Daniel P. 1992. Physicians, cost control, and ethics. *Annals of Internal Medicine* 116: 920–926.

Sulmasy, Daniel P. 2006. Spiritual issues in the care of dying patients "… it's okay between me and God." *JAMA* 296:1385–1392.

Sulmasy, Daniel P. 2008. What is conscience and why is respect for it so important? *Theoretical Medicine and Bioethics* 29: 135–149.

The SUPPORT Principal Investigators. 1995. A controlled trial to improve care for seriously ill hospitalized patients. *JAMA* 274: 1591–1598.

Swick, Herbert M., Szenas, Philip, Danoff, Deborah, et al. 1999. Teaching professionalism in undergraduate medical education. *JAMA* 282: 830–832.

Tavaglione, Nicolas and Hurst, Samia A. 2012. Why physicians ought to lie for their patients. *American Journal of Bioethics* 12(3): 4–12.

Taylor, Janelle. 2003. Confronting "culture" in medicine's "culture of no culture." *Academic Medicine* 78: 555–559.

Teel, Karen. 1975. The physician's dilemma. a doctor's view: what the law should be. *Baylor Law Review* 27: 6–9.

Terasaki, Paul I., Cecka, J. Michael, Gjertson, David W., et al. 1995. High survival rates of kidney transplants from spousal and living unrelated donors. *New England Journal of Medicine* 333: 333–336.

Tervalon, Melanie and Murray-Garcia, Jann. 1998. Cultural humility versus cultural competence: a critical distinction in defining physician training outcomes in multicultural education. *Journal of Health Care for the Poor and Underserved* 9: 117–125.

Thomas, Gerald, Gonneau, Ginny, Poole, Nancy, et al. 2014. The effectiveness of alcohol warning labels in the prevention of fetal alcohol spectrum disorder: a brief review. *International Journal of Alcohol and Drug Research* 3: 91–103.

Thomson, Judith Jarvis. 1971. A defense of abortion. *Philosophy and Public Affairs* 1: 47–66.

Tilburt, Jon C. and Cassel, Christine K. 2013. Why the ethics of parsimonious medicine is not the ethics of rationing. *JAMA* 309: 773–774.

Tolle, Susan W. and Tilden, Virginia P. 2002. Changing end-of-life planning: the Oregon experience. *Journal of Palliative Medicine* 5: 311–317.

Tomlinson, Tom and Brody, Howard. 1988. Ethics and communication in do-not-resuscitate orders. *New England Journal of Medicine* 318: 43–46.

Tooley, Michael. 1972. Abortion and infanticide. *Philosophy and Public Affairs* 2: 37–65.

Toulmin, Stephen. 1981. The tyranny of principles. *Hastings Center Report* 11(6): 31–39.

Truog, Robert D., Brett, Allan S., and Frader, Joel. 1992. The trouble with futility. *New England Journal of Medicine* 326: 1560–1564.

Truog, Robert D., Miller, Franklin G., and Halpern, Scott D. 2013. The dead-donor rule and the future of organ donation. *New England Journal of Medicine* 369: 1287–1289.

Ubel, Peter A. 2000. *Pricing Life: Why It's Time for Health Care Rationing*. Cambridge, MA: MIT Press.

Ubel, Peter A. 2007. Confessions of a bedside rationer: commentary on Hurst and Danis. *Kennedy Institute of Ethics Journal* 17: 267–269.

Ubel, Peter A. and Arnold, Robert M. 1995. The unbearable rightness of bedside rationing. *Archives of Internal Medicine* 155: 1837–1842.

Ubel, Peter A. and Caplan, Arthur L. 1998. Geographic favoritism in liver transplantation – unfortunate or unfair? *New England Journal of Medicine* 339: 1322–1325.

Ubel, Peter A., Zell, Margaret M., Miller, David J., et al. 1995. Elevator talk: observational study of inappropriate comments in a public space. *American Journal of Medicine* 99: 190–194.

United Nations. 1948. The Universal Declaration of Human Rights. Available at: http://www.un.org/en/documents/udhr/. Accessed April 2, 2015.

United Nations General Assembly. 1969. Declaration on Social Progress and Development. Available at: http://daccess-dds-ny.un.org/doc/RESOLUTION/GEN/NR0/256/76/IMG/NR025676.pdf?OpenElement. Accessed April 2, 2015.

US Department of Health and Human Services. 1985. Services and treatment for disabled infants: Model guidelines for health care providers to establish infant care review committees. *Federal Register* 50(72): 14893–14901.

US Department of Health and Human Services. 1996. Waiver of informed consent in certain emergency research. *Federal Register* 61(192): 51531–51533.

US Department of Health and Human Services. 2009. Protection of human subjects. *45 Code of Federal Regulations*, Part 46. Available at: http://www.hhs.gov/ohrp/policy/ohrpregulations.pdf. Accessed April 14, 2015.

US Department of Health and Human Services and US Department of Justice. 2014. Health Care Fraud and Abuse Control Program Annual Report for Fiscal Year 2013. Available at: https://oig.hhs.gov/publications/docs/hcfac/FY2013-hcfac.pdf. Accessed April 1, 2015.

US Department of Health and Human Services, Office for Civil Rights. 2003. *Summary of the HIPAA Privacy Rule*. Available at: www.hhs.gov/ocr/privacy/hipaa/understanding/summary/index.html. Accessed April 14, 2015.

US Food and Drug Administration. 2013. Warning letter to 23andMe, Inc., 11/22/13. Available at: http://www.fda.gov/ICECI/EnforcementActions/WarningLetters/2013/ucm376296.htm. Accessed April 14, 2015.

US National Human Genome Research Institute. No date (a). Cumulative pace of gene discovery 1998–2005. Available at: http://www.genome.gov/Pages/Education/AllAbouttheHumanGenomeProject/CumulativePaceofGeneDiscovery1981-2005.pdf. Accessed April 14, 2015.

US National Human Genome Research Institute. No date (b). Review of the ethical, legal, and social implications research program and related activities (1990–1995). Available at: http://www.genome.gov/10001747. Accessed April 14, 2015.

US National Institutes of Health. 1979. Antenatal diagnosis. Consensus development conference statement. Available at: http://consensus.nih.gov/1979/1979AntenatalDx012html.htm. Accessed April 14, 2015.

US National Library of Medicine. 2015. Gene therapy. In *Genetics Home Reference*. Available at: http://ghr.nlm.nih.gov/handbook/therapy?show=all. Accessed April 14, 2015.

Van der Heide, Agnes, Onwiteaka-Philipsen, Bregje D., Rurup, Mette L, et al. 2007. End-of-life practices in the Netherlands under the Euthanasia Act. *New England Journal of Medicine* 356: 1957–1965.

Veatch, Robert M. 1972. Models for ethical medicine in a revolutionary age. *Hastings Center Report* 2(3): 5–7.

Veatch, Robert M. 1976. *Death, Dying, and the Biological Revolution*. New Haven, CT: Yale University Press.

Veatch, Robert M. 1993. The impending collapse of the whole brain definition of death. *Hastings Center Report* 23(4): 18–24.

Veatch, Robert M. and Sollitto, Sharmon. 1976. Medical ethics teaching. report of a national medical school survey. *JAMA* 235: 1030–1033.

Veatch, Robert M. and Spicer, Carol M. 1992. Medically futile care: the role of the physician in setting limits. *American Journal of Law and Medicine* 18: 15–36.

Von Gunten, Charles F., Ferris, Frank D., and Emanuel, Linda L. 2000. Ensuring competency in end-of-life care: communication and relational skills. *JAMA* 284: 3051–3057.

Vrecenak, Jesse D. and Flake, Alan W. 2013. Fetal surgical intervention: progress and perspectives. *Pediatric Surgery International* 29: 407–417.

Wachbroit, R. 1993. Rethinking medical confidentiality: the impact of genetics. *Suffolk University Law Review* 27: 1391–1410.

Wallis, Claudia. 1983. The stormy legacy of Baby Doe. *Time September* 26: 58.

Warren, Mary Anne. 1998. Abortion. In Kuhse, Helga and Singer, Peter (eds.) *A Companion to Bioethics*. Oxford: Blackwell: 127–134.

Watson, James D. and Crick, Francis H. 1953. Molecular structure of nucleic acids: a structure for deoxyribose nucleic acid. *Nature* 171: 737–738.

Watson, Rory. 2009. Luxembourg is to become third country to allow euthanasia. *BMJ* 338: 738.

Weir, Robert F. 1983. The government and selective nontreatment of handicapped infants. *New England Journal of Medicine* 309: 661–663.

Wendell, Andria D. 2013. Overview and epidemiology of substance abuse in pregnancy. *Clinical Obstetrics and Gynecology* 56: 91–96.

Wenz, Peter S. 1992. *Abortion Rights as Religious Freedom*. Philadelphia, PA: Temple University Press.

Wetterstrand, Kris. 2014. DNA sequencing costs: data from the NHGRI Genome Sequencing Program (GSP). Available at: http://www.genome.gov/sequencing costs. Accessed April 14, 2015.

White, Gladys B. 1998. Crisis in assisted conception: the British approach to an American dilemma. *Journal of Women's Health* 7: 321–327.

Wicclair, Mark R. 1991. Patient decision-making capacity and risk. *Bioethics* 5: 91–104.

Wicclair, Mark R. 2011. *Conscientious Objection in Health Care: An Ethical Analysis*. Cambridge University Press.

Wicclair, Mark R. and White, Douglas B. 2014. Surgeons, intensivists, and discretion to refuse requested treatments. *Hastings Center Report* 44(5): 33–42.

Wijdicks, Eelco F. M. 2002. Brain death worldwide: accepted fact but no global consensus in diagnostic criteria. *Neurology* 58: 20–25.

Wijdicks, Eelco F. M., Varelas, Panayiotis N., Gronseth, Gary S. et al. 2010. Evidence-based guideline update: determining brain death in adults. *Neurology* 74: 1911–1918.

Wilkinson, Anne, Wenger, Neil, and Shugarman, Lisa R. 2007. Literature review on advance directives. Report to US Department of Health and Human Services. Available at: http://aspe.hhs.gov/daltcp/reports/2007/advdirlr.htm. Accessed April 12, 2015.

Wilmut, I., Schnieke. A.E., McWhir, J., et al. 1997. Viable offspring derived from fetal and adult mammalian cells. *Nature* 385: 810–813.

Wojcicki, Anne. 2013. 23andMe provides an update regarding FDA's review. Available at: http://blog.23andme.com/news/23andme-provides-an-update-regarding-fdas-review/. Accessed April 14, 2015.

Wojtasiewicz, Mary Ellen. 2006. Damage compounded: disparities, distrust, and disparate impact in end-of-life conflict resolution policies. *American Journal of Bioethics* 6: 8–12.

Working Group on Incentives for Living Donation. 2012. Incentives for organ donation: proposed standards for an internationally acceptable system. *American Journal of Transplantation* 12: 306–312.

Working Party of the Clinical Genetics Society (UK). 1994. The genetic testing of children. *Journal of Medical Genetics* 31: 785–797.

World Medical Association. 2013. Declaration of Helsinki – Ethical Principles for Research Involving Human Subjects. Available at: http://www.wma.net/en/30publications/10policies/b3/index.html. Accessed April 14, 2015.

Wynia, Matthew K., Cummins, Deborah S., VanGeest, Jonathan B., et al. 2000. Physician manipulation of reimbursement rules for patients. *JAMA* 283: 1858–1865.

Wynn, James J. and Alexander, Charles E. 2011. Increasing organ donation and transplantation: the U.S. experience over the past decade. *Transplant International* 24: 324–332.

Young, Carlton J. and Gaston, Robert S. 2000. Renal transplantation in black Americans. *New England Journal of Medicine* 343: 1545–1552.

Youngner, Stuart J., Jackson, David L., Coulton, Claudia, et al. 1983. A national survey of hospital ethics committees. In President's Commission for the Study of Ethical Problems in Medicine and Biomedical and Behavioral Research, *Deciding to Forego Life-Sustaining Treatment*. Washington, DC: President's Commission for the Study of Ethical Problems in Medicine and Biomedical and Behavioral Research: 443–449.

Zegers-Hochschild, F., Adamson, G. D., de Monzon, J., et al. 2009. International Committee for Monitoring Assisted Reproductive Technology (ICMART) and the World Health Organization (WHO) revised glossary of ART terminology, 2009. *Fertility and Sterility* 92: 1520–1524.

Index